Mac OS X and the Digital Lifestyle

Mac OS X and the Digital Lifestyle

Brad Miser

Premier
Press™

ISBN: 1-931841-74-8

Library of Congress Catalog Card Number: 2001099843 Printed in the United States of America

02 03 04 05 RI 10 9 8 7 6 5 4 3 2 1

Publisher:
Stacy L. Hiquet

Associate Marketing Manager:
Heather Buzzingham

Managing Editor:
Sandy Doell

Acquisitions Editor:
Kevin Harreld

Book Packager:
Justak Literary Services

Editorial Assistant:
Margaret Bauer

User Reviewer:
Brown Partington

Interior Layout:
William J. Hartman

Cover Design:
Mike Tanamachi

Indexer:
Sharon Hilgenberg

Proofreader:
Lara SerVaas

Acknowledgments

A book like this one is definitely a team effort. The following people were a critical part of this book's team:

Kevin Harreld, my Acquisitions Editor at Premier Press, Inc. Kevin was responsible for making this project happen and for allowing me to fulfill the dream I had for this book. Kevin also made sure that the resources needed to complete the project were available. Kevin, thanks for making this book happen!

Marta Justak, the owner of Justak Literary Services. Marta is my agent and was responsible for finding a publisher for the book and for making the business arrangements needed to turn the project into a reality. As if that wasn't enough, Marta also was the book's packager and managed the production process that transformed a bunch of raw Word and TIFF files into the book you are holding in your hands. Marta, I really appreciate your great work (as usual!) on this project. Thanks!

Don Mayer, CEO and Founder; Hapy Mayer, CFO and Co-owner; and especially, Dawn D'Angelillo, VP of Marketing; of Small Dog Electronics. Small Dog provided much of the hardware and software that I needed to write this book. Small Dog is a great Mac-friendly retailer; check them out at www.smalldog.com or call them on 802-496-7171. Also check out the ad at the back of this book. Many thanks to Small Dog for being such an important part of this project.

Brown Partington, an up and coming digital lifestyle guru. Brown did a user review of this book to make sure that the information I provided is actually useful. Brown, you made this book much better and I appreciate your work.

Bill Hartman, who did the production of this book. Bill made this book something that is pleasing to read, and I am amazed at how quickly and accurately he was able to make a book from the files I provided. Thanks Bill!

Sharon Hilgenberg, who did the critical task of creating the index for this book. After all, a computer book is only as good as its index. Sharon, thanks for creating such a good index—I hope the book is worthy of it!

Mike Tanamachi, who designed the cover of this book. Mike created a cover that draws the eye to the book and entices people to pick it up—just what a cover is supposed to do! Thanks!

Premier Press' printing and sales team, who are responsible for getting this book into your hands. Without their work, this project would have remained a pile of electrons that never did any one any good. I really appreciate the support of Premier on this book!

Living with an author during a book project like this one is not an easy challenge, so some thanks to important people in my life are also in order.

To Amy, thanks for putting up with the stress and busyness that this book brought to life.

To Jill, Emily, and Grace who help me focus on what is really important—and who make great subjects for digital lifestyle projects!

About the Author

Brad Miser has been living the Macintosh Way ever since he first glimpsed the mighty Macintosh SE ("say, that's a nice machine, but the screen is so small"). In the years since (not to mention a Quadra 660AV, a Power Mac 8600AV, a couple of DV iMac Special Editions, an iBook, PowerBooks G3 and G4, and several Power Mac G4s running Mac OS 6, 7, 7.1, 7.5, 8, 8.1, 8.5, 8.6, 9, 9.1, 9.2, and now 10.1.3), Brad has written extensively about all things Macintosh. Brad loves to help people get the most out of their Macs, and has even been known to occasionally provide help where none is desired ;-). He hopes that his books help people make the most of the best personal computer on earth. Recently, Brad has been focused on the Mac's incredible ability to transform the analog life into the digital lifestyle.

By day, Brad is an engineer who develops technical documentation, online help systems, and training materials for Mezzia, Inc. (www.mezzia.com). He has also been an engineering proposal specialist for Rolls-Royce, a development editor for Pearson Education, and a civilian aviation test officer for the U.S. Army.

In addition to *Mac OS X and the Digital Lifestyle*, Brad has written many other Mac books including: *Special Edition Using Mac OS X*, *The iMac Way*, *The Mac OS 9 Guide*, *The Complete Idiot's Guide to iMovie 2*, *The Complete Idiot's Guide to iBook*, *The Complete Idiot's Guide to iMac*, and *Using Mac OS 8.5*. Brad has also spoken about living the digital lifestyle at Macworld Expo.

Brad would love to hear about your experiences with this book (the good, the bad, and the ugly). He encourages you to write to him at bradmacosx@mac.com.

Contents at a Glance

Contents

Chapter 13   Adding Digital Tricks to iMovie's Bag 393

Introduction

Living the Digital Lifestyle

From the moment its smiling face first appeared onscreen as it started up, the Macintosh has been all about empowerment. The Mac provides powerful tools that work mostly the way you expect them to. The Mac provides the power to create documents and have them look like they do on the screen when you print them. The Mac was the first, and is still the best, to provide the power to publish from the desktop. The Mac was the first, and is still the best, to provide the power for regular people to surf the Internet and to make their own presence felt on the Internet. Apple's Macintosh has been about making the power of the personal computer available to the rest of us.

Apple has done it again.

With Mac OS X and its digital lifestyle initiative, Apple has made the Macintosh the premiere computer platform to empower you to create, view, and manage digital media. From digital images and music to digital movies to your own DVDs, the Mac gives you the power to transform your life from the analog to the digital.

The Digital Lifestyle Tools

The digital lifestyle is made possible by the superb set of digital lifestyle applications that are available for the Mac. These applications are amazingly powerful, and just like the Mac, they work in a way that the rest of us can understand.

NOTE

It is hard to believe, but you can build a complete set of digital lifestyle tools for less than $50. Most of the applications described in this book are free for Mac OS X users!

QuickTime Makes It All Happen

QuickTime is the Mac's fundamental media technology. QuickTime makes all the other technologies work, and in addition to its behind-the-scenes role, QuickTime provides its own set of features that enable you to view, edit, create, and translate digital media projects (see Figure IN.1). QuickTime provides the common ground upon which all of the other digital lifestyle tools are built and across which they can communicate.

Figure IN.1 *QuickTime Player enables you to view, edit, create, and translate all sorts of digital media.*

iTunes Burns Down the House

iTunes is the Mac's way cool digital music application. Of course, iTunes enables you to do the basics such as listening to CDs, MP3 music, and so on, but it does so much more. You can create your own custom audio CDs, create and manage your own playlists, interface with mobile music players, and so on (see Figure IN.2). iTunes empowers you to master the music in your life.

iPhoto Is Not Your Father's Photo Album

If any application matches the cliché "last but not least," iPhoto is it. While it is the most recent application to be added to the digital lifestyle suite, iPhoto does for digital images what the others do for music, video, and more. iPhoto enables you to do all things with your photos, from the creative, such as making Web sites and slideshows, to the practical, such as providing prints to the important people in your life. From downloading images from a digital camera to publishing your own picture books, iPhoto gives you the tools to take your photos to the limit of your imagination (see Figure IN.3).

Figure IN.2 *iTunes will rock your world.*

Figure IN.3 *iPhoto is your complete digital image studio.*

iMovie Is the Swiss Army Knife of the Digital Lifestyle

If I had to pick only one digital lifestyle tool to take with me on a deserted island, iMovie would be it. That's because iMovie enables you to work with all types of digital media, from still images to digital video to music and sound effects. You can use iMovie's incredible tools to build fantastic movies with which you will amaze even yourself. And I'm not talking about boring home movies here; I'm talking about movies that jump off the screen with titles, transitions, special effects, custom music soundtracks, sound effects, and much more (see Figure IN.4).

Figure IN.4 *Don't let its elegant interface fool you, iMovie includes more features than you might first suspect.*

iDVD Lets You Be Your Own Production Studio

While iMovie is the one application I would take to a deserted island, iDVD is the one that makes me say "Wow!" the loudest. There is something totally cool about putting your own movies and slideshows on a DVD and then playing that DVD on the same player you use to watch your favorite DVD movies. And, just like those movies you rent from your local video store, your DVDs can have cool menus that have motion and sound effects (see Figure IN.5).

Figure IN.5 *The first time you play your own DVD in a standard DVD player, you'll feel like the master of your digital domain.*

iTools Puts Your Digital Life on the Web

The digital lifestyle is a big lifestyle; in fact, you might say that it is a global lifestyle. With iTools, you can share your digital creations with the world. By creating and hosting your own iTools Web site, you can share your digital projects with anyone who lives anywhere and at anytime (see Figure IN.6).

The Digital Lifestyle and You: So Happy Together

Each of the digital lifestyle applications is totally cool and amazing in its own right. But the true power of the digital lifestyle comes when you realize that these tools work together just as well as they work individually. Want to use some music from your iTunes Library on your latest DVD creation? No problem. Want to add that great picture you just took to the iMovie you created last week? That will take you all of a minute to do (if that long). Want to capture an image from a

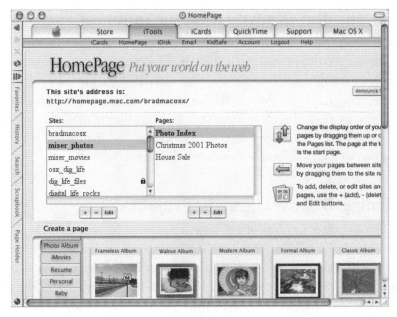

Figure IN.6 *Got Web? With the iTools HomePage service, you definitely do.*

QuickTime trailer from your favorite Hollywood blockbuster and put it on your desktop? No problemo. And on it goes. There are no limits to what you can accomplish when you understand how to use each digital lifestyle application individually and, to an even greater extent, how to make them work together.

That is where this book comes in.

Mac OS X and the Digital Lifestyle

The genesis of this book came when I realized that while there is information on the various digital lifestyle tools, there isn't much to help someone put all the pieces together in a meaningful, practical, and fun way. And, when it comes to the digital lifestyle, the whole is definitely greater than the sum of the parts. This book will help you understand each part and how to put these parts together to form a complete digital life.

To facilitate the stages of your own digital lifestyle, this book is organized into three distinct parts.

Part I: Exploring the Digital Lifestyle Tools

This part consists of seven chapters with each chapter dedicated to a single component of the digital lifestyle toolbox. Each of these chapters provides you with an in-depth understanding about a specific digital lifestyle tool, including QuickTime, iTunes, iPhoto, iMovie, iDVD, iTools, and digital hardware. Because these chapters are packed with information, they are longer than the rest of the chapters in the book. Pick a tool, then pick a chapter, and dig in. There is plenty of information to help you handle these tools like a pro.

Part II: Building Digital Lifestyle Projects

In Part II, you'll start to understand how truly amazing (and fun!) the digital lifestyle is. In this part, there are eight chapters that are each dedicated to a specific type of project. These projects are designed to help you understand how to make the digital lifestyle tools work together to unleash their power. For example, in Chapter 8, you'll learn how to extract video and sound clips from any QuickTime movie to use in your projects (and with the enormous amount of QuickTime material available, this opens up a world of great content for you). As another example, in Chapter 14, you'll learn how to use iTunes and iMovie together to create your own soundtrack audio CD.

Part III: Displaying Your Digital Masterpieces

In Part III, the focus of the book moves to sharing what you have created with the world. Each of the five chapters in this part is devoted to using a different media to share your digital lifestyle with others. The methods you'll learn include videotape, CD, DVD, and the Web. The last chapter even explains how you can organize and maintain all the great content you create.

Special Features of this Book

To make this book more effective in helping you make the most of the digital lifestyle, it contains several special features.

Because this book is more about *doing* rather than just *reading*, it contains many step-by-step instructions that you can follow to learn how to accomplish specific tasks. To help you find these step-by-steps easily, they are offset from the "regular" text as in the following example.

Get a Digital Life

1. Buy *Mac OS X and the Digital Lifestyle* at your favorite bookstore.
2. Put the book next to your Mac and open the book to page 1.
3. Start living the digital life—it is the good life after all.

Sometimes, I like to tell you about something that isn't really necessary for you to do whatever it is you happen to be reading about at the time. In these situations, you'll see a note that looks like the following one:

NOTE

I hope you read the book's notes because I think you'll find them meaningful. However, if you don't read them, you won't hurt my feelings—much.

I want you to be the best you can be so I have included a number of tips throughout the book that provide information to help you work faster, smarter, or simply in another way. The tips in this book are like this:

TIP

Your author is conducting a test of this book's tip broadcasting system. This is only a test. Had this been a real tip, you would have been told something cool to help you be even more powerful with your Mac. This has been a test of this book's tip broadcasting system.

Finally, there are times when you might want to know about something that is related to the chapter's topic, but that goes beyond the chapter's main topic. In these situations, you will see a sidebar, like the one that concludes this introduction.

It's Time to Get on with It

As introductions go, this one's been fun, but it's time that you get on with your own digital life. I hope that you find the information contained in this book to be as empowering to you as your Mac and its digital lifestyle tools are. It's all here, just waiting for you. So, get on and get going.

PART I

Exploring the Digital Lifestyle

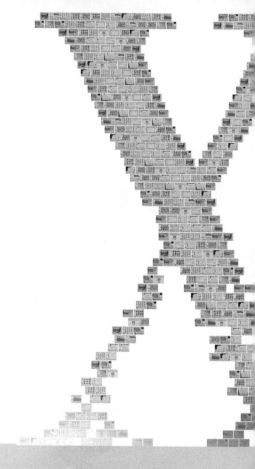

Chapter 1

QuickTime Pro: Making It All Happen

In addition to being fundamental to Mac OS X, Apple's QuickTime technology is also a major part of the digital lifestyle. That's because QuickTime enables all the other aspects and applications that make up the digital lifestyle to work. Without QuickTime, the digital lifestyle would be dead—literally. And so this chapter, the first one in this book, is devoted to this very fundamental (meaning important, not basic) topic.

The QuickTime Way

If you have used a Mac for any significant length of time, you have probably viewed QuickTime movies, whether from a CD-ROM, your hard drive, or the Internet. In technical terminology, QuickTime is a technology that enables a computer to manipulate time-synchronized data. You can use that definition when you want to impress someone with your techno-knowledge, but more simply put, if data "changes" over time, QuickTime takes care of it. The type of data with which QuickTime works includes video, sound, animation, and so on. Because QuickTime data can include different elements, such as video and sound, QuickTime ensures that all the data remains synchronized so that you don't end up with movies in which someone's mouth continues to move 30 seconds after the sounds they were making have stopped.

NOTE

Some good news for Mac users is that QuickTime is cross platform. There is a Windows version of QuickTime that does almost everything that the Mac version does, and Windows users can view the same QuickTime content as Mac users. Even better, QuickTime enables you to work with content that is created in other standard Windows digital media formats, such as the Audio Video Interleave (AVI) format.

QuickTime is both a technology that is built into Mac OS X and an application (QuickTime Player) that you can use to watch and edit QuickTime content. Because QuickTime handles so many different kinds of files, it is also a means you can use to move data (such as movies, music, sound effects, and so on) among the different applications that you use as part of living the digital lifestyle.

There are two "versions" of QuickTime. The basic version of QuickTime, called QuickTime, enables you to view QuickTime content. However, you can't create or change content—you are limited to viewing content, although the variety of content that you can view with QuickTime is pretty amazing. The other version of QuickTime is called QuickTime Pro. This version enables you to do everything that QuickTime does, but it also enables you to create and change QuickTime content, save files in many different formats, work with many more file types, and so on.

Both QuickTime versions enable you to view *streaming* content. This means that you can view data as it is downloaded to your Mac rather than having to wait for a file to download before you can see it. (QuickTime even manages the playback of streaming data so that it doesn't start playing until enough has downloaded to your Mac that you can watch the rest without interruption.) When you create QuickTime content, such as an iMovie project, you can use this feature to stream your own content from the Internet or from a local network.

QuickTime is built into Mac OS X, and you can view QuickTime content to your heart's content. However, QuickTime Pro is an upgrade for which you have to pay an additional fee (about $30). When you pay this fee, you get a registration key that unlocks QuickTime Pro's tools.

If you are at all serious about the digital lifestyle (which I assume you are since you are reading this book), you simply must go "pro." The ability to move data among the various file formats is essential to your digital lifestyle projects. And, with QuickTime Pro, you can convert just about any digital media format into just about any other digital media format. In addition, QuickTime Pro gives you the ability to edit content, save QuickTime movies from the Web, and so on.

NOTE

I must warn you here that much of the information you will get in this book, especially in Parts II and III assumes that you have upgraded to QuickTime Pro. If you haven't, many of the steps in this book won't work for you.

While QuickTime is built into Mac OS X, you use the QuickTime Player application to view, edit, and save digital media content.

Getting Set for QuickTime

If you have used QuickTime at all, you were prompted to set your QuickTime Internet connection preference. This prompt occurs because you will frequently view QuickTime content on the Internet, and QuickTime needs to know how much data flow your Internet connection can handle. QuickTime will adjust how it works to match your connection speed. If you have never set this preference, do so before going any further. If you have already set this preference, you can skip the following steps.

Configure QuickTime for Your Internet Connection

1. Open the System Preferences utility (click its icon on the Dock or choose Apple menu, System preferences).

2. Click the QuickTime icon to open the QuickTime preferences pane.

3. Click the Connection tab (see Figure 1.1).

4. Choose your connection speed on the Connect Speed pop-up menu.

5. If you choose a lower connection speed, such as a 56K modem, the "Allow multiple simultaneous streams" checkbox will be active. Check this checkbox if you want to be able to view more than one QuickTime stream at a time (you probably don't want to allow this if you use a 56K modem because the playback speed will slow to a crawl).

6. Quit the System Preferences utility.

Going Pro with QuickTime Pro

Upgrading to QuickTime Pro is a snap; you don't have to install any software. All you need is a registration code with which to unlock QuickTime Pro's additional features. When it comes to upgrading, you can do it in the following ways:

◆ Go to www.apple.com/quicktime/download/ and click the Upgrade Now link.

◆ Open the QuickTime Player application and choose Preferences, Registration. In the Registration dialog box, click Register On-Line. You will move to the QuickTime registration Web site.

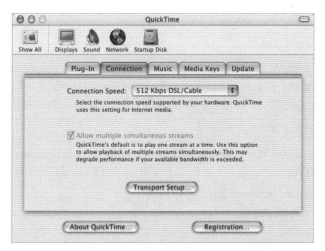

Figure 1.1 *You can use the QuickTime preferences pane to set many aspects of how QuickTime works (if you are lucky, you can use a broadband Internet connection like this one).*

◆ Open the System Preferences utility, open the QuickTime pane, click Registration, and then click Register On-Line. You will move onto the registration Web site.

◆ Call Apple at 1-888-295-0648 to order the upgrade by phone.

Using the Web site to upgrade is quite simple—just follow the onscreen instructions. You will receive your registration code via email. If you register by phone, you will be provided with the registration code directly.

After you have your registration code, you need to register your Pro version information.

Register QuickTime Pro

1. Open the QuickTime pane of the System Preferences utility.
2. Click Registration.
3. Click Edit Registration.
4. Enter the registration information that you received from Apple, including to whom the Pro version was registered, your organization, and the registration number. If you don't enter this information *exactly* as it came to you from Apple, the registration won't work so double-check the information you enter.

5. Click OK. You should now be a "pro."

6. Click Registration again.

7. Make sure that you see the phrase "Pro Player Edition" just above the Registration buttons. If you do, you are all set. If not, re-enter your registration information.

8. Quit the System Preferences utility.

For the remainder of this book, I won't worry about making a distinction about QuickTime Pro versus QuickTime. Since I assume that you have upgraded, I also assume that the differences are no longer important.

NOTE

The QuickTime configuration, including QuickTime Pro registration, is part of the preferences for Mac OS X user accounts. This means that when you configure QuickTime, such as registering the Pro version, your changes affect the current user account only. If you want more than a single user account to be configured for QuickTime, you will need to repeat the QuickTime configuration steps (Pro registration, connection speed, and so on) for each user account.

Viewing QuickTime Movies

You'll find QuickTime movies in all the right places, including on your hard drive, CD-ROMs, DVD-ROMs, and especially, the Web. Although the appearance of the controls that you use to view movies varies a bit between these contexts, the controls work similarly. If you can view a movie from one location, you can view a movie from anywhere.

There are two general ways in which you will view QuickTime content: within the QuickTime Player or from within another application, such as a Web browser.

Viewing QuickTime Content with the QuickTime Player

QuickTime Player is Mac OS X's stand-alone QuickTime viewing application (you also use it to edit and change QuickTime content as well, but you'll get to that a little later in this chapter).

TIP

If you open QuickTime Player Pro directly (by clicking its icon on the Dock, for example), you will see what Apple euphemistically calls hotpicks. Basically, these are ads that QuickTime downloads each time that you start QuickTime Player directly (if you open a movie file, you won't see the hotpicks). If these ads annoy you, you can turn this feature off. From QuickTime Player, choose QuickTime Player, Preferences, Player Preferences. Uncheck the "Show Hot Picks movie automatically" checkbox, and then click OK.

If you use a VCR, CD, or DVD player, you won't have any trouble using the basic QuickTime Player controls to watch movies. Find a QuickTime movie that is on your hard drive or a CD-ROM and open it. (If you need some help finding a movie to view, see the section called "Finding QuickTime Sources Already on Your Mac" in Chapter 8.) A QuickTime Player window will appear, and the movie's poster frame will be displayed. Click the Play button (or press the Spacebar to start the movie (see Figure 1.2).

Figure 1.2 *Using QuickTime Player to watch QuickTime movies is a lot like using a VCR or DVD player.*

Most of the controls in the QuickTime Player window are easy to understand and use. For example, the Review button plays the movie in reverse, the Preview button plays the movie in fast forward mode, and so on.

NOTE

You have to continue pressing the Review and Preview buttons to keep the movie playing at that speed. When you release the mouse button, the movie returns to its previous state (playing or stopped).

However, some of the controls and information might be less familiar to you, especially if you have never worked with digital video. The current frame is shown in the viewing window (if you haven't played the movie, it is the first frame in the movie, which is called the poster frame). Just below the viewing window, you will see the movie's Timeline bar. This represents the total length of the movie. The location of the playhead shows where in the movie the current frame is located. As you play a movie, the playhead moves to the right in the Timeline bar (or to the left when you play the movie in reverse), so that it always shows the location of the frame being shown in the viewing window.

At the left edge of the Timeline bar, you see the timecode. The timecode represents the location of the playhead in the following format: Minutes:Seconds:FrameNumber. For example, if you see 2:34:10, the playhead is located on the 10th frame of the 34th second of the second minute of the movie.

NOTE

The Timeline bar is also known as the Scrubber bar.

You can control the size of the movie by using the commands on the Movie menu. Increasing the size of a movie beyond the size at which it was created will sometimes decrease its image quality and frame rate. With some movies, this is hardly noticeable; with others, increasing the size can make the movie unwatchable. You can experiment to see which size is the best compromise for a particular movie on your specific system.

TIP

You can also change the size of the QuickTime Player window using the Resize handle. The window will remain in proportion to the size in which the movie was created. You can quickly return a movie to its default size by choosing Movie, Normal Size or by pressing ⌘+1.

To watch a movie, click the Play button (or press the Spacebar) and use the Volume slider to adjust its sound level.

TIP

You can mute a movie by clicking the speaker icon at the left edge of the Volume slider.

You can get more control over the movie's sound using the Sound controls; display them by choosing Movie, Show Sound Controls. The Timeline bar will be replaced by sliders for balance, bass, and treble. Use the sliders to make the changes you want. Choose Movie, Hide Sound Commands to return to the Timeline bar view.

Similarly, you can control the brightness of the movie using the Video controls; choose Movie, Show Video Controls to display the Brightness bar. Click and drag on the Brightness bar to the right to make the movie brighter or to the left to make it less bright; choose Movie, Hide Video Controls when you are done.

When it comes to watching QuickTime movies in QuickTime Player, that's about all there is to it. Check out Table 1.1 for some of the other movie playback commands that you might want to use.

NOTE

I've included many keyboard shortcuts in this chapter. As you work more with QuickTime, learn these shortcuts because they can save you a lot of time and mouse movement.

Table 1.1 QuickTime Player Commands for Watching Movies

Command	Keyboard Shortcut	What Happens
Movie, Loop	⌘+L	Makes the movie play in a continuous loop. Choose the command again to make the movie "unloop."
Movie, Loop Back and Forth	None	Makes movie play in a continuous loop, but it plays forward until it reaches the end of the movie. Then it plays in reverse. When it reaches the beginning again, it plays forward again.
Movie, Size commands	⌘+0 through ⌘+3	Changes the size of the movie window. The choices are Half Size, Normal Size, (the size at which the movie was created), Double Size, and Fill Screen (which makes the movie fill as much of the screen as possible).
Movie, Present Movie	⌘+M	When the movie plays, the QuickTime Player window will disappear (as will your desktop) and all you will see is the movie itself. To use this mode, choose the command and the Present Movie dialog will appear. Choose the movie size from the pop-up menu, choose the Normal or Slideshow option, and click Play. When the movie is done, you will return to the QuickTime Player window. If you chose the SlideShow mode, you have to click the mouse button or Spacebar to move through each frame of the movie.
Movie, Play Selection Only	⌘+T	Plays only the frames that you have selected using the crop markers. This is especially useful when you edit movies.
Movie, Play All Frames	None	Causes the entire movie to play, regardless of the frames that you have selected.
Movie, Play All Movies	None	Plays all the movies that you have open.
Movie, Go to Poster Frame	None	Every QuickTime movie has a poster frame; this is the frame that appears when the movie is first opened. By default, this is the first frame in the movie. Choosing this command moves you to the poster frame for the current movie.

Table 1.1 QuickTime Player Commands for Watching Movies (continued)

Command	Keyboard Shortcut	What Happens
Movie, Set Poster Frame	None	Sets the poster frame for the current movie.
Movie, Choose Language	None	QuickTime movies can contain tracks that provide different languages. If the movie that you are watching has multiple language tracks, use this command to choose the language that you want to hear.

Viewing QuickTime Content with Other Applications

QuickTime movies can also be inserted into many types of documents, such as Word files, PowerPoint presentations, and so on. When you view a QuickTime movie in other applications, you will see a "mini" QuickTime controller that enables you to watch the movie that is embedded in a particular document. Applications can add or remove controls to customize the interface that you see in that application, but when you understand how to view movies with the QuickTime Player, you won't have any trouble with these other controllers.

NOTE

Some movies are produced *not* to display any controller. When you open this type of movie, it plays start to end, and you can't control it (other than to quit the application of course).

The other application in which you are most likely to spend time watching QuickTime content is from a Web browser. All Mac OS X Web browsers can use the QuickTime plug-in that enables the browser to display QuickTime movies. The specific way this happens depends on how the movie is created and presented. Most of the time, you see the movie window within the browser along with a QuickTime controller. Other movies are developed with a different interface, but they all work in a similar way. Since there is so much QuickTime content on the Web, you are likely to spend most of your time watching QuickTime on the Web.

Slow Motion Moving Pictures

If you use a relatively slow Internet connection such as a 56K modem, watching movies, such as the movie trailers on the Apple Web site, can be an exercise in patience. High-quality movies files are *big*. Watching them on the Web, even with the streaming feature, can take more time than it is worth. If you use a dial-up account, try watching some movies to see if you can tolerate the length of time that it takes to download enough of the movie so that you can begin watching it. If you can, great. If not, you might have to find smaller movies to watch or, even better, move up to a high-bandwidth connection.

Fortunately, many QuickTime movies are provided in different sizes that are designed for different connection speeds. You usually have Small, Medium, and Large options. Try the options to see which work best for you. If you use a broadband connection, the Large option will usually work great. If you use a dial-up connection, you will probably want to start with the Small option.

One of the best places to view QuickTime movies is at Apple's Movie Trailer site. Here, you can view trailers for the latest creations from Hollywood.

Check out your favorite movie trailer in QuickTime by using the following steps.

Watch QuickTime Movie Trailers

1. Go to www.apple.com/trailers/. You will see an assortment of cool movie trailers.

2. Click a trailer's link to view it. What happens next depends on how the particular trailer has been created. As you read in the previous sidebar, many trailers are offered in different versions, which are sized to be appropriate for various connection speeds.

3. Click the movie size that your connection supports. You will usually see a movie frame with the words "Click to play."

4. Click the movie frame. You will see the movie along with QuickTime controls that you can use to watch the movie (see Figure 1.3). The movie will begin to play as soon as enough has been downloaded to your Mac so that the trailer will play continuously to the end. If you use a fast connection, this will happen quickly. If you use a slow dial-up connection, it can

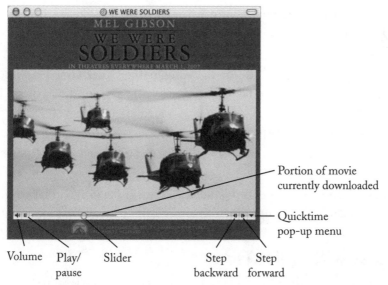

Portion of movie currently downloaded

Quicktime pop-up menu

Volume   Play/   Slider   Step   Step
          pause   backward   forward

Figure 1.3 *For every cool movie, there is a cool movie trailer in QuickTime.*

take some time for enough of the movie to be downloaded to provide a smooth movie experience. You can see how much of a movie has been downloaded by looking at the shaded part of the Timeline bar. You can force a movie to start at any time by pressing the Spacebar. If you don't wait for the automatic start, the movie might stop before it finishes if it "runs out" of downloaded movie before it gets to the end.

5. Use the QuickTime controls to control the movie's playback.

One difference between watching QuickTime movies in QuickTime Player and on the Web is the QuickTime pop-up menu. This menu provides some commands that are unique to movies in a Web browser. The commands on this menu are the following:

◆ **About QuickTime Plug-in**. This choice shows you the version of the QuickTime plug-in that you are using.

◆ **Open This Link**. Opens a link.

◆ **Save As Source**. For a QuickTime movie, this does the same thing as Save As QuickTime Movie. For other types of files, it saves the file as the source's file type.

◆ **Save As QuickTime Movie**. This command enables you to save a movie that you are viewing to your hard drive so that you can view it later.

When you save it to your hard drive, it becomes just like any other QuickTime movie on your Mac (you view or edit it using the QuickTime Player).

◆ **Plug-in Settings**. Enables you to configure the QuickTime plug-in. It takes you to the Plug-in tab of the QuickTime pane of the System Preferences utility.

◆ **Connection Speed**. Enables you to set your connection speed (you should have already set this using the QuickTime pane in the System Preferences utility).

◆ **QuickTime Language**. If the movie has tracks for different languages, you can choose the language in which you want to hear the movie.

Going Further with QuickTime

QuickTime is more than just plain old "watching" movies. You can also use QuickTime to view QuickTime Virtual Reality movies (more commonly called QuickTime VR) and to watch QuickTime TV.

QuickTime Virtual Reality (VR) enables you to interact with movies that simulate panoramic, virtual worlds. You can move around within a movie, and you can even closely examine objects within that movie. QuickTime VR is widely used on the Web so that you can examine products, museums, and other interesting things. When you view a QuickTime VR movie, you won't see the usual QuickTime controls. Instead, you will see special cursors that indicate what you can do with the movie. The standard cursor is a small circle with a dot in the center. When you see this, you know that you are looking at a QuickTime VR movie. To move around the image, simply hold the mouse button down and drag (the cursor will show an arrow to indicate which way you are moving). The image will move accordingly, and you can explore it to your heart's content.

With its streaming capabilities, QuickTime can also be used to watch "broadcasts" from the Web. These can be live events or stored events that have already taken place. You can see live or recorded content on various channels that make their content available in the QuickTime format. The current list of QuickTime TV providers includes CNN, Disney, ABC News, and many more. To watch a QuickTime TV channel, open QuickTime Player and choose QTV, QuickTime TV, and then the channel that you want to watch. When you open a QuickTime channel, you will see the "broadcast" in a new QuickTime window. After the content begins to stream, you can view it.

QuickTime VR and QuickTime TV are pretty cool, but since they are not really relevant to the topic of this book, that is all I will say about them here. Check out Apple's QuickTime Web site if you want to learn more about them.

Making Your QuickTime Player Preferences Known

There are a few QuickTime Player preferences that you might want to set by choosing QuickTime Player, Preferences, Player Preferences. You have the options shown in Figure 1.4 and explained in the following list:

♦ **Open movies in new players**. If you check this checkbox, each movie that you open will appear in a new QuickTime Player window rather than replacing the movie in the current player window. When you edit movies, you will probably have several open at the same time, so you should check this checkbox so that you don't have to keep opening and closing the movies with which you are working.

♦ **Automatically play movies when opened**. If you check this checkbox, movies will begin to play as soon as you open them. When you are editing movies, this setting can interfere with your work, so I recommend that you leave this preference unchecked.

♦ **Play sound in frontmost player only**. This checkbox controls how sound plays when you have more than one movie playing at the same time. If it is checked and you have more than one movie playing, only the movie in

Figure 1.4 *Use the General Preferences dialog to set basic QuickTime Player preferences.*

the frontmost QuickTime Player window will have sound. This is generally a useful setting, unless you prefer the bedlam of having more than one movie providing sound at the same time.

◆ **Play sound when application is in background**. When this checkbox is checked, a movie's sound will continue to play when you move that movie into the background.

◆ **Ask before replacing favorite items**. Checking this checkbox means that QuickTime will present a warning dialog box before you can replace a QuickTime TV favorite channel.

◆ **Show Hot Picks movie automatically**. You know about this one already. Uncheck it to prevent the sometimes annoying "hotpick" ads that appear when you open QuickTime Player directly (before opening a movie).

Configuring and Maintaining QuickTime

One of the great things about QuickTime is that you don't have to mess around with the software itself very much. There are only a few preferences to set, and after they are set once, you'll probably never change them again. QuickTime practically maintains itself, too.

Making Your QuickTime Preferences Known

When you set your connection speed in QuickTime and registered the Pro version, you used the QuickTime pane of the System Preferences utility to do so. (To open this pane, open the System Preferences utility from the Dock or the Apple menu and click the QuickTime icon.) As you probably noticed, this pane contains several other tabs that you can use to configure QuickTime itself.

Configuring the QuickTime Plug-in Tab

This tab has three checkboxes and one button that affect how the QuickTime plug-in works.

The "Play movies automatically" checkbox controls whether QuickTime movies automatically play in your Web browser. This should usually be checked. Check the "Save movies in disk cache" checkbox to have movies that you view on the Web get saved in your browser's disk cache. This is a useful option if you like to view a movie more than once during a single browsing session; subsequent viewings are much faster because the movie is read from your hard disk rather than being downloaded from the Web again. Most users should check this checkbox as well. The "Enable kiosk mode" checkbox hides some QuickTime Player commands so that movies being viewed can't be saved and other changes can't be made. This option is useful if others will be using your Mac to view movies, and you don't want them mucking around with your QuickTime settings or saving movies that they view.

The MIME Settings button is used to configure the specific file formats that are played by the QuickTime plug-in for different types of content. Click MIME Settings to open the MIME Settings dialog. Use the checkboxes to determine which file types are displayed by the QuickTime plug-in (see Figure 1.5).

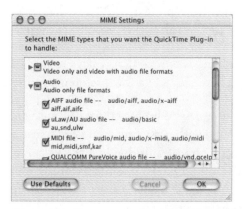

Figure 1.5 *You can use this tab to determine the file types that are displayed in your Web browser by the QuickTime plug-in.*

NOTE

In case you are wondering, MIME stands for Multipurpose Internet Mail Extensions. This is a means of encoding files so that they can be sent over the Internet as plain text files (in the ASCII format) and then reconstructed at the other end. While the format was originally developed for email, it is used by other applications as well, such as Web browsers.

Configuring the Connection Tab

You learned about this one earlier in the chapter. The only option I didn't discuss then was the Transport Setup button. You can use this control to relate specific transport protocols to specific ports. You are unlikely to need to change these settings.

Configuring the Music Tab

QuickTime can play music using different synthesizers (a synthesizer transforms digital or other signals into specific musical notes, tones, and so on). This pane is useful if you work with a Musical Instrument Digital Interface (MIDI) device. By default, the standard QuickTime Music Synthesizer is used. However, you can install various synthesizers and use them to produce the music that is part of QuickTime movie files. If you are involved in creating MIDI files or using a MIDI instrument, you can use this area to select the default synthesizer that should be used.

Configuring the Media Keys Tab

Media keys enable you to manage your access to protected data files. If you need to get to QuickTime files that are secured with passwords, you need to use a password (called a key) to be able to access the files. Individual tracks can also be secured with a key. If you use such secured QuickTime files, you can enter the keys needed to play them in this tab. You aren't likely to ever need to do this, but if you ever are, you at least know where to go to set it up.

Configuring the Update Tab

You use the Update tab to configure how and when QuickTime updates its software. You'll learn about this tab in the next section.

Keeping QuickTime Up-to-Date

Apple continually improves QuickTime, and it is generally a good idea to keep QuickTime at the most current version. You can keep QuickTime current on your Mac in the following ways:

◆ **Use QuickTime Player.** Open the QuickTime Player application and choose QuickTime Player, Update Existing Software.

◆ **Use the Update tab**. Open the Update tab of the QuickTime pane in the System Preferences utility. Click the "Update or install QuickTime software" radio button and then click Update Now. Check the "Check for updates automatically" checkbox to have QuickTime check for updates on its own; this is generally a good idea because you don't even have to bother thinking about it.

◆ **Use Your iDisk**. Open your iTools' iDisk and then open the Software folder. Download any QuickTime updates that you see.

◆ **Use Apple's QuickTime Web site**. You can update QuickTime by moving to www.apple.com/quicktime/.

Understanding QuickTime Quality

The technology underlying QuickTime is complex, but fortunately, Mac OS X manages that complexity for us. However, you do need to understand the primary factors that impact the quality of the QuickTime viewing experience. When you create QuickTime movies of your projects, such as those you create with iMovie and with QuickTime Player, you need to understand how your project settings impact the QuickTime movies you create.

There are three primary factors that affect the quality of your QuickTime movies: resolution, frame rate, and color depth.

QuickTime Movies and Resolution

Just like digital images and everything else you see onscreen, QuickTime movies are composed with specific resolutions. The resolution of QuickTime movies is specified similarly to the way the resolution of your Mac's desktop is, that being X pixels wide by Y pixels high.

NOTE

Pixel is shorthand for PIcture ELement (don't ask me where the "x" comes in. I guess "picel" would not be as cool sounding). Basically, a pixel is a single "dot" on the screen. Every image you see on your Mac's monitor is composed of a number of these "dots." More dots mean more information. Since that doesn't sound nearly technical enough, you should rather say higher resolution images have more information (more pixels).

A movie's resolution determines how much information is stored in a single frame of the movie. More information per frame (higher resolution) means a higher quality image. Higher resolution movies can also be displayed with better quality at larger sizes (given the same desktop resolution).

As you might guess, higher resolution comes with a couple of "costs.' One cost is file size. The other is frame rate (covered in the next section).

Higher resolution movies require larger files because each frame of the movie contains more information (more pixels). File size grows with a multiplication effect because resolution is measured by the number of pixels in the horizontal direction and the number in the vertical direction as in a resolution of 800×600 (a common resolution for smaller monitors). For example, an image with a resolution of 800×600 has 480,000 pixels of information in it. An image with a resolution of 1024×768 has 786,432 pixels of information or 306,432 more pixels of information per frame. Multiply this difference per frame by hundreds or thousands of frames per movie, and you can see why file sizes grow so quickly with higher resolution.

Because higher resolution movies look better, you want to use as high a resolution for your movies as your means of distribution that movie can support. For example, if you are going to email a movie to someone, you don't want the file size to be huge, so you will need to create a lower resolution movie. If you are putting the movie on CD, you can handle a larger file size; therefore, you can create a higher resolution movie. If you are creating a movie for a hard drive, it can be even larger in file size.

Fortunately, you can save movies you create at different resolutions for different purposes (you'll learn how when you get into projects later in the book).

The resolution at which you create a QuickTime movie is called its Normal size (you learned how to change the size at which a movie plays earlier in the chapter).

Because the amount of information in a movie (its resolution) is fixed, it looks the best at its Normal size or smaller. When you play a movie at its normal size, everything looks like it is supposed to. When you make a movie smaller, your Mac can simply "throw away" pixels that it doesn't need to display, and still the image looks good.

However, when you make a movie larger than its Normal size, the image quality can degrade significantly. This is because your Mac has to create pixels that aren't really there to "fill up" the additional viewing area. This can result in a blocky,

---

Size is Relative

A pixel does not have a defined physical size. The size of what you see onscreen depends on the resolution of your display. This is because all monitors have a fixed display area that is determined by the size of the monitor, such as a 17-inch or 22-inch. However, the resolution of the images displayed on a monitor can be changed. When the resolution is increased (say, from 800 × 600 to 1024 × 768), a larger number of pixels must be displayed in the same physical viewing area. The result is that the pixels "get smaller," so an image of fixed resolution will appear to be smaller on a display when it is set to a higher resolution. For example, if you watch a QuickTime movie on a display set to use a resolution of 800 × 600, it will appear to be a certain size (at its Normal size). Take the same movie and play it at its Normal size with a higher display resolution, such as 1024 × 768, and the movie will seem smaller because it is displayed using "smaller" pixels.

When you choose a Normal size (resolution) for your movies, you need to keep the audience in mind. If you think that the audience will be using Macs with a typical display resolution of 800 × 600, you need to size your movie so that it looks good when displayed at this size. If you think most people will be viewing your movie with higher display resolutions, then you need to create higher resolution movies so they will look good then, too.

---

rough looking image (more commonly called a pixellated image because you can see individual pixels).

The bottom line to this is that you need to create QuickTime movies at the largest resolution at which you intend them to be viewed while keeping the file size at a reasonable level for the distribution method you are using. (This all sounds complex, but fortunately, the digital lifestyle applications manage this complexity as you will see when you get into the project chapters later in this book.)

QuickTime Movies and Frame Rate

QuickTime movies—just like their analog counterparts—are actually a series of still images that are slightly different from one another. As these images are shown onscreen, you see the illusion of motion. QuickTime is really just the digital equivalent of the flipbook. The faster these images "flip" on the screen, the smoother and more lifelike the movie appears. The speed at which the images that make up the movie are displayed (are changed) is called the frame rate.

As with resolution, there is a trade-off between the quality of the movie and the resources it requires to be played. The higher the frame rate, the smoother and better the movie appears. However, QuickTime movies with higher frame rates also require more processing power to view and the file sizes are larger. Similar to resolution, you want to use the highest frame rate possible for the file size that you can tolerate.

NOTE

While there is no one standard frame rate, there are standard frame rates that are used. For example, the standard frame rate for QuickTime movies that you create with iMovie is roughly 30 frames per second (fps). This is about the same as the frame rate you will see on television in the United States (Europe uses a slightly different standard). Other media, such as animation, might use a lower frame rate. For example, games are often played at 12 to 20 fps.

When your Mac "flips" to the next image (frame) in a movie, it really only changes the individual pixels that are different from one frame to the next. Often, most of the pixels don't change from one frame to the next. The frame that is used as the "base" from which the following frames are measured is called the key frame. Using key frames more frequently improves the movie's image quality because the motion appears to be more fluid. However, having more key frames also increases file size because more information is required.

Fortunately, you don't have to be as aware of frame rate as you do resolution because most of the digital lifestyle applications handle frame rate for you.

QuickTime Movies and Color Depth

As you read earlier, images on the screen are made up of pixels. Each pixel is composed of three color elements, those being red, blue, and green. The exact color being displayed on any one pixel is determined by a set of numbers that define that color in the particular color space being worked in (when working on the screen, that color space is the red-blue-green or RGB color space). Each color is represented by a number between 0 and 255; all the possible combinations of three numbers between 0 and 255 means that 16 million colors are available.

The number of colors being displayed is called color depth or bit depth. (This is derived from the fact that each pixel requires so many bits of information to be displayed.)

QuickTime movies are created with a specific color depth. Movies with a larger number of colors require more processing power and have larger file sizes. Plus, some Macs are limited in the color depth that they can view. A movie created with a 16 million color depth (more commonly just called millions of colors) might look different on computers that cannot work with that many colors because such machines will have to reduce the number of colors in the movie before the movie can be played.

The number of colors that can be displayed on a Mac is determined by its video hardware and screen resolution. Most QuickTime movies you create will use millions of colors so there isn't usually much you need to do in this area. Just be aware that if you send your movies to someone who has a very old or low-powered Mac, it might not look so good because that Mac might have to display the movie at a lower color depth than that at which it was created.

Editing QuickTime Movies

You can use QuickTime Player Pro to change the contents of existing QuickTime movies and to create new movies. QuickTime Player's editing tools are somewhat limited when compared to other applications, such as iMovie, so you will probably use other tools to do extensive editing work. What QuickTime Player's editing tools are useful for is the preparation of source material for your projects. You can remove unwanted material from a movie, add bits and pieces from other movies to build a new QuickTime movie, and so on.

Editing QuickTime movies is very similar to editing material in other applications; mostly, you will cut and paste frames from movies. You can also manipulate individual tracks of QuickTime movies.

Removing Material from QuickTime Movies

For the purposes of creating source material for your projects, one of the most useful tasks is to be able to remove unwanted material from a movie. About the only tricky part of this is learning to use QuickTime Player's selection tools; after that, it is purely a matter of cutting the material you don't want to leave in the source file.

When you use QuickTime Player to remove material from a movie, you can use the following steps.

Trim the Content in a QuickTime Movie

1. Open the movie with which you want to work. Now make a copy of it so that you can go back to the original if you need to.

2. Choose File, Save As.

3. Name the movie, choose a location in which to save it, select the "Make movie self-contained" radio button, and click Save.

4. Play the movie until you locate the parts that you want to use.

5. Drag the end crop marker to the end of the material that you want to keep (see Figure 1.6).

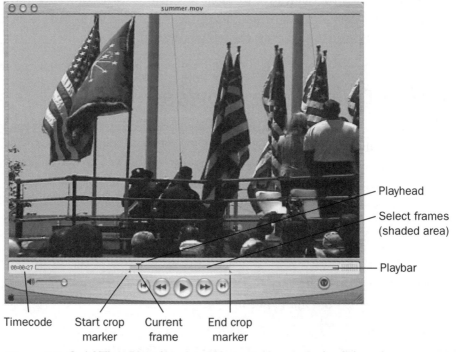

Figure 1.6 *QuickTime Player's tools enable you to do some basic editing of QuickTime movies, such as trimming a movie so that it includes only the frames you want.*

6. Drag the start crop marker to the beginning of the material that you want to keep. When you are done, all of the material that you want to keep should be between the two crop markers. The shaded part of the Playbar shows you the part of the movie that you have selected.

7. Choose Movie, Play Selection Only (or press ⌘+T).

8. Play the movie. Only the selected frames will play. This enables you to really see what you have selected.

9. Adjust the crop markers, as needed; keep selecting and previewing the selection until it contains only what you to want to keep.

TIP

When creating source material, you should usually leave some extra frames at each end. This helps you avoid accidentally clipping frames from the beginning or end of the selected frames when you edit the source in another application.

---

10. Choose Edit, Trim. All the frames that are not part of the selected frames are deleted from the movie. The playbar changes so that what you selected fills it (because it is now the entire movie).

11. Preview the movie one more time, just to make sure the trim is what you wanted (if not, you can undo it).

12. Save the movie.

TIP

When you edit movies in QuickTime Player, you will frequently want to jump to a specific spot in the movie. You can do that by clicking the playbar where you want to move or by dragging the playhead.

Alternately, you can also remove frames from a movie just as easily.

Remove Frames from a QuickTime Movie

1. Open the movie that you want to edit and save a copy of it.

2. Use the crop markers to select frames; this time, choose the frames that you want to delete rather than those you want to keep.

3. Choose Edit, Cut (or press ⌘+X). The selected frames will be removed from the movie.

4. Preview your movie and save it if it is what you want.

TIP

When you drag a crop marker, it becomes larger and has a transparent center so that you can more easily see you have selected it. When you release the mouse button, the crop marker remains selected and the current location marker "sticks" to it. When this happens, you can move the crop marker by pressing the left or right arrow key. This helps you make very fine selections, even down to individual frames (see Figure 1.7).

Current location   Selected crop marker (you can
marker   use the arrow keys to move it)

Figure 1.7 *When a crop marker is selected, you can move it using the left and right arrow keys on your keyboard.*

Creating a New QuickTime Movie with Cut and Paste

You can create a new movie by pasting clips from other movies into it.

Create a New QuickTime Movie with Cut and Paste

1. Open QuickTime Player it if isn't already open.

2. Choose File, New Player. You will see an empty QuickTime Player window. There isn't anything in the viewing area, so it is collapsed and all you see are the QuickTime Player controls (see Figure 1.8).

Figure 1.8 *This QuickTime movie has no content, but you'll soon remedy that.*

3. Open a movie from which you want to copy a clip to paste into your new movie.

4. Use the selection techniques that you learned in the previous section to select the portion of the movie that you want to place in the new movie.

5. Choose Edit, Copy (or press ⌘+C) to copy the selected frames.

6. Move back to the new movie that you created in Step 2.

7. Choose Edit, Paste (or press ⌘+V) to paste the clip into the new movie. The previously empty movie will now show the clip that you pasted into it. Play the clip by pressing the Spacebar.

8. Open another movie and copy a clip from it (or copy a different clip from the same movie).

9. Go back into your new movie and drag the playhead to where you want the next clip to be pasted. You can paste another clip at the beginning, end, or in the middle of your new movie.

10. Press ⌘+V to paste the second clip in the new movie. The frames that you paste remain selected in the new movie. If you don't like the results of the paste, undo it or cut the new frames.

11. Jump to the front of the movie and play it.

12. Keep pasting clips into your movie until it has all the clips that you want in it.

13. Choose File, Save As.

14. In the Save dialog box, click the "Make movie self-contained" radio button, name the movie, choose where you want it to be saved, and click Save. Your new movie is complete.

The new movie takes on the default resolution of the highest resolution clip that you paste into it, even if the movie was not being displayed at its default size when you used the Copy command. For example, if the movie that you copied it from was at Half Size, the new movie will be the Normal Size of the movie from which you copied the clip. You can change the playback size of the new movie, but its default resolution (its Normal Size) is based on the largest resolution clip that you paste into it.

When you include clips of different resolutions, the lower resolution clips will contain space above and below the clip (since they don't fill the QuickTime Player window).

Dependent Movies

When you use resources from one QuickTime movie in another, QuickTime can refer to that information rather than physically placing the material in the movie—this is what happens when you save a movie normally (allowing the movie to depend on the other clip, which QuickTime calls a dependency). This is similar to using an alias to a file. The advantage of this is that the movie file will be much smaller because it is storing only the pointer to the material rather than the material itself in the file. The disadvantage is that if you move the movies around, such as when you email them, the pointer can become invalid, and the movie won't be able to find the referenced material.

If you save a movie with the "Make movie self-contained" radio button selected, the pasted material is actually stored in the file. This means that the movie does not depend on any references. You can move it wherever you want to, and it will work fine.

If you are sure that you won't be moving the clips that you are using, use the "Save normally" option. If you think you might move one or more of the clips, use the "Make movie self-contained" option.

Using Other Nifty QuickTime Editing Tricks

Some other useful editing commands that QuickTime Player offers include the following:

- ◆ **Select All**. Use this to select all the frames in a movie.
- ◆ **Select None**. Use this to quickly unselect any selection.
- ◆ **Add**. This command adds a track onto a movie. For example, if you create some text in a word processor, copy it, move back to QuickTime Player, and choose Add, a text track will be added to the movie.
- ◆ **Add Scaled**. The Add Scaled command scales what you paste to the selection in which you are pasting it. For example, if you add a sound track to a movie, the sound will play for its default length. If you use the Add Scaled command instead, it will be scaled so that it plays only as long as the frames that you have selected do when you paste it.
- ◆ **Replace**. When you use this command, frames that you have copied or cut replace the frames that are currently selected (instead of being added to them as the Paste command does).

Making Tracks with QuickTime

QuickTime movies can contain multiple tracks, where each track contains certain information. For example, a movie can have a video track, a text track, and a soundtrack. You can also have multiple tracks of the same type in a single movie, or you can have a movie with only one track (for example, a soundtrack can be its own "movie"). Using QuickTime Pro, you can manipulate the individual tracks of a movie. For example, you can add new tracks to a movie.

When you play a movie, you can enable or disable tracks to make them play or to hide them, respectively.

Enable or Disable a QuickTime Movie's Tracks

1. Open the movie that you want to play.
2. Choose Edit, Enable Tracks. You'll see the Enable Tracks dialog (see Figure 1.9). Each track in the movie will be listed. Next to the track, you see an On icon if the track will play or an Off icon if that track won't play.

Figure 1.9 *This movie contains only two tracks: video and sound.*

3. Click tracks that are on to disable them or click tracks that are off to enable them.

4. Click OK. When you play the movie, the tracks you turned off won't be included in the movie.

When you enable or disable tracks, the movie is not changed; only what you see or hear is changed.

One of the most useful features of QuickTime tracks is that you can extract tracks from a movie. For example, if a movie contains a soundtrack that you want to use in another project (perhaps you want to use some sounds from a movie trailer that you downloaded from the Web), you can extract that track and create a QuickTime source movie from it.

Extract a QuickTime Movie's Tracks

1. Open the movie containing the track that you want to extract.

2. Choose Edit, Extract Tracks. You will see the Extract Tracks dialog.

3. Choose the track you want to extract and click OK. A new QuickTime Player window will be created, and it will contain the track that you extracted.

4. Edit the new movie to remove any material that you don't want or to add more material to it.

5. Save the new movie.

Working with the QuickTime Properties Tool

A very powerful, but fairly hidden, QuickTime Player tool is the Movie Properties tool. You can use this tool to get all sorts of information about your movie and to change many aspects of it. Because of space limitations, I don't have room to show you much of what this tool can do, but after you use it once, you can explore it on your own.

To see this tool, open a movie and choose Movie, Get Movie Properties (or press ⌘+J). The Movie Properties dialog will appear (see Figure 1.10).

Figure 1.10 *The Movie Properties tool is very powerful; you should take some time to explore what it can do for you.*

The Movie Properties dialog has two pop-up menus at the top of the window. From the left pop-up menu, you choose the element with which you want to work. When you first open the dialog, on the left pop-up menu, you will see Movie, which enables you to work with the movie as a whole. From the right pop-up menu, you choose the aspect of that element that you want to learn more about or that you want to change. The information to view or the controls that you can use appear in the lower part of the dialog.

TIP

You can use the Movie selection in the left pop-up menu to control various aspects of the movie itself. For example, you can set the movie to play automatically when it is opened by choosing Auto Play on the right pop-up menu and then checking the Auto Play Enabled check box. You can use the Controller option to choose a different movie controller (or to display no controller at all).

One of the more useful changes you can make is to change a video track's resolution and orientation. For example, if your viewer will be using a different monitor resolution than that on which you originally created the movie (its "Normal" Size), your movie might not fit on the viewer's screen, or it might appear in postage stamp size.

Change a Video Track's Normal Size or Orientation

1. Open the movie that you want to change and choose Movie, Get Movie Properties.
2. In the Movie Properties dialog, choose a Video Track on the left pop-up menu.
3. On the right pop-up menu, choose Size. You will see size information and controls in the lower part of the dialog (see Figure 1.10).
4. Click Adjust. The movie window will have resizing handles that you can use to change the movie's size (see Figure 1.11). Drag the handle in any corner of the window to resize the movie. As you move the handles, the size shown in the Properties window will be updated. (You might want to minimize the Movie Properties dialog to move it out of the way.)
5. Click the Rotation tool in the center of the window and drag it to rotate the image.
6. Click and drag the Skew tools on each side of the movie to skew it in either direction.

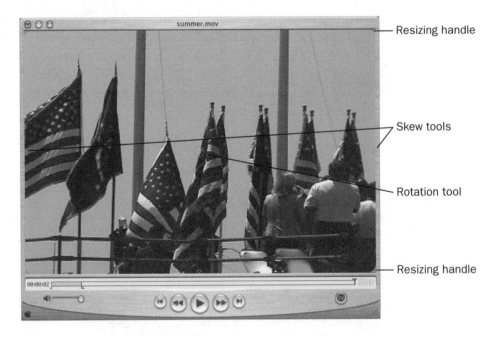

Figure 1.11 *You can use the resizing handles to change a movie's Normal size (its default resolution).*

7. After the size and orientation are correct, click Done.

8. Save your movie. The next time the movie is opened, it will be the size that you set it (the size that you set becomes the movie's Normal size).

TIP

You can "flip" the image horizontally, vertically, counterclockwise, or clockwise using the buttons at the bottom of the Movie Properties dialog.

Converting Files from All Over with QuickTime Pro

One of the most useful things that QuickTime Pro can do is to convert just about any digital media content among a large number of formats. For example, you can convert the soundtrack that you extracted into a format that you can import into iMovie as a sound effect. This one aspect of QuickTime Pro makes it one of the most useful tools in your digital lifestyle toolbox. You'll learn about the formats you will want to use and the details of how to do them in Chapter 8, "Extracting Video and Audio Elements of Any QuickTime Movie for Your Digital Lifestyle Projects" and in Chapter 9, "Converting Digital Media into the Formats You Need for Your Digital Lifestyle Projects."

Working QuickTime Like a Pro

If you want to be a pro with QuickTime Pro, learn to use its keyboard shortcuts. See Table 1.2.

Table 1.2 Useful QuickTime Player Keyboard Shortcuts

Command	Keyboard Shortcut
Add	Option+⌘+V
Add Movie As Favorite	⌘+D
Add Scaled (scale frames to selection)	Option+Shift+⌘+V
Close Player Window	⌘+W
Export	⌘+E
Get Movie Properties	⌘+J

Table 1.2 Useful QuickTime Player Keyboard Shortcuts (continued)

Command	Keyboard Shortcut
Jump crop markers to playhead, play movie forward, and begin selecting frames	Shift+⌘+Right arrow; hold Shift+⌘ keys down to keep going
Loop	⌘+L
Move playhead and crop marker backward one frame	Shift+Left arrow
Move playhead and crop marker forward one frame	Shift+Right arrow
Move playhead backward one frame	Left arrow
Move playhead forward one frame	Right arrow
Move to next crop marker or to end of movie	Shift+Option+Left arrow
Move to next crop marker or to start of movie	Shift+Option+Right arrow
New Player Window	⌘+N
Open URL	⌘+U
Pause movie (movie playing)	Spacebar or Return
Play movie (movie paused)	Spacebar or Return
Play movie at Double Size	⌘+2
Play movie at Half Size	⌘+0
Play movie at Normal Size	⌘+1
Play movie backwards (review)	⌘+Left arrow
Play movie forward at higher speed	⌘+Right arrow
Play movie in Fill Screen mode	⌘+3
Play movie in reverse while moving right crop marker to deselect frames	Shift+⌘+Left arrow; hold Shift+⌘ keys down to keep going
Play Selected Frames Only	⌘+T
Present Movie	⌘+M
Replace selected frames	Shift+Option+V
Select All frames	⌘+A
Select None (no frames)	⌘+B

Table 1.2 Useful QuickTime Player Keyboard Shortcuts (continued)

Command	Keyboard Shortcut
Show Movie Info	⌘+I
Turn volume down	⌘+Down arrow
Turn volume to maximum	Shift+Option+Up arrow
Turn volume to minimum	Shift+Option+Down arrow
Turn volume up	⌘+Up arrow

Using QuickTime Filters

In addition to enabling you to do simple edits to QuickTime movies, QuickTime Player Pro also allows you to apply a variety of effects to movies that you open with it—in QuickTime Player, these effects are called filters. You can use these QuickTime filters for artistic purposes, to improve the quality of a QuickTime movie you have created, and for many other reasons. Because of space limitations, I can't explain the details of how this works nor all the options you have, but a quick example will give you the basic idea—you can explore other options on your own.

Apply an Embossing Filter to a QuickTime Movie

1. Open the movie that you want to emboss.

2. Choose File, Export. You will see the Save exported file as dialog.

3. On the Export pop-up menu, choose Movie to QuickTime Movie.

4. Click the Options button. You will see the Movie Settings dialog.

5. Click the Filter button. You will see the Choose Video Filter dialog. In the left pane, you will see the filters that are available to you. At the bottom left, you will see a thumbnail image of your movie. When you select a filter, its controls appear in the right pane of the window.

6. Click Emboss. The Emboss controls will appear in the window (see Figure 1.12).

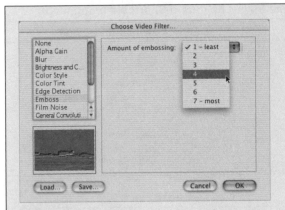

Figure 1.12 *You can use the Emboss filter to emboss a QuickTime movie.*

7. Choose the level of embossing you want to apply on the Amount of embossing pop-up menu. A preview of the embossed image will appear in the thumbnail window.

8. Click OK.

9. Click OK again.

10. In the Save exported file as dialog, name the movie, choose a location in which to save it, and click Save. QuickTime Player will export the movie. If you have applied a complex filter to a large movie, the export process can take a long time. If you use a simple filter on a small movie, the process will be fairly quick.

11. When the export process is complete, view the exported movie to see the results (see Figure 1.13).

If you explore the filters available to you, you will see that you have a lot of options and some appear to be quite complex. However, you can apply any of them by using steps that are similar to those used for the Emboss filter.

You probably also noticed that the Save exported file as dialog includes other menus and options. You will explore many of these in the project chapters in Parts II and III of this book

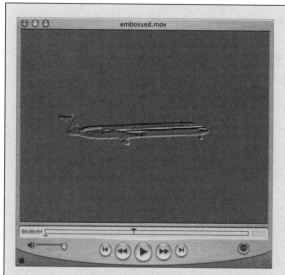

Figure 1.13 *This plane has been embossed giving it a very odd, but somewhat interesting, appearance.*

Chapter 2

iTunes: Burning Down the House

Music is one of the most important parts of the digital lifestyle. From listening to your favorite tunes while you surf the Web to creating soundtracks for your digital lifestyle projects to taking your music collection with you when you are on the move, music makes every aspect of your own digital lifestyle better.

With iTunes, you can take complete control over the music in your digital life. iTunes is a powerful digital music application that enables you to do just about anything with your music, including the following tasks:

◆ Manage your entire music collection

◆ Listen to audio CDs, Internet audio, and MP3

◆ Convert music to and from various audio formats (the most important of which is MP3)

◆ Create and manage custom playlists

◆ Burn audio and MP3 CDs

◆ Download music to a portable MP3 player (the best of which is the iPod)

◆ Convert music into formats you need for your digital lifestyle projects

The iTunes Way

Mastering your digital music with iTunes is key to being able to make your digital lifestyle what you want it to be. Fortunately, iTunes is very well designed and after you become familiar with its interface, you'll probably wonder how you ever got along without it. In this section, you'll learn your way around iTunes and also learn about the amazing things it can do for you.

When you are working with music and sound for your digital lifestyle projects, there are four primary audio file formats with which you will work. Before you jump into iTunes, take a few moments to become familiar with each of these formats.

CD Audio

This is the "native" file format for audio that is recorded on standard audio CDs. You aren't likely to be working with this format directly very much as you will convert it to other formats when you use this type of audio in your projects.

The CD Audio format offers very high quality sound, but the file size that comes along with that quality is quite large. For example, a 3-minute song is about 32MB.

CD Audio files have the file extension .cdda.

MP3 Rocks

MP3 is the abbreviation for an audio compression scheme whose full name is Motion Picture Experts Group (MPEG) audio layer 3. The amazing thing about the MP3 encoding scheme, and the reason that MP3 has become such a dominant file format for audio, is that audio data can be stored in files that are only about $\frac{1}{12}$ the size of unencoded digital music—without a noticeable degradation in the quality of the music. A typical music CD consumes about 650MB of storage space. The same music encoded in the MP3 format shrinks down to about 55MB. Put another way, a single 3-minute song shrinks from its 32MB on audio CD down to a paltry 3MB or less.

MP3's ability to deliver high-quality sound with small file sizes has opened up a world of possibilities. For the first time, music files can be transferred practically over the Internet, even for people who use a dial-up connection. This enables artists to distribute their music to anyone, no matter where they live (as long as they can get online, of course). (This also led to the Napster controversy, but that is another story.)

Because it is quite easy to convert Audio CD files into the MP3 format (this is a one-step operation with iTunes), you can create MP3 files for all of your music and store them on your hard drive. This innovation means that your entire music collection is always available to you, and you never need to mess around with individual CDs. You also get other nifty features, such as playlists, which you will learn about later in this chapter.

The small file sizes of MP3 music also lead to a new type of hardware device, the MP3 player. Because MP3 files can be stored in small amounts of memory, it is possible to store a large amount of music in a small physical device. Some MP3 players don't have any moving parts, thus eliminating any chance for skipping, even under the most rigorous environments. Other devices, such as the Apple iPod, contain their own hard drives so that you can take your entire music collection with you wherever you go.

Because MP3 is such a popular and useful format, you will use it in many of your digital lifestyle projects. You can play MP3 files with a number of applications, including iTunes, QuickTime Player, and so on. You can also use these applications to convert other file formats into MP3 and to convert MP3 files into other formats.

MP3 files have the file extension .mp3.

AIFF, AIFF!

The Audio Interchange File Format (AIFF) also provides high-quality sound, but its file sizes are larger than MP3. As you can probably guess from its name, this format was originally used to exchange audio among various platforms. However, along with that important function, it is now also a useful format in its own right.

The AIFF is supported by most digital lifestyle applications, including iTunes, QuickTime Player, iMovie, and so on. It is also the file format in which Mac OS X's system alerts are stored.

You will frequently use the AIFF format for music, sound effects, and other audio.

AIFF files have the file extension .aiff.

WAV

The Windows Waveform (WAV) audio format is a standard on Windows computers. It is widely used for various kinds of audio, but because it does not offer the quality versus file size benefits of MP3, it is mostly used for sound effects or clips that people have recorded from various sources. There are millions of WAV files on the Internet that you can download and use in your digital lifestyle projects because the digital lifestyle applications can play WAV files and also convert them into other formats.

WAV files have the file extension .wav.

iTunes for the First, but Definitely Not the Last, Time

The first time that you launch iTunes, you move into the iTunes Setup Assistant that does some basic configuration for you. For example, you determine if iTunes should connect automatically to the Internet when you insert a CD to download information about that CD. If you have already used the Assistant, you can skip the remaining material in this sidebar (you'll learn how to configure iTunes manually a little later in this chapter). If not, launch iTunes (for example, by clicking its icon on the Dock) and choose the following Setup Assistant options:

◆ **Internet Playback**. You should choose to have iTunes used when you play MP3 music on the Internet.

◆ **Internet Access**. When you insert an audio CD into your Mac, iTunes can connect to the Internet and look up information about that CD for you. This information includes album title, artist, and so on. You should allow this if possible.

◆ **Find MP3 Files**. iTunes can search your Mac for any MP3 music that is already stored there. You should allow this so that any MP music you already have on your Mac will be brought into iTunes (you can delete it later if you no longer want it).

iTuning Your Music Experience

The iTunes window might look a bit complicated initially, but as you work with the application, you will get comfortable with it quite quickly. The iTunes window has three major areas: the Controls area, the Source pane, and the Content pane (see Figure 2.1).

iTunes Modes

Before you dig into the iTunes interface, you need to understand that iTunes has different modes. In each mode, you will be performing different tasks; iTunes adapts its interface to the task that you are doing, so you will see some different controls when you are in the various modes. The Content pane will also look different to reflect the mode that you are in. The iTunes modes are listed below:

◆ **Audio CD**. As you can probably guess, you use this mode to listen to audio CDs. You also use it to create MP3 files from those CDs.

◆ **Library**. When you create MP3 versions of your music, you store them in your Library. In this mode, you can work with all of the music that you have stored there.

Controls area
Source pane
Content pane
Controls area

Figure 2.1 *iTunes will rock your digital world.*

◆ **Internet Radio**. You can use iTunes to listen to a variety of content that comes from the Internet.

◆ **Playlist**. You'll learn about Playlists in a few pages, but for now know that Playlists are custom music collections that you can create and listen to. You can also burn CDs that contain your Playlists.

◆ **MP3 Player**. In this mode, you can transfer music to an MP3 player, such as Apple's iPod.

iTunes Controls

Above the Source and Content panes, you will see iTunes' major controls. The specific controls that you see depend on the mode you are in, but Figure 2.2 and Table 2.1 explain the controls you will use most often.

NOTE

Some controls that you see are specific to the mode and don't even appear in all modes. For example, when you choose an MP3 player as a source, you will see buttons that are related to specific commands for MP3 players. You'll learn about these commands in the related sections in this chapter (such as the section on using an MP3 player).

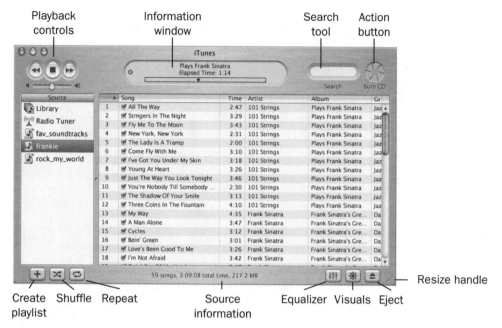

Figure 2.2 *In the MP3 Playlist mode, you see the controls that are shown in this figure; in other modes you might see some slightly different controls.*

Table 2.1 iTunes Controls

Control	What it Does
Playback controls	Control the playback of the selected source. These buttons work just like they do on CD players. From top to bottom and left to right, they are the following: Scan Backwards, which moves you backward through the source at high speed; Play/Pause, which starts or stops the selected source; Scan Forward, which moves you forward through the selected source at high speed; and the Volume slider, which enables you to control the volume level of the selected source.
Information window	This window provides information and controls that are relevant to the mode in which you are operating. See the text following this table for more information.
Search box	When you type text in this box, the Browse pane is reduced so that it includes only those items whose information (such as track name or artist) has the text that you type. This enables you to find specific music with which you want to work quickly.

Table 2.1 iTunes Controls (continued)

Control	What it Does
Action button	This button changes depending on the mode in which you are operating. In the Audio CD mode, this button will be Import, which enables you to create MP3 files. In the Library mode, this is the Browse button, which opens or closes the Browse pane. In the Internet Radio mode, this is the Refresh button, which updates the list of available radio stations. In the MP3 Playlist mode, this is the Burn CD button, which enables you to burn a CD.
Create playlist	You use this button to create new playlists.
Shuffle	This causes the songs in the selected source to play in random order.
Repeat	Click this once to cause the current song to play through and then repeat one time. Click this twice to repeat every song in the selected source.
Equalizer	This opens the Equalizer window (you'll learn about this in the section called "The iTunes Equalizer" a bit later in this chapter).
Visuals	The iTunes window can play visual effects on the screen while the selected music plays. You click the Visuals button to turn on the effects and click it again to turn them off. You can use the commands on the Visuals menu to control the size of the visuals, including making them large enough so that they fill the screen (click the mouse button to return to the iTunes window). You can also add more visuals to those that come with iTunes (but since that won't help you with your digital lifestyle projects, this is beyond the scope of this chapter).
Eject	This ejects a selected CD.
Resize handle	Drag this to resize the iTunes window.

The Information window offers information (as if you couldn't guess that) along with controls that you can use. What you see in this window also depends on the mode in which you are operating. For example, Figure 2.3 shows iTunes while it is creating MP3 versions of the songs on an audio CD.

In other modes, the Information window shows the song currently being played, including both album name and elapsed or remaining time. If you click the Mode Change button, the information shown in the window will change. For example, when you click the button once, the information will be replaced by a graph that displays the relative volume levels of sounds at various frequencies for the left and

Mode Change   Import   Progress   Stop
button   information   bar   button

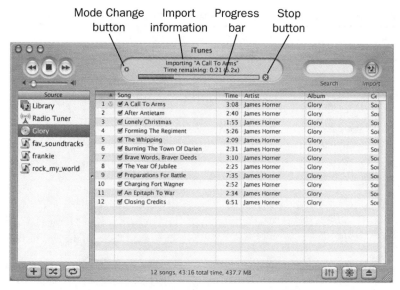

Figure 2.3 *In this mode, the Information window provides information about and control over the MP3 creation process.*

> **TIP**
>
> To see all of the information available in the Information window, click the information that you see, such as the Elapsed Time. The information will change (for example, when you click the Elapsed Time, it changes to Remaining Time).

right channel. When you are converting music to MP3 or when you are burning a CD, you can use the Stop button to stop the process.

Naturally, you can also address iTunes' commands via the application's menus and keyboard shortcuts. Table 2.3 provides a summary of some of the more useful menu commands and their keyboard shortcuts (if available). While some of the commands listed in this table might not be familiar to you now, they will make perfect sense when you have read through this chapter.

Of course, you can also use iTunes' standard Mac OS X commands, such as Hide and Quit. The previous table does not list these because I assume that you are familiar with them.

Table 2.3 Useful iTunes Menu Commands and Keyboard Shortcuts

Menu	Command	Keyboard Shortcut	What it Does
iTunes	Preferences	⌘+Y	Enables you to set iTunes preferences.
File	New Playlist	⌘+N	Creates a new playlist.
File	New Playlist From Selection	Shift+⌘+N	Creates a new playlist containing the songs that are currently selected.
File	Add to Library	None	Enables you to add MP3 files that were created outside of iTunes, such as those you download from the Internet, to your iTunes Library (you'll learn a lot more about the Library in the next section).
File	Update iPod	None	Enables you to synchronize the contents of your Library on an Apple iPod MP3 player.
File	Get Info	⌘+I	Opens the Song Information window for the selected song.
File	Show Song File	⌘+R	Finds the MP3 file located on your Mac for the selected song.
Edit	Show Current Song	⌘+L	Shows the song currently playing in the Content pane.
Edit	View Options	⌘+J	Enables you to determine which columns are shown in the Content pane.
Controls	Play/Pause	Spacebar	Plays the selected song or source.
Controls	Next Song	⌘+Right arrow	Jumps to the next song in the selected source.
Controls	Previous Song	⌘+Left arrow	Jumps to the previous song in the selected source.
Controls	Shuffle	None	Play the songs in the selected source in random order.
Controls	Repeat Off	None	Plays the selected source one time.
Controls	Repeat All	None	Plays the selected source twice.
Controls	Repeat One	None	Plays the current song and then repeats it once.

Table 2.3 Useful iTunes Menu Commands and Keyboard Shortcuts (continued)

Menu	Command	Keyboard Shortcut	What it Does
Controls	Volume Up	⌘+Up arrow	Increases the volume.
Controls	Volume Down	⌘+Down arrow	Decreases the volume.
Controls	Mute	Shift+⌘+Down arrow	Mutes the volume.
None	Unmute	Shift+⌘+Up arrow	Unmutes the volume.
Controls	Eject CD	⌘+E	Ejects the CD.
Visuals	Turn Visuals On/ Turn Visuals Off	⌘+T	Shows/hides the visual display.
Visuals	Small	None	Displays the visuals at the smallest size.
Visuals	Medium	None	Displays the visuals at the medium size.
Visuals	Large	None	Displays the visuals at the largest size.
Visuals	Full Screen	⌘+F	Makes the visuals fill the screen.
Advanced	Open Stream	⌘+U	Enables you to enter a URL for an Internet audio stream to play in iTunes.
Advanced	Convert to MP3	None	Enables you to select files to convert to MP3.
Advanced	Export Song List	None	Exports a text file containing a listing of all the songs in the selected source.
Advanced	Get CD Track Names	None	Connects to the Internet to download information about the audio CD shown in the Source pane. (If you configure iTunes to do this automatically, you'll never need to use this command.)
Advanced	Submit CD Track Names	None	Enables you to upload information about a CD in the event you have a CD that can't be located in the CDDB online database.
Window	iTunes	⌘+1	Shows the iTunes window.
Window	EQUALIZER	⌘+2	Shows the Equalizer window.

TIP

You can also use the Apple Pro Keyboard's media keys (located above the numeric keypad) to decrease the volume, increase the volume, mute the sound, or eject a CD. Note that when you use the keyboard to change the volume, you are changing your Mac's system volume, not the volume of iTunes relative to the system volume, which is what you change when you use iTunes Volume slider, menu commands, or keyboard shortcuts to change the volume.

The iTunes Source Pane

The iTunes Source pane, located along the left side of the window, enables you to choose a source with which you want to work (see Figure 2.4). When you select a source by clicking it, you see its contents in the Content pane. Selecting the source is always the first step in any iTunes activity.

Table 2.4 lists some of the more common sources with which you will work.

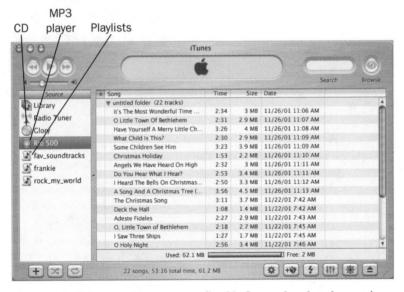

Figure 2.4 *When you choose a source (in this figure, the selected source is an MP3 player), you see its contents in the Content pane.*

Table 2.4 iTunes Sources

Source	What it Is
Library	Contains all of the songs that you have encoded in MP3 or have added to it via the Add to Library command. The Library contains all of the music that you manage with iTunes.
Radio Tuner	Lists Internet radio stations that you can listen to using iTunes.
CD	Enables you to view or listen to the contents of an audio CD.
MP3 Player	Enables you to view and manage the contents of an MP3 player.
Playlist	Enables you to listen to or change the contents of one of your playlists.

The iTunes Content Pane

When you select a source in the Source pane, you will see its contents in the Content pane, which is located on the right side of the iTunes window (see Figure 2.5). You use the Content pane to browse a source as well as to work with it. For example, when you select an audio CD as a source, you will see its songs in the source pane. You can choose songs to import, play songs, and so on. You will learn how to work with the Content pane in its various modes in later sections of this chapter.

Figure 2.5 *Here, I have selected a playlist called "Frankie," and its contents are displayed in the Content pane.*

TIP

To make the size of the Source pane larger or smaller relative to the Content pane, drag the resizing handle (it is a small circle) located in the middle of the border between the Source and Content pane. Drag it to the left to make the Source pane smaller or to the right to make it larger.

The columns that you see in the Content pane work similarly to columns in Mac OS X Finder windows. You can do the following tasks:

◆ **Sort the Content pane**. To sort the Content pane by a column, click its column heading. That column will sort the list of contents; the column heading is highlighted to show you which column sorts the pane. You also will see the sort direction indicator that points up or down. To change the order in which the column is sorted, click the column heading again. The pane will be sorted in the opposite direction.

◆ **Change the order of the columns**. You can change the order in which the columns appear by dragging the columns by their headings. You can move the columns so they appear in any order you'd like.

◆ **Change the width of the columns**. To change the width of a column, point to the right edge of its column heading. The pointer will become a vertical line with an arrow coming out of each side. When you see this, drag to the right to make the column narrower or to the right to make it wider.

◆ **Set the columns that appear in the window**. If you choose Edit, View Options (or press ⌘+J), you can choose the columns that you want to be displayed by checking or unchecking their checkboxes in the View Options dialog. Each source type has its own set of view options (for example, you can select a different set of columns when you select an audio CD than are available when you select a playlist). If you add columns, you can resize the columns to show more of them in the iTunes window.

NOTE

Changes you make to the Content pane apply only for the selected source. You can have a different set of viewing options for each source (for example, you can have a custom set of view options for each playlist).

In several modes, such as when you are working with the Library, a CD, or a playlist, you will see a checkbox next to each song in the source. By default, this checkbox is checked. If you uncheck a song's checkbox, it will be skipped when that source is played. When you check the box again, the song will be played.

The iTunes Equalizer

iTunes includes a graphic equalizer that you can use to fine-tune the music to which you listen. Like hardware graphic equalizers, you can adjust the relative volume levels of various audio frequencies to suit your preferences. Unlike hardware graphic equalizers, you can select different preset configurations, and you can create your own configurations. You can apply an equalizer configuration to your music even down to individual songs so that each tune can have its own equalization.

To see the iTunes equalizer, click the Equalizer button, choose Window, Equalizer, or press ⌘+2. The Equalizer window will appear (see Figure 2.6).

Figure 2.6 *With the Jazz equalizer configuration, both bass and treble frequencies are emphasized.*

Because the Equalizer doesn't really impact your digital lifestyle projects, you won't learn everything about it in this chapter. However, the following list will get you started with it:

◆ To activate the Equalizer, open its window, check the On checkbox, and choose the Equalizer preset configuration you want from the pop-up menu. All iTunes music that you play will be adjusted according to the preset that you selected.

◆ Use the Preamp slider to change the relative volume level for every song. This is useful when a piece of music is recorded at a particularly high or low volume level.

◆ You can create your own Equalizer settings by first choosing Manual from the pop-up menu. Then drag the slider for each frequency to the volume level at which you want that frequency to be played.

◆ You can add your custom Equalizer settings to the pop-up menu by configuring the Equalizer and choosing Make Preset from the pop-up menu. In the Make Preset dialog, name your preset and click OK. Your preset will be added to the list and you can choose it just as you can one of the iTunes default settings.

◆ You can edit the list of presets by choosing Edit List from the pop-up menu. The Edit Presets dialog will appear. You can use to this to rename or delete any of the presets, including the default presets.

You can also associate Equalizer presets with specific songs.

Associate a Specific Equalizer Preset with an Individual Song

1. Select the song to which you want to apply a preset.

2. Choose File, Get Info (or press ⌘+I). The Song Information window will appear.

3. Click the Options tab.

4. On the Equalizer Preset pop-up menu, choose the preset that you want to be used for that song.

5. Click OK. When that song plays, the preset selected will be used.

TIP

Using the View Options dialog, you can have the Equalizer column displayed in the Content pane. This column includes an Equalizer preset pop-up menu from which you can choose a preset for a song.

Making and Using Playlists

Earlier, you learned about the iTunes Library source. This source doesn't actually contain any music—its contents consist of pointers to MP3 files that are stored on your Mac.

While the Library source contains all of the music that you have converted into MP3, you can also create customized sublibraries, called playlists. These playlists act like albums—they contain specific sets of songs. You can create your own playlists and add any songs in your Library to them. You can add the same song to more than one playlist, and you can add a song to the same playlist more than one time.

After you create a playlist, you can listen to it, put it on a CD, or download it to an MP3 player. In fact, you must create a playlist before you can burn a CD. You will be using playlists quite frequently.

Burning Tracks

If you have read this chapter so far, you know that you can use iTunes to create your own audio CDs. First, you create a playlist of music that you want to store on a CD. Then, you burn the CD.

When you create an audio CD, you have two options.

One is to create a standard audio CD that you can play on any CD player, such as the one in your car. The benefit to this format is just that—you can use the CDs you create in any CD player. The downside is that your MP3 files are converted back into the Audio CD format, which means that CDs you create using this format can't store any more music than a standard audio CD can.

The other option is to record music in the MP3 format on a CD. This enables you to store a much greater quantity of music on a single CD. However, to play this type of CD, you must use a CD player that can play MP3 files. While these are becoming more common, they are not nearly as common as players that can play audio in the Audio CD format.

NOTE

Apple maintains lots of good iTunes information on the Web; check it out at www.apple.com/itunes. In addition to information, you can also download the latest updates to the application.

Making Your iTunes Preferences Known

You have everything you need to know in order to start using iTunes to master your music and to use the application for your digital lifestyle projects. However, it will be beneficial if you take a few moments to configure iTunes to suit your preferences. If you don't want to do this now, but prefer to get started using the application, skip to the section called "Making Music with iTunes." You can always come back here when you are ready to fine-tune iTunes.

Similar to other Mac OS X applications, you access iTunes preferences by choosing iTunes, Preferences (or press ⌘+Y). The iTunes Preferences window contains five tabs (see Figure 2.7). The most important settings on each tab are explained in the following sections.

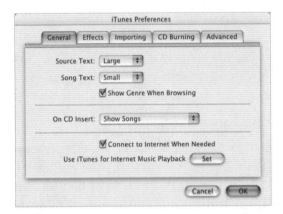

Figure 2.7 *You can use the iTunes Preferences dialog to configure iTunes to your liking.*

Setting iTunes General Preferences

On the General tab, you can set the following preferences:

◆ Use the Display pop-up menus to control the size of the font used in the Source (the Source Text pop-up menu) and Content (the Song Text pop-up menu) panes. Check the "Show Genre When Browsing" checkbox to add the Genre column when you are browsing the Library (you will learn more about this later).

◆ Use the On CD Insert pop-up menu to control what happens when you insert an audio CD into your Mac. The options are to Show Songs, Begin Playing, Import Songs, or Import Songs and Eject. When you start using iTunes, the Import Songs and Eject setting is very useful because it helps you convert all of your CDs into MP3 quickly. After you have all of your CDs converted into MP3, the Begin Playing option is a good choice.

◆ In the Internet section, use the "Connect to Internet When Needed" checkbox to turn off the automatic lookup feature, if you don't want it to be used. Use the Set button to set iTunes as the default application for playing all music on the Internet. Most of the time, both of these options should be on (check the checkbox and click the Set button).

Setting iTunes Effects Preferences

The Effects tab has two preference settings (see Figure 2.8).

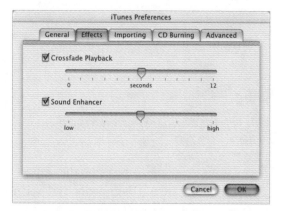

Figure 2.8 *Using the Effect preferences, you can further customize your music.*

Use the Crossfade Playback slider to control the amount of silent time between songs in your playlists. If the slider is set to 0, there will be no silence; one song will fade directly into the next. Set the slider to a value greater than 0 (up to 12 seconds) to have that amount of silence between tracks.

The Sound Enhancer enables iTunes to apply digital effects to your music to improve its quality (that is a matter of opinion, of course). Use the slider to set the relative amount of "enhancing" that iTunes does.

TIP

You can turn off either effect by unchecking its checkbox.

Setting iTunes Import Preferences

The Importing tab is one of the more important tabs because you use it to configure how iTunes will import (convert) your music and sound files (see Figure 2.9).

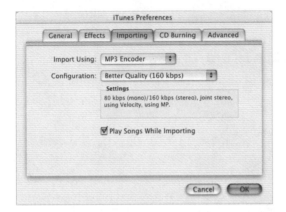

Figure 2.9 *The Importing tab is quite important because you use it to determine how iTunes will convert audio files.*

You first choose the encoder that you want to configure by using the Import Using pop-up menu. You have three options, which are MP3 Encoder, AIFF Encoder, and WAV Encoder. Then you use the controls for each encoder to configure it.

After you have configured one encoder, configuring the others is similar. Since you are most likely to use iTunes to convert files into MP3, some detail on configuring this encoder will be helpful.

Although the default MP3 encoding settings are probably fine, you might want to experiment with the MP3 encoding settings to get the smallest file size possible while retaining an acceptable quality of playback.

Understanding MP3 Encoding

The quality of encoded music is determined by the amount of data that is stored in the MP3 file per second of music playback. This is measured in KiloBits Per Second or kbps. The higher the number of kbps, the better the music will sound. Of course, this means that the file size is larger as well. The goal of MP3 encoding is to obtain an acceptable quality of playback while minimizing the size of the resulting MP3 files.

The encoding level that you should use depends on several factors, which include the following:

◆ **Your sensitivity to imperfections**. If you dislike even minor imperfections in music playback, you should use higher quality encoding settings. If you don't mind the occasional "bump" in the flow of the music, you can probably get away with lower quality settings.

◆ **The music to which you listen.** Some music hides "flaws" better than others. For example, you are less likely to notice subtle problems in the music while listening to grinding heavy metal music than when you listen to classical music.

◆ **How you listen to music**. If you use a low-quality sound system with poor speakers, you probably won't notice any difference between high-quality and low-quality encoding. If your Mac is connected to a high-fidelity sound system, the differences in music quality will be more noticeable.

◆ **How important file size is**. If you are going to be listening to music on an MP3 player, you might be willing to trade off some quality to be able to fit more music on the player. If you are mostly storing music on a hard drive, you can choose higher quality because file size won't be as important.

There are three standard levels of MP3 encoding that iTunes provides: Good, Better, and High. As an experiment, I encoded the same 4-minute song using each of these levels; the results are shown in Table 2.5. These results might or might not match the particular encoding that you do, but they should give you some idea of the effect of quality level settings on file sizes. In this experiment, I couldn't detect much difference between the quality levels on the sound of the music, so I could save almost 0.5MB per minute of music by sticking with the Good quality level.

Table 2.5 Default Encoding Quality Settings Versus File Size

Quality Level	Data Rate (kbps)	File Size (MB)
Good	128	3.8
Better	160	4.8
High	192	5.7

If none of the three standard levels of MP3 coding is acceptable, you can also create custom encoding levels.

Configuring Standard Levels of MP3 Encoding

To configure iTunes to use one of the standard levels of MP3 encoding, use the following steps.

Choose an Encoding Quality Level

1. Open the iTunes Preferences dialog and click the Importing tab.
2. On the Import Using pop-up menu, choose MP3 Encoder (it is selected by default).
3. Use the Configuration pop-up menu to choose the quality level of the encoding; your options are Good, Better, High, or Custom (you'll learn about the Custom option in the next section). When you make your choice, the Settings area of the dialog will provide information about the encoding level that you have selected.
4. If the "Play Songs While Importing" checkbox is checked, the music that you encode will play while you are encoding it.
5. Click OK to close the dialog. When you encode files in the MP3 format, the setting you selected will be used.

TIP

You can vary the encoding quality level that you use from album to album or even from song to song. For example, if you want to play certain songs on a portable MP3 player, you might want to use a lower quality level for those songs so that you can download more of them to the player. Or, you might want to create one version of the tracks at low quality levels and another version at high quality levels. You could then create a low-quality playlist to import to an MP3 player.

Configuring Custom Levels of MP3 Encoding

In almost all cases, you can stick with one of the three standard quality levels. However, you can also customize the MP3 encoder to squeeze the most quality out of the smallest file sizes for the specific kind of music you are dealing with.

To create custom encoding settings, repeat the previous steps up to Step 3. Instead of choosing one of the standard quality levels, choose Custom. You will see the MP3 Encoder dialog (see Figure 2.10).

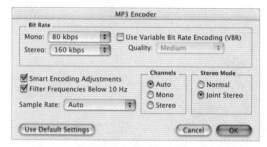

Figure 2.10 *When it comes to MP3 encoding, iTunes enables you to get into the details.*

Going into the details of each of these settings is beyond the scope of this book (besides which, you aren't likely to ever use them). However, if you have the interest and time, you can experiment with these settings to see how they impact file size and playback quality.

Configuring AIFF and WAV Encoding

Configuring the AIFF and WAV encoder is much simpler than the MP3 encoder because you have fewer options. For each of these encoders, your configuration choices are Automatic or Custom. In almost all cases, the Automatic setting is fine. If you want to explore the Custom settings, choose Custom and then set the channels and sample size that you want to use.

Selecting an Encoder

The encoder that you have selected on the Import Using pop-up menu is the one that will be used when you import music or audio into iTunes. For example, if you choose the MP3 Encoder, any music you import into iTunes will be converted into the MP3 format.

Setting iTunes CD Burning Preferences

You can make a few adjustments to how iTunes creates CDs when you burn them by using the CD Burning tab (see Figure 2.11). At the top of the tab, you will see

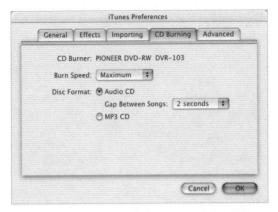

Figure 2.11 *The drive that you use to burn CDs is shown on the CD Burning tab.*

the CD burner that is recognized by your Mac (if you use an external burner, make sure that you have turned it on!).

Use the Burn Speed pop-up menu to select the speed at which you want to burn your CDs. Most of the time, Maximum is the right choice. However, if you have problems burning CDs (especially if you use an external burner), you can set a lower burn speed to see if that solves your problem.

Use the Disc Format radio buttons to choose the type of CDs you will burn. Audio CDs are those that can be played in any CD player, while MP3 CDs require a player capable of playing MP3 files.

If you choose Audio CD, set the amount of silence between tracks on the Gap Between Songs pop-up menu.

Setting iTunes Advanced Preferences

The Advanced tab contains a few, specialized settings (see Figure 2.12).

This tab has the following options:

◆ **Location of imported files**. By default, iTunes stores all the music and audio files that you import in the following location: *shortusername/* Documents/iTunes/iTunes Music/, where *shortusername* is the short name for the current user account. If you open the iTunes folder within your Documents folder, you will see the iTunes Music Library file and the iTunes Music folder. Within the iTunes Music folder, the music files are contained within folders that are named with the artist's name. Within each artist's folder, each album has its own folder. If you prefer to have imported music stored in a different location, use the Change button to set a different location for the files that you import into iTunes.

◆ **Size of streaming buffer.** When you use iTunes to listen to content from a streaming source, such as the Internet, a certain amount of that data is stored in a buffer before it begins to play. This ensures that you can have a constant flow of sound even if the flow of data to your Mac isn't smooth. Use the Streaming Buffer Size pop-up menu to change the size of the buffer you use. For example, if you find Internet content starting and stopping, choose Large to increase the size of your buffer.

◆ **Power conservation.** Check the Battery Saver checkbox if you use iTunes on a PowerBook or iBook running on battery power. This causes iTunes to store music in RAM to lessen the need for the hard drive to spin, thus reducing power use.

NOTE

If you want to share the music that you encode with other users of your Mac, you should store it in your Public folder. Other users can then add that music to their iTunes Library.

Figure 2.12 *The Advanced tab is mostly useful when using iTunes on a mobile Mac.*

Making Music with iTunes

Now that you understand audio file formats, the iTunes application, and how to configure iTunes for the various tasks for which you will use it, it is time to start using the application. In this section, you'll learn how to master your music.

NOTE

For the remainder of this chapter, I have assumed that you have configured iTunes as recommended earlier in the chapter. If you haven't, you might have a slightly different experience. For example, if you don't have iTunes configured to connect to the Internet automatically, you won't see a message telling you that iTunes is looking up the CD, nor will you receive any CD information.

Listening to Audio CDs

Playing audio CDs using iTunes is similar to listening to CDs using any other CD player.

Play an Audio CD

1. Insert an audio CD and launch iTunes, or launch iTunes and insert an audio CD. You'll see a message telling you that iTunes is looking up the CD on the CDDB database. Depending on how you connect to the Internet, this process can take a few moments. If multiple matches are found for the CD, you will be prompted to choose the correct one. Do so, and then click OK. If you have previously listened to the CD in iTunes, you won't see this message because iTunes remembers a CD after it has looked it up one time.

    After the CD is mounted, you will see a listing of its contents in the Content pane—an audio CD is selected as the source automatically when it is mounted (see Figure 2.13).

2. Click the Play button and use the other playback controls to control the music.

Figure 2.13 *The audio CD Glory is selected as the source so its contents appear in the Content pane.*

Here are some additional notes related to playing audio CDs (most of these notes apply to other sources as well):

◆ If you have configured iTunes to play CDs when you insert them, you won't need to click the play button.

◆ You can play a track by double-clicking it.

◆ The track that is currently playing is marked with a speaker icon in the Content pane. You can jump to the current song by choosing Edit, Show Current Song (⌘+L).

◆ If you uncheck the checkbox next to a track's title, it will be skipped.

◆ You can change the order in which tracks will play by dragging them up and down in the window; iTunes remembers this order, and the next time you insert the CD, the same order will be used.

NOTE

When iTunes obtains song information for a CD that you are playing, that information is limited to iTunes itself. If you view the audio CD in a Finder window, the tracks will be named with the ubiquitous "Track 01.cdda," "Track 02.cdda," and so on.

If you click the Maximize button (the green one), the iTunes window will shrink down so that only the playback controls and information window are shown (see Figure 2.14). You can use the Resize handle to reduce the size of the window even further until only the playback and volume controls are shown. Click the Maximize button again to restore the iTunes window to its full size.

Figure 2.14 *When you want to conserve screen space, you can shrink the iTunes window.*

Of course, in the full-size mode, you can manually resize the window by dragging its resize handle. Making it larger will display more information. Making it smaller will display less; the window has a minimum size that is quite a bit larger than the reduced size you get with the Maximize button.

Listening to Internet Audio

You can use iTunes to listen to various Internet radio broadcasts. To do so, use the following steps.

Listen to Internet Radio

1. Select Radio Tuner as the source. The application will download the current list of available genres and present them in the Content pane.

2. Click the Expansion triangle next to a genre to view the channels available in that genre (see Figure 2.15).

3. Select the channel that you want to play and press the Spacebar. The selected channel will begin to stream to your Mac; when the prebuffer is full, it will begin to play.

Here are some notes about listening to Internet audio:

◆ When you first select the Radio Tuner source, iTunes downloads the list of available genres and channels. You can refresh this list at any time by clicking the Action button, which is called Refresh when the Radio Tuner source is selected.

Figure 2.15 *Here, you can see that the Jazz genre currently has 18 channels (streams) for your listening pleasure.*

◆ Some of the channels are live, while some are just large playlists. When you listen to one that is a playlist, it will be repeated until you stop playing it.

◆ The content you see in the Radio Tuner source is actually provided through the Live365 Web site; check it out at www.live365.com.

Building, Listening to, and Managing Your Digital Music Library

Listening to audio CDs and Internet radio with iTunes is okay, but nothing to get too excited about because you can do these tasks just as easily with other tools. Where iTunes separates itself from all the rest is that it enables you to create, listen to, and manage an entire music library. This library can include as much music as you would like—including all of your audio CDs, MP3s that you download from the Internet, and so on.

Building Your iTunes MP3 Library

To build your digital lifestyle music library, you can import files into it.

There are two basic ways to get music into your Library: importing files from audio CDs or adding files to your Library from the Internet or other locations.

There's More to Sound than MP3

In the following sections, I focus on MP3 because that is the format that you are most likely to use with music. However, you can import audio files as AIFF or WAV just as easily.

Earlier, you learned how to configure encoding for these formats—simply choose the encoding that you want to use on the Importing preferences tab.

You can also add AIFF or WAV files to your Library with the Add to Library command.

NOTE

iTunes uses the term "import" for the act of encoding your music in various formats, because when you encode music, it is imported into your Library. In more hip lingo, this process is called ripping a CD.

Encode an Audio CD in the MP3 Format

1. Insert the CD containing the songs that you want to encode. iTunes will connect to the Internet and identify the CD (again, assuming that you haven't disabled this feature or that iTunes hasn't already identified the CD).

2. Select the CD in the Source pane.

3. Check the checkbox next to the title of each song that you want to import—by default, every track is selected.

4. Click the Import button (the Action button becomes Import after you insert an audio CD). iTunes will begin to encode the songs that you select. Depending on how fast your Mac is and the number of songs that you selected, this process can take just a few minutes to a half hour or so. You can see the progress of the encoding process in the iTunes display window (see Figure 2.16). When the encoding process is completed, the song is marked with a green circle containing a checkmark. The resulting MP3 files are added to your Library, and you can listen to them from there, add them to playlists, and so on. When all of the selected songs have been imported, a chime will play.

5. When the selected songs have been added to your Library, eject the CD and repeat the process with other CDs.

Song currently   Encoded   Progress information for song
being encoded   song   currently being imported

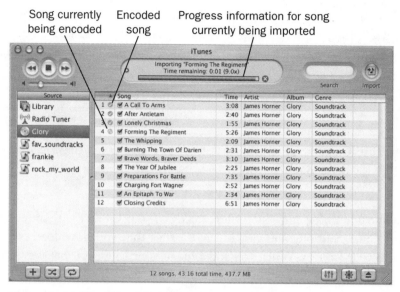

Figure 2.16 *The Glory CD is being added to my Library.*

Following are some notes on importing your CDs:

◆ When you first build your Library, set iTunes to Import Songs and Eject a CD when you insert it (use the General tab of the iTunes Preferences dialog). As iTunes finishes importing a CD, it will eject it. Then you can insert another and add it to the Library. After you have built your Library, choose a different CD insert option or you might end up with multiple versions of the same song in your Library (iTunes enables you to create multiple versions of the same songs in case you want to have songs encoded with different quality levels).

◆ You can cancel the encoding process by clicking the small "x" at the right end of the encoding progress bar in the Information window.

◆ You can listen to the music that you are encoding while you are encoding it. Because the encoding process moves faster than real-time, the import process will be done before the selected songs stop playing. This can be confusing because it seems natural that both should stop at the same time. If you set CDs to eject after they are imported, the end of the importing process will be quite clear (because the CD will be ejected).

◆ You can also listen to other songs in your Library or playlists at the same time that you are encoding songs.

◆ You can find the location of the encoded file for any song in your Library by selecting it and choosing File, Show Song File (⌘+R). A Finder window containing that file that you imported will be opened, and the file will be highlighted.

NOTE

If you purchased a new Mac with iTunes installed on it, your Library might contain quite a few songs already, courtesy of Apple.

You can also add music and sound files directly to your Library without encoding them first. For example, you can add MP3 files that you download from the Internet to your Library. When you add a file to your Library, it behaves just like files that you add by encoding them.

TIP

A good source of MP3 files that you can download is www.mp3.com.

Add Audio Files to the Library Directly

1. Choose File, Add to Library.
2. In the Choose Object dialog box, move to the files that you want to add to your Library, select them, and click Choose. You will see a dialog box explaining that iTunes doesn't actually move the files, but it uses a reference to the files that you choose.
3. Click OK to close the dialog. The files will be added to your Library.

Browsing and Listening to Your Library

After you have built your iTunes Library, you can browse it and then listen to any songs that it contains.

As a source, the Library is unique in that it is designed to hold thousands of songs from hundreds of CDs. Because of this large amount of information it can contain, its Content pane includes a Browse pane that you can use to view the contents of your Library in an organized fashion.

How iTunes Adds Files to the Library

When iTunes adds files to the Library, either through importing them or via the Add to Library command, it doesn't actually add the file to the Library. Rather, it places a reference to the file in the Library. This reference helps iTunes locate the original file when it is needed, such as when you play it.

The application works this way so that you can include the same song in one or more playlists. Rather than making multiple copies of the song, iTunes simply creates another reference to that song each time you want to use it.

When you import music, all of the original files (MP3 files, if you used the MP3 encoder) are located within the iTunes folder, so that iTunes knows where they are. When you add files to the Library, iTunes only adds a reference to that file to the Library. If you move the original file, the reference will become invalid and iTunes won't be able to use the file any more (fortunately, iTunes will help you find the file again so that the reference can be updated). This is why you see the warning dialog when you use the Add to Library command (you can disable the warning by checking the "Do not warn me again" checkbox).

Browse the iTunes Library Source

1. Choose the Library as the source. The contents of your Library will appear in the Content pane.

2. Click the Browse button to open the Browse pane.

3. Drag the Resize handle (the small dot in the border between the panes) until the Browse pane and the Content pane are sized appropriately.

4. In the Browse pane, select the Genre, Artist, or Album in which you are interested (see Figure 2.17). The Content pane of the window will show only the contents of whatever you select in the upper pane of the window. For example, to see all the albums by an artist, click that artist's name. In the Album pane, you will see all the albums for that artist. To see the tracks on an album, click the album name in the Album column. In the Content pane of the window, you will see all the tracks on the selected album. To see all the contents of a selected item again, click All.

5. Select any content to which you want to listen (Genre, Artist, Album, or songs in the Content pane) and click the Play button. The content that you selected will play.

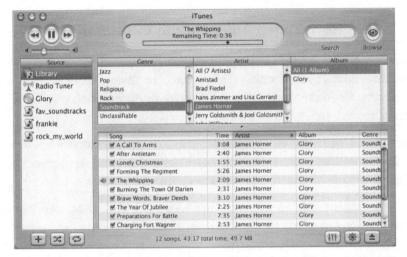

Figure 2.17 *I have selected all tracks by the artist James Horner. In the Album column, you can see that I have only one album by him.*

NOTE

In the columns of the Browse pane, you will see All at the top of each list. When you choose All, all the items in that part of the column will be selected (and played if you click the Play button). For example, if you choose an artist in the Artist column, select All in the Album column, and click Play, then all the albums by that artist will be played. Similarly, if you select All in the Album window and then click Play, all your albums will be played.

The other controls work just as they do for a CD or other source, such as the track checkbox, Shuffle button, and so on. You can also use the track checkbox to skip songs and play a song by double-clicking it just as you do when you listen to a CD.

TIP

To show the Genre column in the Browse pane, check the "Show Genre When Browsing" checkbox in the General tab of the iTunes Preferences window.

Using the Song Information Window

The iTunes Song Information window is a powerful tool that you can use to get information about tracks and to control specific aspects of those tracks. For example, earlier in this chapter, you learned how to associate an Equalizer preset with a specific song. The Song Information window enables you to do more than just this.

To open the Song Information window, select a song and choose File, Get Info (or press ⌘ + I). At the top of the window, you will see the song's title; you can change the song's name by editing the text in this field. This window has the following three tabs:

◆ **Info**. Use this tab to get information about the song.

◆ **Tags**. This tab enables you to apply various tags to the song, such as its artist, album, year, track number, and genre. You can also add comments about the song.

◆ **Options**. Using this tab, you can change the relative volume level of the song, apply an Equalizer preset, and control the start and stop playback time.

At the bottom of the window, you see the Prev Song button, which moves you to the previous song in the selected source; the Next Song button, which moves you to next song in the selected source; the Cancel button, which closes the window without saving your changes; and the OK button, which closes the window after saving your changes.

Making Your Playlists and Checking Them Twice

One of the most useful features of iTunes is the ability to create playlists. Playlists enable you to create your own albums containing as many songs as you'd like in any order that you want. You can repeat individual songs many times in the same playlist and include the same songs in different playlists. You can listen to your playlists just like other sources, and you can move playlists to an MP3 player or burn a CD from them. After you have created playlists, you can continue changing them by adding more songs, removing songs that you no longer want to be included, changing the playback order, and so on. As you use iTunes, you will frequently work with playlists.

Creating a new playlist is very straightforward.

Create a Playlist

1. Click the New Playlist button or choose File, New Playlist (press ⌘+N). You will see a new, untitled playlist in the Source pane.

2. Name your new playlist. Immediately after you create a playlist, the name is in the edit mode and you can name it.

3. Browse your Library to find the songs that you want to include in your playlist. You can browse by genre, artist, or album. You can also use the search tool to find songs.

4. When you find tracks that interest you, drag them onto the playlist that you created in Step 1. The songs that you drop onto a playlist are added to it. You can drop the same song onto a playlist as many times as you like.

TIP

Some standard Mac selection tricks will help you choose songs for a playlist. You can choose a contiguous set of songs by holding the Shift key down, clicking the first song in the group that you want to select, and then clicking the last song in the group that you want to select. You can select multiple noncontiguous songs by holding the ⌘ key down while you click on each song that you want to select. You can select all of the songs in the Content pane by clicking that pane and choosing Edit, Select All (press ⌘+A). To deselect all songs, choose Edit, Select None (press Shift+⌘+A).

5. After you have added several songs, click the playlist you created in the Source pane to see its contents in the Content pane (see Figure 2.18).

6. Drag the tracks up and down in the Content pane to change the order in which they will play.

7. Continue adding and ordering songs until the playlist contains the songs that you want.

TIP

A fast way to start a new playlist and add songs to it is to select a group of songs and choose File, New Playlist From Selection (or press Shift+⌘+N). A new playlist containing the selected songs will be created.

Figure 2.18 *I have created a playlist called "jazz_lives" and placed all of my music from the Jazz genre into it.*

When you select a playlist in the Source pane, information about that playlist appears at the bottom of the iTunes window. This information includes the number of songs in the playlist, their total playing time, and the size of the files that you have referenced in the playlist. This information is very useful when you want to place the playlist on an MP3 device or when you want to burn a CD. You can use the size information to ensure that the playlist will fit in the device's memory. (Playlists themselves contain only file references so they are quite small; however, when you put a playlist on an MP3 player or CD, the actual source files are moved to that device.)

NOTE

Playlists are listed in the Source pane in alphabetical order. You can't change this so if the order in which your playlists appear is important, keep that in mind when you name them.

Listening to a playlist is just like listening to other sources. Select the playlist in the source window and use the playback tools and techniques that you learned earlier in this chapter to listen to it.

There are several ways in which you can change your playlists, including the following:

◆ You can edit playlist names by clicking on them and waiting for a second or so until the name becomes highlighted. When it is highlighted, you can change the name.

◆ You can delete songs from a playlist by selecting the playlist as the source, selecting the songs that you want to delete, and pressing Delete. You will see a warning dialog; click Yes to remove the song from the playlist. The song is not deleted from the Library nor is the source MP3 file affected, so you can always add it to this or other playlists again.

◆ To add more songs to the playlist, select them in the Library's Content pane and drag them to the playlist.

◆ You can delete a playlist by selecting it and pressing Delete.

Removing Songs from the Library

If there are songs that you are sure that you will never want to use, you can delete them from your Library (if you just don't want to hear them, uncheck their checkboxes instead). When you delete songs from your Library, the original MP3 files are also deleted and will no longer be available (you'll have to import them again).

Remove Songs from the Library

1. Select the songs that you want to delete.

2. Press Delete. You will see a warning dialog, just like when you delete a song from a playlist.

3. Click Yes. You'll see a second warning dialog explaining that some of the songs you selected are stored in your Music Library folder—meaning that they are MP3 files you have encoded.

4. Click Yes. The song will be removed from the Library and the related source file will be moved to the Trash. The next time that you empty the Trash, the files will be deleted.

Putting Your iTunes Music on the Move

Mastering your music on your Mac is great, but the digital lifestyle is a mobile one, so why shouldn't you be able to master your music wherever you are? With iTunes, you can.

iTunes enables you to "mobilize" your music (sorry about that, but I just had to write it), in the following ways:

♦ Create your own audio CDs

♦ Put your music on an MP3 player

♦ Put your music on an Apple iPod

Burning Your Own CDs

There is nothing like creating your own audio CDs to provide a musical experience that is tailored to your tastes and musical desires. As you learned earlier, iTunes enables you to create two different types of CDs. You can create an audio CD that can be played in any standard CD player, such as that player in your car. Or, you can create an MP3 CD that contains MP3 versions of your music; of course, you need a player capable of playing MP3 music to play these CDs (the benefit is that you can put a lot more music in the MP3 format on a single CD).

> **NOTE**
>
> It should go without saying that in order to create a CD, you need a drive capable of burning CDs (such as a CD-RW drive). See Chapter 7, "Digital Lifestyle Hardware: Digital Rules, Analog Drools," for information about CD-RW drives.

Burn a CD

1. Create a playlist containing the songs you want to put on a CD.

2. Put the songs in the order on which you want them to be on the CD.

3. Check the information for the playlist that you have created to make sure that it will fit onto a CD. Most CDs can contain up to 750MB of data or 70-80 minutes of music. The amount of songs this includes will depend on the format you are using. If you are creating an audio CD, you will be

limited to the amount of music on a standard audio CD. If you are creating an MP3 CD, you will be able to get much more music on a single CD. In either case, make sure that the size and time shown for the playlist is less than or equal to the amount that you can place on the CD media that you are using.

4. Configure iTunes for CD burning by making sure that iTunes recognizes your CD burner; then choosing the format that you want to use (see the section called "Setting iTunes CD Burning Preferences" earlier in this chapter).

5. Select the playlist that you want to put on the CD. The Action button will become the Burn CD button.

6. Click the Burn CD button. You will be prompted to insert a blank CD. Use CD-R discs for audio CDs that you create rather than CD-RW discs, especially if you will be using the CDs that you create in non-computer CD players. If you create an audio CD using a CD-RW disc, the odds are that you won't be able to play it in a standard CD player. Besides which, CD-R discs are less expensive.

7. Insert a blank CD, close the drive door (unless you have a slot-loading CD-RW drive in which case this isn't necessary), and click the Burn CD button again. iTunes will start burning the CD. Depending on the format of the CD that you are creating, the speed of your CD burner, and your Mac's capabilities, the burning process can take just a couple of minutes to a half-hour or so. When the CD is done, it will be ejected from your Mac.

NOTE

The spinning Burn CD icon gives you a clue as to how fast the data is being transferred to the CD that is being recorded. The faster the icon spins, the higher the data transfer rate is achieved. If the icon slows considerably or stops altogether, you might experience errors because data isn't flowing fast enough to keep the CD burning process fed properly. If this happens, quit all applications that might be accessing any disks on your Mac and make sure that you aren't playing any music in iTunes. This will ensure that the maximum amount of system resources is available for the CD burning process. You can also lower the burn speed to reduce the data flow requirements. Doing so will often alleviate this problem.

Taking Your Digital Music on the Road with MP3 Players

MP3 players are neat because they are really small and can hold the specific music that you want them to. Many are completely RAM-based, which means that they have no moving parts and can never skip. By using the MP3 format, most MP3 players are capable of two or more hours of music and you never have to deal with CDs, which can be a pain when you are on the move.

iTunes makes it easy to move music to and from most MP3 players that are available.

Picking an MP3 Player

There are lots of MP3 players available and explaining all the details associated with these devices is beyond what I have room to cover here. However, the following list provides some guidelines for you:

- ◆ **iTunes compatibility**. By default, iTunes comes with the plug-ins required to support a number of MP3 players, including some of the most popular models. If you are interested in using an MP3 player with iTunes, you should get one of the supported models. To see which models are supported by the current version of iTunes, visit the iTunes Web site at www.apple.com/itunes/. You can also open the following folder: iTunes for Mac OS X/Plug-ins/Device Plug-ins. In this directory, you will see a list of all the plug-ins for the supported MP3 players. If your MP3 player isn't listed, you can add support for it by adding its plug-in to this folder.

- ◆ **Memory**. MP3 players come with a built-in amount of memory. The more memory a model has, the more music that you will be able to store and listen to. Typical models come with 64MB of memory or more, which is enough for about an hour or two of music, depending on the encoding method that you use. Most MP3 players also use some form of removable memory, such as CompactFlash media. Being able to use this type of memory is good because you can expand the amount of music that you can take with you by obtaining more memory cards.

- ◆ **Size and style**. Most MP3 players are really small (the smallest are the Sony models, which are not much larger than a pen). They have a variety of shapes, colors, and so on. Although the style factors don't affect performance, the size and shape of the unit should definitely be a consideration. The whole idea is to carry the unit with you, so you want one that is comfortable for you.

◆ **Cost**. The largest factor in the cost of an MP3 player is the amount of memory that it has. You can get capable MP3 players for around $150. Before paying much more than this, you should consider getting an Apple iPod (you'll learn more about the iPod later in this chapter).

Moving Your Music to an MP3 Player

To listen to music on an MP3 player, you download the music you want from iTunes to the player.

Download Music from iTunes to an MP3 Player

1. Create a playlist containing the songs that you want to put on your player. Use the playlist's information to ensure that the amount of memory contained in the playlist is equal to or less than the memory available in your player.

2. Connect your MP3 player to your Mac and power the player up. iTunes will automatically recognize your player, and it will be selected in the Source pane.

3. If the player has music on it already, select the songs it contains and press Delete to empty the player's memory.

4. Drag the playlist you created in Step 1 onto the player in the Source pane. The music will be downloaded to the player. You can see the progress of the process in the Information window. At the bottom of the Content pane, you will see a memory gauge that shows you the memory status of the player (see Figure 2.19).

Following are some notes to help you work with an MP3 player:

◆ You can drag songs directly from the Library (individual songs or albums) to download them to the player without creating a playlist. However, using a playlist helps you get the most music on the player because you can easily see the memory requirements of the playlist versus the memory capability of the player.

◆ When you select an MP3 player as a source, you will see some additional buttons at the bottom of the iTunes window (see Figure 2.19). Use the Settings dialog to rename your player. You can also upgrade its firmware

Figure 2.19 *The MP3 player (which happens to be a Rio 500) is selected as the source, and you can see the music it contains.*

by clicking the Upgrade Firmware button. Some MP3 players enable you to create folders in which to store music. Use the Create folder button to create a new folder on the MP3 player. Use the Delete button to delete all songs from the MP3 player's memory.

Mastering Your Digital Music with the iPod

While the Apple iPod is an MP3 player, it is much more than most MP3 players. While many MP3 players are limited to 64MB or 128MB of memory, the iPod includes its own 5GB hard drive. This means you can store an entire music collection on the iPod (about 1,000 songs), which eliminates the chore of selecting a small subset of your library to take on the road with you. The iPod uses the FireWire interface to communicate with your Mac, which means that data transfers to and from the iPod much more quickly than it does with most other MP3 players (because most use USB which is much slower than FireWire). iTunes is designed to make managing your mobile music with the iPod even easier than it is with other MP3 players. For example, you can set the iPod up so that it is automatically synched with your iTunes music collection, including the songs in your Library, your playlists, and so on.

The iPod's only downside is its cost, which is higher than many MP3 players (currently about $400). However, if you consider that the iPod is actually a very small 5GB FireWire hard drive and includes a 10-hour rechargeable battery, its price doesn't seem as high. Also, keep in mind that you would have to buy many, many memory cards for most players for them to even approach the amount of music you can store on the iPod.

> **NOTE**
>
> Another cool feature of the iPod is that its battery can be recharged through the FireWire port. This means that you can recharge your iPod just by connecting it to your Mac.

Moving Your Music Collection to an iPod

One of the great things about the iPod is that iTunes is designed to keep the iPod in synch with your music library.

Add Your Music Collection to an iPod

1. Connect the iPod to your Mac using the supplied FireWire cable. Your Mac will recognize the iPod as a new source and iTunes will begin to download all of the music in your Library to the iPod (see Figure 2.20). During this process, the iTunes Information window will display the progress of the process, as well warning you *not* to unplug the iPod while the update is in process. As songs are downloaded, the refresh icon next to them disappears.

2. When the process is complete, disconnect the iPod. Your entire iTunes music library is ready to go with you.

> **NOTE**
>
> iTunes contains a complete online help system for the iPod. To access it, choose Help, iPod Help.

Managing Your iPod Music

As you add music to your Library, create playlists, remove songs, and so on, you will want to keep your iPod current with your iTunes Library. You can control how this is done by setting preferences for the iPod using the Player Options button (see Figure 2.20).

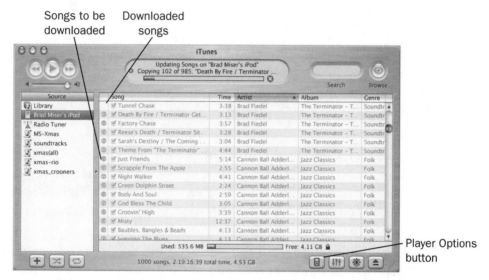

Figure 2.20 *So far, this iPod has only about 556MB of music on it. With 5GB of available disk space, it is just getting started.*

When you click this button, you will see the iPod Preferences window (see Figure 2.21). The options you have in this window are explained in the following bulleted list:

◆ **Automatically update all songs and playlists**. When this option is selected, the entire iTunes music Library will be synchronized with the music on the iPod each time that you connect the iPod to your Mac. This means that the iPod contains a mirror image of the music that you are managing in iTunes.

◆ **Automatically update selected playlists only**. When you choose this option, you select the playlists that you want to be updated. When you

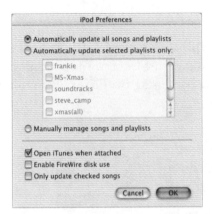

Figure 2.21 *You use the iPod Preferences window to configure how you manage your iPod music collection.*

connect the iPod to your Mac, only the selected playlists are synchronized. This option is useful if there is music in iTunes that you don't really want to carry with you or when you can't fit your entire iTunes Library on the iPod. Create the playlists that you want to keep on the iPod and then have them synchronized automatically.

◆ **Manually manage songs and playlists**. With this option, you must manually move songs to the iPod; you do this just like you do for "regular" MP3 players.

◆ **Open iTunes when attached**. With this button selected, iTunes will open when you attach an iPod to your Mac.

◆ **Enable FireWire disk use**. You can use your iPod as an external FireWire hard disk. To do so, check this checkbox and also the "Manually manage songs and playlists" radio button. When you attach the iPod to your Mac, you can work with it just like other hard disks. (You can't use this method to transfer music to the iPod, though; instead you must use iTunes to do that.)

◆ **Only update checked songs**. This option enables you to prevent songs from being copied to the iPod. Check this checkbox and then uncheck the checkbox next to any songs that you don't want to be copied to the iPod.

That is really all there is to it. The Apple iPod is one of those rare devices that really does work as well as the marketing information claims it will. If you are at all serious about having a mobile music collection, check out the iPod.

NOTE

For more information on the iPod, see www.apple.com/ipod/.

Using iTunes for Your Digital Lifestyle Projects

iTunes is a fundamental part of your digital lifestyle toolkit. In addition to listening to and managing all of your music, you will use iTunes to do the following tasks:

◆ Capture music from audio CDs in the MP3 format for use in your projects.

◆ Translate audio between formats (such as AIFF to MP3).

◆ Put your iMovie soundtracks on a CD.

◆ Create soundtracks for DVDs, slideshows, and other projects.

Chapter 3

iPhoto: Not Your Father's Photo Album

If pictures are worth a thousand words, then iPhoto is worth at least a dozen word processors. With iPhoto, you can take control over digital images that you capture with a digital camera, scan, have developed on CD, or that you acquire from just about any other source. As you build an image library, you can enjoy these images for their own sake and use them in your digital lifestyle projects.

With iPhoto, you can do the following tasks:

- Import images from a digital camera or from other sources
- Organize and catalog your images
- Edit the images by cropping, rotating, removing red-eye, and so on
- Create image books
- Share the images in many ways, such as by printing them, creating slideshows, exporting them, and more

TIP

If you don't already have iPhoto installed on your Mac, go to www.apple.com/iphoto/ and download a copy. The application is free so there is no reason not to use it!

The iPhoto Way

If you read through the previous chapter on iTunes, then you won't have any trouble learning and using iPhoto because the applications are similar in many ways, as you will see in this section.

Like iTunes, iMovie, and the rest of the digital lifestyle applications, iPhoto is both powerful and easy to use. You can use the application to master your digital image library. In the following sections, you'll get a quick tour of iPhoto.

The iPhoto Window

When you open iPhoto, you will see a three-paned window that looks quite similar to iTunes (see Figure 3.1). Also like iTunes, when you select a source in the

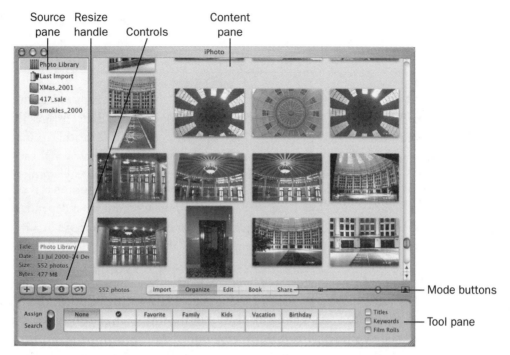

Figure 3.1 *iPhoto helps you make the most of your digital images.*

Source pane, you'll see the contents of that source in the Source pane. You use the Content pane to select the images with which you want to work. Unlike iTunes, iPhoto has five modes, with each mode enabling you to do a specific task with the images that you have selected in the Source pane. When you choose a mode, the Tool pane will contain the tools that you use in that mode. Between the Tool pane and the Content pane, you see iPhoto controls, which include the Mode buttons.

The iPhoto Source Pane

Images in iPhoto can be organized into albums; iPhoto albums are analogous to "analog" photo albums that contain the images in your collection. The iPhoto Source pane shows all of the albums that are contained in your image collection. iPhoto includes two albums that are always present: Photo Library and Last Import. The Photo Library album contains all of the images that you have imported into iPhoto (regardless of how you imported the images). Think of the Photo Library as your entire image collection, and you will understand it correctly. The Last Import album contains the images that you downloaded during the last time you imported images.

To work with an album, you select it in the Source pane and its contents will be shown in the Content pane.

TIP

You can resize the Source pane by dragging the Resize handle to the left or right.

The iPhoto Content Pane

The iPhoto Content pane shows the contents of the source album that is selected in the Source pane. How you see the images in the Content pane depends on the mode in which you are operating. When you are in the Import or Organize modes, you will see thumbnail views of all of the images in the selected album. When you are in the Edit mode, you will see a single image that you have selected in the album (see Figure 3.2). When you work in the Book or Share modes, the Content pane shows a preview of the images that you have selected; you use this preview to set the order and other aspects of the images in the object you are creating, such as a book. You'll learn more about the Content pane in the various modes a little later in this chapter.

Figure 3.2 *In the Edit mode, the Content pane is filled with the image that you are editing.*

iPhoto Controls

Between the Source and Content panes and the Tool pane, you see iPhoto controls that are available in whichever mode you are in (see Figure 3.3).

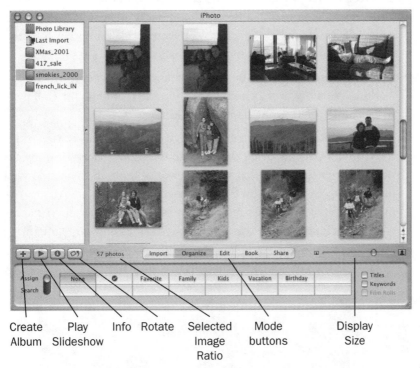

Create   Play   Info Rotate   Selected   Mode   Display
Album Slideshow   Image   buttons   Size
                                Ratio

Figure 3.3 *The controls between the Source and Content pane and the Tool pane are always available to you.*

The controls are explained in the following list:

◆ **Create Album**. You click this button to create a new album. You will learn more about creating albums later in this chapter.

◆ **Play Slideshow**. Click this button and a nice slideshow displaying the images in the selected album will play (accompanied by a music soundtrack).

◆ **Info**. Click this to open or expand the Information area of the Source pane. If the Info area is not displayed, clicking this button once will open it. If it is displayed, clicking this button will expand it. If it is expanded, clicking this button will close it.

◆ **Rotate**. Rotates a selected image by 90-degree increments in the counterclockwise direction. When you select an image and then click this button, the image is rotated in the Content pane; the image assumes the orientation you choose from that point forward (meaning the image itself is changed to be the orientation you select).

◆ **Selected Image Ratio.** This ratio shows the number of images that you have selected compared to the total number of images in the selected album. If you don't have any images selected, this number will be the total number of images in the selected album.

◆ **Mode buttons**. Use these buttons to change the mode in which iPhoto is working. When you click a mode button, the Content and Tool panes will change to reflect the mode you select.

◆ **Display Size.** Drag this slider to change the size of the images you see in the Content pane. Moving the slider to the right makes the individual images larger (meaning that you see fewer of them in the window), while moving it to the left makes the images appear smaller and you can see more images at the same time. The setting of this slider doesn't actually change the image in any way; it only determines how large the images appear onscreen. For example, compare the size of the thumbnails in Figure 3.3 with the same thumbnails in Figure 3.4.

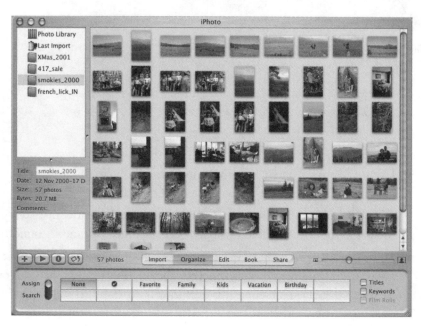

Figure 3.4 *Moving the Display Size slider to the left makes the thumbnails smaller, which means that you see more of your images on the screen.*

iPhoto Modes and Tools

iPhoto is a very powerful application and enables you to do lots of different tasks. For each task, there is a mode. And for each mode, there is a set of tools on the Tool pane.

Import

When you use iPhoto in the Import mode, you import your photos into the application, which places the images that you import into your Photo Library. There are two ways to import images into iPhoto: from a digital camera or from other sources.

When you connect a digital camera to your Mac and click the Import button, iPhoto will recognize the camera and show you how many images it contains (see Figure 3.5). When you import images from other sources, you won't see a camera-connected message, but you will see the other import tools.

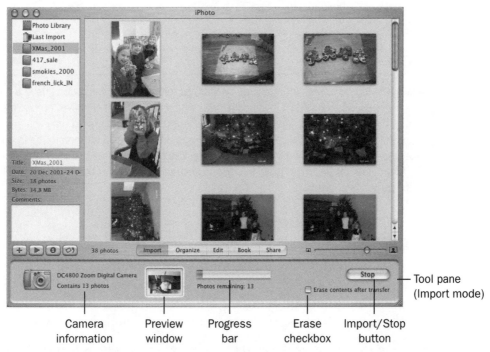

Figure 3.5 *In this figure, you can see that a Kodak DC 4800 camera is connected to the Mac and that there are 13 images available for download.*

In the Import mode, the Tool pane contains the following elements:

◆ **Camera information**. When iPhoto is communicating with a camera, you will see that camera's information, such as its model name. You'll also see how many images are available to be downloaded into iPhoto. When a camera is not connected, you see the "No camera connected" message.

◆ **Preview window**. When you import images, you will see a preview of each image as it is imported in the Preview window.

◆ **Progress bar**. The progress bar displays the progress of the import process. As images are imported, the blue bar fills the progress bar.

◆ **Import/Stop button**. This button is Import when you aren't importing images. When you click the Import button, the import process starts, and the button becomes Stop (the Stop button does just what you think it does).

◆ **Erase checkbox**. If you check the "Erase contents after transfer" checkbox, the images on your digital camera will be erased after they have been imported into iPhoto.

NOTE

Here are two comments on the Erase checkbox for you. First, if you don't have a camera connected to your Mac, it is inactive. Second, even when it is active, I recommend that you don't use it. I suggest that you leave images on your camera until you are sure that they have been imported correctly. Should something happen to the image you import and it is erased from your camera, it is gone forever. After you have verified that your images have been imported successfully, you can delete them by using your camera's controls.

Organize

iPhoto continues its straightforward naming conventions with the Organize mode. You use the Organize mode to organize the images in your Photo Library as well as the albums that you create. Typically, you also start tasks for which you use iPhoto, such as editing images or creating books, from the Organize mode.

When in the Organize mode, the Tool pane contains tools that enable you to assign keywords to images and to find images based on those keywords (see Figure 3.6).

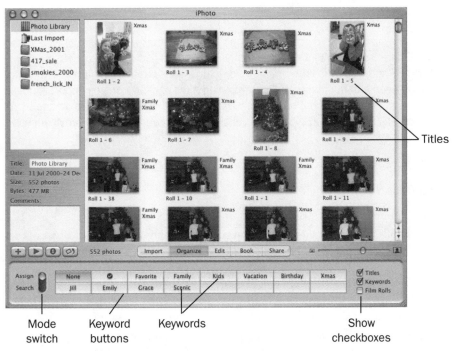

Figure 3.6 *In the Organize mode, you can view the contents of albums selected in the Source pane of your Photo Library; you can also search for specific images.*

The Organize tool pane has two modes; the mode you are in is determined by the Mode switch setting.

When the switch is in the Assign position, you can assign keywords to images (you'll learn how to create and assign keywords to images later in this chapter). When the switch is in the Search position, only the photos with which the highlighted keywords are associated will be shown in the Content pane.

At the far right of the Tool pane, you see the Show checkboxes. When a Show checkbox is checked, the checkbox's label is shown next to the images in the Content pane. For example, in Figure 3.6, you can see that the Titles and Keywords checkboxes are checked and those labels are shown next to the images in the Content pane.

NOTE

In Figure 3.6, you might notice that the images are titled by a sequential number by "roll." iPhoto uses the term "roll" to refer to an import session (the term session might have been a better choice). Like developing a roll of file, when you import images, you do so in chunks, which iPhoto calls rolls. By default, iPhoto names an image by roll number + sequential number. You can change an image's title to be anything you want.

Edit

You can use iPhoto's Edit mode to make changes to your images. While iPhoto is not a full-featured image editing application such as Adobe Photoshop, its tools enable you to make the changes that most people want to make to their images.

To edit an image, you select it and then click the Edit mode button. The image will fill the Content pane, and you will see the Edit mode's Tool pane (see Figure 3.7). For most actions, you will then select the part of the image with which you want to work. You so this by dragging over an area of the image to select it—the selected area of the image appears clear while the unselected part is shaded.

Figure 3.7 *You can use iPhoto's Edit mode to make changes to your images, such as rotating them or cropping them.*

NOTE

Most of the Edit buttons don't become active until you select a part of the image (for example, you must select part of the image before the Crop button becomes active).

The tools you see on the Edit mode Tool pane are the following:

♦ **Rotate**. When you click the Rotate button, the image will be rotated 90-degrees in the counter-clockwise direction. Each time you click the button, the image is rotated another 90-degress, until you click four times at which point it returns to its original orientation.

♦ **Constrain**. You can use this pop-up menu to constrain the portion of the image that you select to a specific size. For example, if you choose 5 x 7, when you select part of the image, the selection will have the 5 x 7 proportion. This makes it easy to crop images to specific proportions for different purposes (such as to print them in 5 x 7). Your choices explained in Table 3.1.

♦ **Crop**. Use this tool to remove any of the image that is outside of the selected area. This helps you get rid of wasted space or parts of the image that you don't want to see.

♦ **Red-Eye**. Use this tool to remove the red from eyes that is often seen when people or animals are looking directly at the camera when the flash goes off. To use this tool, select an area around the eyes that has that certain demon-eyed appearance. When you click the Red-Eye button, the red will be removed from the selected area. Keep your selection to a small area of the image, because the application doesn't really know what is an eye and what is not; it looks for and removes red, whether it is in an eye or elsewhere.

♦ **Black & White**. The button converts the image you are editing into black and white.

♦ **Previous/Next**. These buttons take you to the previous or next image in the selected album.

Table 3.1 iPhoto Constrain Options

Option	What It Does
None	You can choose a selection at any proportion
4 x 3 (Book, DVD)	This proportion is useful when you create books or place your images on DVD
4 x 6	Intended for images that you will use at 4 x 6 inches
5 x 7	Intended for images that you will use at 5 x 7 inches
8 x 10	Intended for images that you will use at 8 x 10 inches
4 x 3 Portrait (Book)	This proportion is useful for portrait-oriented images when you create books or place the images on DVD
4 x 6 Portrait	Intended for images that you will use at 4 x 6 inches in the portrait orientation
5 x 7 Portrait	Intended for images that you will use at 5 x 7 inches in the portrait orientation
8 x 10 Portrait	Intended for images that you will use at 8 x 10 inches in the portrait orientation
Square	Maintains a square selection area

TIP

You can rotate images in any mode. Select the images you want to rotate and then click the Rotate button that is always available just below the Source pane. You can also select images and choose Edit, Rotate, Counter Clockwise (press ⌘+R) or Edit, Rotate, Clockwise (press Shift+⌘+R).

A nice feature of iPhoto is that it maintains the original version of images that you edit so that you can return to the "pristine" version of the photo at any time. When you do this, you lose any changes you have made to the image, but at least you can recover from your "improvements." To return to the original version of a photo that you have edited, select that image and then choose File, Revert to Original. When you click OK in the warning dialog that will appear, the image will be returned to the state that it was in before you started mucking around with it.

Book

In the Book mode, you can create very nice books of your photos in a variety of formats and styles. You can also choose to display a variety of information next to the photos in the book. After you have created a book, you can print it yourself or order a printed copy.

In the Book mode, the Content pane contains a preview of the selected book page above thumbnails of each page in the book. The Tool pane contains the tools you use to build your book (see Figure 3.8).

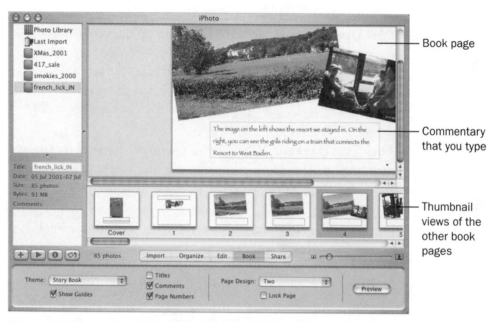

Figure 3.8 *Here, I chose the Storybook theme for the book and am entering comments about the photos on the selected page.*

While you'll get more detailed information about creating books later in this chapter, the following list explains the tools that you see in the Tool pane:

◆ **Theme pop-up menu**. Each book that you create can be on one of six themes. The theme determines how images are displayed on each page of the book. For example, if you choose Story Book, images appear at different sizes and orientations on the pages for a more casual look. If you choose the Year Book theme, thumbnail images will appear on each page of the book. Each theme style also has corresponding text boxes in which you can enter commentary of other information for the book.

◆ **Show Guides checkbox**. When this box is checked, you see blue guidelines around the various text boxes on a page.

◆ **Show checkboxes**. These checkboxes determine which elements of an image's information appear next to the image in the book. If a checkbox is checked, then that information will appear on the book page. However, some themes don't show certain information, even if the checkbox is checked. For example, the Story Book theme doesn't display any of the image's information regardless of the checkbox settings. Instead, that theme provides a separate text box for each page in which you can use text to narrate the book you create.

◆ **Page Design pop-up menu**. Use this pop-up menu to choose a page's design, such as making it the Cover or Introduction, or to choose how many images will appear on that page. If pages are selected when you make a choice on this menu, only the selected pages are affected. If you don't select pages, all the pages are affected. You can choose different designs for each page in the book.

◆ **Lock Page checkbox**. When this box is checked, you can't change a page's design. Use this to prevent accidental changes to a page.

◆ **Preview button**. When you click the Preview button, a separate preview window opens, and you can page through your book as it will be when it is printed. You can also make changes to the book in this window, such as adding text to pages.

TIP

Remember to use the Display Size slider in each mode. For example, when you are editing an image, you can make the image appear larger so that you can make more refined selections. In the Book mode, use the slider to change the size at which the pages you work with appear in the Content pane.

After you create a book, you can print it or you can order a professionally printed book from Apple by using the Share mode.

Share

The Share mode enables you to output your images in a number of ways. The Share Tool pane contains the tools shown in Figure 3.9 and explained in the following list:

◆ **Print**. I bet you can guess what this tool does. Yep, it enables you to print your images. You can configure a number of options for the prints, such as the style (Contact Sheet, Full Page, Greeting Card, or Standard Prints) and the size of the margins.

◆ **Slide Show**. When you click this button, you can show the images in the selected album in a slideshow. You can choose the music that you want to accompany the images, and you can choose the time for which the images are displayed.

◆ **Order Prints**. You can use this tool to order prints from the Kodak Print Service through Apple's 1-Click service. Select the images for which you want to buy prints, click the Share mode button, and then click Order Prints. You will move to the 1-Click setup screen. After your account is set up, you can choose the number and sizes of prints you want to order.

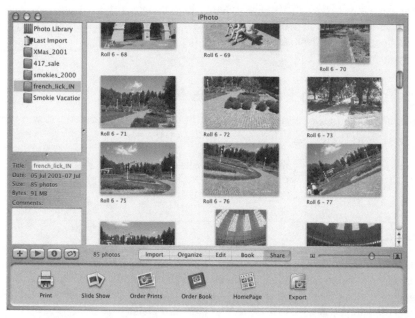

Figure 3.9 *In the Share mode, you can choose the way in which you want to share your images.*

This tool makes it quite easy to get professional-quality prints of your photos delivered to you or other people.

◆ **Order Book**. This tool is similar to the Order Prints function except you get books printed instead of individual photos.

◆ **HomePage**. Use this tool to assemble an iTools Web site displaying your photos. (You'll learn more about this in Chapter 19, "Creating and Hosting a Digital Lifestyle Web Site with iTools.")

◆ **Export**. You use this option to export your images in a variety of ways. You can export images as separate files, in case you want to use them in other applications or for other purposes. You can also export images in a Web page or as a QuickTime movie. This is useful for creating and saving custom slideshows. (You'll learn how to do this in Chapter 15, "Building Digital Lifestyle Slideshows.")

NOTE

The difference between the Slide Show button in the Share tool pane and the Slide Show button just below the Source pane is that with the Slide Show button below the Source pane, you can't choose any options; the slideshow plays with the preferences you have set. When you use the Slide Show on the Share tool pane, you can choose the options for the slideshow.

Making Your iPhoto Preferences Known

Configuring iPhoto is relatively simple. Choose iPhoto, Preferences, and you will see the iPhoto Preferences dialog (see Figure 3.10).

There are three areas of preferences that you can configure: Photos, Double-click action, and Slide Show. These preferences are explained in Table 3.2.

NOTE

When you use the Other option to select more music for your slideshows, the music you select is added to the Music menu so that you can choose it from there when you play future slideshows. If you want to remove music from this menu, choose Edit List, select the songs you want to remove, and then click Delete.

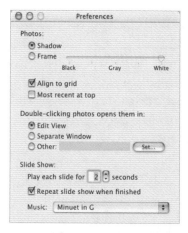

Figure 3.10 *Use this Preferences dialog to configure iPhoto.*

Table 3.2 iPhoto Preference Settings

Preference	Options	What the Options Do
Photos	Shadow	The Shadow option puts a drop shadow behind the thumbnail images in the Content pane when you are in the Organize mode.
	Frame	The Frame option puts each thumbnail in a frame. Use the slider to set the color of the frame (from black to white).
	Align to grid	With this option checked, your images remain aligned to the iPhoto grid.
	Most recent at top	When this checkbox is checked, the photos that you imported most recently appear at the top of the Content pane.
Double-click Action	Edit View	With the Edit View option, when you double-click an image, it opens in the Edit mode.
	Separate Window	With the Separate Window option, when you double-click an image, it opens in a separate window in which you can view the image.
	Other	When you choose Other and then use the Set button to choose an application, the image on which you double-click will open in the application that you select. For example, you might choose to double-click images to open them in another image editing application.

Table 3.2 iPhoto Preference Settings (continued)

Preference	Options	What the Options Do
Slide Show	Play each slide for __ seconds	Use this control to set the amount of time that each image appears on the screen when you click the Slide Show button located under the Source pane.
	Repeat slide show when finished	With this checkbox checked, slideshows will continue to play until you stop them manually.
	Music pop-up menu	Choose the music that plays when you show a slideshow by using the Slide Show button located under the Source pane. You have several default pieces to choose from; you can use Other to select an MP3 file (the application looks in your iTunes music collection by default), or you can edit the list of songs by choosing Edit List.

Building Your Digital Image Library

Moving your images into iPhoto is a simple task, whether you are bringing them in from a camera or from image files that you have from other sources (such as images that you have scanned or that someone has emailed to you).

Importing Images from a Digital Camera

Assuming that you have a digital camera that is compatible with iPhoto, downloading images from the camera into your iPhoto Photo Library is simple.

NOTE

For information about iPhoto-compatible digital cameras, see the section called "Digital Still Camera" in Chapter 8, "Digital Lifestyle Hardware: Digital Rules, Analog Drools."

Download Images from a Digital Camera into iPhoto

1. Open iPhoto if it isn't already open.
2. Connect your camera to your Mac with its USB cable.

3. Power up your camera. If this is the first time that you have connected your camera to iPhoto, you will see a dialog asking you if you want iPhoto to be launched automatically when a camera is attached to your Mac. Unless you use your camera with other applications, which isn't all that likely, click Yes to set that preference.

4. Click the Import mode button—this step won't be necessary if you clicked Yes when prompted about iPhoto being launched automatically when a camera is connected. Your camera will be recognized in the lower left corner of the Import Tool pane, and you will see how many photos are ready to be downloaded.

5. Click Import. The application will begin moving the images from the camera's memory into your Photo Library. As the process proceeds, you can see its progress in the Progress bar (see Figure 3.11).

6. Power down your camera (save them batteries!).

7. Click the Last Import album in the Source pane. iPhoto will move into the Organize mode, and you will see the photos that you just imported.

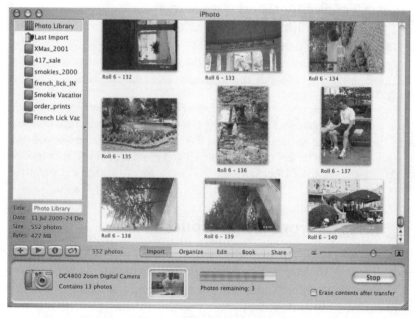

Figure 3.11 *Here you can see that 13 photos are available for download, and that the import process is just about done.*

8. Work with the Organization mode tools to organize and identify the images that you just imported (see the section called "Organizing Your Images" for the steps to do so).

NOTE

If you choose the "Most recent at top" preference, the images you import will appear at the top of the Content pane when you select the Photo Library as the source.

I strongly recommend that you organize and add information to your images as soon as you import them. If you wait, you aren't likely ever to get around to it, and the photos will not be as easy to work with. Make a habit of organizing your images as soon as you import them, and your photo collection won't get out-of-hand (organizing one import session's worth of images is much easier and faster than organizing hundreds of images at the same time).

After you have organized the images that you have imported, use your camera's tools to empty its memory card so that you are ready for your next shooting session. (If you check the "Erase contents after transfer" checkbox before you import the images, this will be done automatically.)

TIP

To remove images from your Photo Library, select the images and press the Delete button. Click OK in the warning dialog, and the image will be deleted from iPhoto. Obviously, you should do this only with images that you are sure you will never want again.

Importing Images from Other Sources

You can also add images from other sources to your iPhoto Photo Library. For example, if you don't have a digital camera that is compatible with iPhoto, then you will have to download images from that camera (such as by using a USB memory card reader) and then import them into iPhoto. Or, you might want to add photos that you have scanned to iPhoto so that you can use iPhoto's great tools to work with them.

NOTE

You can import a wide variety of image file formats into iPhoto, including JPEGs, Photoshop files, and other formats that you are likely to encounter when dealing with digital images.

Import Images from Other Sources into iPhoto

1. Prepare the images that you want to import (for example, scan the photos or download them from a USB memory card reader to your Mac).

2. Choose File, Import (or press ⌘+I). You will see the Import Photos dialog.

3. Move to the files that you want to import and select them. You can select multiple images at the same time by holding the ⌘ key down while you click each image.

4. Click Open (or press Return). The images will be imported into your Photo Library. You can monitor the process by watching the Progress bar—importing images from files is much faster than importing them from a camera so the process moves along pretty quickly.

7. Click the Last Import album in the Source pane. iPhoto will move into the Organize mode, and you will see the images that you just imported.

8. Work with the Organization mode tools to organize and identify the images that you just imported (see the section called "Organizing Your Images" for the steps to do so).

Organizing Your Images

Because you are likely to accumulate a large number of images, it is imperative that you keep them organized and that you use iPhoto's information tools to help you identify your photos so that you can find them when you need them. As you learned earlier in this chapter, iPhoto includes a number of organization tools that help you do just that.

Where iPhoto Stores Your Digital Images

When you import images into iPhoto, from either a digital camera or from other sources (such as photos that you have scanned), the images are stored in the following location:

Yourhomefolder/Pictures/iPhoto Library

As iPhoto imports images into your library, it creates several subfolders and data files that it uses to maintain your image collection. Within the iPhoto Library folder, you will see several data files that iPhoto uses to keep your images organized; these files are Library.data, Library.cache, and Dir.data. You never need to work with these files directly. iPhoto also creates a folder called Albums in which it stores information related to albums that you create. You'll also notice a folder for each year in which photos that you import are captured. Within each year's folder, you will see one or more subfolders that are given numbered names. Within those folders is a Data folder, which contains data that are attached to the images, such as keywords, a Thumbs folder (containing thumbnails of each image), and finally, the images themselves. These images will be named with sequential numbers that iPhoto attaches to the images as you import them.

The organization and naming scheme that iPhoto uses isn't likely to make much sense to you (it sure doesn't to me), but fortunately, you don't need to deal with it directly very often. You can just rely on iPhoto to manage all of the complexity for you. Still, you can move directly to the images within iPhotos folders if you want to. View the folders in a Finder window using the Columns view; when you select an image, you will see a preview of it. This helps you know what the content of a specific image files is (the naming scheme certainly won't tell you!). You can copy image files from the iPhoto folders to other locations to use them for other purposes. (Don't move the files from the iPhoto folders because iPhoto will get confused when it tries to access those images. Copy them instead so that the source file always remains within the iPhoto folders.)

However, when you need to use an image outside of iPhoto, you can easily export the images from iPhoto to work with them in other applications or for other reasons, such as to email them to someone else (you'll learn how later in this chapter).

To help you keep your images organized, you can attach several different kinds of information to your photos. This information includes the following:

◆ **Title**. Each image in your Photo Library can have a title. When you import images, the title that iPhoto assigns to them is a sequential number based on the "roll" number from which you imported them (remember that iPhoto counts each import session as a "roll" of film), such as Roll 10-10, Roll 10-11, and so on. These titles aren't very meaningful; fortunately, you can change them easily.

◆ **Comments**. The application enables you to add comments to each image. For example, you can provide the context for the image so that when you look at it later, you will understand it better; or if you have a poor memory like I do, you can explain where the information was captured. Comments are especially useful when you create books because they include interesting things you've said about those images.

◆ **Keywords**. As you learned earlier, you can attach keywords to your images and use these keywords to find the images that you want to work with only a couple of mouse clicks.

NOTE

You might have noticed that I did not mention adding date and time information to an image. This is because most digital cameras capture the date on which an image is taken, and iPhoto can read this date and attach it to the images automatically. However, if the date isn't automatically read from the image (such as images that you scan and then import), you will probably want to enter the date on which you captured the image as a comment.

Setting the Keywords You Use

Keywords help you find photos because you can search a group of images that are associated with specific keywords. You can use keywords to perform fairly complex searches because you can search by multiple keywords at the same time.

iPhoto includes a number of keywords by default; you will see these in the Tool pane when you are in the Organize mode. However, you can create your own keywords, and you can change any keywords that are available. After you have set the keywords you want to use, you can associate them with your images and use them to search for specific images.

Adding New Keywords

iPhoto's default keywords are okay, but you will probably want to use some that are more specific to your photos. For example, you might want to create a keyword containing a child's name so that you can find photos of that child quickly and easily. To add new keywords to the Organize Tool pane, use the following steps:

Add Your Own Keywords

1. Choose Edit, Edit Keywords (or press ⌘+K). The None button on the Keyword list will be replaced by the Done button to indicate that you are in the keyword edit mode.

2. Move into an empty keyword slot in the Tool pane.

3. Type a new keyword (see Figure 3.12).

4. Repeat Steps 2 and 3 until you have added all the keywords that you want to have available.

5. Click Done, choose Edit, Done Editing Keywords, or press ⌘+K to stop creating keywords.

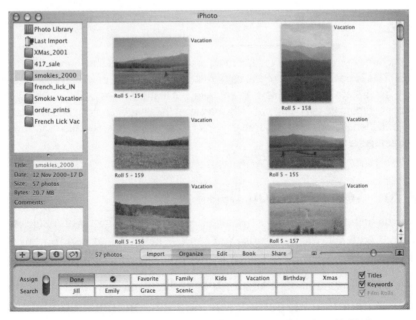

Figure 3.12 *I have added the keyword "Scenic" to my list of available keywords to enable to me find my scenic photos.*

Changing Keywords

You can change existing keywords by using steps that are quite similar to those you used when creating new keywords.

Edit Your Keywords

1. Choose Edit, Edit Keywords (or press ⌘+K).
2. Select the keyword that you want to change. It will become highlighted to indicate that you can edit it.
3. Make changes to the keyword.
4. Repeat Steps 2 and 3 until you have changed all the keywords that you want to.
5. Click Done, choose Edit, Done Editing Keywords, or press ⌘+K to stop editing keywords.

NOTE

When you change a keyword on the Tool pane, it changes where it is associated with any photos automatically.

Adding Information and Keywords to Your Images

After you have set your keywords, add information to your images and associate keywords with them.

Add Information and Keywords to Your Images

1. Click the Organize mode button.
2. Make sure that the Titles and Keywords checkboxes in the Tool pane are checked; these cause iPhoto to display this information next to each image. You might also want to check the Film Rolls checkbox because when you view your Photo Library, the images are organized according to the sessions in which you imported them. This makes finding images easier.
3. Locate the group of images that includes the images to which you want to add information. For example, click the Last Import album to work with images that you imported in the most recent session, or check the

Film Rolls checkbox and scroll in the Photo Library to find the images that you want to work with.

4. Click the Info button located just underneath the Source pane until you can see the Comments box (see Figure 3.13). Depending on your starting point, you might have to click the button once, twice, or not at all if the Comments box is already displayed.

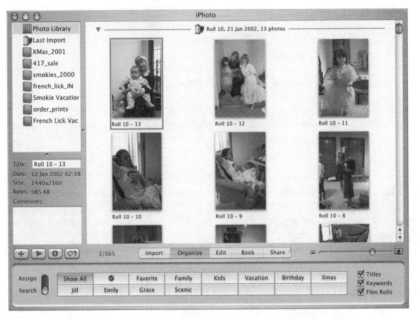

Figure 3.13 *When you open the Information area in the Source pane, you can change an image's title and add comments about the image.*

5. Select an image to which you want to attach information. The image will be enclosed in a box to show that it is selected. In the Info area, you will see iPhoto's default title for the image, the date on which the image was captured (assuming that iPhoto was able to retrieve this information from the source), size (the resolution at which the image was captured), and the image's file size.

TIP

You can adjust the height of the Info area by dragging its Resize handle (the dot between the Source pane and the Info area).

6. Click in the Title box in the Info area and select the default title.

7. Type a new title for the image. Titles should be relatively short, such as four words or less.

8. Click in the Comments box and enter comments about the image.

9. Make sure that the Assign/Search switch is in the Assign position and click the keywords that you want to associate with the image; you can choose as many keywords as you have available. As you click keywords, they remain highlighted to indicate that they will be associated with the selected image.

   If you have the Show checkboxes checked, you will see an image's title and keywords next to it in the Source pane.

10. Repeat Steps 5 through 9 for each image in a roll. When you are done, your images will be more useful because specific images will be easier to find (see Figure 3.14).

This process is a bit of a pain, but it does pay off when you want to create projects using your images. If you do these steps on a roll of images as soon as you create it (such as when you import images from a camera), the process takes just a few

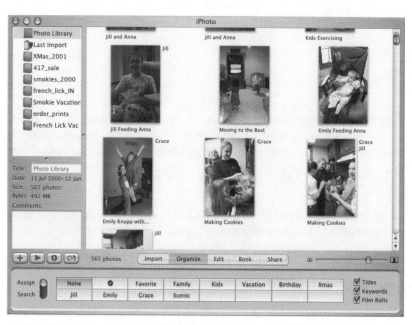

Figure 3.14 *I've associated information and keywords with each image in this roll so I can find specific images more easily.*

minutes. However, if you wait until you have lots of rolls to do, it can take longer and you aren't as likely to actually keep your image information current.

TIP

To remove a keyword from images, select the images that contain the keyword, make sure that the switch is in the Assign position, and click the keyword in the Tool pane. It becomes unhighlighted and will be disassociated from the selected images.

Here are a few tips to make this process go a bit faster:

◆ If you have a group of images that you want to have the same comment, copy the comment for one of the images. As you select other images, you can paste that comment into the Comments box.

◆ Apply keywords to multiple images at the same time. Select the images with which you want to associate a keyword by holding the Shift key down and clicking the first and last image that you want to select (the images between the two will also be selected), or by holding the ⌘ key down while you click each image. When you click a keyword, it will be assigned to each image that is selected at the same time.

NOTE

You might notice that one of iPhoto's default keywords is a checkmark. This is the one keyword that you can't change. The checkmark is intended to be assigned to images temporarily so that you can perform a specific task for those images. For example, you might want to order prints from only a few photos in an album. You can apply the checkmark keyword to each image that you want a print of and then find those images by searching for the checkmark keyword. (The checkmark actually appears in the lower right corner of the image itself instead of next to it.) After you order the prints, you can remove the checkmark keyword (choose Edit, Undo Add Keyword or select the images and click the checkmark keyword again).

Using Keywords to Find Images

After you have associated keywords with your images, it is quite simple to use those keywords to find all the images associated with one or more keywords.

Find Images by Keyword Searches

1. Select the album in the Source pane in which you want to search for images; choose Photo Library if you want to search all of the images that you have imported into iPhoto.

2. Click the Organize mode button if it is not already selected.

3. Move the Assign/Search switch to the Search position. When you are in the Search mode, the None button becomes the Show All button.

4. Click the keywords that are associated with the images that you want to see. For example, if you click the keyword "Vacation," you will find those images to which the keyword "Vacation" has been assigned. You can click as many keywords as you'd like to make your search more specific. For example, clicking "Vacation" and "Scenic" would find only those photos with which both keywords are associated. As you click on keywords, the images in the Content pane will include only those with which the keywords that you clicked are associated (see Figure 3.15).

To view all of the images in the select album again, click the Show All keyword button.

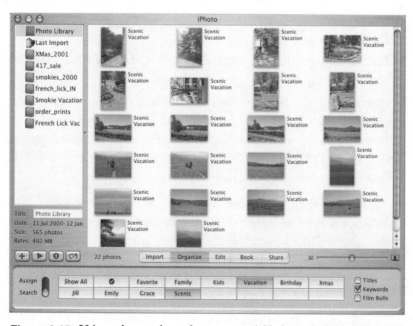

Figure 3.15 *Using a keyword search, you can quickly locate images with which keywords are associated, such as "Vacation" and "Scenic."*

Building and Using Albums

Albums are the tool you use to create collections of images for specific purposes, such as to view specific images or to create slideshows, books, and other projects. You can create albums containing the images in which you are interested and then work with those images by selecting an album in the Source pane.

NOTE

If you have used iTunes' playlists, the concept of albums should be easy to grasp because playlists and albums are analogous.

You can choose any criteria for the photos that you include in an album, and you can include any number of photos in any album that you create.

Create an iPhoto Album and Add Images to It

1. Click the New Album button located just below the Source pane, choose File, New Album, or press ⌘+N. You will see the New Album dialog.

2. Name your album and click OK. The album that you create will appear in the Source pane.

3. Find the images that you want to include in the new album; use the keyword searching technique that you learned earlier to do so.

4. Select the images that you want to include in the album (select multiple images by holding the ⌘ key down) and drag them onto the new album in the Source pane. As you drag the images onto the album, a red circle containing a number will appear—the number is the number of images that you have selected (see Figure 3.16).

5. Continue finding images and dragging them onto the album.

6. When you are done, select the album in the Source pane, and you will see the images that it contains in the Content pane.

TIP

A quick way to select all the images shown in the Content pane is to choose Edit, Select All, or press ⌘+A.

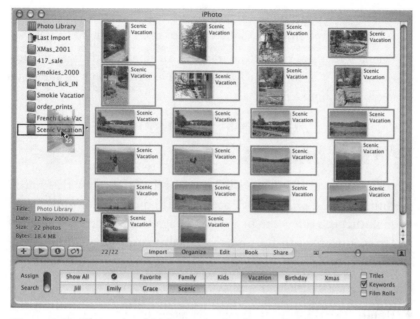

Figure 3.16 *I have placed 22 images in the album called "Scenic Vacation Photos."*

Following are some album tidbits:

◆ Placing images in an album does not remove them from the Photo Library; the Photo Library always contains all of the images that you have imported into iPhoto (unless you have deleted some images from the Library). When you drag an image onto an album, a pointer from the original image to the album is created.

◆ You can create an album by dragging images from the Photo Library or from other albums onto the Source pane. An album called Album-# will be created. You can edit the album name by selecting it, and when it is highlighted, change the name to what you want it to be.

◆ You can place the same image in as many albums as you'd like.

◆ When you select an album, you can select and then drag the images around in the Content pane to change their order. The order in which images appear in an album does affect projects that you create from that album. For example, if you create a book, the images will appear in the book in the same order in which they appear in the album.

- ◆ To remove an image from an album, select it and press Delete. The image will be removed from the album, but not from the Photo Library.
- ◆ Changes that you make to an image in an album, such as associating keywords with it or rotating it, *do* affect the image in all its locations, including in the Photo Library.

Editing Your Images

While you can't do all the image editing tricks that you can with a full-fledged image editing application, such as Photoshop, iPhoto includes some basic image editing tools that you can use to fix up your images. Conveniently enough, iPhoto includes the editing tools that you are most likely to use so that iPhoto can be your one-stop image shop.

iPhoto's editing tools include the following:

- ◆ **Rotate**. Use this to change the orientation of the image.
- ◆ **Constrain**. This pop-up menu enables you to select portions of an image with a specific proportion.
- ◆ **Crop**. Use this tool to remove parts of an image that you don't want to keep.
- ◆ **Red-Eye**. Use this tool to make people or animals in your images look less demonic.
- ◆ **Black & White**. This tool makes an image look like it was taken in the good old days.

Edit an Image

1. Select the image that you want to edit and click the Edit mode button. The Content pane will be filled with the image that you select. You will see the Edit Tool pane that contains the editing tools.

NOTE

If you don't select an image before you click Edit, the first image in the selected album will appear in the Content pane.

2. Use the Rotate button to rotate the image.

3. To select a portion of the image, move the pointer over the image, click the mouse button, and drag. All of the image outside of the selected area will be shaded so that you can clearly see what you have selected. To constrain your selection to a specific proportion, use the Constrain pop-up menu to choose the proportion to which you want to limit your selection. As you drag, this proportion will be maintained.

TIP

You can use the Display Size slider to make the image larger or smaller in the Content pane. For example, drag the slider to the right to zoom in on the image for detailed editing work, such as removing red-eye.

---

4. After you have selected a portion of the image, you can drag your selection around the image to change the area of the image that you have selected.

5. If you need to resize the selection, point to one of its borders—the point will become a hand with a pointing finger. When you see this pointer, drag to resize the selection.

6. Click the editing tool that you want to apply to the selected part of the image. For example, to remove everything that is not selected, click the Crop button. To fix the red-eye in the selected area of the image, click the Red-Eye button. The changes you made are saved as you make them.

7. When you are done editing an image, click Previous or Next to move to the previous or next image in the selected album to edit additional images.

When you edit an image, your changes affect *all* instances of that image in all your albums and in the Photo Library. Fortunately, iPhoto maintains the original image should you ever want to go back to it. Simply select the image that you have edited and choose File, Revert to Original. You will be warned that if you revert to the original, any changes you have made will be lost (which is the whole idea). Click OK, and the image will be returned to the version that you imported into iPhoto.

If you want to have multiple versions of an image, say one cropped and one not, you can create duplicates of images. To create a duplicate, select the images that you want to duplicate. Choose File, Duplicate or press ⌘+D. A copy of the image, including its information and keywords, will be created. This duplicate image is created in the Photo Library and behaves just like the original. You can then perform any actions on the copy that you can on the original, such as adding a title or comments to it, editing it, and so on.

NOTE

You can create as many copies of an image as you'd like, but remember that each image consumes disk storage space. If you are only going to make changes to one version, there is no need to duplicate it since iPhoto maintains the original version for you.

Creating Photo Books

With iPhoto's Book tools, you can create really nice photo books to display your images. You can then print these books yourself or order a professionally printed copy from Apple. Exploring all the details of designing and creating books is beyond the scope of this chapter; however, the following steps will get you started.

Create a Photo Book

1. Create an album containing the images that you want to include in a book.

2. Make the order of those images in the album the same as you want the order to be in the book you are creating (starting from the top left, which will be the first image in the book).

3. Click the Book mode button. The Content pane will include two areas; at the top, you see the first image in the book, which will be its cover. In the lower part of the pane, you will see thumbnails of each page in the book.

4. Choose a theme for the book on the Theme pop-up menu. The book will be redesigned into the theme you select. For example, if you choose Classic, large images will be placed on the pages in a neat and orderly fashion. Choosing Catalog results in thumbnails of each image.

5. Use the Show checkboxes to turn various text on or off. For example, to hide the book's page numbers, uncheck the Page Numbers checkbox. Not all text appears in all book themes (for example, Titles don't appear in the Story Book theme, but they do in the Year Book theme).

6. Select the first page in the book, which is the cover by default. You will see a large size version at the top of the pane.

7. Choose a page design for that page on the Page Design pop-up menu. Typically, you will leave the first page as the Cover page design, but you can change it if you'd like.

8. Edit the text on the page by clicking in the text box that appears on the page. When you do, the page view will be magnified so that it is easier to edit. I recommend that you leave the Show Guide checkbox checked because the guides make the location of text boxes obvious.

9. Choose the next page in the book by clicking its thumbnail image. You will see its preview in the upper part of the pane.

10. Choose a page design from the Page Design pop-up menu. For example, choose the number of images that you want to be displayed on that page. The choices that you have on this menu are determined by the theme of the book.

11. Edit the text that appears on the selected page.

12. To change the order in which images appear on a page or to change the page on which specific images appear, switch to the Organize mode and change the order of the images in the album from which you are creating a book. The images will be reshuffled in the book to match the order of the images in the album. Depending on the number of pages in the book and the page design you use, it can be a bit tricky to get specific images on a specific page, but with a little trial and error, you can do it.

13. Continue working through the rest of the pages until you have selected a page design and added text to each page in the book.

14. Click Preview. A preview window will appear.

15. Click the page forward and page backward arrows to preview each page in the book. Close the Preview window when you are done.

16. Continue selecting pages and making changes until the book is what you want it to be.

After you have created a book, you can print it or order a copy from Apple. You print it by using the Mac's normal print commands. To order a copy from Apple, you use the Share mode tools.

Following are some additional comments about creating photo books:

◆ While I suggested in the previous steps that you add text to the pages in the book as you design them, this was mostly for instructional purposes. A more efficient approach is to design all of the pages first and then go back and add text. This is because your page design can affect the text that is appropriate for a page. For example, if you use the Story Book theme, changing a page design can change your narrative text for a page. Designing the pages first and then adding text will prevent you from having to make as many text changes.

◆ Books remain with the albums from which they are created. You can't save a book as an entity outside of iPhoto. If you change a book that you have created, the previous version is lost. If you want to keep a book, keep the album from which you created it (don't make any changes to the album or you will change the book). If you want to have multiple versions of a book for the same set of images, create a new album for each version of the book that you create.

◆ Books that you order from Apple should include at least 10 pages. If you have fewer than 10 pages in a book that you want to order, add more images or change the theme or page design so that you have at least 10 pages. Otherwise, the book you receive will have blank pages in it.

◆ Before you order a copy of the book from Apple, print it yourself first (even if you only have a black-and-white printer). Books are expensive to order, and you should use your printed copy to make sure that the book you create is worth the cost and that it doesn't have any mistakes.

Sharing Your Images

Viewing images within iPhoto is fine, but sharing them in various ways is even better. Use iPhoto's Share mode to present your images in many different ways. This includes printing them, creating slideshows, ordering prints, ordering books, posting images to your iTools Web page, and exporting them from iPhoto in various formats.

Printing Images

Even an inexpensive inkjet printer can enable you to print photos that are equivalent to the quality of a photo printed by a professional. Printing photos from iPhoto is similar to printing documents from other applications (although the specific settings you use are more important because of their effect on the quality of the printed images).

Print Your iPhoto Images

1. Select the image that you want to print.
2. Click the Share mode button.
3. Click the Print button. You will see the Print dialog (see Figure 3.17).

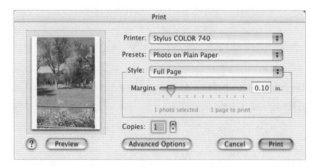

Figure 3.17 *The Print dialog in iPhoto contains more options than it does in most applications.*

4. Choose the printer on which you want to print the image on the Printer pop-up menu.
5. Use the Presets pop-up menu to select preset settings for the selected printer.
6. Use the other controls in the dialog to adjust how your image will be printed. For example, choose a style, such as Full Page, on the Style pop-up menu. Use the Margins slider to set the margins of the printed image.
7. When you are done setting options, click Preview. The image as it will be printed appears in the Preview application.
8. If the image appears as you want it to, print the image. If not, move back into iPhoto and make changes to the print settings.

TIP

Each printer has its own set of printing options. You should explore the user manual included with your printer so you understand its options and how they impact the quality of images that you print.

Printing images with the highest quality will take some experimentation with your specific printer, printer settings, paper, and so on. Minor changes in settings or using a different type of paper can have dramatic effects on the quality of the images that you print. I recommend that you spend some time printing with different combinations of printer settings and paper until you achieve the best results. Then, document the combination that works the best for you so that you can use those same settings the next time that you print images.

TIP

The paper on which you print images might be the single most important factor when it comes to image quality. You should use paper that is designed for printing photos to get the best results.

Creating a Slideshow

An iPhoto slideshow is a great way to view your images on your Mac.

View Images in a Slideshow

1. Select a group of images that you want to see in a slideshow or choose an album to see all of its images in the show. (If you have a lot of time or not many photos, you can select your Photo Library to see all of your photos in the same slideshow).

2. Click the Share mode button.

3. Click the Slide Show button in the Tool pane. You will see the Slide Show Settings dialog (see Figure 3.18).

4. Use the "Play each slide for __ seconds" box and arrows to set the number of seconds that each image will appear on the screen. The default is about 2 seconds, which seems about right for most photos. If you like to linger

Figure 3.18 *You use this dialog to configure an iPhoto slideshow.*

over your photos, increase this number. If you are relatively impatient, change this to 1 second.

5. If you want the slideshow to play through once and then stop, uncheck the "Repeat slide show" checkbox. If you leave this checked, you can stop a slideshow by pressing the Esc button or clicking the mouse button.

6. Choose the music that you want to play on the Music pop-up menu. Choose None to play a silent slideshow. Choose Other to select a song that does not appear on the list. Choose Edit List to delete songs from the menu.

7. Click OK or press Return. Prepare to be impressed as your screen fills with your images and they transition smoothly from one to the next (see Figure 3.19).

8. To stop the slideshow before it finishes or if it repeats, click the mouse button or press Esc.

TIP

You can display an iPhoto slideshow in any mode by selecting your images and clicking the Slide Show button that is located under the Source pane (the Play button). When you click this, the slideshow plays with the settings you have most recently selected in the Slide Show Settings dialog, which are also transferred to the iPhoto Preferences dialog.

When you use iPhoto's slideshow function, you create a temporary slideshow just to view the images on your Mac. You can't save the slideshows that you view with this tool. However, you can use iPhoto to export a series of images as a slideshow

Figure 3.19 *An iPhoto slideshow is a great way to enjoy your photos.*

and then use other digital lifestyle applications to add a sound track, effects, and so on. You'll learn how to export photos in the section called "Exporting Images" a little later in this chapter. You'll learn how to create permanent slideshows in Chapter 15, "Building Digital Lifestyle Slideshows."

Ordering Prints

While most of us have an inkjet printer that is capable of printing fairly nice photos, printing photos can be a bit of a pain, and the results you get aren't always the best. Plus, if you want to share those photos with other people, you have to go through the hassle of mailing them, which might be enough to stop you from sharing them.

To save you the hassle of printing or mailing images, you can order prints from Apple (the prints are actually provided by Kodak). The first time that you order prints, you will use or create an Apple account; after that, you can order prints with a single click by using the appropriately named 1-Click service.

Order Prints of Your Images

1. Select the photos for which you want to order prints (such as by selecting an album).

2. Click the Share mode button.

3. Click the Order Prints button. You will see the Order Prints dialog (see Figure 3.20). Along the left side of the dialog, you will see the photos that you have selected. You can scroll up and down in the dialog to view all of them. In the right side of the window, you see the list of available sizes, prices, and the quantity box.

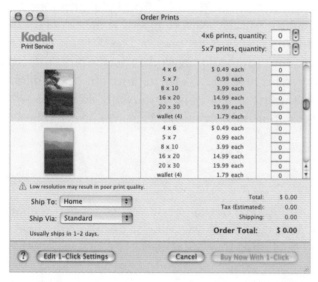

Figure 3.20 *Ordering prints is a great way to share photos with others.*

4. Enter the quantity of each size of photo that you want to order. The total cost of your order will appear at the bottom of the dialog. If you want to order 4 x 6 or 5 x 7 photos of all of the selected images, use the quantity boxes at the very top of the dialog.

5. If you haven't used this service before, open the Ship To pop-up menu, choose Add New Address, and create an address. Add addresses for everyone to whom you will send photos.

6. Choose the address to which you want the current order sent on the Ship To pop-up menu.

7. Choose the shipping method on the Ship Via pop-up menu. Your choices are Standard or Express. Obviously, Express is faster and is also more expensive.

8. When you are ready to order, click the Buy Now With 1-Click button.

9. Follow the on-screen instructions to complete the order. The first time you use this service, you will create or enter information for your Apple account. Then you will work through the remainder of the ordering screens. Your photos will be printed and shipped; Apple keeps you notified of the status of your order via email.

In the Order Prints dialog, you see the cost of each size of print that you can order. Most of these costs are quite reasonable when compared to the cost of the ink and paper required to print images on an inkjet printer. The shipping costs are also reasonable given that you don't have to do any work to get the order shipped anywhere you'd like. However, because it is so easy to order prints, you might find yourself going overboard the first time or two that you order. So before you hit the Buy Now With 1-Click button, take a moment to double-check what you are ordering.

Ordering a Book

Earlier in this chapter, you learned how to create neat books that contain your photos. While you can print these books yourself, you can also order professionally printed and bound books by using the same service that you use to order prints. The process is also quite similar.

Low Resolution Images

If images in a group that you select in an album or individually are low resolution, they will have the low-resolution warning icon placed on them. This icon is a yellow triangle with an exclamation point inside it. An image with this icon might or might not print well in prints or in a book that you order. Be cautious about including low-resolution images in your orders, or you might be disappointed in the results you get.

If you do want to print low-resolution images, keep the print size down to make them look as good as possible.

Order a Professionally Printed Photo Book

1. Build the book (see the section called "Creating Photo Books" earlier in this chapter for details).

2. Print your book and check it. Use the draft or black-and-white mode of your printer to make the process faster and less expensive.

3. When you are *sure* that your book is right, click the Share mode button.

4. Click Order Book. Your book will be assembled. Depending on the number of images and pages in your book, this process can take a few minutes. If your book contains low-resolution images or fewer than 10 pages, you will be warned. When the process is complete, you will see the Order Book dialog. This dialog is very similar to the Order Prints dialog and works in the same way.

5. Select a cover for your book on the Cover Color pop-up menu.

6. Use the Ship To and Ship Via pop-up menus to enter the shipping information. Use the quantity box and arrows to set the number of books you want to order.

7. When you are ready to order, click the Buy Now With 1-Click button and follow the on-screen instructions.

Be aware that ordering books is a relatively expensive proposition. The first 10 pages cost $29.99, additional pages are $3 per page. Shipping for a book is also relatively expensive at $7.99. Take plenty of time to design and check your book before your order it unless you don't mind $40 "experiments."

Building an iTools HomePage

You can use iPhoto to create a HomePage Web site through an Apple iTools account.

> **NOTE**
>
> Before you can post images to an iTools Web site, you need to have created an iTools account. To learn how to obtain and configure an iTools account, see Chapter 6, "iTools: Maybe the Only Internet Tool You Ever Need." You will learn how to create and manage an iTools Web site in Chapter 19, "Creating and Hosting a Digital Lifestyle Web Site with iTools."

Post Images to Your iTools Web Site

1. Select the images that you want to place on the Web (such as selecting an album on the Source pane).

2. Click the Share mode button.

3. Click the HomePage button. You will see the Publish HomePage dialog (see Figure 3.21).

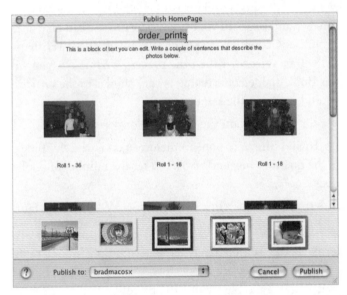

Figure 3. 21 *Using iPhoto's HomePage button, you can create a Web page for your photos in mere seconds.*

4. Select the title text at the top of the page and edit it.

5. Select the page text just below that and edit it.

6. Click a frame style to apply that frame to all of the images.

7. Choose the iTools account to which you want to publish the page on the Publish to pop-up menu.

8. Click Publish. iPhoto will connect to the Internet and transfer your photos to your iTools account. When the process is complete, you will see a completion dialog that provides the URL to the page that you just created.

9. Click the Visit Page Now button and enjoy (see Figure 3.22). You can click any image to see a larger version of it.

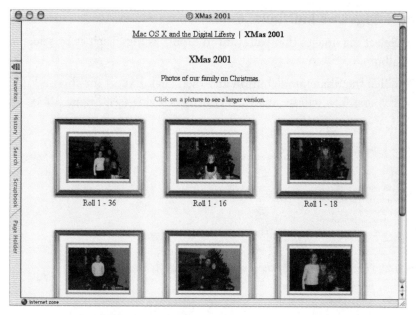

Figure 3.22 *I published these images on a Web page in about 1 minute.*

TIP

If you publish your photos via HomePage, make sure that you have meaningful titles for your images. Otherwise, you get titles like those in Figure 3.22.

Exporting Images

There are a number of ways that you can export images from iPhoto for different purposes. You can export images as separate files so that you can work with them in other applications or to send those files to other people. Or you can export a set of images as a Web site. Another option is to export a set of images as a QuickTime movie.

Exporting Photos as Files

If you want to use iPhoto photos in other applications, such as iMovie, you need to export those images as individual files.

Export Images as Individual Files

1. Select the images that you want to export as files, such as by selecting an album.

2. Click the Share mode button and then click Export (or choose File, Export). You will see the Export Images dialog (see Figure 3.23).

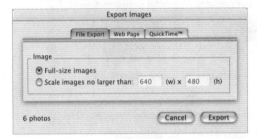

Figure 3.23 *The three export options you have appear as tabs in the Export Images dialog.*

3. Click the File Export tab if it isn't already selected.

4. Click the "Full-size images" radio button to export the files at their current resolution or click the "Scale images no larger than" radio button and enter the resolution with which you want the image files to be exported.

5. Click Export.

6. Use the resulting sheet to choose a location in which to save the images and click OK. Each image will be saved as a JPEG file in the location that you selected.

Exporting Images as a Web Site

Earlier, you saw how easy it is to create a Web site containing photos via iTools HomePage. It is also quite easy to create a separate Web site for your photos so that you can view them on your hard drive, publish the site on a local network, or publish it to a Web site you host with a different Web hosting service.

Export Images as a Web Site

1. Select the images that you want to include in the Web site, for example, by selecting an album.

2. Click Share and then click Export.

3. Click the Web Page tab of the Export Images dialog.

4. Enter the title of the page you are creating in the Title box.

5. Choose the number of row and columns in which you want the images to be displayed on the Web site.

6. Use the Color radio button and bar to set the page background to a color (it is white by default), or select the Image radio button and Set button to choose an image as a background for the page.

7. Use the Thumbnail Max. Width and Max. Height boxes to set the maximum size of the thumbnails of each image.

8. Use the Image boxes to set the maximum size of the images when the viewer clicks on them on the Web site's Home page.

9. If you want the titles displayed, check the Show Title checkbox.

10. Click Export.

11. Select a location to which to save the Web site and click OK. Note that you have to choose a specific folder in which to store the Web site. The Web site will be created in the location you specified.

12. Open the folder you selected in Step 11 and open the index.html file. You will see the page in a Web browser (see Figure 3.24). You can use this site as a stand-alone site or add it to other Web sites you have created.

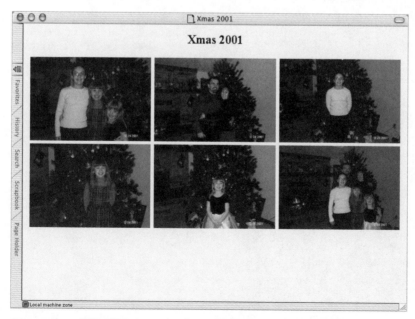

Figure 3.24 *This Web site took all of two minutes to create.*

Exporting Images as a QuickTime Movie

Viewing a slideshow in iPhoto is cool, but it can be even better to create slideshows that you can save and place on DVD, the Web, and so on. To do this, you can export images as a QuickTime movie. The steps to do this are similar to the steps to export image files or a Web page. They are covered in detail in Chapter 15.

Using iPhoto for Your Digital Lifestyle Projects

As you can see, when it comes to digital images, iPhoto is way cool. Whenever you use digital images in your projects, you will be using iPhoto to prepare those images, whether it is to add them to an iMovie project, create a slideshow, put images on a DVD, or create a Web site. When you read the digital lifestyle projects chapters in Parts II and III of this book, you will be returning to iPhoto again and again.

Chapter 4

iMovie: The Swiss Army Knife of Digital Video Software

With due respect to the other "i" applications, iMovie is the application that ignited the digital lifestyle, and it remains the most powerful of them all. iMovie was, and is, revolutionary. Before iMovie, editing video was a task that only people who were either professionals or had lots and lots of time on their hands could do. Video editing applications were complex, and their tools were difficult to learn and use. iMovie changed all that.

iMovie blends power and ease-of-use in a truly remarkable way. With a DV camcorder and a few minutes of time, you can create amazingly sophisticated movies that include titles, transitions, special effects, multiple soundtracks, and much more. And with the range of tools that it provides, iMovie is the heart of the digital lifestyle. You can use it to work with content from other applications, whether you intended to use that media in a movie project or not. For example, you can use iMovie to create sound effects for your desktop. Or you can use it to create soundtracks for slideshows that you create in iPhoto. There is just no limit to what you can do with iMovie and a bit of imagination.

What's more, using iMovie is just plain fun.

The iMovie Way

Unlike other video editing tools, you can be up and creating movies in just a few minutes. However, that doesn't mean that iMovie is a basic tool; it empowers you to do many amazing things with your projects. It's just that the iMovie interface is so well designed that you don't have to spend hours just learning how it works.

iMovie provides an amazing array of tools for you to use. Even better, these tools use a consistent interface so that once you are versed in the iMovie Way, its tools will quickly become second nature to you.

The iMovie Window

The iMovie window contains five main areas, only four of which you can see at the same time (see Figure 4.1).

Figure 4.1 *With iMovie, you can create just about anything that you can conceive of.*

In the upper left corner of the window is the Monitor. Here, you preview and edit your movie, as well as the clips from which you build it. In the upper right, you will see the iMovie Tool pane. At the bottom of the pane, you will see five buttons, with each button opening a palette of tools in the pane. Just below the Tool pane are the disk space tools that you use to manage the disk space with which your project is associated. At the bottom of the window, you will see the viewers of which there are two, those being the Clip Viewer and the Timeline Viewer (you can only see one viewer at a time).

iMovie Modes

iMovie has two basic modes in which you operate: Camera or Edit. The mode you are in is determined by the position of the Camera/Edit mode switch (see Figure 4.1). When the switch is to the left, iMovie is in the Camera mode. In this mode, you work with a DV camera that is attached to your Mac to import video clips from which you will build your movie. When the switch is to the right and iMovie is in the Edit mode, you work with video clips to preview them, edit them, and so on. You will spend most of your iMovie time in the Edit mode.

NOTE

You seldom actually have to move the Camera/Edit mode switch. When iMovie detects that a camera is connected to your Mac, it selects the Camera mode automatically. When you select a video clip to work with it, iMovie switches to the Edit mode automatically.

The Monitor

The Monitor serves two purposes. One is to enable you to view clips and your movie as you work with them. Its second function is to enable you to edit video clips by removing frames, pasting frames, splitting clips, and so on. The controls that you see in the Monitor depend on the mode in which iMovie is operating.

The Monitor in Edit Mode

Since you will spend most of your time in the Edit mode, take a few moments to learn about the Monitor's controls when iMovie is in this mode (see Figure 4.2). Table 4.1 explains the elements of the Monitor window that you need to understand.

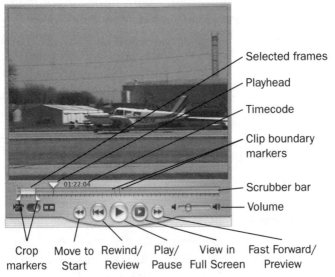

- Selected frames
- Playhead
- Timecode
- Clip boundary markers
- Scrubber bar
- Volume
- Crop markers
- Move to Start
- Rewind/ Review
- Play/ Pause
- View in Full Screen
- Fast Forward/ Preview

Figure 4.2 *When you are in the Edit mode, the Monitor contains the controls you use to edit your clips.*

Table 4.1 Features of the Monitor in Edit Mode

Element	Purpose
Scrubber bar	The Scrubber bar is a visual representation of the timeline for a clip, a group of clips, or your movie (depending on what you have selected).
Playhead	The Playhead shows the exact frame that appears in the Monitor as it appears; you use the Playhead to determine where you "are" in a clip or in your movie. As a clip or movie plays, the Playhead moves across the Scrubber bar.
Crop markers	As with most Mac applications, you select the material that you want to change in some way (in this case, frames of a video clip) and then perform some action on them, such as cutting them out of a clip. You use the crop markers to select the frames with which you want to work. The left crop marker indicates the first frame that you select, while the right crop marker indicates the last frame in the selection.
Selected frames	The selected frames are shown by the gold highlighting between the two markers.
Timecode	The precise location of the Playhead is shown by the timecode that "floats" next to the Playhead. The timecode is an important piece of information that you should get comfortable with. As its name implies, the timecode provides information about the time aspects of a clip or movie. Timecodes appear in the following format:
	Minutes:Seconds:Frames
	If a clip or movie is less than a minute, you will see only two sets of numbers: Seconds and Frames.
	The Frames part of the timecode is a counter that measures the number of frames in a single second of the clip. Most clips that you capture have 30 frames per second, which is the number that is required for smooth onscreen motion. Within each second of the clip, the frames are numbered from 00 to 29 (for a total of 30 frames). The Frames part of the timecode tells you where in each second of the clip you are. For example, a timecode of 36:21 means that the clip is 36 seconds long and has gone 21 frames into the 37th second (so it is actually almost 37 seconds long).
	As you start editing, the timecode becomes very useful, especially when you are able to interpret it immediately. The first few times it can be a bit confusing, but just keep remembering that the last number in the timecode is the frame number; timecodes will become second nature to you as you gain experience.

Table 4.1 Features of the Monitor in Edit Mode (continued)

Element	Purpose
Clip boundary markers	When you have more than one clip selected, the clip boundary markers show the beginning and end of each clip.
Rewind/Review	Click this button to move backward in the selected clips. As the clip is rewound, the Playhead will move rapidly to the left in the Scrubber bar.
Move to Start	Clicking this moves to the start of your movie and unselects any selected clips.
Play/Pause	Click Play to watch and hear selected clips. Click Play again to pause the action. You can also start and stop play by pressing the Spacebar.
View in Full Screen	Plays the selected clips in full-screen mode in which you only see the clips; the iMovie interface disappears.
Fast Forward/ Preview	You can preview (called search forward in iMovie lingo) by clicking the Fast Forward button. The Playhead zooms across the screen until you click the Fast Forward button again.
Volume	Adjust the playback volume using the Volume slider. Note that this only affects the current volume of the clip and in no way changes the clip or the movie itself. This volume setting is temporary and does not affect your movie.

One of the most important iMovie skills you need is the ability to move around in a clip quickly and precisely in order to preview and edit clips. The following are the most important ways to move around:

♦ Click the Playhead and drag it to the right to move forward in the clip (or to the left to move backward in the clip). When you release the mouse button, the Playhead is at the exact position that you left it. The current frame will be shown in the Monitor, and you can see the exact position at which the Playhead is located by the timecode displayed next to the Playhead. Use this method for large but quick movements in the clip, such as moving from the beginning to the middle.

♦ You can move the Playhead much more precisely by using the keyboard; this is essential when you get to detailed editing because you can move by increments as small as a single frame. To move the Playhead one frame at a time, use the Left and Right arrow keys. As you can probably guess, the Right arrow key moves the Playhead forward one frame, and the Left arrow key moves you backward one frame. Use this method to position the Playhead very precisely.

◆ You can move the Playhead forward or backward 10 frames at a time by holding the Shift key down while you press the Left or Right arrow keys. This movement technique is also very useful when you are doing detailed editing because it enables you to quickly move to a precise location in the clip, but you get there a bit faster than by moving one frame at a time.

The Monitor in Camera Mode

When iMovie is in the Camera mode, the features of the Monitor are less complex because importing clips is a relatively simple task (see Figure 4.3 and Table 4.2).

Importing video from a DV camera is a very simple task as you will see later in this chapter.

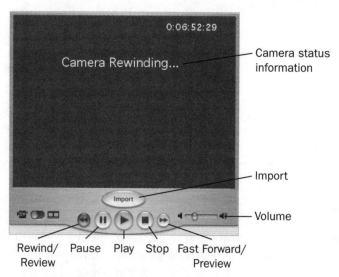

Figure 4.3 *When you are in the Camera mode, the Monitor contains the controls you use to control your DV camera (here, the camera is rewinding) and to import clips from it.*

Table 4.2 Features of the Monitor in Camera Mode

Element	Purpose
Camera status information	When a camera is connected to your Mac, you see information about its status. For example, when you rewind the camera, you see the message "Camera Rewinding." This information helps you control your camera from within iMovie more easily.
Import	Clicking the Import button starts or stops the import process. When you click this button, iMovie plays the DV camera and begins importing video clips.
Rewind/Review	When the DV camcorder is not playing, the Rewind button rewinds the tape at top speed. When the tape is playing, it plays the tape backward (you see the video, but there is no audio). In the Review mode, you have to "hold" the button down to keep the review going (in other words, if you let up on the button, it goes back into Play mode).
Pause	Puts the camera in Pause mode.
Play	Plays the camera.
Stop	Stops the DV camera.
Fast Forward/ Preview	When the tape is not playing, the Fast Forward button moves the tape forward at top speed. When the tape is playing, it plays the tape forward at a high speed (you see video, but don't hear any audio).
Volume	Drag the slider to the right to increase the volume and to the left to decrease it. Note that this affects only the playback volume and doesn't actually change the movie at all.

The Tools Palette

The iMovie Tools Palette contains the tools you use to build a movie from the clips, images, and sound that you import into your iMovie project. You select a palette of tools with which to work by clicking one of the buttons along the bottom of the palette.

The Clips Palette (AKA the Shelf)

When the Clips button is selected, the Palette is in the Shelf mode. In this mode, the Palette contains lots of "boxes" in which the clips and images that you have imported appear. This area serves as a holding area for your clips; they remain here until you place them in your movie (see Figure 4.4). Along the side of the Shelf, you see the scroll bar that you can use to move up and down the Shelf to locate clips in which you are interested.

Figure 4.4 *The Shelf lives up to its name; it holds the clips and images from which you will build a movie.*

The Transitions Palette

The segment between two clips in a movie is called the transition. You can use different transitions to smooth the flow from one clip into the next so that your series of individual clips doesn't look like a series of clips, but rather a movie that flows smoothly from one scene to the next. All movies use transitions of one sort or another.

The three most common types of transitions are the Straight Cut, Cross Dissolve, and Fade To or From Black. The straight cut isn't a transition that you have to apply; this is what happens when you don't add a transition. A Straight Cut transition occurs when one scene runs right into the next one. As long as the adjacent scenes are similar enough, the Straight Cut seems very natural, and you don't even notice it. The Cross Dissolve is also very common. One scene dissolves into the next. This transition can be useful when the adjacent scenes are somewhat similar, but different enough that a straight cut is a bit jarring. The Fade To or From Black are two of the more useful transitions. With the fade, a clip fades to black (or fades in from a black screen).

You can apply these and other transitions to a movie by using the Transitions tools that appear when you click the Transitions button (see Figure 4.5). The Transition tools are explained in Table 4.3.

No matter which transition effect you apply, the general process to add a transition is the same.

1. Select the clip to which you want to apply the transition.
2. Select the transition that you want to apply; you will see preview in the Preview window.

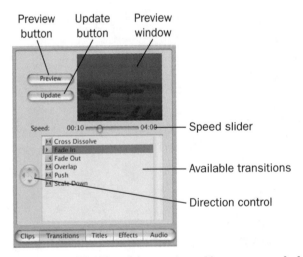

Figure 4.5 *The Transitions tools enable you to smooth the digital flow of your movies.*

3. Use the Speed slider and direction control to configure the transition.
4. Drag the transition into the movie and place it between the clips that you want to transition between.

Table 4.3 iMovie's Transitions Tools

Tool	What It Does
Preview window	When you select a transition on the list of available transitions, a preview of that transition will play in the Preview window. You can use this to get a quick idea of what the transition looks like. You will see the transition applied to the clip that you have selected; if you don't have a clip selected, you will see that transition applied to the first clip in your movie.
Preview button	When you click the Preview button, you will see a preview of the transition applied to the clip shown in the Monitor window. This makes the effect of the transition easier to see because it appears much larger, but it also takes longer to preview.
Update button	You use this button to change a transition that has been placed in a movie. You select the transition clip, use the Transitions tools to make changes to it, and then click the Update button to apply those changes to the transition clip that you have placed in the movie.
Speed slider	You use this slider to control the amount of time over which the transition effect is displayed. Moving the slider to the left makes the transition last a shorter amount of time. Moving it to the right stretches the transition out so that it takes longer to play. After you release the slider, you immediately see the transition in the Preview window. In the lower-right corner of the Preview window, you can see how long the selected transition takes with the current setting of the Speed slider.
Available transitions	This list shows the transition effects that are currently available to you. To work with a transition effect, you select it.
Direction control	When a transition has a directional component, such as a push effect, you use the direction controls to set the direction of the transition. For example, when you use the Push transition (where one clip "pushes" the previous one off the screen), you click the arrow for the direction in which you want the push to occur.

Transitions are fairly sophisticated effects, and they require your Mac to do a lot of work to apply them to a clip. This process is called rendering. When your Mac renders a clip, it applies the proper amount of transition effect to each frame of the clip. When you apply a complex transition with a long duration, this can take a while. Fortunately, you can continue to work while your Mac renders your transition in the background.

The Titles Palette

The Titles tools enable you to add all sorts of text to your movies. Although adding onscreen text is called titling, this term refers to much more than just the movie's name. Basically, titling is iMovie's term for overlaying all sorts of text on the screen. The titles that you might want to use in your movies include the following:

◆ **Captions**. You can use "clip captions" to add information to the images that are appearing on the screen. You might want to add some explanation of what is happening onscreen, the date on which the clip was captured, or you can even add subtitles if you want to.

◆ **Credits**. I'm sure that you are quite familiar with credits, because most modern movies have several minutes of credits at the end. Credits are just what the term implies: the opportunity to take, or give, credit for something in the movie.

◆ **Titles**. Titles are introductory text that can introduce a movie, a scene, or anything else you think warrants an introduction. Titles normally appear at the beginning of something, whether it is a movie or a clip.

To work with titles, you click the Titles button (see Figure 4.6). The elements of the Titles palette are explained in Table 4.4.

The tools and options that you see on the Titles palette depend on the title style that you use. Some styles (for example, Centered Multiple) allow you to add more lines or blocks of text. With these styles, the Add button is active. Other styles (for example, Scrolling Block) involve motion for which you can set the direction; the direction arrows are active for these types.

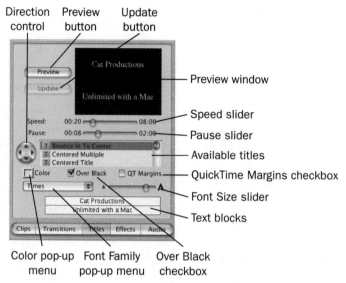

Figure 4.6 *The Titles tools enable you to add text to your movies.*

Table 4.4 iMovie's Titles Tools

Tool	What It Does
Preview window	This works just as it does on the Transitions palette. When you click a title style, you see a preview of it in the Preview window.
Preview button	When you click this button, you see a preview of your title in the Monitor.
Update button	If you make changes to a title that you have already placed in your movie, click this button to update the title to include the changes that you have made.
Speed slider	Just like transitions, all titles have a set amount of time that it takes for the title effect to occur. You use the duration slider to set this time. Drag it to the left to make the title faster or to the right to make it slower.
Pause slider	If there is a pause element in a title's motion, use the Pause slider to control how long that pause lasts. Drag the slider to the right to make the pause last longer or to the left to make it a shorter pause.
Direction control	Some styles let you set motion. You choose a direction for that motion by clicking one of the active arrows on the direction control.

Table 4.4 iMovie's Titles Tools (continued)

Tool	What It Does
Available titles	This list shows the titles that are currently available.
Color pop-up menu	Click this to change the color of the text in the title (it also affects the stripe color in Stripe Subtitle).
Over Black checkbox	If you prefer the title to appear over a black background instead of appearing on a clip, you can check the Over Black checkbox. Instead of being applied to a clip in your movie, the title appears in a new black clip that is added to your movie wherever you drop the title.
QuickTime Margins checkbox	A QuickTime movie has different proportions than a standard TV screen. For title styles that appear on the bottom edge of the screen, this can be a problem because those titles can get cut off when the movie is viewed on a TV. Unchecking the QT Margins checkbox moves the title up on the screen so that it won't be cut off when you show the movie on a TV. Checking it moves the title back down again so that it appears in a better location on the screen when viewing the movie in QuickTime Player. You should leave this unchecked unless the style you use places text at the bottom of the screen. The only styles for which you need to use this are Music Video and Stripe Subtitle.
Font Family pop-up menu	You can choose a font family for a title using this pop-up menu.
Font Size slider	This slider enables you to make the selected font larger (drag it to the right) or smaller (drag it to the left).
Text blocks	You type the text for your title in the text blocks that appear on the palette. You see two or more styles of text block, depending on what style you use. Most styles use single lines of text. Others use a larger text block into which you can place a fair amount of text.
Add/Remove Text Blocks	Some titles can contain multiple text blocks. When you select one of these, the Add (+) and Remove (-) text blocks buttons will appear. Click the Add button to add text blocks to your title. Click Remove (-) to remove text blocks.

The general steps to apply a title to a movie are the following:

1. Decide what sort of text you want to add (caption, credit, date, or title) and to which clip you want to apply the text (or whether you want to apply it to a black background).

2. Based on the kind of text you add and where you apply it, decide on a title style to use.

3. Open the Titles palette and click a title style to select it. You will see a preview in the Preview window.

4. Type the text for the title in the text boxes for that style. Use the Add button (if available) to add more text blocks to the title.

5. Choose a font, color, and size for the title.

6. Set the direction of the motion (if applicable).

7. Set the speed and pause (if applicable) of the title.

8. Preview the title in the Preview window and by clicking the Preview button (to preview it in the Monitor).

9. Make adjustments to the title until it is what you want.

10. Place the title in your movie.

The Effects Palette

The fifth button on the iMovie Tool palette is the Effects button; Effects is short for special effects and that is precisely what this palette enables you to apply to your movies (see Figure 4.7).

Unlike the Transitions and Titles palettes, the effects available on the Effects palette are related to each other only in that they all appear on the same palette. Each effect is unique, and the controls that appear for one effect might or might not be the same as those that appear for another. For example, the Adjust Colors effect includes sliders for Hue Shift, Color, and Brightness while the Sepia Tone effect doesn't have any tone adjustments. Fortunately though, all the effects do work similarly even though the controls you see for various effects might be a bit different.

The available effects on the Effects palette are described in Table 4.5.

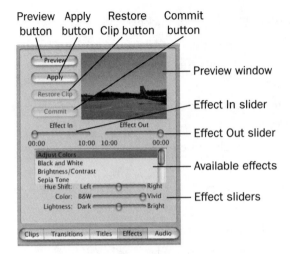

Figure 4.7 *The Effects palette is special indeed.*

Table 4.5 Special Effects Available on the Effects Palette

Effect	What It Does	When To Use It
Adjust Colors	Enables you to adjust the hue, color, and lightness of a clip	When a clip has poor color or seems somewhat dingy
Black and White	Converts a clip into black and white	For artistic effects
Brightness/Contrast	Enables you to adjust the brightness and contrast of a clip	When a clip is too dark, too bright, or has poor contrast
Sepia Tone	Applies a "wood grain" texture to the clip	For artistic effects (often used to make a clip appear as if it were filmed in the past)
Sharpen	Adjusts a clip's sharpness	When a clip is too "fuzzy"
Soft Focus	Applies a blur to the images in a clip	For artistic effects
Water Ripple	Makes the image look as if it is being shot through water; can also be used to apply a "heat shimmer" effect	For artistic effects

Many of the controls on the Effects palette are similar to those on the other palettes as you can see in Table 4.6.

Table 4.6 iMovie's Effects Tools

Tool	What It Does
Preview window	When you click an effect, you see a preview of it in the Preview window.
Preview button	Click this button to see a preview of the selected effect in the Monitor.
Apply button	Click this button to apply the selected effect to the selected clip.
Restore Clip button	This button is unique to the Effects palette. When you apply an effect to a clip, iMovie reworks that clip using the effect that you apply. However, it also saves the original clip so that you can go back to it if you want (this is like an undo that you can use at any point in the future). If you decide that you don't want an effect any more, you can click Restore Clip. The clip is returned to the condition in which it was before you applied the effect to it.
Commit button	Saving two versions of a clip (the one to which an effect has been applied along with the original one) consumes extra disk space that you might not be able to afford. When you click the Commit button, the original clip (the one that doesn't have the effect applied) is deleted. Avoid using the Commit button as long as you can. Being able to go back to a pristine version of your clip is often desirable in the event that you mess up a clip (of course, you can always reimport it from your camcorder, too). After you are sure that the changed clip is what you want, click Commit to free up some disk space.
Effect In slider	The Effect In slider controls the number of frames over which the effect is applied. When the slider is all the way to the left, the effect is applied in full force from the start of the clip. As the slider is moved to the right, the effect "fades in" and is applied gradually over the time selected on the slider up to the maximum amount of time on the slider (10 seconds). For example, if you wanted to apply the black-and-white effect to a clip that is surrounded by two color clips, you might want the color of the clip to slowly fade away so that the transition to black-and-white isn't jarring.
Effect Out slider	The Effect Out slider controls the time over which the effect "fades out." When the slider is all the way to the right, the effect remains in full force until the end of the clip. As the slider is moved to the left, the effect begins to fade out from the point at which the slider is set (the maximum amount is 10 seconds before the end of the clip).

Table 4.6 iMovie's Effects Tools (continued)

Tool	What It Does
Available Effects	This area contains the list of effects from which you can choose. You can use the scroll box to see all the available effects.
Effect sliders	Various sliders appear when you select certain effects, such as Soft Focus, for which the Amount slider appears. These sliders enable you to change some aspect of the effect. In the case of Soft Focus, the Amount slider enables you to adjust the amount of softness that is applied to the clip. Some effects don't have an effect slider; the effect is either on or off.

The Audio Palette

Ah, what would a movie be without sound? A silent movie, of course. The Audio palette provides tools you can use to apply audio effects to your movie (see Figure 4.8).

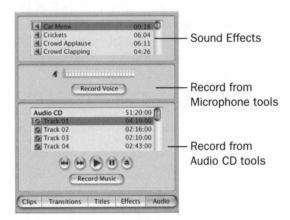

Figure 4.8   *Using the tools on the Audio palette, you can make your movie sing, laugh, cry, bark, or make just about any other noises that you desire.*

As you can see in Figure 4.8, the Audio palette includes the following three areas:

◆ **Sound Effects**. In the Sound Effects area, you see sound effects, which are actually AIFF files that you can include in your movie. By default, iMovie includes a number of different sound effects, such as a cat meowing, crowd applause, thunder, and so on. You can easily add more sound effects to the palette (you'll learn how in Chapter 13, "Adding Digital Tricks to iMovie's Bag"). To preview a sound effect, click it, and it will play.

◆ **Record from Microphone**. The Record from Microphone tools enables you to record sound from a microphone, such as an external USB microphone or from a Mac's built-in mike. The sound level bar shows you the relative sound level of sound coming into your Mac. You use the Record Voice button to start and stop recording. This tool can be used to record a voice, such as to narrate your movie, and it can be used to record any other sound through a microphone as well.

◆ **Record from Audio CD**. These tools enable you to record from an audio CD. Before the advent of iTunes, this function was very useful, but since you can use iTunes to convert music on a CD into formats that you can import into iMovie, this tool isn't as useful as it once was. However, it still comes in handy when you want to grab a short clip from an audio CD.

NOTE

The Record Voice button isn't among the best named buttons in the world. It should actually be Record from Microphone, but I guess that text was too long to fit in the button.

The Clip Viewer

Just below the Monitor and Tools palette are the two Viewer tools; the viewer that you can see depends on the tab that is selected. When the Eye icon is selected, the Clip Viewer appears (see Figure 4.9).

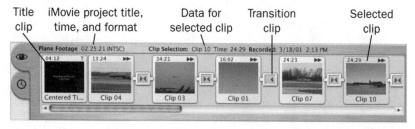

Figure 4.9 *The Clip Viewer is where you build the video track of your movie.*

The Clip Viewer is where you build your movie. After you have placed clips on the Shelf, you drag them onto the Clip Viewer to place them in the movie. You do the same thing for transitions and title clips. The Clip Viewer enables you to view thumbnails of each clip in your movie in the order in which they appear. Conveniently, you can also change the order in which clips appear in a movie by rearranging the clips on the Clip Viewer.

The Timeline Viewer

When you click the Clock tab, the Timeline Viewer appears (see Figure 4.10).

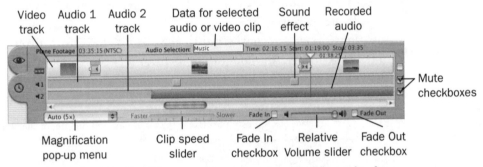

Figure 4.10 *The Timeline Viewer enables you to view all of the tracks of your movie at one time.*

As you can probably guess, the Timeline Viewer shows you the timeline for your movie. While the Clip Viewer is designed for the gross (meaning large, not disgusting) assemblage of your movie, the Timeline Viewer shows you all of your movie's details. It includes the three tracks that your movie can have, which are the video track plus two audio tracks. You also have tools that you can use to create your movie's soundtrack and to synchronize the elements of your movie with one another. The tools on the Timeline Viewer are explained in Table 4.7.

TIP

Here's a little secret for you. You can do everything in the Timeline Viewer that you can in the Clip Viewer plus a lot more. You don't ever really have to use the Clip Viewer, although it seems a lot easier to use it to build your movie initially.

Table 4.7 iMovie's Effects Tools

Tool	What It Does
Video track	The top track on the Timeline Viewer displays the video track for the movie. You can see each clip in the movie, including video clips, transitions, and titles. This information is exactly the same as in the Clip Viewer, although it looks a bit different.
Audio 1 track	You can place any sound on the Audio 1 track, including sound effects, sound that you record, and music. The sound on the track is represented by blue blocks when the sound is a sound effect or by a colored bar when the sound is recorded sound or music.
Audio 2 track	The Audio 2 track is the same in function as the Audio 1 track.
Magnification pop-up menu	You can choose the magnification of the Timeline Viewer by using the Magnification pop-up menu. When the value on this menu is lower, you see more of the movie's timeline, but the elements you see are smaller and are more difficult to work with. When you choose a higher value, you "zoom in," and you can see elements in greater detail. As you edit a movie, you can use this pop-up menu to change the view to be appropriate for the task you are doing. For example, when you are synchronizing sound, you might want a close-up view so you can position objects in precise relative positions. When you are recording sound from an audio CD, you might want to see more of the movie so that you can see how much longer the sound you are recording will play relative to the movie's length.
Clip speed slider	This slider enables you to change the speed at which a video clip plays. Moving the slider towards Faster makes the clip play faster and provides a fast forward effect. Moving the slider in the other direction makes the clip play more slowly in a slow motion effect. When the slider is in the center, the clip plays at its original speed.
Fade In checkbox	When an audio clip is selected and this checkbox is checked, the clip's sound fades in.
Relative Volume slider	This slider enables you to set the relative volume of clips. For example, you might want narration in your movie to be louder than the music score. You use this slider to set the relative volume levels of various audio elements. Unlike the Volume slider in the Monitor, this slider *does* change the movie. It is called a relative slider because you change only the relative volume levels of elements in your movie, not the actual volume of the movie itself (which is controlled by the viewer when your movie is played).

Table 4.7 iMovie's Effects Tools (continued)

Tool	What It Does
Fade Out Checkbox	When checked while an audio clip is selected, this control makes the audio fade out.
Mute checkboxes	The Mute checkboxes determine whether the audio contained in a track is audible or silent. When a track's Mute checkbox is checked, the sound contained in that track is heard. Conversely, to mute a track's sound, you uncheck its Mute checkbox.

There are two audio tracks on the Timeline Viewer because you will often want to use several kinds of sound in the same movie, such as sound effects, narration, and music. It is easier to manipulate these sounds when you have two tracks to work with. For example, you might want to put sound effects on the Audio 1 track and music on the Audio 2 track. When you can see the elements more clearly, it is easier to work with your movie's sound. Two tracks also enable you to have alternate soundtracks for your movie.

The Disk Gauge

iMovie projects are big, really big. DV clips consume tremendous amounts of disk space, and you can expect a movie's files to consume several GBs of disk space (even with a relatively short movie). The Disk Gauge, which is located between the Tools palette and the viewers, is a tool you use to monitor the disk space that is available on the disk on which the iMovie project is stored (see Figure 4.11).

Figure 4.11 *This disk has 393MB of space available—when it comes to an iMovie project, this is not a whole lot of room to work in.*

Along with the numeric value shown, the gauge uses a color code scheme to keep you informed about the available disk space for your project. When the gauge is green, iMovie thinks you have plenty of room left. When the gauge turns yellow, the disk is starting to fill up, and you need to keep a close eye on the situation. When the gauge turns red, the disk is either full or getting very close, and your project is about to come to a grinding halt.

The iMovie Trash

iMovie has its own Trash. When you delete clips, cut frames from clips, and otherwise dispose of material, iMovie moves that material to its Trash (see Figure 4.12). For example, when you cut frames from a clip, they are moved to the Trash. The material remains here until the Trash is emptied. This enables you to undo things you have done, up to the last 10 actions you have performed.

Figure 4.12 *At least iMovie's Trash doesn't smell bad.*

> **NOTE**
>
> Unlike the Mac OS Trash, you can't drag items from the iMovie Trash back into your project. You can only retrieve them by using the Undo command.

While being able to undo actions is good, items in the Trash do consume disk space. When you are running low on disk space, you should empty the iMovie Trash to free up more room on the disk. To empty iMovie's Trash, choose File, Empty Trash. Be aware that iMovie empties its Trash whenever you quit the application so make sure that nothing is there that you will need before you quit iMovie.

Making Your iMovie Preferences Known

There are three areas in which you can set preferences to control how iMovie works: Import, Views, and Advanced. You set your iMovie preferences by choosing iMovie, Preferences. The iMovie Preferences window has three tabs, which not coincidentally, correspond to the three areas I listed previously (see Figure 4.13).

Setting Import Preferences

The Import tab contains the preference controls explained in Table 4.8.

Setting Views Preferences

The View preferences tab contains the controls explained in Table 4.9.

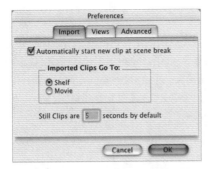

Figure 4.13 *There aren't many iMovie preferences that you will want to change in the beginning, but you might want to make some changes as your iMovie expertise grows.*

Table 4.8 iMovie's Import Preferences

Preference	What It Does
Automatically start new clip at scene break checkbox	By default, this checkbox is checked. As iMovie imports video clips from a DV camera, it starts a new clip each time there is a break in the video coming in; basically, a clip starts when you pressed the Record button on the camera and stops when you pressed the camera's Record button again to stop recording. If this checkbox is unchecked, iMovie imports the video as one clip (up to 2GB at which point iMovie starts a new clip anyway). Usually, you want iMovie to break the clips for you.
Imported Clips Go To radio button	By default, iMovie places clips that you import on the Shelf, from which you can drag them to the Clip Viewer or Timeline Viewer to place them in your movie. If you choose the Movie radio button instead, iMovie places clips on the Clip Viewer instead of the Shelf, and you can build a movie as you import clips. I recommend that you leave the Shelf selected because it makes building a movie easier.
Still Clips are 5 seconds by default	You can import still images into your iMovie projects to use them in a movie. The value in this text box determines how long those images appear on the screen before the next clip starts. The default value is 5 seconds (which is usually a bit too long), but you can make it whatever you want. Note that you can manually change the amount of time any still image appears on the screen; this value sets the initial time for all still images that you import.

Table 4.9 iMovie's Views Preferences

Preference	What It Does
Shown Thumbnails in Timeline checkbox	When this box is checked, you see a thumbnail image at the center of clips on the Timeline Viewer. This helps you understand your clips better so you should leave this on.
Use Short Time Codes checkbox	When this box is checked, leading zeros in timecodes that are less than one minute are hidden. Since leading zeros don't add any information, you might as well turn this on.
Show More Details checkbox	When turned on, this control causes more information to appear in the video clips shown in the Timeline Viewer, including clip title, timecode, effects icons, and so on. Generally, you should turn this on (it is off by default).
Show Locked Audio Only When Selected checkbox	You can lock audio clips to specific points relative to the Playhead's position in a movie. When you do this, you can move other elements around in the movie, and the audio remains in sync with the element to which you locked it. When this checkbox is checked, you see the locked icon only when an audio clip that has been locked has been selected. I like to leave this off since it is helpful to see which audio is locked when you are looking at a movie in the Timeline Viewer.

Setting Advanced Preferences

The Advanced preferences tab contains the settings detailed in Table 4.10.

Table 4.10 iMovie's Advanced Preferences

Preference	What It Does
Extract Audio in Paste Over checkbox	You can paste video over an existing video segment. When this checkbox is checked, the audio track for the video over which you are pasting a clip is extracted, and it is not included in the resulting video. For example, suppose that you have a clip containing narration that you don't want to maintain, but you want to replace part of the video that you shot with another clip. With this option on, when you paste in the new segment, the underlying narration is removed. With this option off, the audio of the clip in which you are doing a paste over is maintained.

Table 4.10 iMovie's Advanced Preferences (continued)

Preference	What It Does
Filter Audio from Camera checkbox	With this option on, iMovie filters the sound that it imports from a DV camera. Unless you have a very specific reason that you don't want this to happen, you should allow this to happen because the quality of your audio will be better.
Video Play Through to Camera checkbox	If you have a DV camera connected and powered up while you edit a movie, when you play clips or the movie, this preference causes what you play to be displayed on the DV camera as well as on the Mac's screen. For example, you might want to do this to preview what you play in your DV camera's monitor to give you a better perspective of how the video will appear on a television screen.

Building a Movie in iMovie

Creating a movie that is worth watching involves more than just slamming video clips into your Mac and plopping them on the Clip Viewer. If you really want to create movies that people (including you) will actually want to watch, you should use a disciplined process that consists of the following steps:

1. Plan your movie.
2. Build a basic video track.
3. Improve the video track by adding transitions, title, and special effects.
4. Build a soundtrack.
5. Polish the movie.
6. Export the movie.

Skipping over or skimping on any of these steps will result in a movie that isn't as good as it could have been. Practice the skills you need in each of these steps so that they become second nature to you and your movies will not only be pleasing to watch, but you'll create them more quickly as well.

Planning a Movie

In a cruel twist of irony, while planning your movie is the most important step in the whole process, I don't have room in this chapter to give it even a basic treatment (this chapter is about using iMovie rather than making movies). I have room only to tell you that planning *should* be done and to explain how to prepare an iMovie project. If you are serious about making movies, you should learn more about the planning tasks associated with the movie-making process.

NOTE

If you want to learn more about making movies with iMovie, including planning them, see my book *The Complete Idiot's Guide to iMovie 2*.

Deciding What Your Movie Will Be

There are two general kinds of movies you will make: spontaneous or scripted. In spontaneous movies, you usually have a set of clips that you have captured with a camcorder, and you want to make a movie from those clips. In scripted movies, you actually have a script that controls the contents of the movie, by defining what happens on the screen, who says what, and so on. Creating a scripted movie is not what most people do with iMovie, so I'll focus on spontaneous movies.

Most of the time, you will be using iMovie to create a movie from video that you have taken at some event, but some of the best movies can be made from video taken during those "everyday" moments that we all take for granted.

While the contents of the video you capture might not be "known" before you capture it, your movie's contents should be known before you crank up iMovie and start building the movie in iMovie. Create a rough plan for your movie by doing the following steps.

Plan a Movie

1. Decide the general content of the movie. For example, if you took video during a vacation, decide what parts of the vacation you want to include in the movie. You might want to include the whole vacation, or you might want to create movies about specific activities that you did during the vacation.

2. Watch the raw video that you captured.

3. As you view the video, create a log that generally describes the contents of the video at various timecodes. This log is essential while you make your movie, but it is even more important for cataloging the raw footage in your collection so that you can find it again (this concept is explained further in Chapter 20, "Organizing and Archiving Your Digital Media").

4. In your log, include a notation for clips that contain footage that you think you will want to include in your movie. This notation will help you avoid spending time importing clips that you were never going to use anyway.

When you shoot a movie, keep the following tips in mind:

◆ When you shoot at any specific time (such as an event), try to keep the total amount of video to 30 minutes or less (preferably less). The more video footage that you have to work with, the longer the movie will take to create and the more effort you'll spend doing it. This makes it harder to get the movie done, and projects can linger forever and never get finished. For example, if you have one hour of raw footage, it will take quite a while just to preview that video to see what you actually have. It's better to have a shorter but finished movie than a longer one that is never seen.

◆ When you shoot, try to vary camera locations so that you have shots from different perspectives that can be put together. A movie shot from the same perspective can be less interesting than one that includes a variety of shots.

◆ Try to keep camera motion while you are shooting to a minimum. When you move the camera, stop shooting while you are moving, unless it is essential to move and shoot at the same time. Footage that you capture on the move is not likely to be pleasant to watch. You should also avoid using the camera's Zoom control while you are shooting for the same reason. Stop taping, change the camera position or zoom, and resume taping again. Try to use a tripod whenever possible.

Preparing the iMovie Project

When you have planned your movie, you are ready to get into iMovie and start making the movie by creating an iMovie project.

Create an iMovie Project

1. Open iMovie. If you have not used iMovie before, you will see a dialog box with three buttons: New Project, Open Project, and Quit. In this dialog box, click the New Project button. (If you have previously worked with iMovie, it remembers your last project and automatically opens it for you. In that case, start a new project by choosing File, New Project.)

2. In the Create New Project dialog box, name your project. Move to the volume on which you are going to store it and click Create.

3. Open the project folder that you just created, and you will see two items: a folder called Media and an iMovie file that has the same name as the project you created (see Figure 4.14). The media folder is used to store the clips, images, additional sounds (such as a music track), and other components that you use in your project. The iMovie file is a small pointer file that contains references to all the files in the media folder that you are using. If you want to open your project by double-clicking something, this file is the icon that you double-click.

Figure 4.14 *This iMovie project is called "Moving By Air."*

When you choose a location in which to store a project (by selecting a location in the Create New Project dialog), make sure that you choose a volume with plenty of free space to store your iMovie project. If you have a partitioned hard disk, you might need to move outside of your Home directory to store your project in order to have enough room. In the ideal situation, you will have a dedicated hard disk or volume on which to store your project. If your movie will be more than a couple of minutes, you should have at least 2GB available for your project. Running out of disk space will put a major crimp in your movie-making process.

NOTE

The steps in the remainder of this chapter assume that iMovie is configured with the preferences as I like them and as described in the section called "Making Your iMovie Preferences Known." If you set your preferences differently, the steps you need to use might be slightly different than what is shown in this chapter and what you see on your screen might look different. For example, if you have imported clips placed on the Clip Viewer instead of the Shelf, you won't end up with clips on the Shelf like my steps do. While you are learning iMovie, keep your preferences the same as mine. After you know your way around the application, you can change your preferences to suit your, well, preferences.

Building a Basic Video Track

Your next step is to create the basic video track. To do this, use the following general steps:

1. Import the clips and images that you will use in your movie.
2. Edit the clips you imported.
3. Build the basic video track from your edited clips.

Stocking the Shelf with Clips

There are three sources of clips that you will place on the Shelf and from which you will build your movie:

♦ Video clips from a DV camera

♦ QuickTime clips

♦ Still Images

Importing clips from each of these sources requires slightly different tasks.

Adding Video Clips from a DV Camera

The really neat part about an iMovie-compatible DV camcorder is that you can control your DV camcorder by using iMovie's controls. The Play, Fast Forward, Stop, and other buttons in the iMovie Monitor actually control your DV camcorder. Importing clips from a DV camcorder is a snap.

Import Clips from a DV Camcorder

1. Open your iMovie project.

2. Turn the DV camera on and set it to its output setting (this is sometimes labeled VCR or VTR).

3. Connect the FireWire cable to the DV camcorder and your Mac. You will see a message in iMovie's Monitor window confirming that iMovie is in touch with your DV camcorder. In addition to the "Camera Connected" message, the button just under the Monitor is now Import, which means that you are ready to begin importing your clips into iMovie.

4. Use iMovie's controls to control the DV camera to move to the first segment on the tape that you want to import into your project; this is where the log you created when you planned your movie comes in. Use your log to get to a point just before the clip that you want to import.

5. Click the Import button (or press the Spacebar); iMovie starts the camcorder and begins capturing the clips. It stores the first clip in the first available slot on the Shelf. When it gets to a scene break (the point at which you hit the Stop Recording button on the DV camcorder), it ends that clip and immediately begins capturing the next scene, which it places in the next available slot on the Shelf (see Figure 4.15). iMovie names each clip Clip # where # is a sequential number.

   iMovie continues this process until it runs out of video to import or out of disk space to store clips, whichever comes first.

6. If you don't want to wait that long, click Import again to stop the capture process (or press the Spacebar).

7. Use the iMovie controls to move the tape to the next set of scenes that you want to capture, and begin again.

8. Continue this process until you capture all the scenes that your movie plan calls for. Your Shelf now has some nice clips (and probably some not-so-nice ones), ready for you to edit and use in your movie.

TIP

As you import clips, keep an eye on the Disk Gauge. If it turns yellow or red, you need to make more room on the disk on which your project is stored before you can capture more clips.

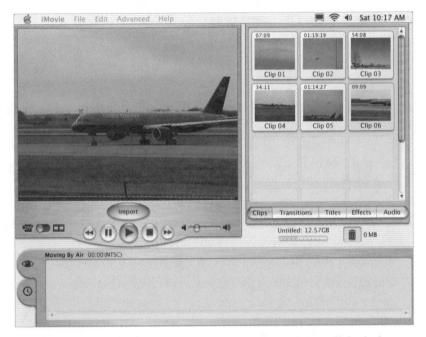

Figure 4.15 *Capturing clips from a DV camera is easy because iMovie does the work for you.*

9. When you have captured the clips you need for your movie, disconnect your camera and turn it off.

NOTE

If you don't use an iMovie-compatible camcorder, you might still be able to import clips, but you probably won't be able to control your camera by using iMovie's controls.

Adding QuickTime Clips to Your iMovie Movie

A great source of material for your iMovie projects is QuickTime movies that you create or that you obtain from other sources. As you learned in Chapter 1, "QuickTime Pro: Making it All Happen," you can use QuickTime Pro to convert any QuickTime movie into the DV format that, conveniently enough, is a format that you can import into iMovie. The steps to import a QuickTime movie into iMovie aren't all that much more involved than those to capture a clip from a DV camera.

First, save the QuickTime movie clip in the DV Stream format.

Save a QuickTime Movie in the DV Format

1. Open the QuickTime movie that you want to use in your iMovie project.
2. Use the QuickTime Player controls to edit the movie so it contains only that material you want to import (of course, you can import the whole thing and edit it in iMovie as well, but getting rid of material first makes the process faster). You might want to work on a copy so that you don't you mess up the original.
3. Choose File, Export.
4. In the Save exported file as dialog, choose Movie to DV Stream on the Export pop-up menu.
5. Name the clip, choose a location in which to save it, and click Save. The DV clip will be created in the location that you selected.

After the clip is in the DV Stream format, import it into iMovie.

Import a DV Clip into iMovie

1. Choose File, Import File.
2. In the Import File dialog box, choose DV Stream file from the Show pop-up menu.
3. Move to the clip that you converted into the DV Stream format in the previous steps.
4. Select the DV stream clip and click Import. You will see a progress bar showing you how the import is moving along. If your clip is fairly lengthy, this process can take a few moments. When the importing process is complete, the clip appears on the Shelf, and it is automatically selected so that you see it in the Monitor. From this point on, it behaves in the same way as any other clip on the Shelf, such as those you imported from your DV camera (see Figure 4.16).

Putting Still Images on the Shelf

You might want to use still images in your movie; a strategically placed still image can make a nice transition between scenes, or you might want to include still images related to a particular clip. You can use images in the usual image file formats, such as JPEG, TIFF, and so on.

Figure 4.16 *I have captured a clip of Huey helicopters from the movie "We Were Solders" to use in my iMovie project (you see the first frame of the clip in the Monitor).*

Import Still Images into iMovie

1. Prepare the images that you want to import outside of iMovie. For example, you can export images from iPhoto for this purpose.

2. Jump back into your iMovie project and choose File, Import File to see the Import File dialog box.

3. Move to the folder in which you saved the photos that you want to use in your movie.

4. Hold the Shift (to select a series of images next to each other) or ⌘ (to select individual images) key down and click all the images that you want to import.

5. When they are selected, click Import. A progress window appears; and after a few moments, you will see your images on the Shelf (see Figure 4.17). You work with images just like you do video clips; for example, you place an image in your movie by dragging it to the Clip Viewer.

Figure 4.17 *The selected clip is a still image of an F-15 that I imported into my project (you can see several other images on the Shelf).*

Images in iMovie

Images that you import into iMovie will be converted into the 640 x 480 format in the landscape orientation. If you import images larger than this, iMovie will do the conversion itself, and the results might not look very good. For best results, you should use an image editing application to put your images in the 640 x 480 format before importing them into iMovie. For portrait-oriented photos, you might want to place the image over a 640 x 480 background and save the combined image. Otherwise, iMovie will stretch a narrower image to fill the screen, and that probably won't look very good either.

Hacking (AKA Editing) Your Clips

After you have your source material (your clips) stored on the Shelf, you should edit them. Your goals should include the following:

◆ Preview clips you want to include in the movie.

◆ Delete any clips you won't use.

- Rename clips that will appear in your movie and get information about them.
- Split clips into parts so you can work with each part individually.
- Edit any clips you will use in your movie.

Previewing Clips

To preview a clip, do the following steps.

Preview a Clip

1. Select a clip by clicking it on the Shelf. The clip is highlighted with a yellow border, which means that the clip is selected. More telling is the first frame of the clip that shows in the Monitor. Also notice that when you select a clip, iMovie also moves into the Edit mode, in which you can manipulate your clips (if it isn't in the Edit mode, slide the Camera/Edit switch to the right).
2. Use the iMovie controls to play the clip, to rewind it, and so on. One of the fastest ways to preview a clip is by clicking the Preview (Fast Forward) button.
3. Decide if the clip has usable material in it or not.

TIP

Remember that there are many ways to move around a clip. You can use the play controls, drag the Playhead, and use the keyboard shortcuts. Get really comfortable moving around because this is one of the most important skills you need to learn.

Deleting Clips

When you identify clips that you aren't going to use in your movie, it is best to get rid of them right away so that they aren't wasting disk space.

Delete a Clip

1. Select the clip.
2. Press the Delete key. The clip will be moved to the Trash.

3. Continue deleting clips until you have rid your projects of the useless clips.

TIP

You can also delete a clip by dragging it from the Shelf to the iMovie Trash.

Changing a Clip's Information

iMovie enables you to rename clips so that they have more meaningful names than those assigned by iMovie.

Rename a Clip

1. Select a clip on the Shelf.
2. Double-click the clip, choose File, Get Clip Info, or press Shift+⌘+I. The Clip Info window will appear.
3. Rename the clip in the Name field. Just under the name you will see its Media File name and size (see Figure 4.18).

TIP

You can also rename a clip on the Shelf by selecting its name so that it becomes highlighted and then typing a new name.

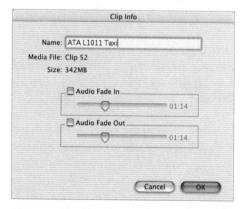

Figure 4.18 *I've given this clip a meaningful name.*

4. Click OK to rename the clip. When you return to the Shelf, the clip will have the name you gave it.

NOTE

The Media Name is the actual name of the file in the Media folder that is within the project's folder. If you wanted to use the clip's file outside of iMovie (such as by importing it into QuickTime Player), you could find it by opening the project's Media folder and looking for the Media Name of the clip that you want to use.

Splitting Clips

In certain situations, you might want to split a clip so that you can work with each part independently. When you split a clip, the two resulting clips behave just like clips you have created by capturing them from a DV camera or importing them.

Split a Clip

1. Select the clip that you want to split. It will appear in the Monitor.
2. Drag the Playhead to the point at which you want to split the clip.
3. Choose Edit, Split Clip at Playhead or press ⌘+T.
4. The clip will be split into two clips at the point in the clip at which the Playhead was located. A new clip with "/1" will be appended to the first segment's name and will be added to the Shelf (for example, if the clip's name was Clip 43, the new clip will be named Clip 43/1). You can treat the two clips independently because they are now separate clips.

Editing Clips

Editing your clips is one of the most important tasks you will do. When you edit a clip, you remove everything from that clip that will detract from, rather than add to, your movie. Editing your clips is fundamental to creating good movies.

You can edit clips at any time, but in my opinion you are better off if you edit your clips *before* you place them in a movie. Building a movie from edited clips gets you to a completed movie faster because you deal with less material when you actually build your movie.

NOTE

Even if you edit your clips before you place them in your movie, you should expect to have to do some minor editing on some clips after you build your movie. However, you can get clips very close to their final condition before you even place them in a movie.

Edit a Clip

1. Click the clip on the Shelf that you want to edit to select it; the clip appears in the Monitor.

2. Preview the clip and locate a part of the clip that should be removed.

3. Drag the Playhead to the point at which you want to start removing frames from the clip.

4. Move the pointer between the underside of the Scrubber Bar and the Monitor's playback controls, and click and hold the mouse button down; two Crop Markers will appear.

5. Continue holding the mouse button down and drag to the right. When you do, the Start Crop Marker's location becomes fixed at the point at which you clicked the mouse button. Drag to the right to move the End Crop Marker to select a series of frames. As you drag the End Crop Marker, you can see the frames that you are selecting in the Monitor. The area of the clip that you have selected is indicated by the gold-colored portion of the Scrubber bar (see Figure 4.19). When you release the Crop Markers, the Playhead jumps to the End Crop Marker.

    When the Playhead is aligned with a Crop Marker, it "sticks" to it. This enables you to make very fine selections, even down to the individual frame. When the Playhead is "stuck" to a Crop Marker, you can make very fine selections by using the arrow keys. To increase the selected frames by a single frame, press the Right arrow key one time (to shorten the selection by one frame, press the Left arrow key once). To change the selection by 10 frames at a time, hold the Shift key down while you press the appropriate arrow key.

    You can also make the Crop Marker stick to the Playhead by dragging the Playhead so that it is directly over a Crop Marker (a small line extends down from the Playhead so that you can see precisely where it is located).

Start Crop Selected Pointer End Crop Playhead
Marker   Frames   Marker

Figure 4.19 *The frames contained between the two Crop Markers are selected and action can be taken on them.*

TIP

When the Playhead is stuck to the End Crop Marker, you can move it by clicking another location on the Scrubber bar.

---

6. To remove the selected frames from the clip, choose Edit, Cut (or press ⌘+X). The Crop Markers disappear, as do the selected frames, and they are removed from the clip.

7. Play the clip to see how it is without the frames that you just cut. If you don't like the result, you can undo it by choosing Edit, Undo (⌘+Z).

8. If you want to remove everything that is *not* selected instead, choose Edit, Crop instead of Cut. This is useful when you want to remove frames from both the beginning and end of a clip at the same time. Select the portion of the clip that you want to *keep* between the Crop Markers; when you crop it, all the frames outside of the clip are removed.

9. Preview the edited clip and continue editing it until you have removed all the chaff from it.

NOTE

By the way, copy, paste, and other editing commands work in iMovie just like they do in other Mac applications. If you select a series of frames and choose Copy instead of Cut, the frames are moved to the Clipboard, and you can paste them in the same clip or in another clip.

Continue editing your clips until they are close to how you want them to be in your movie. It's usually a good idea to leave a couple of spare frames at each end of the clips so that you have some "extra" to work with when you do the final editing. Your goal should be to have a set of edited clips from which to build a movie. When you are done editing clips, you should have shorter and fewer clips than you did after you imported all the clips into the project.

TIP

The Clear command removes selected frames without placing them on the Clipboard. Technically speaking, you should use Clear rather than Cut because then memory resources aren't wasted by placing the selected frames on your Clipboard. However, I prefer to use Cut because it has a keyboard shortcut, whereas Clear does not. And practically speaking, you notice any performance problems if you leave frames on your Clipboard.

Building the Video Track

After you have edited your clips, you are ready to being building a movie from those clips. You assemble your movie by placing clips on the Clip Viewer in the order that you want them to be in the movie.

Place Clips in a Movie

1. Click the Clip Viewer icon to bring the Clip Viewer to the front (it will probably be in the front already).

2. Drag the first clip from the Shelf onto the Clip Viewer. You will see the clip's thumbnail on the Clip Viewer. This means that the clip is now part of the movie.

3. Drag the next clip from the Shelf onto the Clip Viewer and place it before or after the first clip that you placed there.

4. Continue moving clips from the Shelf to the Clip Viewer until you have placed all of the clips that you want to use in your movie (see Figure 4.20).

Figure 4.20 *Here, you can see that I moved most of the clips from the Shelf to the Clip Viewer.*

5. Preview the movie by playing it. Make sure that no clips are selected and press the Play button. The movie will play; you haven't added any transitions yet so all the clips run right into one another (the Straight Cut). Sometimes, this will look fine; sometimes it won't. You will add transitions in the next phase.

As you build your basic video track, keep the following points in mind:

◆ When you select one or more clips on the Clip Viewer, the Monitor will show the clips that you have selected. Vertical lines in the Scrubber bar mark the boundaries of each clip. If you don't have any clips selected, the Monitor will show the contents of all the clips on the Clip Viewer, in other words, your entire movie.

◆ If the Clip Viewer gets full, use its scroll bar to reveal empty space for more clips.

◆ You change the order in which clips appear by dragging them around the Clip Viewer. When you move a clip between two other clips, they will slide apart to make room for the clip you are moving. Similarly, you can drag a clip from the Shelf to the Clip Viewer to be between clips that are already there.

◆ When you have built your movie, choose Edit, Select None (or press ⌘+D) to deselect any clips that are selected. Press the Home key to move to the start of your movie. To preview your movie, press the Spacebar. Your movie will play.

◆ You can use the same movement and editing controls with an entire movie as you can when dealing with an individual clip (such as fast forward).

◆ You learned earlier that you can easily include still images in your movies. Rather than using a frame rate, still images use a duration, which is the amount of time the image appears onscreen. By default, this is 5 seconds, meaning that the still image appears for 5 seconds. You can change the duration for a still image when you add it to your movie. To do this, add the image to your movie by dragging it from the Shelf and placing it on the Clip Viewer. Select the image in the Clip Viewer and edit the value in the Time field (located at the top of the Clip Viewer toward its right end) to be the new duration for the image.

◆ You can play or edit a single clip again by selecting it on the Clip Viewer. The timecode shown next to the Playhead in the Monitor for the selected clip becomes the timecode for the movie and shows you the location of that clip in the movie.

◆ You can remove a clip from your movie and place it back on the Shelf by dragging it from the Clip Viewer to the Shelf. You can delete a clip by selecting it and then pressing Delete.

◆ To see your movie in full-screen mode, click the View in Full Screen button. Your movie plays back so that it takes up the entire screen. This helps you focus on your movie without any distractions from the iMovie interface. To stop your movie and return to iMovie before your movie has finished, click the mouse button or press the Spacebar.

Continue placing clips in the Clip Viewer until you have all the clips that you want to appear in your movie in the order that you want them to play. You don't have to use all the clips on the Shelf; you can leave clips there for later use or delete them when you are sure that you won't use them in this movie.

Building a Better Video Track

Now that you have the basic video track for your movie, it's time to polish your movie's video track by adding titles, transitions, and special effects. And you can add some iMovie trick effects to really liven things up.

Explaining Yourself with Titles

In the section called "The Titles Palette" earlier in this chapter, you learned about how you can use iMovie's titling tools to add all sorts of text to your movie, such as opening and closing credits, captions, and so on. In that section, you will find all the detailed information you need to add titles to your own movies. However, a couple of examples will lock this information in for you so that you will be able to add any titles that you would like to add.

Adding Opening Credits

Most movies contain opening credits that introduce the movie.

Add Opening Titles to a Movie

1. Click the Title button to open the Title palette.

2. Click Centered Title to choose it. You will see a preview of the title in the Preview window (the text will be some filler that iMovie has inserted for you).

3. Click the Over Black checkbox if it isn't already selected. This makes the title appear over a black frame instead of being applied over a video clip.

4. Type the title text in the text boxes (with the Centered Title style, you can have two lines of text).

5. Choose a font for the title on the Font pop-up menu.

6. Choose a size for the title by using the Font Size slider. Each time that you make a change, a preview of the title appears in the Preview window to show you the effect of your change.

7. Choose the color of the text by using the Color pop-up menu. (White is the default color and is usually the best choice for titles over a black background).

8. Use the Speed slider to set the title's duration. The Speed slider determines how long the title appears on the screen. Moving the slider to the right causes the title to appear on the screen for a longer time.

9. Use the Pause slider to set the amount of time the text actually appears on the screen. With the Centered Title style, the text fades in and then fades out. The farther to the right you place the Pause slider, the longer the text appears on the screen relative to the length of the title clip.

10. When you think that the title is getting close to being ready, click Preview to preview it in the Monitor.

11. Continue making changes to the title until you are satisfied with it.

12. Drag the title style from the Titles palette to the Clip Viewer and place it before the first clip in the movie (see Figure 4.21). When you place the title clip on the Clip Viewer, it will be rendered. While the rendering process is occurring, you can continue to work on your movie (however, you won't be able to save the movie until all rendering has been completed).

13. Select the first couple of clips on the Clip Viewer and press Play to preview the movie with the title clip.

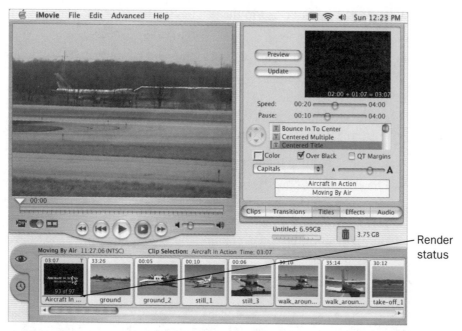

Figure 4.21 *The first clip in the Clip Viewer is a title clip.*

Adding a Caption to a Clip

Another example of a commonly used title effect is a caption, which means that text appears on a clip (presumably to place the clip in context or to explain it).

When you place a title on a clip (which is what happens unless the Over Black checkbox is checked), it's applied over the clip that is selected in the Clip Viewer or on which you drop the title. When you place the title on a clip, the clip will be split into two clips. One clip contains the title effect and the other contains the remainder of the clip. If you want the title to appear in the first part of the clip, drop the title on the left side of the clip. If you want the title to appear on the end of the clip, drop it on the right side of the clip. The adjacent clips slide apart to indicate where the title clip is placed.

Add a Caption to a Clip

1. On the Clip Viewer, select the clip to which you want to add a caption.
2. On the Title palette, select the Stripe Subtitle title style.
3. Uncheck the Over Black checkbox. The Preview window now shows the selected clip with the title applied to it.
4. Enter the caption's text in the text boxes (this style also allows two lines of text).
5. Use the Font and Color pop-up menus and the Size slider to configure the text.
6. Use the Speed slider to set the amount of time that the caption appears on the screen.
7. Click Preview to preview the caption in the Monitor.
8. Continue refining the title until it is ready for your movie.
9. Drag the title to the left of the clip to which you want to apply it (this should be the clip that is selected). The clip will be split in two, and the part containing the title will be rendered (see Figure 4.22). The name of the segment of the clip containing the title will be part of the title's text.

NOTE

Title clips behave just like other clips on the Clip Viewer. You can move them around, delete them and so on. Of course, if you have applied a title to a clip (such as a caption), moving the title to a different clip can have unanticipated effects.

Figure 4.22 *A caption has been applied to this clip; notice that two clips are selected on the Clip Viewer, the first contains the title while the second one contains the remainder of the clip.*

Changing a Title Clip That Had Been Placed in a Movie

Making changes to a title clip that has been placed in a movie is similar to creating the title clip in the first place.

Change a Title Clip Included in a Movie

1. Select the title clip that you want to change.
2. Use the tools on the Titles palette to make changes to the title, such as changing its text, speed, font, and so on.
3. When you are satisfied with the changes you have made, click Update to apply those changes to the title clip. It will be rendered again, and the changes you have made will be part of the movie.

NOTE

iMovie includes a basic set of titles and transitions by default. You can add more titles and transition effects to iMovie to expand the tools that you have available to you. You'll learn all about your ability to expand iMovie's tools in Chapter 13.

Making Your Movie Flow with Transitions

Back in the section called "The Transitions Palette," you learned about iMovie's powerful transitions tools that you can use to add transition effects to your movies. Adding transitions is quite similar to adding titles, as a couple of examples will demonstrate.

Adding a Fade Out Transition

One of the more useful transition effects is the fade out technique where a clip fades to a black screen. This transition is great for those times when there is a substantial change between two clips or at the beginning or ending of a segment of your movie. The fade gives the viewer a clear indication that a change is coming, but does so in a smooth way.

Add a Fade Out Transition

1. Click the Transitions button to open the Transitions tool palette.

2. Click the Fade Out transition. You will see a preview in the Preview window.

3. Set the speed of the fade by using the Speed slider. Moving the slider to the right makes the transition last longer, which means the clip to which you apply it fades out more slowly. Moving the slider to the left makes the clip fade more quickly.

4. Click Preview to preview the fade in the Monitor. The fade out transition will be shown on the clip with which you most recently worked or with a clip that is selected.

5. If the transition is what you want, drag the transition to the right side of the clip on the Clip Viewer that you want to fade out (see Figure 4.23). The transition clip appears as a green box with arrowheads that indicate the direction of the transition. The transition will be rendered and will become part of the movie.

Figure 4.23 *I have added a fade out transition to the second clip that is called "walk_around."*

Like titles, when you add a transition to a clip, the clip is actually split into two parts. One segment contains most of the clip to which you apply the transition while the second clip contains a portion of the original clip with the transition effect applied to it.

Even though they look a bit different than video or image clips, transition clips can be handled in the same way. For example, you can apply a transition clip to a different clip by moving it to a new location on the Clip Viewer. And you can delete a transition clip by selecting it and pressing Delete.

Adding a Cross Dissolve Transition

In a cross dissolve, one clip fades out while the next clip fades in (the screen never goes to black). The cross dissolve is often used when the location of the scene isn't changing, but time is, in other words, to indicate the passage of time between two clips. It can also be a good effect to transition between clips showing different images, but that are part of the same event. For example, if you are filming an air show, a cross dissolve is a good way to transition between different airplane routines.

Apply a Cross Dissolve Transition

1. In the Clip Viewer, select the clip after which you want the cross dissolve transition to appear and move the Playhead to the end of the clip.

2. Open the Transitions palette and click Cross Dissolve to choose it; then watch the preview in the Preview window.

3. Set the transition's duration with the Speed slider; try placing the slider in the middle of its range. If that is too long or too short, use the slider to set the proper amount of time for the transition.

4. When the timing looks close, click Preview to see how it looks on the Monitor.

5. After you are satisfied with the transition, drag the transition from the Transitions palette to the Clip Viewer and drop it between the two clips that you want to transition between.

NOTE

The amount of time over which a transition can be applied depends on the length of time of the clip to which you apply it. A transition effect can't last longer than the clip to which it is applied. If you try to add a transition that is longer than the preceding clip, you will see an error message, and you will have to shorten the transition or apply it to a longer clip.

Changing a Transition That Has Been Placed in a Movie

Changing a transition after it has been placed in a movie is just like changing a title clip that is part of a movie.

Change a Transition Clip

1. Select the transition clip that you want to change.

2. Use the transition tools to change the transition, such as changing its duration. You can change the transition style if you want to.

3. When you are done making changes, click Update to implement your changes in the movie. The clip will be rendered again.

Some Transition Rules to Create By

Transitions are fun to add to a movie, but there are some general guidelines you should follow so your movies make good use, but not overuse, of transition effects.

◆ You can place two transitions adjacent to one another. For example, to have one clip fade out and then the next fade in, place a Fade Out and a Fade In between two clips.

◆ Don't feel as though you need to have a transition effect before and after every clip in your movie. Sometimes (dare I say most of the time?), the default straight cut works just fine. This is where your creativity comes in, so experiment until you achieve an outcome that is pleasing to you.

◆ Certain transitions tend to cause viewers to expect certain things. For example, a fade transition usually implies a longer break in the action, such as a major scene change. A cross dissolve is usually used where a minor scene change is taking place. A straight cut should be used when you want to call as little attention to the transition as possible. Keep these guidelines in mind when you use transitions so you don't stray too far from your viewer's expectations.

◆ Don't use transitions just for the sake of using them. Adding transitions is fun, and you might be tempted to put them everywhere. When transitions are done properly, the viewer shouldn't even notice them. If you find yourself or your audience being wowed by your transitions, something isn't right. Also, avoid the so-called ransom note effect resulting from applying every kind of transition—just because you can.

Making Your Movie Special with Special Effects

Special effects are a good way to enhance the quality of your movie's clips or to add artistic touches to your movie. While there are a variety of effects that you can apply, they all work similarly. The two examples in this section will demonstrate how you can apply any of the special effects to your clips. (See the section called "The Effects Palette" for all the details about the Effects tools available to you.)

Making New Clips Look Old

A useful special effect is the application of Sepia tone to a clip. This gives the clip a beige-tinged, wood grain effect that viewers will interpret as being old.

Add Sepia Tone to a Clip

1. Select the clip to which you want to apply the Sepia Tone effect.

2. Click the Effects button and from the list of available effects, click Sepia Tone. You see a preview of the effect in the Preview window.

3. Use the Effect In slider to set how long the effect takes to transition in; if you want the whole clip to be in Sepia Tone, leave the slider set all the way to the left. The further to the right that you drag the slider, the longer it takes for the full effect to kick in.

4. Use the Effect Out slider to determine when the effect begins to go away, thus returning your clip to its previous appearance. If you leave the slider all the way to the right, the clip remains in Sepia for its duration. The farther you move the slider to the left, the earlier in the clip the effect begins to disappear.

5. When you think that you are close to where you want to be, click Preview. You see a preview of the affected clip in the Monitor.

6. Continue refining the effect until you are happy with it.

7. When you are satisfied with the effect, click Apply and the effect is applied to the clip.

Improving a Clip's Brightness and Contrast

You can adjust a clip's brightness and contrast for artistic effect or to correct problems with the clip.

Adjust a Clip's Brightness and Contrast

1. Select the clip that you want to correct.

2. Click the Brightness/Contrast effect. You will see a preview in the Preview window.

3. Use the Effect In slider to set how long the effect takes to transition in; if you want the whole clip to be affected, leave the slider set all the way to the left. The farther to the right that you drag the slider, the longer it takes for the full effect to kick in.

4. Use the Effect Out slider to determine when the effect begins to go away, thus returning your clip to its previous appearance. If you leave the slider all the way to the right, the clip will remain as you adjust it for its

duration. The further you move the slider to the left, the earlier in the clip the effect begins to disappear.

5. Use the Brightness slider to change the clip's brightness.

6. Use the Contrast slider to change the clip's contrast.

7. Click preview to see the changed clip in the Monitor.

8. Continue adjusting the effect until you are happy with it.

9. Click Apply to apply the effect to the clip.

Committing to or Removing a Special Effect

After you have applied an effect to a clip, live with the clip for a while. Preview it several times.

If you decide that you want to return to the original version, select the clip and click Restore Clip. The effect will be removed, and the original version of the clip will be restored.

When you are sure you want to keep the clip as you've changed it, select the clip to which the special effect has been applied and click the Commit button. This removes the original version of the clip and frees up the disk space it was consuming.

Using Smart iMovie Tricks to Liven Things Up

Several iMovie tricks will help you make your movie even more interesting. These include changing the speed at which clips play, changing the direction in which a clip plays, adding an instant replay to a movie, and adding a freeze-frame.

Speeding Clips Up or Slowing Them Down

iMovie enables you to change the rate at which a clip plays; you make clips play faster than "normal" or slow them down in a slow motion effect. For example, you might choose to speed a clip up to make it move along faster when the actual content isn't so compelling. Or, you might want to slow a clip down to make its detail easier for the viewers to spot.

Change the Speed at which a Clip Plays

1. Click the Timeline Viewer icon to reveal the Timeline Viewer.

2. Use the Magnification pop-up menu to choose a viewing magnification that is comfortable for you (the automatic value might be just fine).

3. Select the clip whose speed you want to change (you can select the clip on the Clip Viewer and then open the Timeline Viewer if you prefer).

4. Move the Clip Speed slider to the left to make the clip play faster or to the right to make it play more slowly (see Figure 4.24). A speed change marker will appear on the clip, and it will lengthen or shorten in the timeline depending on whether you slowed it down or sped it up.

Figure 4.24 *The selected clip has been sped up; you can tell by the fast forward indicator in the clip on the Timeline Viewer.*

5. With the clip selected, preview it in the Monitor.

6. Continue adjusting the speed until you have achieved the effect that you desired.

To return a clip to its original speed, repeat the previous steps except this time, place the slider in the center of the range.

> **TIP**
>
> Changing a clip's speed also changes its audio. If you don't want the audio to be affected by the speed change, extract the audio from the clip first (you'll learn how to do that later in this chapter).

Changing Direction

You change the direction in which clips play by using the following steps.

Change a Clip's Direction of Play

1. Select the clip whose direction you want to change.
2. Choose Advanced, Revese Clip Direction (or press ⌘+R). The clip will be marked with a reverse direction marker and will play in the opposite direction.
3. Preview the clip in the Monitor.

Adding Instant Replay

You can combine the previous two tricks to create an instant replay effect.

Create Instant Replay

1. Select the portion of the clip that you want to replay and copy it; to make the most realistic effect, include the very end of the clip in your selection.
2. Move to the viewer and use the Paste command twice so that you have the three clips in a row. The first clip should be the original while the next two should be the segment that will be replayed.
3. Choose the middle clip (the first replay segment) and make it play in reverse.
4. Use the Clip Speed slider to make this "rewind" really quickly.

When you play this section of your movie, it will appear as if the clip is rewound at high speed before replaying, thus looking just like an instant replay.

Creating a Freeze-Frame

An interesting transition effect is to "freeze-frame" the last image in a clip before the transition to the next clip.

Add a Freeze-Frame Effect

1. Select the clip that you want to freeze-frame.

2. Move to the end of the clip on the Monitor.

3. Choose Edit, Create Still Clip (or press Shift+⌘+S). A still image clip of the frame that was visible on the Monitor will be created on the Shelf. This clip is just like a still image clip that you imported into iMovie.

4. Select the image clip you just created and enter its duration in the Time box at the top of the viewer (either one).

5. Place the image clip at the end of the clip from which you created it. When you play this section of the movie, the scene will "freeze" for the duration of the image clip.

TIP

You can apply transitions to image clips just as you can to other clips. Inserting a freeze-frame and then applying a fade out or cross dissolve transition to it makes a very interesting transition.

TIP

You can export any frame in a movie as an image file by moving to that frame in the Monitor and choosing File, Save Frame As (or press ⌘+F). In the resulting dialog, choose a save location, file name, and format (JPEG or PICT). Click Save and the frame will be exported from iMovie, and you can work with it just like other image files you have.

Pasting Over a Clip

There might be situations in which you want to replace some or all of the frames in one clip with frames from another clip. For example, suppose that you have shots of the same scene that are taken from different perspectives. You can use one shot as the master and paste in scenes from the other perspective over them.

Paste Over a Clip

1. Select the frames that you want to paste into another clip and copy or cut them.

2. Select the clip into which you want to paste the frames that you copied or cut.

3. Place the Playhead at the point at which you want the paste over to start. You can also use the Crop Markers to select the area in which to paste the copied or cut frames.

4. Choose Advanced, Paste Over at Playhead (or press Shift+⌘+V). The frames that you cut or copied will be pasted over the selected area in the original clip.

Building a Sound Track

Sound is a very important part of any movie; in fact, good sound can make any movie better. When working with iMovie projects, you can use the following kinds of sound:

◆ **Native sound.** When you import clips into iMovie, any sound that was part of those clips comes in, too. If your clips had sound, you've already heard it numerous times while you were assembling your movie from those clips. You can use iMovie tools to control some aspects of your movie's native sound.

◆ **Sound Effects**. You can add sound effects to your movie to bring it to life. You can use iMovie's built-in sound effects, and you can import other sound effects to use.

◆ **Narration and other recorded sound**. If you want to explain what is happening in a movie or add your own commentary, you can record narration for your movie. You can also use the narration tool to record sounds from a tape player or other audio device.

◆ **Music**. The right music makes a movie a better experience. You can import music to your movies from many sources, such as audio CDs, MP3 files, and so on.

While you can work with a movie's video track in either the Clip Viewer or the Timeline Viewer, when you work with sound, you use the Timeline Viewer exclusively. As you have seen, the Timeline Viewer includes three tracks. The top track represents the video track and the native sound of the video included in the movie. The lower two tracks are for audio that you add to your movie, such as sound effects, music, recorded sound, and so on. At the right end of each track, you will see the Mute checkboxes. When a track's Mute checkbox is checked, the audio in the track plays; if a track's checkbox is unchecked, the track is mute.

Going Native (Native Sound That Is)

Most of the video that you import into iMovie will contain native sound that presumably goes along with the video. You can do several tasks to make the most of the native sound included in your video track. Many of the tools and techniques you will learn in this section are equally applicable to the other sounds included in the movie.

When you edit a video clip that contains native sound, the sound is also edited. For example, if you remove frames from a clip, the audio from those frames is removed too. When you crop a clip, copy frames and them paste them in another clip, or other tasks, the audio in the clips is affected in the same way as the video. For this reason, you should also listen to clips while you edit them to make sure that you aren't removing or changing audio in unanticipated ways. (You can extract the sound from a clip to work with it separately as you will learn later in this section.)

Muting Native Sound

The most basic change that you can make is to mute the Native track so that you don't hear any of its sound. To do so, uncheck the Mute checkbox located on the right end of the Native track. Now when you play your movie, you don't hear any Native sound from it. To hear the native sounds again, check the Mute checkbox.

NOTE

When you mute a checkbox and then export your movie, the sound is not included in the exported version. While this detracts from the experience of your movie, it also makes the resulting file size smaller.

Changing the Relative Volumes of Native Sound

Because the clips in your video clip probably came from different sources or were recorded under different conditions, the sound level from one clip to the next might vary quite a bit. Although some variation is natural (you expect the roar of a jet plane to be louder than a cat walking across the road), too much variation (or the wrong variation, such as if the cat is louder than the airplane) can be annoying or distracting. You can use the Relative Volume slider to set the relative sound levels of the various sound clips that make up the Native track.

Set the Relative Volume Level of the Native Sound in a Movie

1. On the Native track (the top track on the Timeline Viewer), select a clip that should be at the "average" volume level of your movie; after you do, the clip's bar on the track becomes highlighted in yellow to show that it is selected.

2. Move the Relative Volume slider toward the middle of its range. This sets the volume level of the selected clip at an "average" level.

3. Now move through each clip in the movie and use the Relative Volume slider to set its volume relative to your "average" sound level. Select the first clip in your movie that has native sound (assuming that your first clip isn't also your average clip, of course).

4. If you want the sound of the selected clip to be louder than the sound level of your "average" clip, drag the Relative Volume slider to the right of the position that you set as the average volume level; if you want it to be quieter, move the slider to the left. Or, if you want it to be about the same, place the slider in about the same position as it is for the average clip.

5. Continue this process with all the clips that have native sound.

6. Preview your movie to hear the results of your work. Hopefully, all the sound makes sense. Loud sounds should be loud while quiet sounds should be quiet. If not, continue with the previous steps until the native soundtrack is what you want it to be.

TIP

You can change the relative sound levels for several clips at once by holding the Shift or ⌘ key down while you select the clips. With the clips selected, move the Relative Volume slider. The relative volume of all the selected clips will be set at the level you choose.

Fading Native Sound

You can use iMovie's Fade controls to make the sound of a clip fade in or out smoothly. If you make a clip's sound fade in, it starts completely silently and smoothly comes to its full level. Similarly, if you fade out a sound, its volume smoothly becomes quieter until by the end of the clip, it has faded to silence.

Fading sound from clip to clip can make your movie flow more smoothly if it includes native sound because the sound of the component clips fades in and out rather than going through a jarring transition as one clip's sound runs into the next.

NOTE

If you add a Fade Out or Fade In transition to a clip, its sound also fades, so you don't need to use the Timeline Viewer fade controls on that clip.

To make a clip's sound fade in, select the clip and check the Fade In checkbox. If you want it to fade out, check the Fade Out checkbox.

If you want to control the fade duration (how long it takes sound to fade in or fade out), you can use a clip's Info window to do so.

Set the Duration of a Sound Fade

1. Select the clip whose sound you want to fade in or fade out.
2. Choose File, Get Clip Info (or press Shift+⌘+I). The Clip Info window will appear.
3. To make the audio of the selected clip fade in, check the Audio Fade In checkbox.

4. Use the Audio Fade In slider to set the duration of the fade in. Move the slider to the left to make the sound fade in more quickly. Moving the slider to the right makes the clip fade in more slowly.

5. In a similar way, use the Audio Fade Out controls to set the audio's fade out.

6. Click OK to close the Info window and to set the fade properties.

7. Preview the clip to hear the affect of your fades. Make changes if the results are not satisfactory.

Extracting Native Sound

You can extract the audio portion of a clip that contains native sound so that you can work with that sound independently from the video clip. For example, you might want to remove some frames from a clip while keeping the underlying sound intact. You can extract the sound from that particular clip and then edit the video without changing the sound that you extracted from the clip. Extracting the audio from a clip also enables you to move the sound relative to the video clip. This is useful if you don't want to use all of the audio, but want to keep all of the video in the clip.

TIP

One of the best uses for the extracting audio feature is when you have a clip containing background music that should be at least somewhat synchronized with the video, such as a ballet performance. You can extract the audio, and then you can edit the video part of the clip without hacking up the music that goes with it. You can then "spread" the extracted music so that the single music clip covers all of the video. Although the music may not exactly match what is happening in the video anymore, this is much less distracting than music that jumps around as the edited scenes play.

Extract a Clip's Native Sound

1. Select the clip from which you want to extract sound on the Timeline Viewer.

2. Choose Advanced, Extract Audio. The audio portion of the clip is extracted, and it is placed on the Audio 1 track. When you extract it, it's still in synch with the video clip from whence it came (see Figure 4.25).

You can tell this by the Locked icons that appear at the beginning of the video and audio clips. You'll learn more about locking and unlocking audio clips to video in the section called "Building a Soundtrack that Rocks" later in this chapter.

Locked icons

Extracted audio

Figure 4.25 *The audio shown in the Audio 1 track was extracted from the clip called "land_4."*

After the audio clip is extracted, you can use the audio editing techniques that you learn about in the rest of this chapter to work with it. For example, you can move it around, lock it in place, and so on. After the audio has been extracted, it behaves just like other sound that you add to your movie.

When you extract audio from a video clip, the audio actually is copied to the audio track rather than being cut from the video clip. The volume of the audio that is part of the video clip is set to zero so that you never hear it again. Does this matter? Not really, but you shouldn't extract an audio clip unless you really need to. Because it is not actually removed from the video clip, your movie file will be larger than if you didn't extract the audio (because iMovie will carry two versions of that sound around). If you only want to mute the audio associated with a video clip, set its relative volume to zero instead of extracting it.

This also means that you can hear the sound of a video clip from which you have "extracted" the sound by selecting that clip and using the Relative Volume slider to increase the sound of the clip again. You can use this for some interesting sound effects because you can have multiple versions of the sound playing at the same time, with each being slightly out of synch with the others.

Livening Up Your Movie with Sound Effects

One of the more fun aspects of making a movie is adding sound effects to it. There are two ways to add sound effects to a movie: you can add iMovie's built-in effects or you can create and add your own sound effects.

> **NOTE**
>
> The differences between a sound effect and other sounds in iMovie are that sound effects are relatively short and the only aspects of a sound effect that you can change are its location and relative volume.

Adding iMovie's Built-in Sound Effects

To add a built-in sound effect to your movie, do the following steps.

Add a Built-in Sound Effect

1. Click the Audio palette to reveal the Audio tools.
2. Review the list of available sound effects in the top pane of the audio palette.
3. Preview sound effects by clicking them. The sound effect will play.
4. To place an effect in your movie, drag the sound effect from the Audio palette to one of the Audio tracks on the Timeline Viewer. When you move the sound over the track, a yellow line appears on the track where the clip will be placed when you release the mouse button; this line indicates the point at which the sound effect will start playing. In other words, where you place the effect on the track determines where in the movie the effect is heard.

5. When you reach the point at which you want the sound to begin playing, release the mouse button. A blue square will appear on the track on which you placed the sound effect. This square represents the sound effect that you have added to the movie (see Figure 4.26).

Sound effect information

Sound effect

Figure 4.26 *Here, a sound effect has been added just after the current location of the Playhead.*

6. Select the sound effect that you added (when selected, the effect's blue box will become darker). You will see its name, duration, the timecode at which it starts playing, and the timecode at which it stops playing in the Audio Selection area at the top of the Timeline Viewer.

7. Drag the Playhead to just before the sound effect icon and play the movie to preview the sound.

8. Select the sound effect again and use the Relative Volume slider to set its volume level relative to the other sound occurring in the same location in the movie (by default, the sound effect will have the maximum relative volume setting).

9. Adjust the starting point of the sound effect by dragging its icon to the left on the audio track. The effect will begin playing earlier in the movie.

10. Continue adjusting the location and the volume level of the sound effect until it is "just right."

NOTE

You can add sound effects to either audio track. They work the same way no matter which track you place them in. The purpose of providing multiple soundtracks is that you can more easily work with a variety of sound in your movie, such as sound effects, music, and narration because you have more room in which to work.

Want some more tips about working with sound effects?

◆ To delete a sound effect from a movie, select it and press Delete. If the sound effect is one that came from the Audio palette, the sound effect remains available for you to add again.

◆ You can add the same sound effect as many times as you'd like.

◆ You can also overlap sound effects. To do so, simply drag one effect on top of another. For example, to have lots of people clap, drag the Crowd Applause sound effect to the Timeline Viewer several times. At those moments where the sound effects overlap, all the overlapped sound effects will play. You can more easily manage overlapped sound effects by placing some in the Audio 1 track and others in the Audio 2 track.

◆ To keep a sound effect in synch with the video, you should lock the sound effect in place. You'll learn how later in this chapter.

◆ Unlike other sounds with which you will work, a sound effect's icon does not reflect the length of the sound effect. All sound effects have the same size icon. By visual clues, you can only tell where a sound effect will start, not where it will stop. To tell where it stops, preview the portion of the movie in which it occurs or use the Audio Selection information that appears at the top of the Timeline Viewer.

Adding Your Own Sound Effects

iMovie's built-in sound effects are fine, but you can add any audio clip as a sound effect in your movie.

First, create an AIFF file that contains the sound that you want to use as a sound effect. You can do this with QuickTime or iTunes (see Chapter 9, "Converting Digital Media into the Formats You Need for Your Digital Lifestyle Projects" for the detailed steps to do this).

Then import the sound into iMovie.

Add Your Own Sound Effects to a Movie

1. Choose File, Import File (or press ⌘+I).

2. In the resulting Import File dialog, move to the AIFF file that you want to use as a sound effect, select it, and click Import. The sound effect, which is represented as a purple bar, will be placed on the Audio 2 track (see Figure 4.27).

— Imported sound effect

Figure 4.27 *The hueys.aif sound has been imported into this movie.*

3. Use the audio editing techniques you learn in this chapter to make changes to the sound, such as cropping it, changing its location, setting its relative volume, and so on.

TIP

You can change the track on which audio tracks appear by dragging from one track to the other.

Making Your Movie Sing with Music

Music is one of the best things that you can add to a movie (just imagine *Star Wars* without its music, and you'll understand instantly the value of adding music to a movie). There are two ways that you can add music to an iMovie project: you can import an MP3 file that you have created in iMovie, or you can record music directly from an audio CD.

Importing MP3 Files

You can import MP3 music files that you have created with iTunes to be a music soundtrack for your movie. The steps to do this are quite similar to importing an AIFF sound effect that you have created.

Add MP3 Music to a Movie

1. Move the Playhead to the point in the movie at which you want the music to begin playing (you can always adjust this later).
2. Press ⌘+I to open the Import File dialog.
3. Move the MP3 file that you want to import (by default, MP3 files that you used iTunes to create are located in the following directory: Home/Documents/iTunes/iTunes Music).
4. Select the MP3 file you want to include in your movie and click Import. The music will be placed on the Audio 2 track (see Figure 4.28). The music is represented by a purple bar that has a crop marker on each end. (Use the Magnification pop-up menu to decrease the amount of magnification if you can't see the entire bar.)
5. Edit the music clip with the techniques listed next.

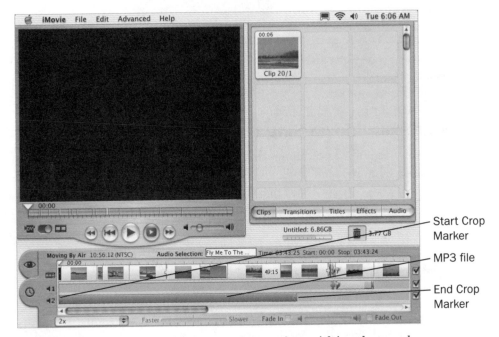

Figure 4.28 *This movie now has some music to go along with its other sounds.*

You can edit music and other sound clips (all sound except those sound effects on the Audio palette) by doing the following tasks:

◆ Name the clip by selecting it (the bar darkens to indicate that it is selected) and typing a name for it in the Audio Selection box. If the song's title is already there (because you have previously identified the song title), you will see the name in the Audio Selection box.

◆ Position the clip by dragging it on the track. Align the Playhead with the left or right Crop Marker to make it stick to the clip, and then use the arrow keys to precisely position it. When it is properly aligned, use the Lock Audio at Playhead command to lock it relative to the video clip.

◆ Use the Fade In, Fade Out, and Relative Volume slider controls just as you did with the native sound and the sound effects. To use these, select the music clip and then use the appropriate control to apply it. (The Info window works with these music clips too.) Most of the time, you will end up using the Fade Out control on music clips, unless you get lucky, and they end at precisely the right time.

◆ You can crop a clip if it is too long or if you want to remove either or both ends of it. Select the clip that you want to edit. Move the Crop Markers so that the music that you want to keep is between them. Now, only the portion between the crop markers will play. When you are ready to remove the sound that doesn't play, select the sound clip and choose Edit, Crop. The sound outside the Crop Markers is removed from the track.

NOTE

Generally, all the music that you listen to, unless you created it yourself, is protected by some sort of copyright. Mostly, these copyrights prohibit you from distributing the copyrighted work as your own or profiting from its distribution. Be aware of any copyright issues related to the music you use in your movies. Usually, as long as you keep your movies to yourself or distribute them to just a few other people, you will be okay copyright-wise. However, if you distribute your movie to many people or use it for any sort of profit-generating work, make sure that you have sufficient licenses to cover that use of the music.

Recording from Audio CD

Should you not want to use iTunes to convert music into MP3 for some reason (perhaps you don't want to listen to the music outside of your iMovie project), you can record directly from an audio CD.

Add Music from an Audio CD to a Movie

1. Open the Audio palette.

2. Insert an audio CD into your Mac's CD or DVD drive.

3. Use the Play, Rewind, and Fast Forward controls on the Audio palette to find the song that you want to use in your movie.

4. Now move the Playhead to the point in your movie at which you want the music to begin. You don't have to be terribly precise here because you can always move the music around on the audio track later.

5. Use the CD playback controls on the Audio palette to get the music to a point just before you want to start recording.

TIP

You can jump to a specific track on a CD by clicking it on the Audio palette.

---

6. Click the Play button and start recording by clicking the Record Music button. Your movie begins to play as the music is recorded. You see the purple music clip being laid down in the Audio 2 track. Note that you won't hear the other sounds in your movie while you are recording from a CD.

7. When you are done recording, click Stop. The Audio CD track will be imported into your movie.

8. Edit the music you recorded using the techniques presented in the previous section.

TIP

You can also drag a track from the CD window on the Audio palette onto either of the Audio tracks to add the entire CD track to your movie.

Recording Your Own Sounds

Using the Audio palette's Recording tool, you can record your own sounds to play during your movie. One obvious use for this is to add narration to various parts of your movie, but you can also record your own sound effects.

To be able to record sound from an external source, you need to have some sort of microphone attached to your Mac. Some Macs have built-in microphones. Other Macs have microphone jacks (although these sometimes require that you use a PlainTalk microphone). However, the best way to record sound is to use an USB microphone. To record narration, use a headphone type microphone, such as those included with voice recognition software. Or, add a USB sound input device that enables you to connect a standard microphone to it (many headphone type microphones include such a port).

NOTE

If the device you use has an audio in port (sometimes you can use the microphone jack), you can connect the output of an audio device, such as a cassette tape player, to it to record sound from that audio device.

Record Narration or Other Sounds for a Movie

1. Open the Audio palette.

2. Test your microphone setup by speaking into it or making the other kinds of sound you will be recording. If everything is working, you'll see a sound level bar in the area just above the Record Voice button that shows you the level of the sound that is being input. This bar should be moving to levels at least above halfway across the bar. If it isn't, move closer to the microphone so it gets better input.

3. Drag the Playhead to the point in your movie at which you want to begin recording.

4. Click Record Voice. Your movie will begin playing. Speak into the microphone or make the sound that you are recording. An orange bar will appear on the Audio 1 track to represent the sound you are recording.

5. When you have recorded all the sound you want, click Stop.

6. Edit the recorded sound using the same techniques that you use for other sound, such as music.

Building a Soundtrack that Rocks

After you have added various sounds to your movie, you are likely to have quite a cacophony of sound. The final step in creating a soundtrack is to mix all this sound together so your movie sounds the way you want it to.

When you mix a soundtrack, you want to make sure that the following characteristics are true:

- ◆ Sounds start and stop at the right time.
- ◆ Relative volume levels are correct.

◆ Sounds enhance one another (instead of detracting from one another).

◆ The soundtrack complements the video track (for example, sound effects occur at appropriate moments).

Play your movie from start to finish and pay careful attention to the sound. Use the editing techniques you have learned throughout this chapter to make changes to the soundtrack until you are happy with the results.

Locking Sound

As you continue to work on your movie, you are likely to make some minor adjustments to it (or even some major ones). If these changes involve changing the video track, sounds that you have carefully placed in your movie can become unsynchronized.

You can lock audio to a specific point in a video clip so that when you move the video or when it moves because of edits you make elsewhere in the movie, the audio goes along for the ride and always remains in synch with the video.

To lock a sound in place, do the following steps.

Lock Sound in Synch with Video

1. Select the sound that you want to lock (you can select any type of sound).

2. Place the Playhead at the point at which you want to synchronize the sound.

3. Choose Advanced, Lock Audio Clip at Playhead (or press ⌘ + L). The Locked icons will appear (see Figure 4.29). One icon appears at the beginning of the locked audio and the other appears at the point in the video track to which the audio is locked.

When audio has been locked to a Playhead position, when the movie plays and that position is reached, the audio will play, even if you change the video track (such as by removing frames from a clip).

To unlock an audio clip again, select it and choose Advanced, Unlock Audio Clip (or press ⌘ + L).

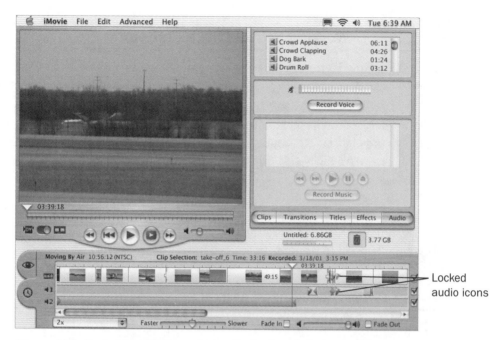

Locked audio icons

Figure 4.29 *Locked icons indicate that audio has been locked to specific points in the video track.*

Exporting Your Movie

The only point of making a movie is to be able to watch it yourself and to share it with others. While you can watch a movie in iMovie (use the Play Full Screen button to play it in full screen mode), the application is not really designed as a movie player. You can export your finished movie in three basic ways:

- ◆ **To Videotape**. You can record your movie back to your DV camera so that you can then record it on VHS tapes.

- ◆ **To QuickTime**. You can create QuickTime versions of your movie to send to others, put on the Web, place on CD-R, put in documents, and so on. You can use QuickTime Player or other applications to watch these versions.

- ◆ **For iDVD**. You can export your movies for iDVD so that you can view them on most standard DVD players (and also by using a DVD-ROM equipped Mac).

Working iMovie Like a Hollywood Pro

In creating a movie, there are literally hundreds of tasks that you will do. While you can use your mouse to do any of these tasks, using a mouse is relatively inefficient. As you become more iMovie-savvy, try to learn to use the keyboard as much as possible. This will help you work more efficiently so that you can complete projects faster. And the keyboard often enables you to work more precisely so your movie is better than it might have been. Table 4.11 lists the most important keyboard shortcuts that you should learn and use.

The techniques required to output your movies in these ways are described in detail in Chapters 16 through 19.

Table 4-11 iMovie Keyboard Shortcuts

Task	Keyboard Shortcut
Create Still Clip	Shift+⌘+S
Crop	⌘+K
Decrease volume	Down arrow
Export Movie	⌘+E
Extract Audio	⌘+J
Fast Forward	⌘+]
Get Clip Info	Shift+⌘+I
Import File	⌘+I
Increase Volume	Up arrow
Lock Audio Clip at Playhead	⌘+L
Unlock Audio Clip	⌘+L
Move audio clip backward by 1 frame	Click audio clip; then Left arrow
Move audio clip backward by 10 frames	Click Audio clip; then Shift+Left arrow
Move audio clip forward by 1 frame	Click audio clip; then Right arrow

Table 4-11 iMovie Keyboard Shortcuts (continued)

Task	Keyboard Shortcut
Move audio clip forward by 10 frames	Click audio clip; then Shift+Right arrow
Move backward 1 frame	Left arrow
Move backward 10 frames	Shift+Left arrow
Move Crop Marker backward by 1 frame	Click Crop Marker; then Left arrow
Move Crop Marker backward by 10 frames	Click Crop Marker; then Shift+Left arrow
Move Crop Marker forward by 1 frame	Click Crop Marker; then Right arrow
Move Crop Marker forward by 10 frames	Click Crop Marker; then Shift+Right arrow
Move forward 1 frame	Right arrow
Move forward 10 frames	Shift+Right arrow
Move Playhead to beginning of clip/movie	Home
Move Playhead to end of clip/movie	End
Paste Over at Playhead	Shift+⌘+V
Play/Stop (Edit mode)	Spacebar
Reverse Clip Direction	⌘+R
Rewind	⌘+[
Save Frame As	⌘+F
Select All	⌘+A
Select None	⌘+D
Split Clip at Playhead	⌘+T
Start/Stop Capture (Camera mode)	Spacebar

Using iMovie for Your Digital Lifestyle Projects

In addition to enabling you to create all sorts of cool movies, iMovie is a very useful tool for other tasks as well. For example, you can use iMovie to create soundtracks for slideshows that you create by using other applications. You can also use iMovie to create alert sounds for your Mac, capture desktop pictures, and many other uses. In fact, iMovie is likely to be the digital lifestyle application that you use most often for your projects, and you will be returning to it frequently throughout Parts II and III of this book.

Chapter 5

iDVD: The Power of a Movie Production House in Your Mac

The Mac is the premiere digital media platform precisely because it has a set of "jaw-dropping, holy-cow-that-is-way-cool" applications that are groundbreaking in many ways. iDVD is another amazing application in that set. With iDVD, you can put your digital lifestyle projects on DVD for playback on your Mac or, even better, on most standard DVD players. This enables you to move your projects from the computer room to the living room.

Since DVD players are almost as common as VCRs these days and most households now have them, putting your great (and even not-so-great) projects on DVD is a fantastic way to share those projects with other people.

What's more is that not only can you place your projects on DVD, but the DVDs you create can contain custom, motion menus and buttons, just like those that appear on commercially-produced DVD movie discs. You will be amazed at how cool your DVDs can be. What's more #2 is that using iDVD is mostly a matter of drag-and-drop so that you can create these amazing DVDs in just a few minutes.

NOTE

iDVD is the one digital lifestyle application that requires specific hardware. That hardware is a DVD Recordable (DVD-R) drive that you use to write to DVD-R discs. In fact, if you don't have a DVD-R drive, iDVD will not even open. The good news is that all desktop Macs now have the Apple SuperDrive as an option; this drive includes a DVD-R drive. There are also third-party DVD-R drives available (although for maximum compatibility, an Apple SuperDrive is your best option). If you don't have a DVD-R drive, reading this chapter might provide the motivation you need to get one! (Besides, you were looking for a reason to get a new Mac anyway!) For more information on DVD-R drives, see the section called "DVD-R Drives" in Chapter 7, "Digital Lifestyle Hardware: Digital Rules, Analog Drools."

The iDVD Way

Looking back over the hundreds of applications that I have used in my Mac life, iDVD is among the few that took my breath away when I first saw it (talk about being happy to be a Mac user!). iDVD is a picture of power and elegance wrapped up in a very attractive package.

On the surface, iDVD appears to be relatively simple, which is a good thing because this makes creating DVDs easy and fun. In the background, iDVD manages the complexity of encoding and writing DVDs for you so that you can focus on the more creative aspects of the process.

The iDVD Window

When you launch iDVD, you see the iDVD window (see Figure 5.1). Like iMovie, iDVD automatically opens the last project on which you worked. If you haven't used it before, you can create a new project.

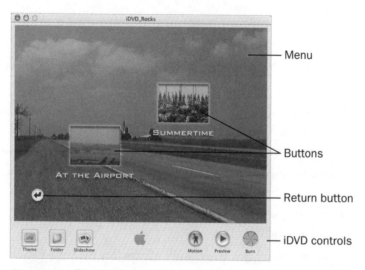

Figure 5.1 *The iDVD window is elegantly designed; it combines simplicity with power.*

The top pane of the window is called the menu. This is the area that appears onscreen when the DVD is played. Buttons represent each project that has been placed on the DVD; you select a button to view the content with which it is associated. Each menu can include up to six buttons; a disc can contain multiple menus so that you can store as many projects on a disc as you have room for on the DVD.

Each menu has a theme that determines how the menu looks and sounds. At the most basic, a theme is simply a static image that is the menu's background. However, menus can contain motion, which means that a movie can play as the menu's background while the menu appears on the screen (if you have watched

DVD movies, you have, no doubt, seen examples of motion menus). Motion menus can include a movie with sound, a movie without sound, or a static image with sound. You can apply one of iDVD's default themes to your menus, and you can create and save your own themes.

Buttons can also have motion, which means that the content that is accessed by that button plays within the button itself while the button is being viewed. This type of motion provides a preview of the content without the viewer having to actually open it. (Again, if you have viewed commercially produced DVD movies, sometimes the chapter buttons contain motion and show you part of the chapter associated with the button).

iDVD Controls

Along the bottom of the iDVD window, you will see the six iDVD control buttons, which are the following:

- **Theme**. This button opens or closes the iDVD Drawer (which you will learn about in the next section).
- **Folder**. When you click this button, you create a new folder that represents an additional menu on the DVD. When you open a folder, you see the new menu.
- **Slideshow**. Use this button to create a slideshow. When you click it, iDVD moves into the Slideshow mode.
- **Motion**. This button toggles the motion effects (for both menus and buttons). When the button is "on," it is green and motion effects play. When it is "off," it is gray and no motion effects play. Because motion effects can be annoying while you are designing a CD, it is helpful to turn them off.
- **Preview**. This button puts iDVD in the Preview mode that enables you to view the DVD as it will be when you burn it.
- **Burn**. Click this one to burn a DVD.

The iDVD Drawer

When you click the Theme button, the iDVD drawer appears (see Figure 5.2). The drawer contains controls and information that you use while you design a DVD.

View Themes pop-up menu

Figure 5.2 *The iDVD drawer enables you to work with themes and buttons while you are designing a DVD; you can also use the Status tab to see the encoding status for projects.*

The drawer has the following three tabs:

◆ **Themes tab**. The Themes tab displays the themes that are available to you (see Figure 5.2). These themes include the default themes that are included with iDVD and any themes that you have created and saved. You can choose the type of themes you want to see by using the View Themes pop-up menu; for example, if you choose Motion, you will see only those themes that include motion. Your other choices are All, Picture only, Picture with audio, or Favorites (favorites are themes that you create).

◆ **Customize tab**. The Customize tab contains controls you can use to design the themes and buttons that are used on your DVD (see Figure 5.3).

◆ **Status tab**. The Status tab shows the total duration of the DVD that you are creating along with the encoding status of each project that you have placed on the DVD (you'll more about encoding in a couple of paragraphs).

Figure 5.3 *With the Customize tab, you can design many aspects of how your DVD will look and sound.*

iDVD Modes

As you work with iDVD, you will encounter its three different modes of operation:

◆ **Design**. This is the mode in which you design the look and feel of your DVD. You see the contents of your DVD organized into its various menus, buttons, and so on (see Figure 5.3).

◆ **Slideshow**. In the slideshow mode, you create slideshows from images that you place in the slideshow window (see Figure 5.4).

◆ **Preview**. In the preview mode, you see the DVD as it will be when you burn it and play it in a DVD player (see Figure 5.5). When you preview a DVD, a controller that simulates the controller used to view DVDs (on a computer or on a standard DVD player) appears. You use the controls on the controller to watch your DVD. Use this mode to carefully preview a DVD before you burn it. After you burn a DVD, you can't change it—the preview mode helps you avoid wasting DVD discs (after all, how many coasters does one need?).

◆ **Burn**. When your DVD is ready for production, you use iDVD's tools to burn it.

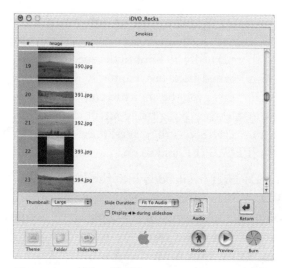

Figure 5.4 *Using iDVD, you can create very nice slideshows displaying your images.*

Figure 5.5 *When it comes to making DVDs, there is at least one rule to remember, preview before you burn!*

iDVD Projects

Similar to iMovie, when you create a DVD, you first create a project. The project determines what content will appear on the DVD as well as its look and feel.

The content that you place on a DVD will consist of either movies (in the QuickTime format or in the DV format) or slideshows. Because you can place any QuickTime content on a DVD, there is really no limit to the specific content that you can place on a DVD. As you learned back in Chapter 1, "QuickTime Pro: Making it All Happen," QuickTime gives you the ability to convert just about any content into the QuickTime format, thus making that content eligible for DVD. You can also create slideshows from a series of still images; these images can be in the usual image formats, such as JPEG, TIFF, and so on.

When you place content on a DVD, it is encoded into the MPEG-2 format, which is the standard for DVD. MPEG-2 provides very high quality with relatively small file sizes (thus making digital movies on DVD possible). Fortunately, iDVD manages the encoding process for you and does it automatically. You'll learn how to assess the encoding status of the content on a DVD that you are creating later in this chapter.

A DVD created with iDVD 2 can contain up to 90 minutes of content. However, iDVD uses a higher-quality encoding scheme when the content in a DVD project is 60 minutes or less—you should try to keep your DVDs within this limit, if possible. (You might think that 60 minutes isn't much, but you will find that creating 60 minutes of *good* content takes a bit of doing.) Again, iDVD manages this for you; the application chooses the 90-min or 60-min format for you automatically.

> **NOTE**
>
> Just like iMovie, iDVD uses the term *render*. However, in iDVD, render refers to the process of encoding the project content into the MPEG-2 format.

Making Your iDVD Preferences Known

There aren't that many iDVD preferences that you need to set (see Figure 5.6).

The options you have are the following:

- ◆ **Video Standard**. There are two primary video standards. NTSC, which stands for National Television Standards Committee, is the primary video format in the U.S. PAL, which stands for Phase Alternating Line, is the primary video format in Europe. Each format has its own parameters, such as frame rates and such, but you really don't need to worry about the details. If you are creating projects that will be displayed on U.S. equip-

Figure 5.6 *It won't take long to configure your iDVD preferences.*

ment, choose the NTSC radio button. If you are creating projects for display on European systems, choose PAL. If you change formats, the change you make will apply to new projects, so make a preference choice before you start a new iDVD project.

◆ **What to do with rendered files**. If you check the "Delete rendered files after closing a project" checkbox, iDVD will delete the files that it encodes when you close your iDVD project. Choosing this option can save you some disk space, but if you want to recreate a DVD from an iDVD project, you will have to have iDVD re-render its contents before you can burn another DVD.

◆ **Show Watermark**. This option turns the Apple logo on (checked) or off (unchecked). If you want to proudly display your Mac colors on your DVD's menus, you can leave this turned on. However, for most projects, you will probably want to turn this off.

NOTE

There is also a third video format that will eventually overtake the other two. That is High-Definition Television or HDTV. This format provides higher quality than the others and is designed to use the same screen proportions that movies in the theater do (16 x 9). While, iDVD does not yet support this format, it probably will someday.

Making DVDs with iDVD

Making a DVD with iDVD consists of the following four steps:

1. Prepare your content.
2. Design the DVD.
3. Preview the DVD and fix any problems you find.
4. Burn the DVD.

Preparing Content for DVD

As you learned earlier, there are two basic types of projects that you can put on DVD: QuickTime movies or slideshows. In both cases, the process works better if you prepare all of your content before diving into iDVD. If you do this prep work first, the process of creating your DVD in iDVD will go more smoothly and more quickly because you can focus on the DVD itself.

Preparing QuickTime Movies for DVD

In Chapters 1 (QuickTime), 3 (iPhoto), and 4 (iMovie), you learned a number of ways that you can create movies. Any content that you create or translate using these tools can be put on a DVD. See those chapters to learn the details of using those applications; in Parts II and III of this book, you'll learn even more techniques that you can apply to create great movie projects.

Both QuickTime and iMovie also enable you to save your content in the DV (Digital Video) format. When you have this option, you should use it because your results will be the best possible (however, the results you get with movies in the QuickTime format will also be quite good, depending on the specific project—you might not even notice the difference). Refer to Chapter 1 to learn how to save any QuickTime movie in the DV format. Refer to Chapter 4 to learn how to save iMovie projects in the DV format.

TIP

If you are going to have many different movies or slideshows on your DVD, consider making a list of each project that you want to place on the DVD. Without such a list, you might end up forgetting to add all of the projects that you intended to.

Putting a Slideshow on DVD

There are two ways in which you can place slideshows on DVD. One is to create a QuickTime or DV movie version of the slideshow. The other is to use iDVD tools to create the slideshow.

There are many ways to create slideshows as QuickTime movies. You can use QuickTime Pro, iPhoto, and iMovie to do so; each tool has its own advantages and disadvantages (see Chapter 15, "Building Digital Lifestyle Slideshows" for the details of each method). When you create a slideshow using these methods, you treat the result just like other QuickTime or DV movies that you want to place on DVD (for example, you can save the slideshow as a DV file).

You can also use iDVD's own tools to create a slideshow. The slideshow can include images that you have captured using a digital camera and have exported from iPhoto (see Chapter 3 for the details) or from many other sources. You can use images in the common image file formats in an iDVD slideshow, including JPG, TIFF, and so on.

While you don't have to be too concerned about the file format of the images you include in an iDVD slideshow, you do need to be aware of the resolution of the images that you include. iDVD will scale your images to the 640 x 480 resolution when it creates a slideshow. If an image does not have this proportion, black bars might appear at the top and bottom or left and right sides of the image when it appears on the screen.

If this bothers you, you should resize your images to the 640 x 480 size before you place those images in iDVD. You can use an image editing application to do this, or you can choose to limit your images to this size when you export them from iPhoto.

You'll learn how to use iDVD's slideshow tools in the section called "Creating a Slideshow," later in this chapter.

Designing a DVD

After you have prepared your DVD's content, you are ready to design your DVD. Designing a DVD requires that you first plan the contents of your DVD. Then you create your iDVD project. After you start working with your project, you organize its contents. Then you add the content to the DVD. Lastly, you design and build your DVD's menus and buttons (this just might be the most fun part).

Planning Your DVD

To get started, organize your content by menu; think about a menu as being a folder for specific content, and you'll get the idea. Each menu appears in its own window on the DVD. For example, you might choose to group projects related to specific time periods on different menus, or you might want to put all of a DVD's movies on one menu while its slideshows appear on another. Remember that you can have up to six buttons on a single menu. Also remember that a button can represent a project (such as a movie) or a submenu (analogous to a subfolder on your desktop) that contains additional projects or submenus. Create a list of each menu and its contents so that you have a guide to design your DVD (see Figure 5.7). Each menu can have a name; use this name to help the viewer identify the type of content that is included under that menu. For each menu, list the specific files (as in QuickTime movie files), slideshows (that you will create with iDVD), or submenus that will appear on that menu.

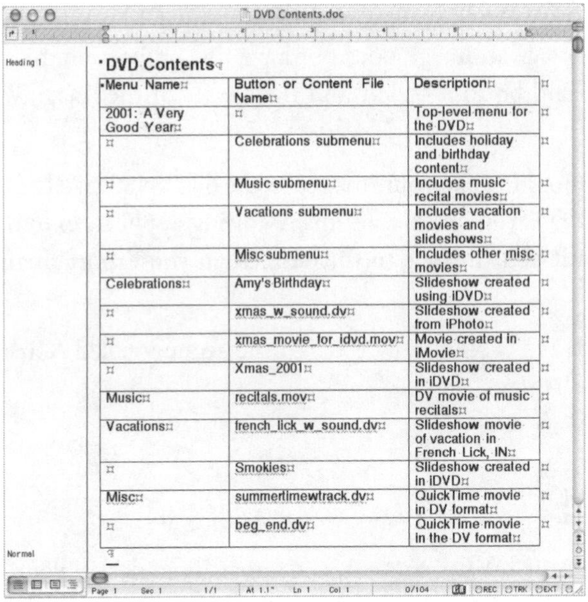

DVD Contents

Menu Name	Button or Content File Name	Description
2001: A Very Good Year		Top-level menu for the DVD
	Celebrations submenu	Includes holiday and birthday content
	Music submenu	Includes music recital movies
	Vacations submenu	Includes vacation movies and slideshows
	Misc submenu	Includes other misc movies
Celebrations	Amy's Birthday	Slideshow created using iDVD
	xmas_w_sound.dv	Slideshow created from iPhoto
	xmas_movie_for_idvd.mov	Movie created in iMovie
	Xmas_2001	Slideshow created in iDVD
Music	recitals.mov	DV movie of music recitals
Vacations	french_lick_w_sound.dv	Slideshow movie of vacation in French Lick, IN
	Smokies	Slideshow created in iDVD
Misc	summertimewtrack.dv	QuickTime movie in DV format
	beg_end.dv	QuickTime movie in the DV format

Figure 5.7 *Create a guide to your DVD's contents before you start placing that content on your DVD; this guide will save you time and will help you create a better DVD.*

You might be tempted to skip over the creation of this content guide. You can do so, but creating a good DVD will be much harder because you will have to organize its contents on the fly. A little planning will go a long way towards improving both the speed and quality of your project.

TIP

If you want to be really organized, create a folder in which you place the contents of the DVD you will create. Within that folder, create a folder for each submenu on the DVD and place the QuickTime movies and images that you will store on each submenu in its respective folder. This makes adding the right content to the right menu simple.

For best DVD writing performance, make sure that all of the media that you will put on the DVD is located in the same folder on your Mac, preferably on your Mac's internal hard drive. After you have added content to a DVD, don't move it until you have burned the DVD. Doing so can cause iDVD to lose track of the content (and thus it won't appear on the DVD). Later in this chapter, you'll learn how to check for missing content before you burn a DVD.

Creating an iDVD Project

Armed with your DVD planning document, you are ready to jump in to iDVD and create your DVD.

Create a New iDVD Project

1. Launch iDVD.
2. Choose File, New Project.
3. Name your project, choose a location in which to save it, and click Save.

You can name your project anything you'd like because the name you choose won't appear when the DVD is played (names of individual menus on the DVD do appear).

Where you save your project is an important consideration. The files that iDVD creates (and which you will put on DVD) can be quite large for a DVD with a significant amount of content on it. Make sure that the disk on which you store your project has plenty of room. Typically, you will need several GBs of disk space for the project folder that iDVD creates. While the specific amount of disk space you will need depends upon your content, you shouldn't try to store an iDVD project on a disk with less than 3-4GB available. This does not include the space that is required to store your content files; this space is for the rendered versions of your content that iDVD creates when it prepares a DVD.

Organizing Your DVD

After you have created a new project, an empty menu window will appear—this menu will have one of iDVD's default themes applied to it, but it won't contain any content (see Figure 5.8). If the theme for that menu includes motion, it will begin to play. Because this can be distracting, click the Motion button (located at the bottom of the iDVD window) to turn the motion effects off for now.

Figure 5.8 *When you create a new project, an empty menu window will appear.*

TIP

If the Motion button is green, the motion effects are on. If it is gray, they are not.

The title that you see at the top of the menu window (in Figure 5.8, it is Brushed Metal) is the name of the theme that was applied to that menu when you created the new project.

Don't worry about how the first menu looks; you will apply a theme to it after you first set up the submenus that will appear on the DVD. In other words, first create and name all the containers for the content that you are going to place on the DVD; then you will apply the themes to those menus.

Refer back to your DVD design document to determine what you will call the top-level menu, how many submenus you will need, and what the name of each submenu is.

NOTE

The menu that iDVD creates when you create a new project is called the main menu because it is the one from which all others originate.

Change the name of the main menu to what you want it to be.

Change the Main Menu Name

1. Click on the main menu name. It will become highlighted.
2. Type the menu name that you want to use.

Now, add each submenu to the main menu.

Create Submenus on the DVD

1. Click the Folder button. A new empty folder button will appear (it will be titled "My Folder"). Remember that a folder is a submenu.
2. Select the folder's name so that it becomes highlighted. A colored box will appear around the folder icon to show you that it is selected, and you will see a slider at the top of the icon.
3. Type the submenu's name.
4. Repeat Steps 1 through 3 until you have created all the submenus that appear on the main menu (see Figure 5.9).

If any of the submenus that you create has its own submenus, add them to the DVD.

Add Submenus to the DVD

1. Double-click the submenu to which you want to add a submenu. The submenu will open, and you will see the default theme and menu title again.

Figure 5.9 *While this main menu doesn't look very appealing yet, it now contains the four submenus that will appear on the DVD.*

2. Use the previous steps to add the submenus.

3. When you are done, click the Return button (curved arrow that faces to the left) to move back to the previous menu.

Repeat these steps until you have added and named all of the submenus that will appear on your DVD. Now you have an organized DVD that is ready for you to add content. After you do so, you can apply themes and design the buttons.

Adding Content to the DVD

After you have organized the DVD, you will be ready to add your content to it. As you learned earlier, there are two types of content you can add: QuickTime movies or an iDVD slideshow.

Adding QuickTime Movies to the DVD

Most of the content that you place on a DVD will probably be in the form of QuickTime movies (whether you have saved them in the QuickTime or DV formats). As you learned in the previous chapters and will learn in later chapters of this book, there are many ways to create QuickTime movie content.

Add QuickTime Movies to a DVD

1. Open the main menu or submenu to which you want to add a QuickTime movie. To open a submenu, double-click its folder icon. To move back to the previous menu, click the Return button.

2. Drag the QuickTime movie file from your desktop to the iDVD menu window. A button will be created on the menu; its icon will be the first frame in the movie. The name of the button will be the name of the file.

3. Click the Motion button to turn motion effects on. The first few seconds of the QuickTime movie will play inside the button to provide a preview of the movie.

4. Click the Motion button again to turn off the motion effects because they can be distracting when you are designing the DVD. In a later section, you will learn how to configure the motion effects for each button.

5. Select the button name by clicking it; it will be highlighted.

6. Change the button name to be what you want to be displayed onscreen. For example, if the movie is of some event, use the event name as the button name.

7. Repeat Steps 2 through 6 until you have placed the QuickTime movies that you want on the menu.

8. Click the Motion button to preview the menu (see Figure 5.10). Click it again when you are done.

9. Repeat Steps 1 through 8 until you have placed all the QuickTime movies on the DVD.

As you place QuickTime movies on the DVD, iDVD begins to encode them automatically in the background (all content must be encoded before you can burn a DVD). Fortunately, iDVD handles this task for you so you don't really need to think about it much. The encoding process goes on whenever iDVD is open until all of the content has been encoded. However, if you want to see where the encoding process stands, use the following steps.

Check the Status of the Encoding Process

1. Click the Theme button. The iDVD drawer will appear.

2. Click the Status tab. On this tab, you will see movies that you have added to the DVD. Each movie has a progress bar that displays the current state

of the encoding process for that movie. At the top of the Status tab, you will see the amount of content that is currently on the DVD. For example, in Figure 5.11 you can see that the DVD currently has about 31 minutes of content.

Figure 5.10 *This menu has two QuickTime movies on it.*

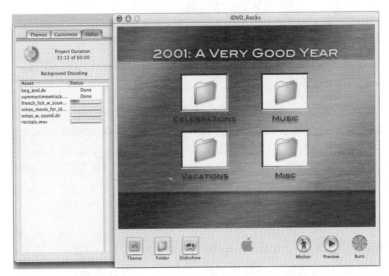

Figure 5.11 *As iDVD encodes each movie, you can view its progress on the Status tab of the iDVD drawer; here you can see that I have added six movies to the DVD and that two of them have been encoded.*

As you place your QuickTime movies on the DVD, keep the following points in mind:

◆ Each menu can contain up to six buttons (a button can represent a movie, slideshow, or submenu). But, you can add as many submenus as you need to be able to place your content on the DVD.

◆ You can also add QuickTime content to the DVD by choosing File, Import, Video. In the resulting dialog, move to the movie that you want to add, select it, and click Open. The movie will be added to the DVD just like when you drag it there.

◆ The total length of content (movies and slideshows) must be less than 90 minutes. For best quality, keep the total content to 60 minutes or less. Use the information on the Status tab of the iDVD drawer to monitor the length of the DVD as you create it.

Creating iDVD Slideshows for the DVD

iDVD's slideshow tools enable you to transform a set of images that you have prepared for the slideshow into a slideshow with a soundtrack that you select. (See the section called "Putting a Slideshow on DVD" earlier in this chapter for information about preparing the images for your slideshow.)

NOTE

If you want to make more complex soundtracks for a slideshow, including sound effects and narration, for example, you can use iPhoto to create the image part of the slideshow, iMovie to create the sound track, and QuickTime Pro to combine those elements into a slideshow (saved as a QuickTime movie). That process will be described in Chapter 15.

Create a Slideshow Using iDVD's Slideshow Tools

1. Open the menu on which you want to place a slideshow.

2. Click the Slideshow button. A button entitled "My Slideshow" will appear.

3. Select the slideshow name so that it becomes highlighted and rename the slideshow.

4. Double-click the slideshow's button. You will see iDVD in the Slideshow mode; the name that you gave the slideshow's button will appear at the top of the window (see Figure 5.12). Just above the iDVD toolbar, you will see iDVD's slideshow tools.

Figure 5.12 *You use the slideshow tools to build a slideshow for your DVD.*

5. Drag the images that will be in the slideshow from your desktop to the iDVD window. The order in which you place them in the iDVD window will determine the order in which they appear in the slideshow, with images at the top of the window appearing in the slideshow first. You will see a progress dialog as the images are imported into iDVD. When the process is complete, you will see thumbnails of the images in the window.

6. To make the thumbnails larger so that you can see the images better, choose Large on the Thumbnail pop-up menu (see Figure 5.13).

NOTE

You might notice that the images shown in Figure 5.13 have numbers for their names. When you export images from iPhoto, it uses a numeric value as the file name of each image. You can rename the images before you import them into iDVD if you want to. The names you give the files will appear in the File column in iDVD. However, the file names have no effect on the slideshow itself, so leaving them as you find them works, too (and is easier).

Figure 5.13 *This slideshow now contains the images shown in the window.*

7. If you want to change the order of any images in the window (and thus in the slideshow), drag the images up or down in the window and release the mouse button. As you move an image between other images, they will slide apart to "make room" for the images that you are moving.

8. To remove an image from the slideshow, select it and press Delete.

9. Continue reordering and deleting images until the window contains only the images that you want in the show in the order in which you want them to appear.

10. Add a soundtrack to the slideshow by dragging an audio file, such as an MP3 that you have created with iTunes, onto the Audio well that is located next to the Slide Duration pop-up menu. You should choose music that "goes with" (according to your own artistic taste of course) the images and is about the length that you want the slideshow to be (you will match the duration of the slideshow to the length of the soundtrack).

11. Now set the duration of the slideshow. If you add a soundtrack, the Slide Duration pop-up menu defaults to Fit To Audio that adjusts the amount of time that the images are displayed onscreen so that the total duration of the slideshow matches the length of the slideshow. For most slideshows you create, this is the best option. However, you can also choose the amount of time that you want each image to appear onscreen

by choosing a value on the Slide Duration pop-up menu (such as 3 seconds). If you choose a duration, the soundtrack might end before or after all the images have been displayed. I recommend that you use the Fit To Audio for any slideshow with a soundtrack. If you don't include a soundtrack, use the pop-up menu to set the image display time for the slideshow.

12. Click the Preview button. Your slideshow will fill the iDVD window.

13. To stop the slideshow, click the Preview button again.

14. Continue making changes to the slideshow until it is done.

15. Click the Return button to move back to the menu from which you started.

Continue adding slideshows until you have created all that you want on the DVD. As you do this, keep the following points in mind:

◆ You can also import images into a slideshow by choosing File, Import, Image. Use the resulting dialog to select images that you want to import and click Open. The selected images will be placed at the end of the slideshow.

◆ You can also import a soundtrack into a slideshow by choosing File, Import, Audio. Use the resulting dialog to select MP3 file that you want to import and click Open. The selected audio will be placed in the Audio well, and you will see an MP3 icon located there.

◆ To remove a soundtrack, drag its icon out of the Audio well. It will disappear in a puff of smoke.

◆ If you want to be able to move through the slideshow at your own pace, choose Manual on the Slide Duration pop-up menu and check the "Display <> during slideshow" checkbox. When you play the slideshow, you can use the left and right arrows that will appear on each image to move to the previous or next image respectively.

◆ You can create title slides for your slideshow by adding text to images using an image editing application, such as Photoshop. Just drag the title images onto the slideshow where you want the titles to appear. Solid black (or other color) screens with white text make nice title slides.

Making the DVD Look Marvelous

Now that you have filled the DVD with great content, you can finish the package by changing the appearance of the menus and buttons. You can also add motion to menus and buttons to really "wow" your audience.

Creating Themes for DVD Menus

A theme determines what a menu looks like onscreen. A theme includes two elements: a background and an audio track. The background can be as simple as a static image, or it can be a video clip (which plays when Motion effects are on). The audio track (which is optional) can be an MP3, AIFF, or other audio file. On the simple end, a theme consists of a static image with no sound. On the complex end, a theme consists of a video clip and separate soundtrack.

You'll need to apply a theme for each menu on your DVD. When you apply a theme for a menu, you have two options: use one of iDVD's default themes or create your own theme. And, you can apply a different theme to each menu or use the same theme for all the menus in your project.

As you design and lay out your menus, it is a good idea to keep the viewing platform in mind. If you intend to view the DVD on a television, you should work in what iDVD calls the TV Safe area (if you intended to view the DVD only on a Mac, you don't have to worry about this area because your Mac will display the entire contents of the iDVD window without cutting any of it off). This area is what is certain to appear on any TV on which you view the DVD. If objects are outside of this area, they might or might not be shown completely on the screen. To see the TV Safe Area, choose Advanced, Show TV Safe Area (or press ⌘+T). A red box will appear in the iDVD window; inside this box is the TV Safe area. Keep everything that you want to be displayed on the television screen inside this box.

Start the process of applying themes with the main menu. After you have completed its theme, apply a theme to each submenu on the DVD. These menus can be the same, similar, or completely different. It all depends on the look and feel that you want for the DVD.

Let me offer one word of caution here. Just because you can have all sorts of motion effects on a menu doesn't mean that you should use them all the time. You can also have motion in the buttons on a menu; using motion effects in both places can be overwhelming. Sometimes, it is better to make your menus static when you use motion in the buttons or use motion in the menus when you use static buttons.

iDVD includes a number of default themes that you apply to your menus with a single click of the mouse button.

Apply a Default Theme to a Menu

1. Open the menu to which you are going to apply a theme.

2. Click the Theme button to open the drawer. If the Themes tab is not selected, click it. The available themes will appear on the Themes tab (see Figure 5.14). The theme currently applied to the menu will be highlighted. Themes that have motion effects have the Motion icon in the lower right corner.

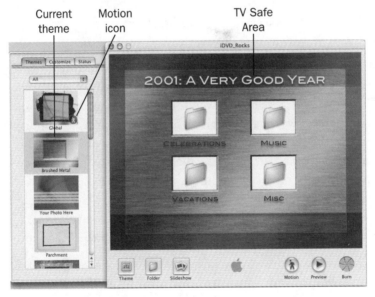

Figure 5.14 *The Brushed Metal theme is currently applied to this menu.*

3. Use the pop-up menu at the top of the tab to select the themes you want to view by category; your choices are All, which shows you all the available themes; Motion, which displays only themes that contain motion effects; Picture only, which displays themes that contain only a static

image; Picture with audio, which displays only themes that have a static image and a soundtrack; or Favorites, which displays the themes you have created.

4. Use the tab's scroll bar to preview the available themes in the selected category.

5. Apply a theme to the menu by clicking it. After a moment, the menu's appearance will be updated to the new theme.

6. If the theme you select has motion effects, click the Motion button to preview the theme (see Figure 5.15).

Figure 5.15 *The menu now has the Global theme applied to it.*

7. Continue applying and previewing themes until you find the one you want.

8. To apply a theme to the submenus, open the submenu and repeat Steps 3 through 7.

TIP

If you want to apply the same theme to every menu on the DVD, choose Advanced, Apply Theme to Project.

iDVD's default themes are okay, but you can express your own creativity by designing your own themes. After you have created a theme, you can save it as a favorite so that it will appear on the Themes tab (and thus, you will be able to reuse that theme at any time).

TIP

You can apply and modify iDVD's default themes and then save those modified themes as favorites. If one of the default themes is "close" to what you want, this can be a timesaving way of creating a theme.

Create a Custom Theme

1. Open the menu for which you want to create a custom theme.

2. Open the drawer if it isn't open already (click the Theme button to open or close the drawer).

TIP

You can also open or close the drawer by choosing Project, Show/Hide Theme Panel or by pressing Shift+⌘+B.

3. Click the Customize tab (see Figure 5.16). You can use the tools on this tab to design your theme. The tab is organized into three areas: Background, which you use to apply a background to your theme; Title, which you use to format the menu's title; and Button, which you use to design the menu's buttons (you'll learn about designing buttons in the next section). At the top of the tab, you will see the Motion Duration slider that controls the length of time that motion effects play—if the theme has them. At the bottom, you will see the Save in Favorites button that you use to save a customized theme on the themes tab.

4. To apply an image or a movie clip to the theme's background, drag an image or movie file from the desktop to the Image/Movie well. For the image, you can use files of the usual types, such as JPEGs, TIFFs, and so on. For movie backgrounds, you can use QuickTime movie or DV files. The icon in the well will be replaced by a thumbnail view of the file you placed there.

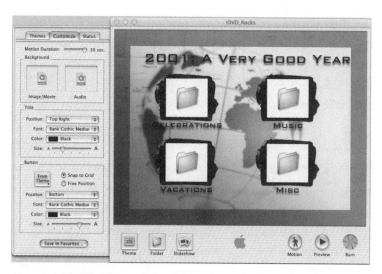

Figure 5.16 *The Customize tab contains tools that you can use to design your menu themes.*

5. To apply a soundtrack to the menu, drag an MP3 or AIFF file onto the Audio well. An icon that represents the audio file will be displayed in the well.

TIP

To remove a background movie, image, or soundtrack, drag its icon out of the respective well. To replace a background movie, image, or soundtrack, drag a new file onto the respective well.

6. If either the background or soundtrack contains motion effects (video or soundtrack), use the Motion Duration slider to set the amount of time that the effects play until starting over—the maximum is 30 seconds. If you use a clip or audio file longer than 30 seconds, you can only play up to the first 30 seconds of the file. The motion effects will loop continuously while the menu is being displayed. For example, if you choose 10 seconds on the slide, the first 10 seconds of the background movie will play and then repeat.

7. Use the Title Position pop-up menu to set the location of the menu title. You can choose a specific location, such as Top Center. Or choose Custom and then drag the title to place it anywhere on the menu. Choose No Title to remove the title from the menu.

8. Use the Title Font pop-up menu to choose the font used in the menu title.

9. Use the Title Color pop-up menu to set the color of the menu's title.

10. Use the Title Size pop-up menu to choose the size of the text in the title.

11. If your theme uses motion effects, click the Motion button to preview them. The background movie and soundtrack will play.

12. Select another menu on the DVD and repeat Steps 4 through 11 to customize its theme. Continue customizing themes until you have done each menu (see Figure 5.17).

Figure 5.17 *This menu will look much better when the buttons are designed; for now, it contains a background movie and soundtrack.*

TIP

If you want to apply a custom theme to every menu on the DVD, choose Advanced, Apply Theme to Project.

Following are some additional tips about customizing menu themes:

◆ You can use the commands on the File, Import menu (your choices are Audio, Image, Background Video) to apply the background and sound-track to a menu.

◆ If a menu's buttons will contain motion, it is often better to use a relatively plain image as the background. Otherwise, the motion of each button and the background can be chaotic.

Designing the DVD's Buttons

You can also design how each button on each menu looks and sounds. Remember that there are three types of buttons available in iDVD. A button can represent a folder (a submenu), a movie, or a slideshow. Designing buttons is quite similar to designing menus, but how you design a button also depends on what kind of button you are working with.

First, design the general style for all of the buttons on a menu; then configure each button individually.

Design the Buttons on a Menu

1. Open the menu containing the buttons you want to design.
2. Open the drawer and click the Customize tab.
3. Use the pop-up menu in the Button area to select the shape of the buttons. If you choose From Theme, the shape will be based on the default theme that was most recently applied to the menu. Otherwise, the shape you choose on the pop-up menu will be applied to each button.
4. If you want to locate each button on the screen, click the Free Position radio button. If you want the buttons to be organized according to iDVD's grid, click the Snap to Grid radio button.
5. Choose the title position for each button on the Button Position pop-up menu.

TIP

If you choose Text Only on the Button Position pop-up menu, buttons will contain only their title text.

6. Use the Button Font, Color, and Size controls to set the text properties of each button title (see Figure 5.18).

Figure 5.18 *Now that the general button design has been applied, this menu is starting to shape up.*

After you have done the general button design for a menu, you can design the contents of each button individually. How you do this depends on the kind of button you are working with.

Design a Movie's Button

1. Select the button for a movie. It will become highlighted and a slider and checkbox will appear above it (see Figure 5.19).

2. If you want the movie to play inside its button, check the Movie checkbox. If this checkbox is unchecked, a single frame of the movie will be displayed instead.

3. Use the slider to set the frame at which the movie will begin to play (if the Movie checkbox is checked) or to select the frame that will be displayed in the button (if the Movie checkbox is unchecked). If the Movie checkbox is checked, the movie will play inside the button when motion effects are on; the Motion Duration Slider on the Customize tab determines the amount of the movie that will play before it loops.

Figure 5.19 *Use the slider and checkbox to configure a movie's button.*

Design a Slideshow's Button

1. Select the slideshow's button. A slider will appear above the button.

2. Drag the slider to the image that you want to appear in the button.

TIP

You can also drag an image file onto a slideshow button. That image will appear in the button.

Design a Folder's (Menu's) Button

1. Select the button that you want to design.

2. Drag an image or movie file onto the button.

3. If you place a movie file on the button, use the button's slider to set the beginning frame for the button's motion.

TIP

You can apply the design of the buttons on a menu to all of the folders on the DVD by choosing Advanced, Apply Theme to Folders.

Continue designing the buttons on each menu until you have designed them all (see Figure 5.20).

TIP

To delete a button, which also deletes its contents from the DVD, select it and press the Delete button.

Figure 5.20 *When motion effects are turned on, this menu has a lot of action.*

Saving and Using Favorite Designs

Some of your custom menu designs will be pretty good. So good in fact, that you might want to reuse them. To do so, you can save a design as a favorite.

Save a Menu Design as a Favorite

1. Open the menu that contains the custom theme that you want to save.
2. Open the drawer and click Save in Favorites.
3. In the resulting sheet, name the custom theme you are saving.
4. If you want the custom theme to be available to everyone who uses your Mac, check the "Share for all users" checkbox.
5. Click OK.

To see the custom themes you have saved, click the Themes tab and choose Favorites on the pop-up menu. You can apply your favorite themes to other menus just like you apply iDVD's default themes.

TIP

There is no way to delete a favorite theme from within iDVD. To remove a theme that you have created, open the following folder:

Home/Library/iDVD/Favorites

Drag the theme that you want to delete to the Trash to get rid of it.

Previewing and Fixing a DVD

Before you hit the Burn button, take some time to check out your DVD to make sure it is what you want it to be. First, preview the DVD.

Preview a DVD

1. Turn the motion effects on by clicking the Motion button (if they aren't on already).

2. Click the Preview button. The drawer will close, and you will see a DVD controller (see Figure 5.21). Use the controller's buttons to view the DVD. Most of the controls you see (Stop, Pause, Volume, and so on) are self-explanatory. Use the arrow buttons to select various buttons on a menu; use the enter button to choose a button that you want to view. If the button is a movie or a slideshow, that item will play in the iDVD window. If the button is a submenu, that submenu will open.

3. Continue previewing your DVD until you have seen *all* of its content. You might be getting tired of your DVD by now, but take the time to check it carefully anyway. After you burn the DVD, you can't change it so now is the time to fix any problems you find or to make improvements in the way the DVD looks and sounds.

4. When you are done previewing the DVD, click Preview again.

Figure 5.21 *Watching your DVD in iDVD before burning it will help you avoid wasting DVD-R discs.*

TIP

When you preview a disc, make sure that the TV Safe Area is shown. This will often reveal problems with the content on the DVD, such as people's heads being cut off in images in a slideshow. If you find such problems, you have to go back to the content source files and fix them. Then re-add the content to the DVD (you will also have to reset the content's button design).

As a final check, make sure that all of the media for your DVD is included in the project.

Ensure That All Media for an iDVD Project Is Available

1. Choose Project, Project Info. The Project Info window will appear (see Figure 5.22). Each file in your project will be listed along with its status.

2. Scroll down the window and make sure that every file has a checkmark in the Status column. If it doesn't, you need to fix that file before you create the DVD. For example, if you have moved a movie file since you placed it on the DVD, iDVD won't be able to find it, and you will have to replace it on the appropriate menu.

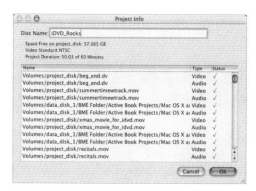

Figure 5.22 *Check your project out to make sure it has all the files it needs.*

Burning a DVD

Your DVD is all done, and you have checked it carefully by previewing it. You are now ready to click the Burn button and create your disc, right? Not necessarily. Remember that you can write to a DVD-R disc only once. After you burn a disc, you can't change it—if something is wrong, the disc you burned becomes a somewhat expensive coaster. Before clicking the Burn button, leave your project for a while and go do something else. After some time has passed, come back to the project and preview it again. Make any changes that are needed. Now you are ready to make it real.

Burning a DVD is *very* Mac-intensive. Because the process also tends to be a bit finicky, you should make sure that iDVD has all of your Mac's resources available to it during the burning process. For the best chance at creating a good DVD, do the following tasks:

- ◆ Quit iDVD and any other applications that are open (save your changes first).
- ◆ Restart your Mac.
- ◆ If any applications open upon login, quit them. This includes the classic environment (to stop it, open the Classic pane of the System Preferences utility and click Stop).

NOTE

Hopefully, all of the media that will be placed on the DVD is located in the same folder on your Mac, preferably on your Mac's internal hard drive. This enables your Mac to access this data as quickly as possible, which helps the data writing speed.

Burn a DVD

1. Open your project and make sure that the motion effects are on.
2. Save your project.
3. Click the Burn button. Its icon will become active.
4. Click the Burn button again.
5. At the prompt, insert a blank DVD-R disc into the drive. The burn process will start, and iDVD will manage it from start to finish. Expect the process to take some time; usually around three times the length of the content on the DVD. For example, if your DVD contains an hour of content, burning the DVD will take about three hours.

When the burning process is complete, your DVD will be ready to play. You can play it on your Mac using the DVD Player application, or you can play it in most standard DVD players.

NOTE

After you burn a DVD, check it out using your Mac's DVD Player. If it plays fine, you have created a good DVD. If it doesn't play properly, something went astray, probably in the burning process (for example, another application might have taken too many resources away from iDVD). Check out the project carefully to make sure that all the media is available. Preview it again to make sure it plays okay within iDVD. Then try burning the disc again, making sure to use the list you read earlier to maximize your chances of creating a good disc.

Recovering Disk Space

If you have limited disk space available, after you are *sure* that your DVD is right and that you have made all the copies you want, you can delete the iDVD project file. These files are large so if you don't have the space to store them permanently, getting rid of them will free up disk space. You can also delete the individual content files if you no longer want to store them. Ideally, you will have a tape backup system to which you can archive this data, but if not, you will have to decide which is more important—hard disk space or keeping all of the files. Try to save the content files if you can because you can more easily recreate the DVD than you can recreate the individual content files.

Using iDVD for Your Digital Lifestyle Projects

DVD is such a great way to view and store your projects that you are likely to want to store many of the digital lifestyle projects that you create on a DVD so that you view them easily. And fortunately, you can do so since most of the digital lifestyle projects you create can be exported as QuickTime or DV movies. Plus, putting projects on DVD is a great way to store completed projects so they don't consume valuable hard disk space.

Chapter 6

iTools: Maybe the Only Internet Tool You Ever Need

iTools is a suite of Internet services that is provided by Apple for people who use Mac OS 9 and later versions (at no charge by the way!). This suite includes an email account, a virtual disk on which you can store files (called iDisk), and, most importantly for the purpose of this book, a Web site. You can use your iTools Web site to display your digital lifestyle projects, provide files for people to download, and so on. While it's not an application that you store on your Mac like iTunes, iMovie, or iDVD, iTools is an equally important part of the digital lifestyle.

> **NOTE**
>
> By the way, only Mac users can access iTools services, but Windows users can bene-fit from the great content that Mac users create with iTools, such as an iTools Web site.

The iTools Way

The three primary iTools services are the following:

◆ **Email**. Using iTools provides you with a free account that you can use to send and receive email. The really cool thing about an iTools email account is that your address ends in "@mac.com." When you use an iTools email account, you show the world that you are proud to be a Mac user.

◆ **iDisk**. The iDisk is a virtual disk space that you can use to store files on servers maintained by Apple. As you will learn in this chapter, you can use your iDisk in a number of ways.

◆ **HomePage**. The HomePage service enables you to design, create, and publish a Web site or a group of Web sites that can contain your digital lifestyle content. The tools with which you build a site are very simple to use, and you don't need to learn any HTML, nor do you even need to learn to use an application. This is because you can build your Web sites by using Apple's Web-based tools.

All three of these services are extremely useful, but for the purposes of the digital lifestyle, you'll learn about iDisk and Homepage in the remainder of this chapter. You will use your iDisk to store your digital lifestyle content, and you will use HomePage to build a cool Web site to show off your creations.

Putting iTools to Work for You

The only requirements for using iTools are the following:

◆ A Mac running Mac OS X or Mac OS 9.

◆ An iTools account configured on your Mac.

Since you are reading this book, the first requirement doesn't require an additional explanation—you are already using the best digital lifestyle computer, so take full advantage of it!

Getting an iTools account isn't hard either. To start using an iTools account, you must first create your account and then configure your Mac with your account's information.

NOTE

If you already have an iTools account and have configured it on Mac OS X, skip to the section called "Working with Your iDisk."

Getting an iTools Account

You can create an iTools account on Apple's iTools Web site. When you are ready to create your iTools account, you have the following options:

◆ Use a Web browser to move to www.apple.com/itools and click the Sign Up button.

◆ Open the System Preferences utility, click the Internet icon, click the iTools pane, and then click the Sign Up button.

◆ When you install Mac OS X and reach the iTools configuration page, click the Sign Up button.

All three options lead you to the iTools information page in which you enter your personal information to create your iTools account (see Figure 6.1). Enter your information on this screen and then follow the on-screen instructions to create

Figure 6.1 *When you see this form, you are near your own iTools nirvana.*

your iTools account. You will have to provide personal information and accept a license agreement. The only information you really need to think about is the Member Name and password for your account.

You should put some thought into your Member Name. The Member Name that you choose will be part of your iTools email address (which will be member-name@mac.com), and it will also be part of the URL to your iTools Web site (which will be homepage.mac.com/membername). Typically, you should choose some variation of your name so that people can easily remember your email address and URL, and so that they can easily associate both with you.

NOTE

In case you are wondering, my Member Name is bradmacosx. So you can send email to me at bradmacosx@mac.com. You can also visit my Web site at homepage.mac.com/bradmacosx. I have also created a Web site for this book at homepage.mac.com/bradmacosx/osx_dig_lif.

You will need to create a password and password hint question for your account. You must enter your password when you sign on to the HomePage tools to create or manage your Web site; for other iTools services, you can have Mac OS X enter your password for you. Your password has to be between six and eight characters long, and you can use special characters if you want to. The password hint question enables you to identify yourself if you forget your password (and if you have a memory as poor as mine is, you will!). Try to use a question that you can answer only one way, such as your birth city or your mother's maiden name.

After you have successfully created an account, you will see a page that provides your Member Name, Password, Email address, and Email server information. You should print this page so that you will have the information if you need to retrieve it at a later time.

TIP

You can also save your iTools account information page by using your browser's Save As command. In Internet Explorer, use the Web Archive option to retain the page's formatting. In Internet Explorer, you can also save the page to the Scrapbook.

Making Your iTools Preferences Known

After you have created your iTools account, you should configure it in Mac OS X so that you can access your iTools email and your iDisk without having to log in to your iTools account on the iTools Web site.

NOTE

When you installed Mac OS X, you were prompted to enter your existing iTools account information or to create an iTools account. If you entered your iTools account information or created an iTools account at that time, you are all set and can skip to the next section.

Configure Your iTools Account in Mac OS X

1. Open the System Preferences utility and click the Internet icon.
2. Click the iTools tab (see Figure 6.2).

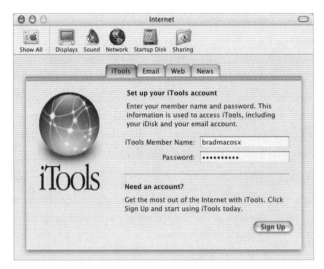

Figure 6.2 *Configuring Mac OS X to access your iTools account is a snap.*

3. Enter your member name and password in the appropriate fields.

4. Close the System Preferences utility.

That's all there is to it. Now Mac OS X can log into your iTools account for you. And if you use Mac OS X's Mail application, your iTools email account will be configured for you automatically.

Using Your iTools Account

To use iTools services, you first log in to your iTools account. Because you have configured your iTools account, you won't have to do this process manually when you want to use your iDisk, or when you use your iTools email account. However, when you build your HomePage, or when you want to mount your iDisk manually, you will need to log in to your iTools account on the iTools Web page.

Log In to the iTools Web Page

1. Open a Web browser and move to www.apple.com and then click the iTools tab. You will move to the iTools page.

2. Click the Login button. You will see the iTools login page (see Figure 6.3).

3. Enter your member name and password.

4. Click Enter. You will see the iTools services page from which you can access the various iTools services, such as HomePage.

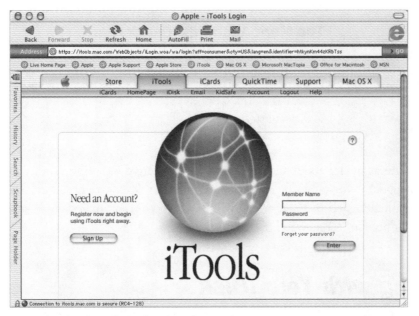

Figure 6.3 *Cool globe, eh?*

TIP

Internet Explorer includes a favorite to the iTools site in the Favorites bar. Click this to jump directly to the iTools Web site.

After you have logged in, you can sometimes return to your iTools services page without having to log in again. If you can move directly to one of the services pages, such as the HomePage page, you are already logged into your account. If you see the Login page instead, you have to log back into your account before you can use a service. (At the time of this writing, this behavior seemed to be a bit inconsistent so you just have to try it for yourself.)

TIP

You can log in to your iTools account from any computer running Mac OS 9 or later by visiting the iTools Web page and logging in to your account.

The More Accounts, the Merrier

Each user account on your Mac can have its own iTools account. The iTools settings in the Internet pane of the System Preferences utility of one account do not affect the other accounts. The steps to work with other accounts are exactly the same as those to work with the first one that you created.

If you are a stickler about such things, when you are done using iTools, you can click Logout to log out of your account (although it doesn't seem to hurt anything to remained logged in because you will be logged out automatically if you don't use your account for a period of time).

Working with Your iDisk

Your iDisk provides you with hard disk storage space on servers that Apple maintains for you. This storage space is where you store content that you place on a Web site that you create with the iTools HomePage service. You can also use your iDisk to share files with other users.

TIP

You can use your iDisk as a place to back up important files. Just store them on your iDisk, and you can retrieve them from any computer that you can use to access your iTools account.

Your free iTools account includes up to 20MB of storage space on your iDisk. If you plan to create a Web site with much content, especially content from your digital lifestyle projects, this space won't be enough. Fortunately, you can upgrade your iDisk storage space economically. At the time of the writing, the cost was about $1/MB per year up to 1 GB.

Lack of Speed Sometimes Kills (Your Patience, That Is)

Using an iDisk over a slow Internet connection can be an exercise in futility. When you move files to an iDisk—especially movie files—you move a large amount of data from your computer to the iDisk. Using a dial-up account or other slow Internet connection, this can be quite frustrating—even simple tasks such as opening the iDisk can seem to take forever. If you use a dial-up connection to the Internet, try to use the iDisk at less popular times of the day (such as early in the morning) so that the performance will be as good as it gets. The speed might still annoy you, but at least you stand a better chance of being able to tolerate it.

The good news is that using the iDisk is much faster under Mac OS X than it was using previous versions of the Mac OS.

Accessing Your iDisk

To use your iDisk, you mount it on your Mac, just like the hard disks that are physically connected to your machine. There are several ways to do this. These include the following:

- ◆ Open a new Finder window and choose Go, iDisk (or press Option+⌘+I).
- ◆ Add the iDisk button to your Finder toolbar and then click that button.
- ◆ Log into your iTools account, click the iDisk button, and then click Open Your iDisk.

NOTE

To learn how to configure the Finder's toolbar, see my book *Special Edition Using Mac OS X.*

Your Mac will connect to the Internet, and your iDisk will be mounted on your Mac. If you have configured Mac OS X to show mounted volumes on the desktop, you will see it there. You always see your mounted iDisk in the Computer folder (see Figure 6.4). Your iDisk will have your iTools member name as its name.

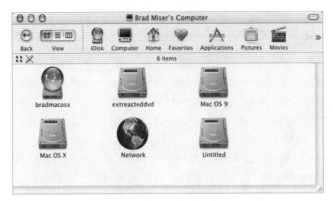

Figure 6.4 *When your iDisk is mounted on your Mac, you can work with it just like you use disks that are physically connected to it.*

In addition to being included on the Go menu, your iDisk also appears as a choice on the Where pop-up menu in Mac OS X Save sheets in many applications so that you can store documents directly to your iDisk (see Figure 6.5). This enables you to quickly store documents on your iDisk and to work with them from there (again, just like a disk physically connected to your Mac).

Your iDisk remains mounted on your Mac until you log out of your user account (such as when you shut your machine down). Until that time, it remains mounted on your desktop, and you can use it as needed. Fortunately, data is transmitted to

Figure 6.5 *You can export movies from iMovie directly to your iDisk.*

or from your iDisk only as you move files back and forth. You can disconnect your Internet connection without affecting your iDisk. When you use the iDisk again, your Mac will reconnect to the Internet as it needs to.

What's in an iDisk?

After your iDisk is mounted on your Mac, you can work with it just like the other volumes and disks on your machine. Open your iDisk and you will see the following folders:

◆ Documents

◆ Movies

◆ Music

◆ Pictures

◆ Public

◆ Sites

◆ Software

The Documents, Movies, Music, and Pictures folders contain elements for Web pages that you might want to add to your iTools Web site. For example, if you want to include QuickTime movies on your site, store them in the Movies folder.

The Public folder is where you can store files that you want other iTools users to be able to access.

The Sites folder is where you store your own HTML pages to be served from the iTools Web site (rather than using the HomePage service's tools to create your Web site).

The Software folder contains software that you can download to your Mac. Apple stores system and application software updates here so that you can easily access and download them. To see what software is available, simply open the Software folder. To download any of the files that you see to your Mac, drag the file from the Software folder to a folder on your machine. For example, there is a folder called Mac OS X Software that contains applications that you can download to your Mac by simply dragging them from the folder to your hard drive. The contents of the Software folder do not count against the 20MB size limit (or other size if you have increased it) of your iDisk.

Bigger is Better

Although being able to store 20MB of data on your iDisk for free is a great value, you might need to have more space available. In fact, if you want to create a Web site with lots of movies, music, and photos on it, 20MB isn't likely to be enough for you. As you learned earlier, you can increase the amount of iDisk storage space you have by upgrading it.

Increase the Size of Your iDisk

1. Log in to your iTools account on the iTools Web site.

2. Click the iDisk icon to open your iDisk page.

3. Click the Upgrade Now button. You will see the iDisk Upgrade page; at the top of the page, you will see the size your iDisk is currently (see Figure 6.6).

4. Click the icon for the size of iDisk you want.

5. Follow the on-screen instructions to complete the upgrade process.

6. If your iDisk is currently mounted, unmount it (select its icon and press ⌘+E) and then mount it again to make the new space available to you.

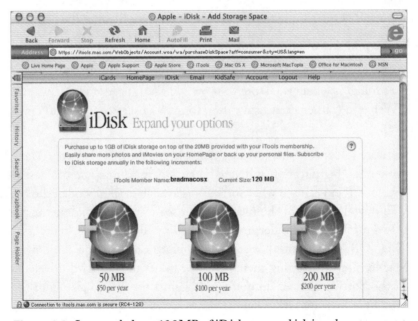

Figure 6.6 *I currently have 120MB of iDisk space, which is a decent amount for creating a digital lifestyle Web site.*

Building Your HomePage

Because the digital lifestyle tools enable you to create such cool projects, you aren't likely to want to keep them to yourself. Using the iTools HomePage service is a great way to create your own digital lifestyle Web site. Your iTools Web site can include one or more Web sites that each can contain one or more pages (see Figure 6.7).

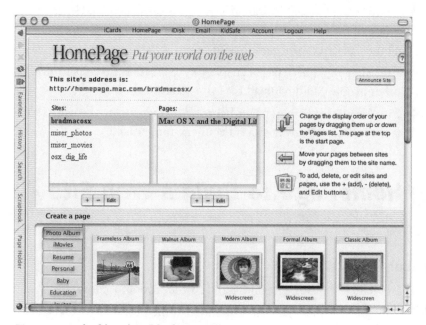

Figure 6.7 *At this point, I had created four Web sites under my iTools account (you can see them listed in the Sites window).*

To build a Web site using the HomePage tools, you first create a site (one site is created for you when you create your iTools account—this site has your member name as the end of its URL). Then you add pages to each site, one page at a time. When you add a page to one of your sites, you choose a template for that page. Then you select the contents for the page, edit it as needed, and publish it.

You can use HomePage templates to add any of the following pages to your site:

◆ **Photo Album**. I bet that you can guess what you store on these pages. When you create share photos from iPhoto to the Web, the pages use the Photo Album templates.

◆ **iMovies**. You can serve iMovies that you create so that others can watch them over the Web.

◆ **Resume**. You can create a resume to land you your next big job.

◆ **Personal**. These pages are formatted as personal newsletters.

◆ **Invites**. You can use these pages to create custom Web invitations.

◆ **Baby**. Use these pages to make a grandparent's day.

◆ **Education**. These pages are designed for those involved in education. Some of the template pages include pages for school events, school albums, teacher information, and so on.

◆ **File Sharing**. These pages enable you to create FTP sites from which other people can download files you place on the site.

◆ **Site Menu**. Site menu pages help you organize your Web site so that visitors can find their way around your site more easily.

Using HomePage to Build a Web Site

Here are the general steps to use HomePage to build a Web site.

Build an iTools Web Site

1. Move to the iTools site and log in to your iTools account.

2. Click the HomePage button to move to the HomePage screen (see Figure 6.8).

3. Use the site tools at the top of the page to add a Web site.

4. Use the page tools to add a page to the site.

5. Edit the template for the page type that you choose to add.

6. Add the content to the page.

7. Preview the page and correct any mistakes you find.

8. Publish the page.

9. Use the page tools to add more pages to a Web site and to organize the pages that it contains.

10. Use the site tools to add more sites and to organize the sites under your iTools account.

Page creation tools   Site tools   Page tools

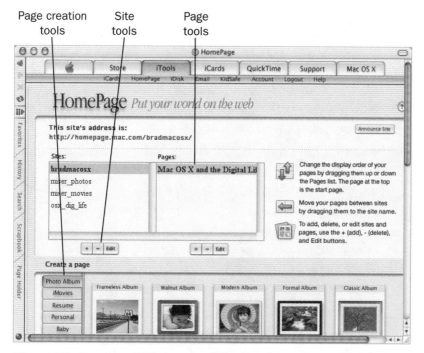

Figure 6.8 *Creating a Web site using HomePage is mostly a matter of point and click.*

Because an iTools Web site is such a great way to distribute your digital lifestyle projects, Chapter 19, "Creating and Hosting a Digital Lifestyle Web Site with iTools," is devoted to that topic.

Using iTools for Your Digital Lifestyle Projects

You can use iTools to share your digital lifestyle projects with other people. Using HomePage, you can build a Web site that will enable you to really show off what you have done. You can use your iDisk or an FTP site to share files with others just as easily. iTools truly enables you to make the digital lifestyle a global one.

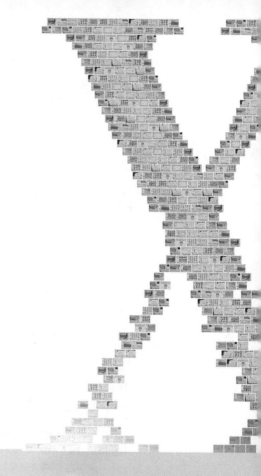

Chapter 7

Digital Lifestyle Hardware:
Digital Rules, Analog Drools

Digital hardware makes the digital lifestyle possible. From your trusty Mac to the latest and greatest digital camcorder, you will use many different hardware devices while creating your digital lifestyle projects. The purpose of this chapter is to give you a *brief* introduction to the major types of hardware that you might want or need to use at some point in your digital life. You'll also learn about some of the basic technologies with which you have to deal, such as USB, PCI, and lots of other TLA.

> **NOTE**
>
> While this chapter provides a good overview of digital lifestyle hardware, I don't pretend that it covers the details of each type of hardware discussed in it. That would require one or more books, let alone a single, short chapter. However, if you are unfamiliar with a specific kind of device, this chapter will help you understand enough to be able to decide which type of device is best for you. If you are hardware-savvy, you will probably only need to scan most of this chapter; read the sections about hardware with which you aren't familiar in detail.

Macintoshes for the Digital Life

Ah, where would we be without the Mac? We wouldn't be living the digital lifestyle in such ease and comfort, that's for sure. Because Mac hardware is powerful, reliable, and even elegant, and it runs the great tools that you learned about in Chapters 1 through 6, there is nothing better than having and using a Mac.

There are four families of Mac hardware (Power Macs, iMacs, PowerBooks, and iBooks); the good news is that every current Mac brings plenty of power to the digital table. While each Mac family offers a different set of features, they all share some basic technology that you should understand. A summary of this technology is provided in Table 7.1.

Table 7.1 Mac Technology Basics

Technology	Description
Processor	The processor is the central device that performs the computations and manages the data that make up a Mac's operation. There are two types of processors used in modern Macs: G4 or G3. The G4 is the more powerful of the two processors, and all Macs except the iBook use the G4. The G3 is also powerful, but doesn't match the G4 in processing power. Using a Mac containing a G4 processor makes all your work go faster, and the results will be better. Within the processor families, there are a variety of speeds available; faster speeds are better (duh). Some Macs also feature multiple processors, which enables these Macs to really fly.
RAM	Random Access Memory is the area to which your Mac stores information as it works with it. A larger amount of RAM means that your Mac can handle larger amounts of data, and operations on the data happen more quickly. There are various types of RAM used in modern Macs, but the general rule of RAM is that more is better. RAM is measured in MB; if a Mac has enough RAM to run Mac OS X, then it has enough to do digital lifestyle projects. However, adding additional RAM to a Mac is one of the best ways to improve its performance.
Hard Drive	Hard drives are used to store data that your Mac doesn't need to work with as quickly as the data it stores in RAM, as well as the data you keep on the machine (such as the OS, applications, and documents). Hard drives come in various sizes, with 20 GB being the smallest size in modern Macs. There are also different types of hard drives, from internal ATA drives to external FireWire drives. As with RAM, more hard drive space is better. Since digital lifestyle projects consume large amounts of storage space, you will need to have plenty of hard drive space available.
CD-ROM	Compact Disc Read Only Memory drives enable your Mac to read from compact discs, including audio CDs, application CDs, data CDs, and so on. These drives are useful to display data that has been recorded on them.
DVD-ROM	Digital Versatile Disc Read Only Memory drives enable a Mac to read DVD discs, such as those on which movies are stored or that you create with iDVD. These drives are useful to display digital data.

Table 7.1 Mac Technology Basics (continued)

Technology	Description
CD-RW Drive	Compact Disc Recordable reWritable drives enable your Mac to read CDs and to record information onto CD-R or CD-RW discs.
	In addition to displaying data on CD, these drives also enable you to record information on CD. You can burn audio CDs or put your digital lifestyle projects on CD to distribute them.
Combo Drive	The combo drive includes a CD-RW and DVD-ROM drive.
SuperDrive	The SuperDrive adds a DVD-R (Digital Versatile Disc Recordable) drive to the combo drive. Putting your digital lifestyle projects on DVD is way cool; the ultimate digital lifestyle Macs include the SuperDrive.
Expandability	This is a general term that refers to the ease with which components can be added to a Mac. The mobile Macs are somewhat limited in that you can't easily add much to their "innards;" the iMac is similar. The Power Mac G4 is very expandable and you can add many types of internal devices to it.
	However, just because you can't add much internally to some Macs, you can always expand your system by adding external devices.
USB	Universal Serial Bus is an input/output technology that is used by many kinds of input devices, including keyboards, mice, cameras, and so on. USB is plenty fast for many tasks and USB devices are inexpensive.
	All Macs include USB ports to which you can attach USB devices.
FireWire	FireWire is a high-speed input/output technology that you can use to attach devices that move large amounts of data, such as hard drives, digital camcorders, and so on.
	All Macs also include at least one FireWire port.

iBook

The iBook is one of the two mobile Mac families. In addition to being excellent "everyday" Macs, iBooks are also pretty good digital lifestyle Macs. The downside to the iBook is that they use the G3 processor, which isn't as fast or as powerful as the G4, and that they currently can't include a SuperDrive.

PowerBook

The PowerBook is the other mobile Mac family. In addition to being one of the coolest pieces of hardware ever produced, the PowerBook is also powerful. It includes a G4 processor and has all the features you need to take your digital lifestyle on the road. Like the iBook, the PowerBook doesn't currently offer a SuperDrive so you won't be able to create DVDs with it (unless you add an external DVD-R drive). Also, it isn't as fast or expandable as a Power Mac, but it sure is a lot easier to carry around!

iMac

The iMac has been groundbreaking in many ways, and the newest iMac proves that no one produces cooler hardware than Apple (see Figure 7.1). In addition to being a treat for the eye, the iMac offers everything you need, including a G4 processor, lots of disk space, plenty of RAM, and the option of a SuperDrive. About the only limitation to the iMac is that it isn't as expandable as the Power Mac.

Power Mac

If you want the most out of the digital lifestyle, the Power Mac provides it. Including one or more G4 processors, powerful supporting hardware (internal data buses, memory caches, and more), and lots of room to add internal devices, the Power Mac is the pinnacle of processing power for the desktop.

Figure 7.1 *Is it a work of art or a powerful digital lifestyle computer? The answer is both, of course.*

NOTE

Because I have assumed that you already have a Mac, I haven't gone into much detail about specific Mac models. If you want to get into the specifics, visit www.apple.com/hardware.

Data Storage Devices

The digital lifestyle involves data, lots and lots of data. You need places to store this data; data storage devices provide the space you need. The following are three general types of data that you need to store:

◆ **Active projects**. As you work on a project, you need room to store all of the files associated with it. For example, when you create a DVD, you need several GBs just to store the iDVD project itself. You need more to store the actual content of the DVD.

◆ **Back-ups**. Unless you enjoy redoing your work, you should obtain and use a back-up storage device. As you work with your projects, you should keep them backed up regularly.

◆ **Archives**. No matter how complex it is, you will eventually finish every project. After you have output that project, such as to a DVD, you aren't likely to have the luxury of enough room to store the project's data along with the projects on which you are actively working. Archiving data means removing that data from your active storage area and putting it a place that you will be able to retrieve it should you need it, but that doesn't limit what you are currently doing.

Dealing with data storage devices means dealing with some of the technology described in Table 7.2.

Table 7.2 Storage Device Technologies

Technology	Description
Internal ATA	The AT Attachment interface is used for the internal hard drives in most modern Macs. ATA hard drives are plentiful and inexpensive and their performance is adequate for all but the most demanding applications. You can add one or more internal ATA hard drives to Power Mac computers. Other models include a single ATA hard drive.

Table 7.2 Storage Device Technologies (continued)

Technology	Description
External FireWire	External FireWire data storage devices come in different types, including hard drives, CD-RW drives, DVD-R drives, tape drives, and so on. FireWire drives offer excellent performance, and they are easy to connect to Macs (just connect to the drive to the Mac with a FireWire cable).
External USB	USB data storage devices include CD-RW drives, Zip drives, and so on. USB data storage devices are easy to use, but their performance is not as good as that of FireWire devices (not surprisingly, USB devices tend to be less expensive than FireWire devices).
Internal or External SCSI	The Small Computer Serial Interface was standard on previous generations of Macs. SCSI provides very high performance, but its cost made Mac hardware more expensive than it needed to be—once ATA drives performed well enough to be useful for Mac users. SCSI is still available, but it is typically used only when the fastest speed is needed.
Size	All data devices can store an amount of data, which is the drive's size. Hard drives are limited to their size, such as 60GB, but drives that use removable media, such as CD-RW drives, have an unlimited capacity because you can always use additional media. The size parameter of such drives refers to the size of the media to which they write. For example, a CD-RW drive can write 700MB to a disc while a tape drive can often store 20GB on a single tape.
Speed	Speed is critical to those storage devices that you use for active projects, which are typically hard drives. The speed at which the drive turns, the speed at which data can be read from or written to the drive, and the speed at which the device communicates, determine how "fast" the drive is. For other devices, such as CD-RW or tape drives, speed is not quite as important because you don't use those devices while you are working on a project. However, faster devices are still better.
R vs. RW	Recordable drives can write to recordable media. Recordable media, such as a CD-R disc, can't be erased. Once it is written to, the disc is no longer recordable. Rewritable drives can also write to rewritable media, which means it can be erased and used again. Recordable media is less expensive than rewritable media is.
	All recordable CD drives today are CD-RW drives so that you can use either type of media in them. However, there are DVD-R drives, such as the Apple SuperDrive, and DVD-RW drives, which enable you to erase DVD-RW discs.

Hard Drives

Every Mac has at least one internal hard drive, either the ATA or SCSI variety. Internal hard drives are fast, and you don't have to make sure that they are connected to your Mac and are powered up when you want to use them (if the Mac's on, the drive is on). Hard drives should be used primarily for active projects along with your OS, applications, and so on.

If you have a Power Mac, you can add additional internal hard drives to it to increase the amount of storage space available to you. If you have other kinds of Macs, you can only replace the original hard drive (which I don't recommend unless you absolutely have to do so).

The good news is that you can add an external FireWire hard drive to any Mac. These drives offer excellent performance and are simple to connect and use (see Figure 7.2). They are also relatively inexpensive; you can obtain a 60GB drive for as little as $250. Adding such a drive that you can dedicate to specific digital lifestyle projects is a great way to make sure you have plenty of room in which to work.

An external FireWire hard drive is also a good way to keep your active data backed up. These drives are very fast so that the back-up process is also fast. The

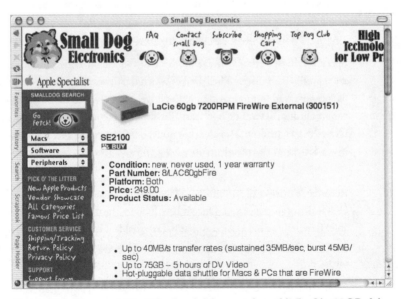

Figure 7.2 *External FireWire hard drives, such as this LaCie 60GB drive, are an easy way to add more hard drive space to your system.*

downside to using such a drive as a back-up device is that you need to have enough space to back up all of your important data; this usually means duplicating all of your Mac's other hard drives. This option isn't feasible for most Mac users.

Archiving your data on a hard drive is not practical for many reasons, including cost, reliability, and so on.

CD-RW Drives

A CD-RW drive is at least an option for all Macs (it is standard in most Mac models). In addition to reading audio CDs, CD-ROMs, and so on, CD-RW drives enable you to write data to CD-R and CD-RW discs. Several Mac models offer the Combo drive or SuperDrive, both of which include a CD-RW drive.

You can add external FireWire or USB CD-RW drives to any Mac with FireWire or USB ports. These drives are simple to configure and use, and are relatively inexpensive. Unless cost is a critical factor, obtain a FireWire drive instead of a USB drive because FireWire drives are much faster.

Any CD-RW drive is relatively slow—much too slow to store data for active projects. However, writing completed projects to CD-R discs is a great way to distribute them to others.

CD-RW drives are also useful for backing up and archiving your data. Their drawback in this area is that you can't store that much data (relatively speaking) on them. While 700MB is sufficient for outputting many projects, it is not usually sufficient to back up or archive the data that makes up the project. The result is that you have to use multiple discs, which can be time-consuming and makes managing the media more difficult. Still, if you have a CD-RW available, using it to back up your data is much better than not backing up at all.

NOTE

For backing up and archiving data, get a copy of Dantz's Retrospect. This is the ultimate back-up application and every Mac user should have a copy. Retrospect enables you to back up and archive any type of data to just about any type of storage device. Get more information about Retrospect by visiting www.dantz.com.

DVD-R and DVD-RW Drives

DVD-R and DVD-RW drives are similar to CD-RW drives except that they write to DVD discs. These discs hold much more data than do CD-R or CD-RW discs—4.7GB as compared to a CD's 700MB. This huge data storage capacity makes all sorts of things possible, the most important of which is the ability to store hours of digital video.

A DVD-R drive is part of Apple's SuperDrive that is offered on Power Mac and iMac models. When it comes to writing to DVD, the Apple drives are your best bet because they will be the most compatible with Apple applications, including iDVD.

You can add an external FireWire DVD-R or DVD-RW drive to any Mac that has a FireWire port. However, iDVD 2 works only with the Apple SuperDrive. Many of these third-party drives come with DVD writing software that will enable you to create DVD discs, but frankly, none of this software is nearly as good as iDVD. Some of these drives are supported by the Pro version of iDVD, DVD Studio Pro. At the time of this writing, DVD Studio Pro is available only for Mac OS 9, but an update for Mac OS X is very likely.

An Apple SuperDrive is most useful for using iDVD to create your own DVD movie discs. However, it can also be used to store any sort of data on the disc, just like CD-R and CD-RW discs. The capacity of DVD-R discs is large enough to use for backing up data; however, their cost and the fact that you can't use an Apple SuperDrive to write to DVD-RW discs makes them impractical as a back-up device for most users. However, even at its relatively expensive cost, a DVD-R disc can be an excellent way to archive important data, such as all of the data for a particularly important iDVD project.

Tape Drives

Tape drives write data to magnetic tapes of varying sizes and capacities—the Travan 20GB format is a common one (see Figure 7.3).

Tape drives are relatively slow; they are much too slow for data on which you are actively working. In fact, tape drives are really only good for two purposes, which are to back up or archive your data. While being limited in scope, they excel in function. In fact, because tapes are relatively inexpensive for the large capacity they offer, a tape drive is the ultimate back-up and archival system.

Figure 7.3 *A tape drive, such as this iMation FireWire Travan drive, makes a great back-up system.*

External FireWire tape drives are available for any Mac with a FireWire port. If protecting your data in the short-term and keeping it for the long term is important to you, consider adding a tape drive to your system.

NOTE

Tape drives usually include a copy of Retrospect so you get a complete back-up and archival system in one package.

Digital Input Devices

Moving data into your Mac is a critical part of the digital lifestyle. Digital data input devices that you should consider are the following:

- ◆ Digital video camera
- ◆ Digital still camera

- ◆ Scanner
- ◆ Microphone

These devices enable you to capture content that you can use in your digital lifestyle projects.

As with data storage devices, digital input devices share some common technology and terminology that is summarized in Table 7.3.

Table 7.3 Digital Input Device Technology

Technology	Description
Resolution	The resolution of a digital input device is a very important factor. Resolution determines how many pixels (picture elements) of data are captured in an image (whether a video or still image). Resolution is measured in number of pixels in width by number of pixels in height.
	Higher resolution devices are better because they capture higher quality images resulting in better looking projects. However, as you might expect, higher resolution devices are also more expensive.
USB or FireWire	Digital input devices include either USB or FireWire ports. Digital video cameras use FireWire while digital still cameras and microphones use USB. Scanners are available for either USB or FireWire.
Compatibility	The most important factor in any digital input device is compatibility with the hardware and software that you want to use with it. Make sure that any digital input device is compatible with Mac OS X and with the specific applications that you want to work with. For example, any digital still camera you consider should be compatible with iPhoto, while you should only consider digital video cameras that are compatible with iMovie.

Digital Video Camera

A digital video camera, also known as a digital camcorder or DV camera, enables you to capture your own video and easily import clips into iMovie via FireWire. A DV camera is a critical part of the digital lifestyle because it enables you to create video content for your digital lifestyle projects. If you don't have a DV camera, you should get one as soon as possible.

Obtaining a DV camera can be a baffling and sometimes intimidating process. There are many brands, and each offers many models with dozens of different features. This adds up to more choices than you might want to deal with.

However, by assessing a few specific factors, you can quickly reduce the dozens of choices you have to just a few.

◆ **iMovie compatibility**. Compatibility with iMovie should be the most important factor that you consider when you choose a DV camera. What does iMovie compatibility mean? Basically, it means that you have the easiest time and get the best results using that camera with iMovie. This is because you can control the camera from within iMovie, which makes transferring clips from the camera into iMovie a snap.

Apple maintains a list of iMovie-compatible DV cameras on the iMovie Web page. To see this list, go to www.apple.com/imovie/compatibility.html. You will have the best results if the camera that you choose is on this list.

◆ **Format**. Many video camera formats are available. The good news is that you need to consider only two formats: Digital8 and MiniDV. The difference between them is (as you probably surmised) size. Digital8 cameras use a digital tape that is the same physical size as an 8mm tape. MiniDV tapes are considerably smaller, and MiniDV cameras tend to be considerably smaller, as well. Because of the size benefits and the fact that MiniDV has become the standard for DV camcorders, I recommend that you consider only cameras that use the MiniDV format. However, if you already use an 8mm video camera and have lots of 8mm tapes, a Digital8 camera can be a good choice because you can use those tapes in the Digital8 camera.

◆ **Cost**. How much you have to pay for a camera is likely to be one of the first things that you think about. And it might indeed be the most important factor of all. To find out how much specific models cost, make a note of some of the models you see on the supported camera's list. Go to your favorite retail Web site—such as www.smalldog.com—and search for the models that you noted to see how much they cost.

◆ **Size, shape, and comfort**. How often you shoot video with a camera is usually a matter of how convenient it is to carry and use. Fortunately, MiniDV cameras are very small; in fact, a few are almost pocket-size!

Make sure that the camera you get is small enough that you're willing to haul it with you.

◆ **Magnification**. The power of the lens determines how close you must be in order to shoot something. Two values are quoted for DV cameras. One value is for optical zoom, and the other is for digital zoom. Optical zoom uses the physical lenses to achieve magnification; digital zoom uses digital enhancements to make the image larger. Optical zoom provides higher quality, but both are useful. For both values, bigger numbers are better (for example, a 20X optical zoom is better than a 10X optical zoom).

If it comes down to a choice, larger optical magnification is more important than a larger digital magnification. Optical magnification actually improves the image, whereas digital magnification uses the same amount of data to generate the image. For example, a 20X optical zoom with a 75X digital zoom is probably preferable to a 15X optical zoom with a 250X digital zoom.

◆ **Lighting options**. Some models have built-in lights to use when you shoot in low-light conditions. Others feature shoes into which you can plug external lights, such as those used for high-quality still cameras. Some models are designed to use the same lights as their 35mm film-based still-image cousins.

◆ **Input and output ports**. In addition to the FireWire port, other ports are available to get information into or out of the camera. These include a microphone jack so that you can connect and use a higher-quality or focusable microphone, additional audio/video input/output ports, and so on.

Make sure that the DV camera that you get has a port that enables you to record from an external source. This is usually called an A/V port. Often, this is the same port that is used to export video from the camera (the same jack is used to record from a source as is used to export the video to a VCR). This feature enables you to use an analog source to capture clips for your movies (in effect, such camcorders function as digitizers). For example, you can record from a VCR and then use FireWire to transfer that footage through the DV camera into iMovie so that you can use it in your movies. This is easy to do, and the quality is very good (better than with most consumer digitizing devices). Even better is a model that enables you to pass-through a signal so that you don't even have to record it with your DV camera because the signal passes through the DV camera into your Mac (via FireWire). This means that you get a higher-quality first generation recoding in your IMovie movie rather than a second-generation recording (as you would if you have to record the video on the DV camcorder before you import it into iMovie).

NOTE

Some video cameras also enable you to capture still images (two devices in one). If this capability is important to you, check the resolution of the still images that the digital camcorder is able to capture to make sure that it is high enough for your purposes.

Digital Still Camera

Second only to the DV camera in usefulness, the digital still camera enables you to capture still images to use in your digital lifestyle projects. A digital still camera offers many benefits over its film-based cousins, including the following:

◆ **Cost-free shooting.** There is no film or development cost associated with images that you capture with a digital camera. You simply download the image from the camera to your Mac. Because each shot costs you literally nothing, you might find yourself being much more liberal with the capture button than with the shutter button on a film-based camera. It is easy to delete any images that aren't what you want, and poor shots don't cost you anything. This frees you to be more creative when you shoot photos.

◆ **Customization**. Because the images that you capture are digital, you can use an image editing application to customize those images in any way that you can imagine. You can also easily correct flaws such as red-eye, bad background images, and so on.

◆ **Multiple uses**. The power of digital images and the applications that you can use to work with them enables you to use digital images in many ways. You can create digital photo albums, make slideshows, add them to your digital movies, and so on (you can even print them with the same quality as images captured on film).

◆ **Share images easily**. Unlike film photos that you have to copy and mail, you can easily (and instantly) provide your digital photos to just about anyone via email or on the Web.

Like obtaining a DV camera, obtaining a digital still camera can be intimidating. Hundreds of models are now available, and more seem to come into the market every day. These cameras range in price from $100 to over $1,000. Also like DV cameras, you can greatly limit the number of models from which you will want to choose by considering the factors described in the following list:

◆ **iPhoto compatibility**. If the camera that you are considering supports the Picture Transfer Protocol (PTP), you can use it with iPhoto. The good news is that many modern digital still cameras support this protocol.

To see models that are iPhoto-compatible, go to www.apple.com/iphoto/compatibility/.

◆ **Resolution**. Resolution is the single most important factor affecting digital image quality. The higher resolution the camera has, the more pixels that it captures in each image and thus the quality of the image is higher. Unlike some devices, it is common to measure the resolution of digital cameras by the total number of pixels in their images. Usually, this is referred to in millions of pixels or mega-pixels. And using the shorthand 2 mega-pixel or 3 mega-pixel further simplifies this. Because their quality is too low for printing, don't consider any camera in the 1-mega pixel range. Cameras that are 2-mega pixels will be suitable for all but the most demanding print jobs, such as 8 x 10 images. Three-mega pixel cameras capture images that are suitable for any purpose. Only professionals need cameras above 3-mega pixels in resolution.

All cameras enable you to change the resolution at which they capture images (they usually have low, medium, and high resolution settings). So the resolution of the camera is really its maximum resolution; depending on the photos that you are taking during a session, you might or might not take the highest resolution images possible.

◆ **Memory capacity and format**. All those pixels that a camera captures have to be stored in some form of memory. And, as with your Mac, more memory is better. In the case of a camera, having more memory available enables you to take more photos without having to download them to your Mac. Some cameras have built-in or fixed memory, but most modern cameras use some form of removable memory. There are three memory formats used in digital still cameras: CompactFlash, SmartMedia, and Sony's Memory Stick. These formats are similar, and you can obtain memory cards in various capacities, such as 128MB (which enables you to store about 120 images taken at the 3-mega pixel resolution). If you have other devices that also use such memory, it can be convenient to choose a camera that uses the same format so that you can share memory cards among your devices.

◆ **Price.** This factor probably goes without saying, but better cameras generally cost more. The prices of these cameras have fallen dramatically in the past year. Currently, you can obtain a good quality 2-megapixel camera for about $300 and a 3-megapixel camera for about $500.

◆ **Feel factor**. The physical characteristics of a camera might be one of the most important factors in your decision. If you are going to use it regularly and well, a camera must be suitable for carrying with you, and it should "feel" right in your hands. For example, the size and shape of the camera is a very important consideration. If you plan on taking plenty of photos on the move, you need a camera that is easy to carry. If portability is extremely important, you might want a camera that will fit in a pocket.

◆ **Features**. Digital cameras offer more features than even film-based cameras do; in fact, the sheer number of features can be overwhelming. Usually, you can limit the number of features that you have to consider by first using the other criteria (such as resolution, memory, and price) to eliminate most models from consideration. After you have a "short list" of possible models, you have to decide which features are the most important to you. You aren't likely to find a single model that offers exactly the features that you want, so you are looking for the best mix of features to best suit your needs.

NOTE

Just in case you are wondering, I use a Sony DCR-PC100 DV camera and a Kodak DC4800 still camera. Both of these are excellent cameras that offer great quality, lots of features, and excellent controls.

Scanner

A scanner enables you to capture physical images and convert them into an electronic format. In these days of digital cameras, the scanner has lost much of its usefulness. However, if you have lots of photos in hard copy or you want to continue using a film camera, a scanner can be a useful tool for your digital lifestyle projects (see Figure 7.4).

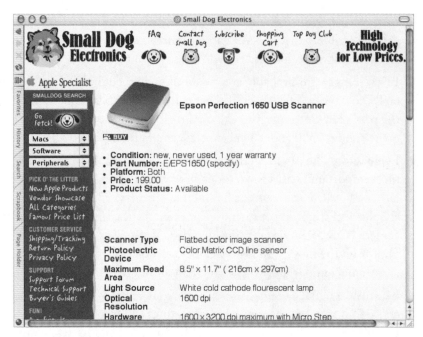

Figure 7.4 *A scanner such as this Epson Perfection 1650 can be a useful addition to your digital lifestyle toolkit.*

When choosing a scanner, consider the following factors:

◆ **Mac OS X compatibility**. Any scanner you obtain should be compatible with Mac OS X. Although in some cases, you can use the Mac OS X Classic environment to work with scanners that are Mac OS 9 compatible.

◆ **Resolution**. Just like other imaging devices, scanners offer a variety of resolutions with higher resolution devices being able to capture higher quality images. Typical scanner resolutions include 600 x 1200, 1200 x 1220, and so on. A good general-purpose scanner should have a resolution of no less than 1200 x 1200.

◆ **Interface**. Scanners can use either USB or FireWire to transfer data to your Mac. If you will be using the scanner frequently, consider a FireWire scanner, which will be faster than a USB scanner (it will be more expensive, too).

◆ **Price**. While price is always an important factor, scanners are among the more inexpensive devices. You can obtain a very nice scanner for less than $200.

◆ **Features**. Scanners offer a variety of features in which you might be interested. For example one-touch scanning enables you to scan images with the press of a button. Some scanners take their power from the interface they use (such as USB) so that you only have to deal with one cable (a particularly nice feature when the scanner won't always be connected to your Mac).

Microphones

A microphone can be useful when you want to capture "live" sound for your digital lifestyle projects. The most obvious example is narration for slideshows and movies, but you might also want to capture sound effects (slamming doors, creaking floors, and so on).

There are two basic types of microphones that you can use.

One type uses USB to connect directly to your Mac. This type is commonly mounted on a headset that you can wear and is frequently included with voice-recognition software. The headset type is very useful for recording narration because they are designed to capture voice sounds at a very high quality.

The other type is a USB adapter than enables you to connect standard analog microphones to your Mac. This is useful because you can use any sort of microphone to capture sound, such as a focused microphone when you want to capture sound effects.

NOTE

You probably have noticed by now that most of the figures in this chapter are screenshots of Small Dog Electronics' Web site. Small Dog Electronics is a very pro-Mac retailer that offers an excellent selection of product (new, used, and refurbished), good prices, and excellent service. Because they are so pro-Mac, I strongly recommend that you check Small Dog out whenever you need hardware or software. You can contact Small Dog at www.smalldog.com or 802-496-7171. Small Dog also provides several neat newsletters that you can sign up for; check out the Web site to do so.

Display Devices

Because you use them in each and every digital lifestyle project, the display (also known as monitor or more colloquially as the screen) you use is perhaps the most important device in your system (next to your Mac that is). The display you use is critical to both the creation of your projects and their display once they are created.

The technology and terminology associated with displays is summarized in Table 7.4.

Flat Panel Displays

Flat panel displays, also known as LCDs, made mobile computers practical. Because flat panel displays are thin and light, it is possible to equip a portable computer so that it becomes a laptop machine that can be carried easily.

Initially, LCD displays didn't offer very good image quality, and they were also very expensive. They were used solely for their physical benefit; for example, they were small enough to be carried around. As the technology improved, the quality of the flat panel displays increased while their prices decreased. Eventually, the quality/price balance overtook that of CRT monitors.

Why Bigger Looks Smaller

When you increase the display resolution that you are using, an interesting thing happens. The images and text that you see on the screen actually appear to get smaller. Why is this? A display has a fixed physical dimension, such as 17-inches. When you increase the resolution being displayed, more pixels are being displayed in the same physical space (which is the display size of the monitor). Pixels don't have a physical size; they are simply a "dot" on the screen. When you increase the number of pixels in the same physical space, each pixel "gets smaller" thus enabling more pixels to be displayed on the screen. The amount of information you see (the total number of pixels) increases and thus your desktop looks much larger and you can see more of your documents at the same time. But, the size of everything decreases. Choosing the resolution at which you work requires you to trade off the amount of information you can see on the screen versus the size of the images and text that your eyes are comfortable viewing.

Table 7.4 Display Device Technologies

Technology	Description
Display Type	There are three fundamental types of displays available for Mac systems. Flat panel displays, also know as liquid crystal displays (LCDs), are becoming the dominant type on the Mac and offer many benefits over the other types. Cathode Ray Tube (CRT) devices were the dominant type for many years and are still quite common. The recent drop in price and improvement in quality have made projector devices a feasible addition to many Mac users' systems.
Display Size	Display size is second only to type in importance. Bigger displays are better because you can see more information at the same time, and that is always a good thing. Standard display sizes (in inches) are 15, 17, 18, 19, 21, and 22.
Interface	Displays use one of three types of interfaces to connect to your Mac. Modern desktop Macs include the Apple Display Connector (ADC) that combines a high-quality video signal, power, and even USB connections over a single cable. The Video Graphics Array (VGA) interface is also standard on most Macs (including PowerBooks); this is the standard display interface for PCs and enables Macs to use many kinds of monitors. The Digital Video Interface (DVI) is used on many third-party flat panel displays. Most Macs do not support the DVI interface; you can add additional graphics cards to desktop Macs to enable them to use DVI displays. (Some new Power Mac models include a graphics card with built-in DVI support.)
Supported Resolutions	The combination of graphics hardware and display capability determines the resolution that can be displayed on a display device. Just like other devices, a display's resolution is measured as the number of pixels in width by the number of pixels in height. The greater the number of pixels that can be displayed, the more information you can see on the screen at the same time. (You choose the current resolution of your display on the Displays pane of the System Preferences utility.) Larger displays can typically support larger resolutions, but all displays support multiple resolutions. Common display resolutions on the Mac are 800 x 600, 1024 x 768, and 1280 x 1024.

The result of this evolution is that flat panel displays are becoming the standard; in fact, this is now the only type that Apple produces. And, if you have seen one, you know why. Flat panels are not only smaller than their CRT counterparts, but their image quality far exceeds any other type. Flat panel displays offer sharper, brighter, and more vivid images than other display types.

There are two basic types of flat panel displays available for Macs, those produced by Apple and those produced by other companies.

Apple's flat panel displays feature stylish design, superb image quality, and the Apple Display Connector (see Figure 7.5). Apple flat panel displays come in 15-inch, 17-inch, and the monster 22- and 23-inch models.

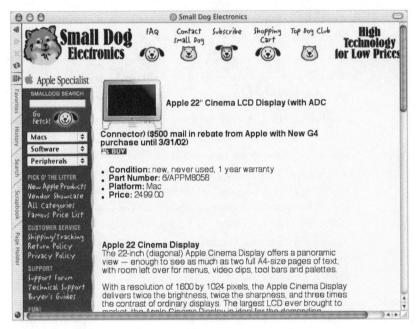

Figure 7.5 *Want an ultimate display? Apple's 22" Display is simply spectacular.*

Apple isn't the only producer of flat panel displays; most monitor companies also produce them. Flat panel displays produced by other companies have more variable display quality, but some rival the Apple flat panel displays. The most important difference between Apple flat panels and those produced by other companies is that the standard interface for non-Apple flat panel displays is the DVI connector. Most Macs do not support this interface without the addition of a graphics card that includes the DVI interface. However, Power Macs equipped with the GeForce4 Titanium graphics card include both an ADC and DVI interface so that you can connect either type or one of each type.

Because of their superior image quality, you should consider adding a flat panel display to your Mac.

> **NOTE**
>
> Modern Power Macs feature two display interfaces. Some include an ADC and VGA port while the newest feature an ADC and DVI port. Most Power Macs with dual video ports can support multiple monitors with no additional hardware needed (see the sidebar later in the chapter for information about adding and using multiple monitors).

CRT Monitors

CRT monitors generate an image by an electron "gun" spraying the backside of a specially coated piece of glass. As the beam strikes the coating, phosphors generate light and the image is displayed. CRT monitors come in many sizes and quality levels. Generally, when it comes to a CRT monitor, you get what you pay for.

CRT monitors use the VGA interface, which is the current standard on PC computers and most Macs.

> **NOTE**
>
> PowerBooks, iMacs, and iBooks offer a VGA port so that you can attach an external monitor to them.

While they used to dominate the computer world, CRT monitors are being rapidly replaced by flat panel displays (in fact, the newest Power Macs no longer support CRTs without the addition of a DVI/VGA adapter). Still, CRT monitors are a viable option for most Mac users, especially when adding a second (or third) display to your system.

> **NOTE**
>
> One parameter that is significant for CRT displays is their dot pitch, which is basically a measure of the size of the dots that appear on the screen. Smaller dot pitches result in higher quality images and more expensive monitors.

Projectors

Once priced in the stratosphere, projectors were an option only for businesses for which the ability to make presentations was worth the cost of such devices. Now, projectors have decreased in price and increased in quality so that they are a feasible option for many Mac users.

As their name implies, a projector projects an image onto a screen, wall, or other flat surface. The main benefit of a projector is that the image size is infinitely variable from very small to huge (most projectors are capable of projecting an image of 100 inches or more).

A projector enables you to transform your Mac into a digital movie theater, and you can show your digital lifestyle projects "on the big screen." Of course, they are also way cool for watching DVD movies, playing games, and even surfing the Net.

Projectors vary greatly in quality and price with the low end being around $2,000 (the sky is the limit on the high end). The good news is that many projectors support both computer inputs and many others, such as component video used for home theater applications. This means that you can share such projectors with your Mac and your home theater equipment (see Figure 7.6).

Figure 7.6 *You can use this Mitsubishi LVP-X80U with your Mac and with your home theater.*

Two or More Monitors Are Much Better Than One

When it comes to working with digital media, working room is always at a premium. You usually have more than one application open; some of the digital lifestyle applications, such as iMovie, take up the whole screen. One of the best things you can do for your own productivity is to add a second (or even third) monitor to your system. This enables you to dramatically increase the size of your desktop working area. Instead of being limited to a single monitor's display area, you can spread your work over two monitors at the same time. For example, you might have iMovie open on one screen and your iTools Web site and iTunes open on another.

There are two basic Mac types to which you can add multiple monitors: Power Macs and Macs with built-in screens (iMacs, iBooks, and PowerBooks).

Many Power Macs include a graphics card that has two video out ports, such as one ADC port and one VGA port or one ADC port and one VGA port. On many of these machines, you can attach a monitor to each port; that's all there is to it. Your desktop space is expanded instantly. For those Power Macs that only have one video out port or on which you can't use both video out ports simultaneously, you can add a graphics card to a PCI slot. Then you attach a second monitor to the video out port on the PCI graphics card.

For those Macs with a built-in screen, such as PowerBooks and iBooks, you can add an external monitor to the VGA port (some iBook models call this the AV port).

To configure multiple monitors, open the Displays pane of the System Preferences utility. You can choose the arrangement of the displays to determine which monitor is the main monitor that includes the menu bar. You can also set the resolution of each display independently. If you want the same image to appear on both screens, for example to project your Mac's desktop on a projector while it also appears on a display, you can turn on video mirroring. When video mirroring is turned off, the displays are independent.

Speakers

When it comes to the digital lifestyle, sound is at least half the experience. While all Macs have at least one built-in speaker, the sound you hear out of these speakers is not worthy of the digital lifestyle. You should definitely add external speakers to your system so that you can enjoy all the great sounds that are part of your digital lifestyle projects (not to mention music and movies that you enjoy on your Mac). This includes iTunes music, the soundtracks of your iMovie projects, DVD sounds, and so on.

NOTE

The best built-in speakers in Macs are those in the later generation of G3 iMacs. These iMacs have two Harman Kardon speakers built-in that produce fairly good sound. When an iSub sub-woofer is added, you have a decent sound system.

When adding a speaker system to your Mac, you should only add systems that have at least three speakers, with two being satellites and one being a powered sub-woofer.

There are two basic types of speaker systems that you can add: analog or digital.

Analog speakers connect to your Mac's headphone or speaker jack and use analog signals to produce sound. There are many such speaker systems available, and they are easy to install and use. Analog speakers also tend to be less expensive than digital speakers. However, they don't produce as good a quality of sound as digital speakers do, nor can you take advantage of some of the more advanced features of digital speakers.

Digital speakers connect to your Mac's USB port and handle all audio digitally. These speakers can offer additional features, such as the ability to play alert sounds through your Mac's internal speakers and other output sound through the speakers (if you have even been knocked out of your chair when an alert sound played while you were listening to loud music, you know why this is a good thing). Among the best sounding and certainly most cool looking speaker systems are the Harman Kardon SoundSticks (see Figure 7.7).

NOTE

If you have a Power Mac, you can add a PCI sound card, such as the Creative Labs Soundblaster Live, to produce even better sound. These systems enable you to connect four or more speakers to your Mac so that you can have surround sound capabilities.

Figure 7.7 *When you add a set of SoundSticks to your Mac, be prepared to answer questions about what the sub-woofer is (you'll be surprised at what people might think it might be!).*

Recording and Exporting Devices

Recoding and exporting devices enable you to move your digital lifestyle projects outside of your Mac. These devices include the following:

◆ **DV Camera**. A digital video camera can be the ultimate link between your Mac and other devices. For example, you can output your iMovie projects to the DV camera and then attach the camera to a VCR to record your projects to VHS tape, or you can connect your DV camera to your home theater to display your work. You can also use a DV camera to capture content from other sources, such as a VHS movie.

◆ **VCR**. The VCR is also a useful addition to your digital lifestyle toolkit. Because VCRs are everywhere, putting your projects on videotape is a great way to make them available for viewing. (You'll learn how to get your projects on videotape in Chapter 16, "Exporting Your Projects to Videotape.")

◆ **iPod**. The iPod is not only a great way to take your music collection with you—you can also put any sounds that you have created on the iPod so that sound goes with you. For example, suppose you captured a concert that you attended using your DV camera and wanted to be able to listen to the music that you recorded. You can move the music from iMovie to iTunes and then onto the iPod. You can also use the iPod to move audio files from one Mac to another.

NOTE

There are other input and output devices that can be useful for the digital lifestyle, but that I don't have the room to cover in this chapter. For example, you can add a PCI or USB TV tuner to your Mac so that you can watch TV on the desktop. You can add hardware that enables you to connect a VCR to your Mac to capture its output or to display your Mac's output on a TV (some Macs, such as PowerBooks, have a built-in S-video port that you can use for this purpose). Hardware exists for just about any purpose of which you can conceive.

Using Hardware for Your Digital Lifestyle Projects

Digital hardware is fundamental to the digital lifestyle. At the heart of the digital lifestyle is the Macintosh from which all digital goodness flows. But as you create your digital lifestyle projects, you will use much more—everything from inputting digital video from a digital camcorder to showing the great movies you have created via a digital projector; digital hardware enables you to live the digital lifestyle in style.

PART II

Building Digital Lifestyle Projects

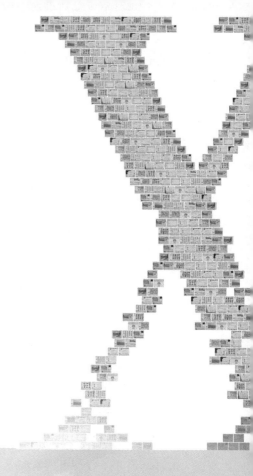

Chapter 8

Extracting Video and Audio Elements of Any QuickTime Movie for Your Digital Lifestyle Projects

As you learned in Part I of this book, QuickTime is the software technology that ties all of the other elements of the digital lifestyle together. In fact, QuickTime is a key enabler for all digital media applications on the Mac. One benefit to this is that every digital lifestyle application can "speak" QuickTime. This means that QuickTime is the great link between and bridge among the digital lifestyle applications.

Because of this, you can move QuickTime elements among the various projects that you do. For example, you can extract sounds from a QuickTime movie and use those sounds in your other projects, such as in an iMovie project. Or you can capture video clips from QuickTime movies to create other QuickTime movies or for import into another application, such as iDVD.

In this chapter, you'll learn how to do the following tasks:

◆ Find QuickTime movies that you can use as a source of video and audio clips

◆ Import files into QuickTime

◆ Edit your QuickTime source clips

◆ Extract selected tracks of QuickTime source movies

◆ Export movies into formats you need for your projects

What You Need for This Project

To use QuickTime to extract video and audio clips for your projects, you need to have the following:

◆ QuickTime movies that you are going to use as sources

◆ iMovie and a digital camcorder to create your own QuickTime source files

◆ QuickTime Pro to manipulate your source files

Developing Your QuickTime Sources

The first step in extracting QuickTime material to use in your projects is to locate QuickTime content that you want to use. Fortunately, QuickTime is widely used for the distribution of lots and lots of content. You should have no trouble locating QuickTime content that contains some gems that you want to extract for your own purposes. Of course, you can use the digital lifestyle tools to create your own QuickTime content. However, you can also find interesting content that other people have created, such as trailers for the latest movies from Hollywood or even the most recent commercial from Apple.

Rolling Your Own QuickTime Source Movies

One of the best places to find great QuickTime content that you can reuse is from your own projects. For example, you can export any iMovie project as a QuickTime movie and "slice" content from it.

As an example of how this can be done, suppose that you have some interesting footage of aircraft taking off and landing at a local airport. You think some of this material has some video and sound that you might like to use elsewhere so you want to create a QuickTime source movie from it.

> **NOTE**
>
> If you don't know your way around iMovie yet (you must not have been following along!), check out Chapter 4, "iMovie: the Swiss Army Knife of Digital Video Software," for an iMovie primer.

Create a QuickTime Source Clip from Your Own Video Source

1. Fire up iMovie and create a new project; name your project so that you will be able to tell what the QuickTime content is without actually viewing it. (In this example, I used the oh-so-clever title, "Plane Footage.")

2. Connect your digital camcorder to your Mac. You should see the Camera Connected message in the Monitor.

3. Use iMovie's controls to move to the point at which you want to start capturing footage.

4. Click the Import button (or press the Spacebar). iMovie will capture the footage and place it on the Shelf; by default, iMovie will break the footage into clips based on the start and stop points in the tape.

5. When you are done, click the Import button again (or press the Spacebar).

6. Continue gathering clips from the raw footage until you have the clips you want to include in your source movie (see Figure 8.1).

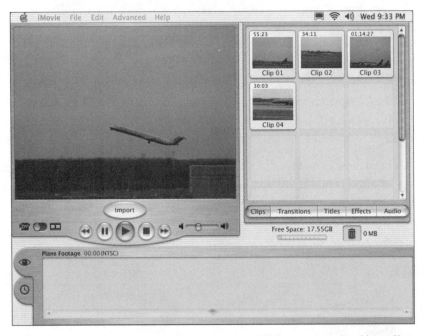

Figure 8.1 *Here I have captured some footage of different aircraft taking off from a local airport.*

7. Identify the clips you captured that you want to include in your QuickTime source movie (come now, not all of that footage will be worth keeping!).

8. Edit those clips to remove the portions that you won't want to reuse.

9. Now build a basic movie by dragging the clips onto the Clip Viewer; the order in which you place them doesn't matter much since you will be extracting pieces from the source movie rather than using it as a complete movie.

Now, add some black space in between the clips of your movie so that pieces of it will be easier to select and edit in QuickTime Player Pro. A simple way to do this is to place a title clip between the source clips (you can include text describing the clip or just leave the title clip blank).

Add Transition Space Between Clips in a QuickTime Source Movie

1. Click the Titles button on the Tools palette.

2. Click one of the title clip styles (it doesn't matter which you choose since it will only be a spacer between clips).

3. Check the Over Black checkbox (this places the title clip on a black screen instead of over a clip).

4. If you want to add text describing the clip, do so.

5. Drag the title clip between each video clip (change the text in the title clip before you drag it onto the Clip Viewer if you are including text).

6. Repeat Step 5 to add a transition between each clip. When you are done, your source movie will have black screen transitions between each clip (see Figure 8.2).

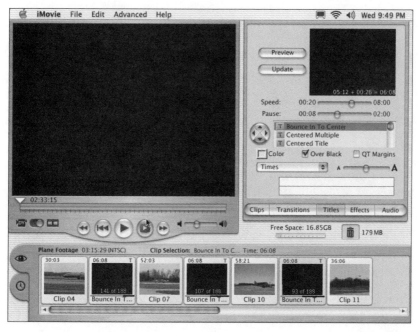

Figure 8.2 *I used the Bounce In To Center title clip with no text to separate my clips.*

Finally, export your movie as QuickTime to create the QuickTime source movie.

> ### NOTE
>
> Although I use the term QuickTime throughout this chapter when writing about source material, you should understand that almost any content could be imported into QuickTime directly, even if it isn't actually a QuickTime movie, thus becoming QuickTime source material. At the end of this chapter, you will find a table that lists most of the files formats that you can import into QuickTime Player (and thus export in other formats that you can import to and use in your projects).

Export the QuickTime Source Movie from iMovie

1. Choose File, Export Movie.
2. Choose To QuickTime on the Export pop-up menu.
3. Since you want your source movies to be as high quality as possible, choose Full Quality, Large on the Formats pop-up menu (see Figure 8.3).

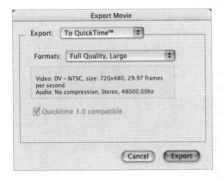

Figure 8.3 *Since you want your source movies to be high quality, use the Full Quality export setting to create the QuickTime movie.*

4. Click Export.
5. In the Save As dialog, name your source movie, choose a location in which to save it, and click Save. The QuickTime source movie will be created in the location you indicated.

Now you have a QuickTime movie that you can use as source material for other projects (see Figure 8.4).

Figure 8.4 *Here is a QuickTime source movie playing in QuickTime Player.*

Why Not Keep It in iMovie?

You might wonder why you shouldn't just keep the material in iMovie instead of exporting it to QuickTime. The reason is because it is easier to manage the source material as a single QuickTime movie rather than a bunch of individual clips in iMovie. Plus, you can use the QuickTime movie to extract elements you might want to use outside of iMovie, such as to create an alert sound. (You'll learn about that in Chapter 12, "Customizing Your Mac OS X Desktop with Digital Media.")

Downloading Source QuickTime Movies from the Web

If you've spent any time on the Web, you've probably seen many QuickTime movies including those made by "regular" people as well as movies produced by Hollywood professionals (well, at least the trailers) along with everything in-between. As you saw in Chapter 1, you can watch all of this great (and some not-so-great) content from your favorite Web browser, courtesy of the QuickTime plug-in. The good news is that with QuickTime Pro, you can download many of these movies to your Mac and then use them as source material for your projects.

Here are two ways in which you can download QuickTime movies from the Web:

◆ Many movies are set up to stream. A streaming movie can be viewed as it is downloaded to a computer. This makes the online movie watching process faster because the entire movie doesn't have to download before it can be viewed. Streaming movies are even better when viewed over a broadband connection because there is little delay between when the movie starts to download and when it starts to play (over a slow connection, this time lag can be lengthy for large movie files). For streaming movies, use the QuickTime pop-up menu to download the movie to your Mac.

◆ Some movies are provided as downloadable files rather than as streaming movies. Download this type just like you download any other file from the Net (see Figure 8.5).

Figure 8.5 *On* The Lord of the Rings *Web site, you have your choice—watch the trailer as a streaming movie or download it.*

In either case, downloading QuickTime movies from the Web is quite simple. As an example, suppose that you want to use the sounds of a light saber duel as an alert sound. You can grab a QuickTime movie trailer from a *Star Wars* movie and then extract the sound (you'll learn how to do that part later in this chapter).

Copyright—Not the Only Warning You'll Read in this Book

As you go about gathering great QuickTime clips to use in your projects, keep in mind that most of the material you discover on the Web or in other places is protected by copyright (unless you have created that material yourself). Most copyrighted material prohibits you from distributing it in any form. Sometimes, you can legally use the material for your own purposes; in other words, if you keep it to yourself, no one is likely to complain (or to sue you!). As you locate QuickTime material that you want to use in your projects, be aware of copyright restrictions that might be placed on it; your projects will be limited by that copyright if you include that copyrighted material in them. Be especially careful if you intend to distribute your projects over the Web or on CD or DVD. Basically, if you keep the material on your own Mac, you don't have to worry about copyright all that much. But, if you distribute material via any means, you need to be very much aware of copyright issues. I doubt anyone will come after you if you create one or two DVDs that you send to someone close to you for their viewing, but if you make your projects widely available, you really need to be aware of the copyright limits on source material that you use in those projects.

Download a QuickTime Movie from the Web as a Source File

1. Find the QuickTime movie that you want to download. For example, visit www.apple.com/trailers/for lots of great movie trailers that are available as QuickTime movies.

2. Preview the trailers until you find one that contains material you want to use (see Figure 8.6).

3. Click the QuickTime pop-up menu located at the end of the QuickTime Player control bar (see Figure 8.6).

4. Choose Save As QuickTime Movie.

5. Choose a location in which to save the movie and click Save. The movie will be saved to your Mac.

You won't be able to download every movie you find because some are provided without the QuickTime controls, and you might not be able to save them to your Mac. However, you will be able to save the vast majority of movies that you find on the Web.

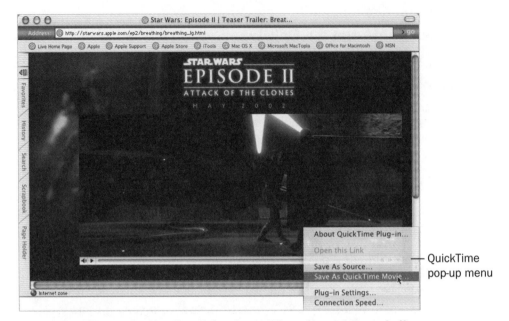

QuickTime pop-up menu

Figure 8.6 *The sounds of battling light sabers might make a great sound effect for some projects.*

> **NOTE**
>
> If the commands on the QuickTime pop-up menu are disabled, you aren't using QuickTime Pro. You have to be using QuickTime Pro to be able to save QuickTime movies to your Mac.

Finding QuickTime Sources Already on Your Mac

The odds are that you have a number of QuickTime movies on your Mac already. You can use Sherlock to search your Mac to find QuickTime source material that is already stored on your machine.

Use Sherlock to Find Potential QuickTime Source Files Already on Your Mac

1. Click the Sherlock icon on the Dock or choose File, Find when you are working in the Finder. You will see the Sherlock search window.

2. Click the Files icon to put Sherlock in the local search mode (the Files icon looks like a hard drive).

3. Choose the sources that you want to search by checking their On checkboxes. Since you want to make a complete search, check all the On checkboxes you see.

4. Click the Custom radio button.

5. Click the Custom pop-up menu and choose Edit. You will see the More Search Options dialog.

6. Click the triangle next to the Advanced Options text to open the Advanced search options.

7. Check the file type checkbox, select it on the pop-up menu, and then enter the file type for QuickTime movies, which is *MooV*, in the text box.

8. Click OK. Your search will be ready to run (see Figure 8.7).

9. Click the Search button. All the QuickTime movies on your Mac will be listed. In Figure 8.8, you can see that my search results included the plane_footage.mov movie that I created earlier along with some unexpected movies located on my Mac OS 9 volume (see Figure 8.8).

Figure 8.7 *This search will find all files of file type MooV on all disks on this Mac.*

Figure 8.8 *The spExmple movie that Sherlock found on the Mac OS 9 volume might be useful someday (if you ever need a nice voice saying "What time is it?").*

Explore the QuickTime movies that Sherlock finds for you to see if any of them will be useful as source material. This technique works equally well to explore CD-ROMs, DVD-ROMs, and other sources of content. For example, many multimedia CD-ROMs use QuickTime; you can locate the MooV files on such discs and use them as source material.

NOTE

To explore the movies that Sherlock finds, double-click a movie in Sherlock's Search Results pane. The movie will open in QuickTime Player, and you can preview it. Then jump back into Sherlock to continue your exploration.

Bringing Content into QuickTime

Because QuickTime provides a bridge among so many file formats, you can use it to import all sorts of content in many different file formats. After you have imported content into QuickTime, you can use that content in your projects by either saving it as a QuickTime movie or exporting it.

Knowing One Format From Another

Listing all of the file formats that are supported by QuickTime would be a big exercise, and it isn't really necessary. Table 8.1 provides a list of the major file formats that you can bring into QuickTime quickly and easily.

What this table means is that you can use files in *any* of these formats in your projects by first importing them into QuickTime. As an example, consider the WAV file format, which is a standard audio format. There are literally millions of WAV files on the Internet that contain any sort of sound that you can imagine (and plenty of others that you probably can't imagine), such as sound effects, clips from movies and television, and so on. You can download any of these files, import them into QuickTime, and then use QuickTime to edit them. When you are done, you can export the files into formats that you need to use, such as AIFF so you can move them into iMovie.

Table 8.1 Useful File Formats That Can Be Imported into QuickTime

File Format	Format Abbreviation	Mac OS X File Name Extension	Type of Content
Audio CD	Audio CD	.cdda	Audio used on standard audio CDs
Audio Interchange File Format	AIFF	.aiff	Audio
Audio Video Windows PCs Interleave	AVI	.avi	Video standard on
Digital Video	DV	.dv	Digital video
Graphics Interchange Format	GIF	.gif	Compressed graphics
Joint Photographic Exports Group	JPEG	.jpg	Compressed still images and graphics
Moving Pictures Exports Group Layer 1	MPEG-1	.mpg	Compressed video and audio
Moving Pictures Exports Group Layer 3	MP3	.mp3	Compressed audio

Table 8.1 Useful File Formats That Can Be Imported into QuickTime (continued)

File Format	Format Abbreviation	Mac OS X File Name Extension	Type of Content
Musical Instrument Digital Interface	MIDI	.midi	Digital audio
Photoshop	Photoshop	.psd	Images created by Adobe Photoshop
Picture	Pict	.pct	Still images and graphics
Picture Series	PICS	.pics	Series of images, as in a slideshow or animation
QuickTime	QuickTime	.mov	Video, audio, animation, and much more
Tagged Image File Format	TIFF	.tiff	Still images and graphics
Virtual Reality	QuickTime VR	.mov	Three-dimensional "worlds" that can be explored
Windows Waveform	WAV	.wav	Standard for Windows audio

Importing Files into QuickTime

Importing files into QuickTime is about as simple as things get. You can use QuickTime Player Pro to directly open most of the file formats you see in Table 8.1. In this section, you will see a couple of examples of how this works.

Open WAV Files in QuickTime Player Pro

1. Move to your favorite WAV site, such as http://new.wavlist.com/.
2. Find a Wav file that you want to preview and click it. Depending on the Web browser you are using and how it is configured, the results can be different. In most cases, a new QuickTime Player window will appear and the sound will play (see Figure 8.9).

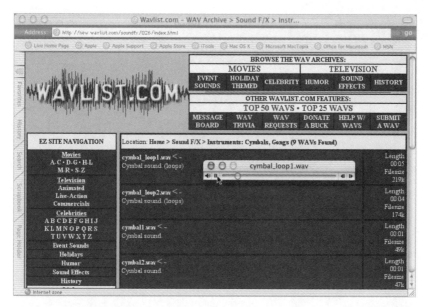

Figure 8.9 *In this example, I clicked the file called cymbol_loop1.wav; the file opened in the QuickTime Player window that enabled me to play the sound.*

3. When you find a sound that you want to keep for later use, download it to your Mac by choosing File, Save As.

4. Name the file, make sure that QuickTime Movie is selected on the Format pop-up menu, choose a location in which to save the movie, and click Save. The file will be saved in the location you chose.

5. Find the file that you just downloaded and open it. QuickTime Pro will open, and you can play the file (see Figure 8.10).

After the file is saved as a QuickTime movie, you can play it, edit it, export it, and so on.

As another example, suppose that you find a Photoshop image that you want to use in a project, but you don't have a copy of Photoshop on the machine on which you are working. With QuickTime Pro, this is not a problem. Just use QuickTime Player to open the image; then you can export it in a format for which you *do* have an available image editing application or export it in a format that you can use in your project.

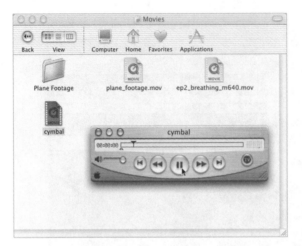

Figure 8.10 *Here you can see the cymbal sound effect file that I downloaded in QuickTime Player in the foreground and the Finder folder containing the file in the background.*

Open a Photoshop Image in QuickTime Player Pro

1. Open the QuickTime Player.

2. Choose File, Open Movie in New Player.

3. Use the Open dialog to move to the Photoshop image that you want use and open it (see Figure 8.11). The image will open in a new QuickTime Player window (see Figure 8.12).

Figure 8.11 *Don't have Photoshop? No problem, just open the image in QuickTime Player.*

Figure 8.12 *This is a Photoshop image file; by opening it in QuickTime Player, there is no limit to how you can use the image in your projects.*

Even though these examples are simple, they demonstrate the remarkable ability that QuickTime Pro provides to open just about any file in the formats that you want to use in your digital lifestyle projects.

Editing QuickTime Movies in QuickTime Player Pro

You can use QuickTime Player Pro to edit QuickTime movies, which is useful in preparing content for your projects because you can eliminate all of the material that you don't want from a source file quickly and easily.

Going back to the cymbal WAV file that I converted into QuickTime earlier in this chapter, suppose that I want to use the sound as a sound effect in a movie, but it is currently too long (I want only one cymbal crash instead of several crashes). I can use QuickTime Player Pro to cut out the extra sound.

NOTE

Because QuickTime Player's editing tools are relatively basic compared to other applications, such as iMovie (for example, you can't fade audio in QuickTime Player Pro as you can in iMovie), you aren't likely to use it for fine editing work. But for cropping out content that you don't want to use, QuickTime Player Pro is just fine.

TIP

I recommend that you always make a copy of a source file before you edit it. If you happen to mess up the file while editing it, you can always go back to the original version and start over.

Use QuickTime Player Pro to Remove Material from a QuickTime Source File

1. Open the file that you want to edit; in this example, I opened the cymbal file that I converted into a QuickTime movie.

2. Make a working copy of the file by choosing File, Save As. You will see the Save dialog.

3. Give the file that you will edit a new name. Use a name that will help you identify what the file is when you reuse it. In this example, I used the name single_cymbal_crash.mov.

4. Choose a location in which you want to save the file.

5. Click the "Make movie self-contained" radio button and click Save. You will have a copy of the source file that you can hack. The file will be opened in a QuickTime Player window.

6. Play the file and identify the segment that you want to keep.

7. Drag the crop markers so that they contain that segment.

8. Choose Movie, Play Selection Only (or press ⌘+T). This causes QuickTime Player to play only the portion of the movie that is between the crop markers.

9. Play the movie. You will hear the part that is selected.

10. Continue playing the clip and adjusting the crop markers until the sound is exactly what you want (see Figure 8.13).

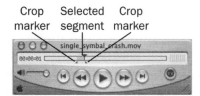

Figure 8.13 *Here, I have selected a single cymbal crash.*

11. Choose Edit, Trim. Everything outside of the crop markers will be removed.

12. Save the movie. You now have a source file containing only the sound that you want to use in a project (in this case, a custom alert sound).

Extracting the Tracks You Need

If you read Chapter 1, you know that QuickTime movies can have multiple tracks; each track can contain a specific type of data. For example, a movie can have a video track, one or more soundtracks, and so on. You can extract one or more tracks from a QuickTime movie to reuse elsewhere.

Now suppose that you want to use a sound effect from a movie trailer that you have downloaded. In this example, I want to capture the sound of a light saber battle from the movie *Star Wars: Attack of the Clones*.

Extract Tracks from a QuickTime Source File

1. Use the steps you learned earlier in this chapter to download the movie trailer to your Mac.

2. Using the technique from the previous section, edit the movie so that you have a source file that contains only the segment that you want to use. The movie trailer has three tracks: sprite, video, and sound. I'm only interested in the sound track so that's what I'll extract.

NOTE

A sprite track can be used for animation.

3. Choose Edit, Extract Tracks. You will see the Extract Tracks dialog (see Figure 8.14).

Figure 8.14 *This movie has three tracks, but I only want the Sound 1 track because it contains the light saber battle sounds.*

4. Choose the track that you want to extract and click Extract. The track will be opened in a new, untitled QuickTime Player window.

5. Play the sound to preview it.

6. Edit the sound, if necessary.

7. Save the movie (choose the self-contained option).

8. Select the file in Finder window in the Columns view and preview it (see Figure 8.15).

After you have edited and extracted the part of the source file that you want to reuse, you can export it into the format you need for your project, which leads us to the next section.

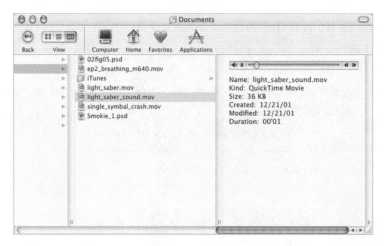

Figure 8.15 *The file called light_saber_sound.mov contains the sounds of battle.*

Exporting QuickTime Tracks for Other Applications

Now we get to the point of this chapter—moving content out of QuickTime into formats that you can use in your projects. Just as QuickTime Pro can import a large number of formats, it can also export a number of formats that you will be able to use elsewhere (see Table 8.2).

Table 8.2 Export Options for QuickTime Movies and Where You Can Use the Resulting Content

Export Option	Resulting File Format	What You Get	Where You Can Use the Content
Movie to DV Stream	DV file	Digital video file	IMovie iDVD
Movie to Picture	PICT file	A PICT file containing the image currently appearing in the QuickTime Player window	Desktop picture iMovie iDVD
Sound to AIFF	AIFF file	Sound file	iDVD iMovie iTunes System alert sound

TIP

The export options listed in Table 8.2 are those that you are most likely to use with Mac OS X digital lifestyle applications. However, there are some other really useful options that aren't listed. For example, you can use the Movie to AVI file to export .avi versions of your QuickTime movies that can be played with Windows Media Player, which is part of all standard Windows installations. Another example is the Sound to Wave option that enables you to create WAV sound files.

Exporting content in different file formats is not much of a challenge. You simply export the file in the format that you need.

Suppose that I want to use the cymbal WAV file that I prepared earlier in the chapter as a system alert sound. From Table 8.2, you can see that alert sounds are in the AIFF format. A couple of quick steps will produce the file in that format so I can install it and use it as my alert sound.

Convert a File's Format

1. Open the QuickTime movie version of the sound file.
2. Choose File, Export. You will see the Save export file as dialog.
3. Use the Export pop-up menu to choose Sound to AIFF (see Figure 8.16).
4. Choose a location in which you want to save the sound and click Save.

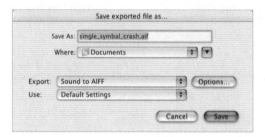

Figure 8.16 *With these options, the movie will be saved as an AIFF file.*

TIP

You don't need to change the file name because QuickTime Player will replace the file extension .mov with .aif automatically. This means that your source file remains unchanged.

After the AIFF is created, you can install it as an alert sound (you'll learn how in Chapter 12), or you can use it in other ways, such as in an iMovie project.

Options, Options

In Figure 8.16, you might notice the Use pop-up menu and Options button. These tools enable you to change various aspects of the file that you are exporting. For example, when you export a sound to an AIFF file, you can use the Use pop-up menu to select the sampling rate, size, and stereo/mono characteristics of the resulting sound file. You can use the Options button to open the Sound Settings dialog to choose a compressor, set the Use options, and set any options for the compression mechanism that you choose for the exported file.

Much of the time, the default settings will be what you need, especially in the case of a simple export, such as a short sound that you are going to use as a system alert. However, when you export a large file that you will use in a project, you might want to use some of these options to better match your media to the project, to reduce file size, and so on. While covering the details of all the options possible is beyond the scope of this book, you will learn about some of the export options in other project chapters

Chapter 9

Moving Your Digital Media into and out of the Digital Lifestyle Applications

f I had to choose one skill that I would like for you to take away from this book, this chapter has that skill set. When you finally understand how to move various types of digital media between the digital lifestyle applications, you can use those applications together to create amazing digital lifestyle projects. Being able to move your data across the applications enables you to use the right application for each kind of work that you do as you build your projects.

One of the most amazing things about the digital lifestyle applications is that they share so many different types of data. If one application can't import the kind of file you need for a project, you can probably use one of the others to convert that file into a format that you can import where you need it. In this chapter, you will learn how to move the image, video, and audio files from which you build your digital lifestyle projects among the "big 4" digital lifestyle applications.

NOTE

As you read this chapter, you'll notice that it is dominated by QuickTime Pro. That's because QuickTime Pro is a primary tool you should use to convert files into different formats. QuickTime Pro includes all the tools that you need to convert files from many formats into the formats you need for your digital lifestyle projects.

What You Need for This Project

In order to move data among the applications, all you need is the data that you want to move and the major digital lifestyle applications that you use to build your projects. Just in case you have forgotten what those applications are, here's the list:

◆ QuickTime Pro
◆ iTunes
◆ iPhoto
◆ iMovie

> **NOTE**
>
> Before getting into the meat of this chapter, you should understand that this chapter is a bit different than the others in this part of the book. While most of the chapters are focused on doing projects, this chapter is more informational in nature. Here you will learn about various file formats you will encounter in the digital lifestyle in order to understand which formats you can import or export in the various digital lifestyle applications. You should use this chapter as a reference whenever you need to figure out how to open or how to translate a file format for a project on which you are working.

Moving Digital Data into and out of QuickTime Pro

Of all the applications and services that you learn how to use in this book, QuickTime Pro can be considered the hub of everything you do in the digital lifestyle. Because QuickTime technology underlies all the digital lifestyle applications, it is accurate to say that without QuickTime, the digital lifestyle wouldn't exist.

In addition to being the foundation upon which the digital lifestyle is built, QuickTime Player Pro provides an amazingly powerful set of tools you can use to translate almost any type of data into almost any format. When you need to change the format of a file for a digital lifestyle project, QuickTime Pro should be your first stop.

> **NOTE**
>
> In this section, you will learn about many of the file formats that are supported by QuickTime Pro. However, I have included only those formats that you are most likely to use in your digital lifestyle projects. QuickTime actually supports even more file formats, believe it or not.

Moving Image Files Into and Out of QuickTime Player Pro

You probably associate QuickTime mostly with moving images, but it can also work with many types of still images just as well.

Importing Image Files into QuickTime Player Pro

You can open a wide variety of image files in QuickTime Pro as defined in Table 9.1.

Opening an image file using the QuickTime Player is rather simple.

Open an Image File in QuickTime Player Pro

1. Open QuickTime Player.
2. Choose File, Open Movie in New Player or File, Import.
3. Move to the image that you want to open, select it, and click Open. The image will appear in the QuickTime Player window (see Figure 9.1).

After you have opened an image, you can export it as another format, use it in a QuickTime movie, and so on.

Figure 9.1 *You can view images, such as this JPEG image, in QuickTime Player.*

Table 9.1 Image File Formats You Can Open in QuickTime Player Pro

File Format	Abbreviation/File Name Extension	Where It Is Used
Bit-mapped Graphics	BMP .bmp	Standard image format on Windows computers
FlashPix	FPX .fpx	Image file format developed by Kodak that offers advanced features, such as the ability to store multiple image resolutions in the same file
Graphics Interchange Format	GIF .gif	A graphics format originally developed by AOL for presenting images online; GIF files are widely used on the Internet for simple images, such as buttons and other graphic elements
Joint Photographic Experts Group	JPEG .jpg	A compressed image file format that achieves excellent quality with substantially smaller files; JPEG is the standard image format for most digital cameras as well as most image applications, such as iPhoto
MacPaint	MacPaint	The format of the original Mac graphics application; you aren't likely to run into many MacPaint files (I included it mostly for old time's sake)
Photoshop	Photoshop .psd	Adobe's Photoshop is the standard for editing digital images on any platform
Pictures in Sequence	PICS .pics	Format containing still images in a slideshow format (images shown in a sequence)
Picture Format	PICT .pct	The bit-mapped graphics format standard on Macs
QuickTime Image File	QuickTime Image .qtif	Image format native to QuickTime
Text	Text .txt	File format for text; you can import text as a text track in QuickTime movies
Tagged Image File Format	TIFF .tiff	Uncompressed image file format that maintains maximum image quality, but that also has relatively large file sizes

Exporting Image Files from QuickTime Player Pro

You can use QuickTime Player to convert image files that are open in QuickTime Player into formats that you need for your projects. Table 9.2 lists some of the file formats into which you can convert images that you open in QuickTime Player.

Using QuickTime Player to convert an image file into a different format isn't any harder than opening that file in the first place.

Table 9.2 Image File Formats You Can Export from QuickTime Player Pro

File Format	Abbreviation/File Name Extension	Where It Is Used
Bit-mapped Graphics	BMP .bmp	Standard image format on Windows computers
Joint Photographic Experts Group	JPEG .jpg	A compressed image file format that achieves excellent quality with substantially smaller files; JPEG is the standard image format for most digital cameras as well as most image applications, such as iPhoto
Photoshop	Photoshop .psd	Adobe's Photoshop is the standard for editing digital images on any platform
Picture Format	PICT .pct	The bit-mapped graphics format standard on Macintoshes
QuickTime Image File	QuickTime Image .qtif	Image format native to QuickTime
Text	Text .txt	File format for text
Tagged Image File Format	TIFF .tiff	Uncompressed image file format that maintains maximum image quality, but that has relative large file sizes

Convert an Image File from One Format to Another

1. Open the image file that you want to convert.

2. Choose File, Export.

3. Choose a location in which to save the file.

4. On the Export pop-up menu, choose the format into which you want to convert the image file (see Figure 9.2).

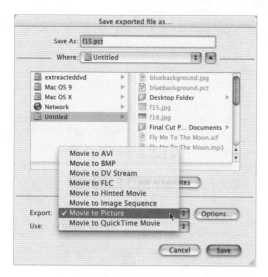

Figure 9.2 *With this selection, the image will be converted from the JPEG file format to the PICT file format.*

5. Click the Options button and choose the options for the format that you have selected or open the Use pop-up menu and choose the settings that you want to use for the export.

6. Change the file name as needed (generally, you should leave the file name extension that QuickTime Player adds to the file name).

7. Click Save. The image file in the format you select will be ready for you to use.

Moving Video Files Into and Out of QuickTime Player Pro

As you have learned in earlier chapters of this book, QuickTime is made for motion. QuickTime Player Pro enables you to work with all of the video file formats that you are likely to need for your digital lifestyle projects.

Importing Video Files into QuickTime Player Pro

You can use QuickTime Player to open many video file formats, including those listed in Table 9.3.

Table 9.3 Video File Formats You Can Open in QuickTime Player Pro

File Format	Abbreviation/File Name Extension	Where It Is Used
Audio Video Interleave	AVI .avi	A standard video format for Windows computers; for example, Microsoft's Media Player application uses AVI as its standard format
Digital Video	DV .dv	In most applications that support digital video, such as iMovie
Motion Picture Experts Group Layer 1	MPEG-1 .mpg	A video compression scheme that provides high quality video in relatively small file sizes
QuickTime Movie	QuickTime .mov	QuickTime's native video format
QuickTime Virtual Reality	QTVR .qtvr	A format that simulates three-dimensional worlds by using a panorama of images in which the viewer can move around

Opening a video file is similar to opening an image or any other file.

Open a Video File in QuickTime Player Pro

1. Open QuickTime Player.
2. Choose File, Open Movie in New Player or choose File, Import.
3. Move to the file that you want to open, select it, and click Open. The file will appear in the QuickTime Player window, and you can use QuickTime Player's tools to work with it.

Exporting Video Files from QuickTime Player Pro

QuickTime Player Pro also enables you to convert movies that you open in it into the formats described in Table 9.4.

Converting a movie from one file format to another requires only a few steps.

Table 9.4 Video File Formats to Which You Can Convert Movies Opened in QuickTime Player Pro

File Format	Abbreviation/File Name Extension	Where It Is Used
Audio Video Interleave	AVI .avi	A standard video format for Windows computers; for example, Microsoft's Media Player application uses AVI as its standard format
DV Stream	DV Stream .dv	Format required to import QuickTime movies into iMovie or iDVD
QuickTime Movie	QuickTime .mov	QuickTime's native video format

Convert Video Files from One Format to Another

1. Open the video file that you want to convert into another format.

2. Choose File, Export.

3. Choose a location in which to save the converted version of the file.

4. On the Export pop-up menu, choose the file format into which you want to convert the file. For example, choose Movie to AVI to convert the move into the AVI format.

5. Click the Options button to open the Settings dialog for the format that you selected (see Figure 9.3).

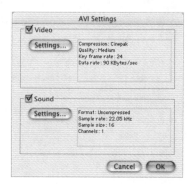

Figure 9.3 *You can configure the settings used for a file format into which you are exporting a file by opening its Settings window.*

6. Use the controls in the Settings window to configure the file that you are exporting. For example, to remove the sound from the movie when it is exported, uncheck the Sound checkbox. Use the Settings button to configure the settings for each property, such as Video for the video track, in detail (see Figure 9.4).

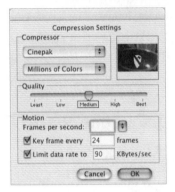

Figure 9.4 *You can use the Video Settings dialog for the AVI format to choose the compressor used, quality level, and other parameters of the AVI file that you create.*

7. After you have configured each property for the file that you are exporting, click OK to close the Settings dialog.

8. Rename the file as needed (maintain the file extension that QuickTime Player adds to the file).

9. Click Save. The Exporting Movie progress bar will appear and will display the progress of the export. When it is complete, the video file will be ready for your use.

TIP

Converting a movie into the AVI format is a great way to share a movie with a Windows user who doesn't have QuickTime installed on their computer. (QuickTime is also a standard on Windows machines, but is not installed with the Windows OS since it is for the Mac OS.)

In the Export dialog, the Use pop-up menu enables you to choose a set of export settings to use for the file that you are creating. The set of options on this pop-up menu changes depending on the type of file format in which you are exporting a file. Most options include Default Settings, which are the default settings for the selected file format, and Most Recent Settings, which enable you to quickly return to the most recent settings used for that format. There are other options for various formats as well. For example, when converting a movie to the AVI format, you can choose 2x CD-ROM, which configures the AVI movie to play with good quality on a machine capable of playing a CD at faster speeds (this configuration uses a relatively high frame rate, for example).

Moving Audio Files into and out of QuickTime Player Pro

Working with audio files in QuickTime Player Pro isn't much different from image or video files. Of course, when you use QuickTime Player for audio files, you don't see any video track.

Importing Audio Files into QuickTime Player Pro

QuickTime Player Pro enables you to open many audio file formats, including those listed in Table 9.5.

Open an Audio File in QuickTime Player Pro

1. Choose File, Open Movie in New Player or choose File, Import.
2. Move to the file that you want to open, select it, and click Open. The audio file will open in the QuickTime Player window (see Figure 9.5). After you have opened the file in QuickTime Player, you can work with it, such as converting it into a different format.

Figure 9.5 *While it isn't much to look at, this audio file from an audio CD is beautiful to listen to.*

Table 9.5 Audio File Formats You Can Open in QuickTime Player Pro

File Format	Abbreviation/File Name Extension	Where It Is Used
Audio	AU .au	Audio file format for UNIX; also used widely in Java
Audio Interchange File Format	AIFF .aif .aiff	Standard audio file format that is supported by most digital media applications; you will use this format frequently in your digital lifestyle projects
Audio CD	Audio CD .cdda	Audio format for standard audio CDs
Musical Instrument Digital Interface	MIDI .mid	A format for creating and playing music via digital synthesizers; MIDI files are very small and can produce decent sounding music
Motion Picture Experts Group Layer 3	MPEG-3 .mp3	A revolutionary audio format that provides nearly audio CD quality in files that are about a tenth as large
Waveform Audio File	WAV .wav	Standard audio format on Windows computers; there are millions of WAV files on the Internet that you can download and use in your projects

Exporting Audio Files from QuickTime Player Pro

If you've read the previous sections, exporting audio files from QuickTime Player Pro will seem very familiar to you. Table 9.6 lists some of the files formats into which you can convert audio files.

Table 9.6 Audio File Formats into Which You Can Convert Audio Files by Using QuickTime Player Pro

File Format	Abbreviation/File Name Extension	Where It Is Used
Audio Interchange File Format	AIFF .aif .aiff	Standard audio file format that is supported by most digital media applications; you will use this format frequently in your digital lifestyle projects
Musical Instrument Digital Interface	MIDI .mid	A format for creating and playing music via digital synthesizers; MIDI files are very small and can produce decent sounding music

Table 9.6 Audio File Formats into Which You Can Convert Audio Files by Using QuickTime Player Pro (continued)

File Format	Abbreviation/File Name Extension	Where It Is Used
System 7 Sound	System 7 Sound	Sounds that can be used as system sounds under Mac OS 9 and earlier versions
Waveform Audio File	WAV .wav	Standard audio format on Windows computers; there are millions of WAV files on the Internet that you can download and use in your projects

Convert an Audio File into Another Format

1. Use QuickTime Player to open the audio file that you want to convert into a different format.

2. Choose File, Export.

3. Choose the audio format into which you want to convert the file on the Export pop-up menu, such as Movie to AIFF.

4. Use the Options button or Use pop-up menu to configure the settings for the format that you selected.

5. Choose a location for the resulting file, name it if needed (maintain the file extension), and click Save. The Exporting Movie progress bar will show you the progress. When it is done, the audio file will be ready for you to use.

Moving Audio Files into and out of iTunes

Unlike QuickTime Pro, iTunes can only work with audio files. Still, while more limited in function (from the file conversion viewpoint that is), iTunes is the primary way you should use to convert audio CDs into MP3 files that you can use in your projects.

iTunes can work with (import or export) the audio formats listed in Table 9.7.

In Chapter 2, you learned how to convert files on an audio CD into the MP3 format. However, you can also use iTunes to convert audio files into AIFF, MP3, or WAV files.

Table 9.7 Audio File Formats Supported by iTunes

File Format	Abbreviation/File Name Extension	Where It Is Used
Audio Interchange File Format	AIFF .aif .aiff	Standard audio file format that is supported by most digital media applications; you will use this format frequently in your digital lifestyle projects
Audio CD	Audio CD .cdda	Audio format for standard audio CDs
Motion Picture Experts Group Layer 3	MPEG-3 .mp3	A revolutionary audio format that provides nearly audio CD quality in files that are about a tenth as large
Waveform Audio File	WAV .wav	Standard audio format on Windows computers; there are millions of WAV files on the Internet that you can download and use in your projects

Using iTunes to convert an audio file into a different format consists of the following two steps:

1. Move the audio file into iTunes in the format you want it to be in.
2. Find the file you converted in the Finder.

Moving Audio Files into iTunes

First, choose the format into which you want to convert an audio file by setting the Encoder that iTunes uses to open the file.

Configure the Encoder iTunes Uses to Import Audio Files

1. Launch iTunes.
2. Choose ITunes, Preferences.
3. Click the Importing tab.
4. On the Import Using pop-up menu, choose the format that you want to use. Your options are MP3 Encoder, AIFF Encoder, or WAV Encoder.
5. Use the Configuration pop-up menu to configure the settings for the encoder that you select.
6. Click OK to close the iTunes Preferences dialog.

To convert files from an audio CD into the format you selected, the steps are the same as those presented in Chapter 2.

Use iTunes to Convert an Audio File on an Audio CD from One Format to Another

1. Choose the audio CD as the source.

2. Select the songs that you want to import.

3. Click Import. The selected songs will be moved into the iTunes Library in the format that you selected by using the iTunes Preferences window.

Use iTunes to Convert an Audio File Not on an Audio CD from One Format to Another

1. Choose Advanced, Convert to Format, where Format is the encoder that you choose in the iTunes Preferences dialog.

2. In the Choose Object dialog, move to the file that you want to import, select it, and click Choose. The file will be imported into the iTunes Library in the format that you selected.

Moving Audio Files out of iTunes

The title of this section is a bit misleading. After you have converted an audio file into a different format in iTunes, you don't need to export it from iTunes. When you import a file from any source into the iTunes Library, a file in the format that you select is created automatically. To use that file, you simply find it in your iTunes music collection.

There are a couple of ways to do this:

◆ Use the Sherlock application to search for the specific file by name.

◆ Browse for the file in the Finder.

To browse for the file that you converted, use the following steps.

Locate Audio Files You Have Converted with iTunes

1. Open a new Finder window.

2. Open your Home folder.

3. Open your Documents folder, then open the iTunes folder, and finally open the iTunes Music folder.

4. Look in the artist folder for the artist who created the music file that you converted. If you converted audio other than from an audio CD, check the Unknown Artist folder.

5. Browse the artist's album folders or the Unknown Artist folder to find the file that you converted. The file is ready for you to use in your projects (see Figure 9.6). Just drag it to a new location or copy where you want to use it.

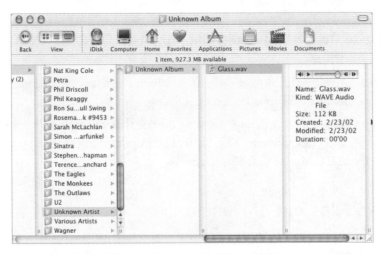

Figure 9.6 *I used iTunes to convert the Glass.AIFF alert sound file into the WAV format.*

Moving Image Files into and out of iPhoto

Similar to iTunes, iPhoto can work with only one type of file—images. Using iPhoto to convert image files from one format to another is also quite similar to using iTunes to convert audio files from one format to another. The process also requires the following two general steps:

1. Import the image into the iPhoto Library.

2. Export the image from iPhoto in the format into which you want to convert it.

Moving Image Files into iPhoto

There are two ways to get image files into the iPhoto Library. One is to import them from a digital camera (you can learn how to do that in Chapter 3). The other way is to use iPhoto's Import command.

You can import a variety of image file formats into iPhoto. The most likely formats that you will want to import are listed in Table 9.8.

Table 9.8 Image File Formats That You Are Likely to Import into iPhoto

File Format	Abbreviation/File Name Extension	Where It Is Used
Bit-mapped Graphics	BMP .bmp	Standard image format on Windows computers
Joint Photographic Experts Group	JPEG .jpg	A compressed image file format that achieves excellent quality with substantially smaller files; JPEG is the standard image format for most digital cameras as well as most image applications, such as iPhoto
Picture Format	PICT .pct	The bit-mapped graphics format standard on Macs
Tagged Image File Format	TIFF .tiff	Uncompressed image file format that maintains maximum image quality, but that also has relative large file sizes

Import an Image File into the iPhoto Library

1. Launch iPhoto.
2. Choose File, Import.
3. In the resulting Import Photos dialog, move to the image that you want to import, select it, and click Open. The image will be added to the iPhoto Library, and you can use iPhoto's tools to work with it, such as the Editing tools (see Figure 9.7).

Moving Image Files out of iPhoto

You can use iPhoto to convert images into the formats listed in Table 9.9.

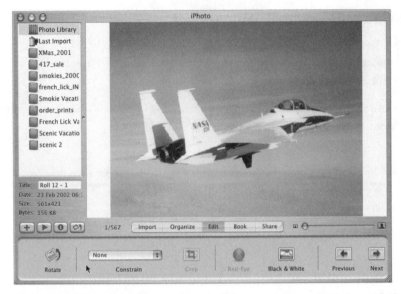

Figure 9.7 *If you have been paying attention, you have seen this image before.*

Table 9.9 Image File Formats That You Can Export from iPhoto

File Format	Abbreviation/File Name Extension	Where It Is Used
Joint Photographic Experts Group	JPEG .jpg	A compressed image file format that achieves excellent quality with substantially smaller files; JPEG is the standard image format for most digital cameras as well as most image applications, such as iPhoto
Tagged Image File Format	TIFF .tiff	Uncompressed image file format that maintains maximum image quality, but that also has relative large file sizes
Portable Network Graphics	PNG .png	A compressed bit-mapped image format that is similar to GIF and is becoming widely used on the Web

Use iPhoto to Change the File Format of an Image File

1. Select the images that you want to export.
2. Click the Share button.
3. Click the Export button.

4. In the Save Selected Photo dialog, name the image (you don't need to add a file name extension, iPhoto will handle that for you).

5. Choose the location in which you want to save the image file that you are exporting.

6. Use the Format pop-up menu to choose the format in which you want to save the image, such as PNG (see Figure 9.8).

Figure 9.8 *Here I am converting this image into the PNG format.*

7. If you choose the JPEG format and want to scale the image, click the "Scale no larger than" radio button and choose the scale at which the image should be exported.

8. Click Save. The image will be converted into the format that you selected and stored in the location you selected. You can then use that file in your projects.

Moving Digital Data into and out of iMovie

iMovie ranks a close second to QuickTime Pro in its ability to work with many different file types. And like QuickTime, iMovie can work with image, video, and audio files. However, unlike QuickTime, iMovie always has a video track (which you can remove from QuickTime movies that you create in iMovie by using QuickTime Pro if you don't want it). And its export options are limited for the purposes of converting file types from one to another. However, there might be times when it is the best tool for the job (the most common of which is when you want to create an audio file to use as a soundtrack that includes many different sounds).

Moving Files into iMovie

Back in Chapter 4, you learned how to import files into iMovie for your iMovie projects. Importing files into iMovie for the purpose of converting them into different formats involves the same steps. The file formats that you can import into iMovie include those listed in Table 9.10.

Table 9.10 File Formats You Can Import into iMovie

File Format	Abbreviation/File Name Extension	Where It Is Used
Image Files		
Bit-mapped Graphics	BMP .bmp	Standard image format on Windows computers
Graphics Interchange Format	GIF .gif	A graphics format originally developed by AOL for presenting images online; GIF files are widely used on the Internet for simple images, such as buttons and other graphic elements
Joint Photographic Experts Group	JPEG .jpg	A compressed image file format that achieves excellent quality with substantially smaller files; JPEG is the standard image format for most digital cameras as well as most image applications, such as iPhoto
Photoshop	Photoshop .psd	Adobe's Photoshop is the standard for editing digital images on any platform
Picture Format	PICT .pct	The bit-mapped graphics format standard on Macintoshes
Video Files		
DV Stream	DV Stream .dv	Format required to import QuickTime movies into iMovie or iDVD
Audio Files		
Audio Interchange File Format	AIFF .aiff	Standard audio file format that is supported by most digital media applications; you will use this format frequently in your digital lifestyle projects

Table 9.10 File Formats You Can Import into iMovie (continued)

File Format	Abbreviation/File Name Extension	Where It Is Used
Audio CD	Audio CD .cdda	Audio format for standard audio CDs (by recording from an audio CD using the Record tool)
Motion Picture Experts Group Layer 3	MPEG-3 .mp3	A revolutionary audio format that provides nearly audio CD quality in files that are about a tenth as large

Importing a file of any of the types listed in Table 9.10 into iMovie requires the following steps.

Import Files into an iMovie Project

1. Choose File, Import File (or press ⌘+I).
2. In the Import File dialog, move to the file that you want to import, select it, and click Import. The file will be placed on the Shelf if it is an image or video file or on the Timeline Viewer if it is an audio file.

In the Import File dialog, you can choose All Importable files on the Show pop-up menu. iMovie will then indicate which files you can import by graying out all those that you can't import. Or you can choose a specific file format on the Show pop-up menu, and iMovie will gray out all files other than that format.

NOTE

Oddly, you can import MP3 files into iMovie, although they are not listed on the Show pop-up menu as a valid choice.

Moving Files out of iMovie

iMovie isn't really designed to be a conversion tool; however, you can export any files that you import into iMovie in the QuickTime format. After the file is in QuickTime, you can use QuickTime Player Pro to convert that file into the formats that you learned about earlier in this chapter. This technique has several uses. For example, in Chapter 10, "Creating Soundtracks for Digital Lifestyle Projects," you'll learn how to create an audio file that combines different sounds (such as sound effects, music, and so on) to use as a soundtrack for slideshows or other movies that you create in QuickTime Player or another tool.

> **NOTE**
>
> You can also export movies from iMovie to a DV camera or as a DV file (to use in iDVD, for example). These capabilities are very useful for creating and displaying projects; however, they don't help you convert files from one type to another (unless you want to convert a file into the DV format, which case, iMovie does the job).

Chapter 10

Creating Soundtracks for Digital Lifestyle Projects

Sound is an important part of almost all digital lifestyle projects. From QuickTime movies to slideshows on DVD, what your audience hears is as important as what they see on the screen (and sometimes more important). You can use iTunes and iMovie to create sophisticated soundtracks for any of your digital lifestyle projects, including the following:

- QuickTime movies
- iPhoto slideshows
- DVD slideshows
- iDVD menus

The soundtracks that you develop for these projects can include music, of course, but you can also add sound effects, different layers of music, recorded sounds, and just about any other sound that you can hear.

The general steps to creating a digital lifestyle soundtrack are the following:

1. Design the soundtrack that you need.
2. Use iTunes to produce the music for the soundtrack.
3. Use iMovie to combine the music with sound effects and other sounds that will be part of the soundtrack.
4. Prepare the soundtrack for use.
5. Add the soundtrack to the project.

What You Need for This Project

To produce soundtracks, you need the following:

- The project to which you will add the soundtrack
- iTunes
- The music that you want to use in the soundtrack
- iMovie

◆ Sound effects that you want to use in the soundtrack

◆ QuickTime Pro

◆ The application in which you created the project (such as iDVD)

NOTE

Particularly fun types of sounds to add to your projects are sounds that you capture from VHS and DVD movies. You'll learn how to capture such sounds in Chapter 11, "Adding Video and Sound from Movies or Television Shows to Your Digital Lifestyle Projects."

Designing a Soundtrack

Just like most digital lifestyle projects, the first step in creating a soundtrack is planning it.

Obviously, you need a project if you are going to create a soundtrack for a project.

After you have selected your project, figure out precisely how long you need your soundtrack to be. You might want the soundtrack to occupy the entire project's length, or you might want it to cover only a portion.

To keep your soundtrack project organized, create a folder in which to store the elements that you use in it. This will save time when you create the soundtrack because you won't have to hunt for the "pieces" you will use; they will all be located in the same place.

Selecting the Music for a Soundtrack

If your soundtrack will include music, select the music that you want to include— this task requires some thought. The music you select should enhance your project. For example, if the project includes action (or if you want to make the project seem like it includes more action than it actually does), use music that has a driving beat, such as rock or jazz. If the project involves a special occasion, such as a holiday, choose music that is associated with that holiday. If the project is a slideshow of miscellaneous images, a mellow instrumental piece can be a good choice.

Many digital lifestyle projects involve trips or vacations in different parts of the world. Most areas of the world have specific types of music associated with them; the music associated with an area that you have visited can be a nice complement to a project that you create about that area. For example, when creating a project about a trip to the Smoky Mountains in Tennessee, use music associated with the people who first lived in that area (something featuring banjos is a good choice). Keep your eye out for audio CDs offered in areas that you visit; these can provide unique music for your soundtracks that you might not be able to find elsewhere.

NOTE

When you select your music, make sure that you keep the means by which you will distribute your project in mind. If you are creating a project that you plan to distribute widely, you probably don't want to use music that is copyrighted. You need to use music that you have a license to distribute or license-free music instead. At the end of this chapter, you'll learn about an application called SmartSound Sonicfire Pro that you can use to create a licensed music soundtrack for your digital lifestyle projects. In addition to providing tools you can use to really customize the music in your soundtracks, you will be able to distribute projects that include that music in any way you'd like.

Gather all the music that you will be using; if you are using multiple tracks, make a notation about where you want each track to start and stop in your project. This information will help you when it comes time to mix your soundtrack in iMovie.

Selecting Sound Effects for the Soundtrack

As you plan your soundtrack, identify sound effects that you might want to add. For example, if your project includes images of animals, you might want to add those animals' sounds to the soundtrack. If your project includes vehicles of some kind, sounds from such vehicles might make a nice addition.

As your learned in Chapter 9, "Converting Digital Media into the Formats You Need for Your Digital Lifestyle Projects," you can convert almost any audio file into a format that is compatible with the digital lifestyle applications so when it comes to sound effects, the world (literally) is available to you. For example, many Web sites provide WAV files that you can download and use as sound effects in your projects. When you locate sound effects that you will use or even that you think that you might use, place them in the folder for your soundtrack that you created earlier.

As you learned in Chapter 4, "iMovie: the Swiss Army Knife of Digital Video Software," you can record your own sound effects either directly in iMovie or by first recording them on an external device and then recording them in iMovie.

Just like the music, sound effects should enhance what appears on the screen. Don't go crazy with sound effects; sound effects should be used sparingly because too many sound effects can overwhelm the rest of the project. While music playing throughout a project is usually just fine, you should include sound effects only at key points.

TIP

If you want to get the best results, create a script for your soundtrack that ties specific sounds to specific points in the project. Use this script to guide the creation of your soundtrack.

Using iTunes to Produce the Music Track

After you have selected your music, use iTunes to prepare the music for your projects. To do this, you encode the music in the format you need for your projects. For most projects, you should encode the music in the MP3 format.

If the music you are using is already in your iTunes Music Library, you don't need to encode it because it is already encoded. If the music isn't part of your iTunes Library, you need to add the music to your Library to encode it (see Chapter 2, "iTunes: Burning Down the House" for the steps to do this).

After the music has been encoded, you can open your iTunes Music Library folder to find it.

Find iTunes Music Files

1. In the Finder, open your Home folder.
2. Open the Documents folder.
3. Open the iTunes folder.
4. Open the iTunes Music folder. Within this folder, you will see all of the music in your library. The music is organized into folders with the artist's name that is associated with that music in iTunes (see Figure 10.1).

Figure 10.1 *Your iTunes Music folder contains all of the music you have stored in your iTunes Library.*

Within those folders, you will find folders for each album from that artist that is contained in your Library.

5. Open the album folder that contains the tracks that you want to use.

6. Make copies of the music tracks you will use in your soundtrack in the soundtrack's folder that you created earlier. By making copies, you can freely edit the music without changing the original that remains safely in your Library.

TIP

To make a copy of a file in a new location, such as your soundtrack's folder, hold the Option key down while you drag the file to the location in which you want to store the copy.

Using iMovie to Create the Soundtrack

You should now have a plan for your soundtrack, as well as a folder that contains the music and sound effects that you will use in it (see Figure 10.2).

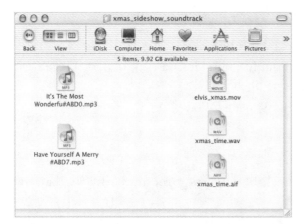

Figure 10.2 *The folder for my soundtrack contains two music tracks and a couple of sound effects in different formats.*

Now it is time to use iMovie to build the soundtrack from the elements that you have selected.

Creating the iMovie Soundtrack Project

Create the iMovie project for your soundtrack.

Create an iMovie Soundtrack Project

1. Launch iMovie.
2. Choose File, New Project.
3. Name the project, choose a location in which to save it, and click Create.

If you are creating a soundtrack for a QuickTime movie in one form or another, import the movie into iMovie. You can use the movie to time the soundtrack you are creating, even if you don't end up using the video track that you import. For example, in Chapter 15, "Building Digital Lifestyle Slideshows," you'll learn how to create slideshows that are of a higher resolution than iMovie can produce; you can create the slideshow in another tool (such as iPhoto) as a QuickTime movie.

Convert the QuickTime movie for which you are creating the soundtrack into a DV Stream file by using QuickTime Player Pro. After you have the DV Stream version of the file, import it into iMovie.

Import a DV Stream File into iMovie

1. Choose File, Import File (or press ⌘+I).

2. Move to the DV Stream file, select it, and click Import. The file will be imported to the iMovie Shelf.

3. Drag the movie to the Timeline Viewer.

Importing the Music

Start creating the soundtrack by importing the music tracks that you have selected.

Import Music Tracks for the Soundtrack

1. Move the Playhead to the position in the movie where you want the first music track to start playing.

2. Choose File, Import File.

3. Move to the first MP3 track that you want to include in the soundtrack, select it, and click Import. The track will be placed in the Audio 2 track of your movie, starting at the current location of the Playhead.

4. Move the Playhead to the location where you want the next music track to start playing.

5. Choose File, Import File.

6. Move to the second MP3 track that you want to include in the soundtrack, select it, and click Import. The track will be placed in the Audio 2 track of your movie, starting at the current location of the Playhead.

7. Repeat Steps 5 and 6 for each music track that you want to include in the soundtrack (see Figure 10.3).

Music tracks

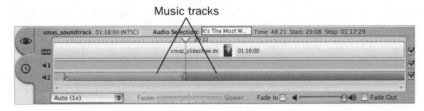

Figure 10.3 *I've added two music tracks to the soundtrack that I am creating.*

Adding Sound Effects

Now add the sound effects to the soundtrack.

Add Sound Effects to the Soundtrack

1. Place the Playhead at the location where you want the first sound effect to begin playing.
2. Choose File, Import File.
3. Move to the first sound effect that you want to place, select it, and click Import. The sound effect will be placed on the Audio 2 track. If there is music over the same portion of the track, the two sounds will play at the same time.

NOTE

If you use a sound effect from iMovie's Audio palette, you can drag it to either Audio track.

---

4. Drag the sound effect to the Audio 1 track so that the sound clips are easier to work with.
5. Repeat Steps 2–4 until all of the sound effects are included in the sound-track (see Figure 10.4).

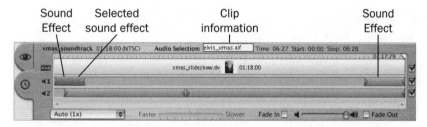

Figure 10.4 *This soundtrack includes two sound effects that are located in the Audio 1 track.*

Adding Recorded Sounds

Use iMovie's recording tools to record narration or other sounds effects if those are called for in your soundtrack's script. (See Chapter 4 to learn how to record sound in iMovie).

Mixing the Soundtrack

After you have placed all the sounds in the soundtrack, it is time to mix the soundtrack. Using the sound editing skills that you learned in Chapter 4, do the following tasks:

- Crop sounds that are too long.
- Move sounds on the Timeline Viewer to change the time at which they play.
- Change the relative volume level of the various sound clips.
- Fade sounds in or out.

If you have imported a video track to use to time the sound effects, you can use that track to ensure that sounds play at the right time and that the soundtrack is the right total length for your project.

If you aren't using a video track as a timing tool, you will have to keep a close eye on the timecode information for your movie. You can select a sound clip and view its information at the top of the Timeline Viewer to see when that sound starts and stops (see Figure 10.5). You can also use the movie's timecode information to monitor the total length of your soundtrack.

Continue mixing your soundtrack until it matches the plan you have for your project.

Figure 10.5 *If you don't have a video track that you can use to time your soundtrack, you have to pay close attention to the time information provided in the Timeline Viewer.*

Preparing the Soundtrack

After you have developed the soundtrack in iMovie, you will need to prepare it for the project in which you will be using it. First export the soundtrack as a QuickTime movie. Then convert it into the format you need for your project.

Exporting the Soundtrack as a QuickTime Movie

First export the soundtrack as a QuickTime movie.

Export the Soundtrack as a QuickTime Movie

1. Choose File, Export Movie (or press ⌘+E).

2. In the Export Movie dialog, choose To QuickTime.

3. On the Formats pop-up menu, choose Expert.

4. In the Image Settings area, enter 10 for the width and the height of the movie's image. Since you aren't going to be using the video track at all, there is no reason to export a lot of data so you should make the video track very small. If you haven't used a video clip as a timing tool, all you will have is a black screen as the video track anyway.

5. In the Audio Settings area, click the Settings button to open the Sound Settings dialog (see Figure 10.6). You will use this dialog to maximize the quality of the soundtrack that you export.

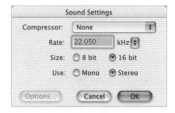

Figure 10.6 *You use the Sound Settings dialog to configure sound properties of the movie soundtrack that you are exporting.*

6. Choose None from the Compressor pop-up menu.

7. Click the pop-up button at the right end of the Rate field and choose 48 kHz. This sets the sampling rate to as high as possible.

8. Make sure that the 16 bit and Stereo radio buttons are selected.

9. Click OK to close the Sound Settings dialog.

10. Click OK to close the Expert QuickTime Settings dialog.

11. Click Export.

12. In the resulting Export QuickTime Movie dialog, name your soundtrack movie, choose a location in which to save it, and click Save. iMovie will

export your movie; the application will display a progress window to let you see how the export is proceeding. When the process is complete, you will have a QuickTime movie containing a very small video track and your soundtrack.

After you have created the QuickTime version of your soundtrack, you need to get rid of the video track.

Delete the Video Track from the Soundtrack Movie

1. Open the soundtrack movie that you created in QuickTime Player.
2. Choose Edit, Delete Tracks.
3. In the Delete Tracks dialog, select Video Track and click OK. The video track will be removed from the movie.

Now, you have a QuickTime version of your soundtrack (see Figure 10.7). If the project for which you have created the soundtrack can work with QuickTime movie files, you are done and are ready to add the soundtrack to your project.

Figure 10.7 *A QuickTime movie version of your soundtrack is useful in many different ways.*

If the project for which you have created the soundtrack can't work with QuickTime movie files, you will need to convert the soundtrack into the format you need.

Converting the Soundtrack to AIFF

Almost every tool that works with sound can handle AIFF files. To convert your QuickTime soundtrack into AIFF, use the following steps.

Convert the Soundtrack into AIFF

1. Open your soundtrack in QuickTime Player.
2. Choose File, Export.

3. In the "Save exported file as" dialog, choose Sound to AIFF on the Export pop-up menu.

4. Click the Options button. The same Sound Settings dialog that you saw when you exported the soundtrack from iMovie will appear.

5. Make sure that the quality is the maximum possible (48kHz as the rate and the 16 bit and stereo radio buttons selected).

6. Click OK to close the Sound Settings dialog.

7. Name the AIFF file, choose a location in which to save it, and click Save. QuickTime Player will export the file as an AIFF file. The progress dialog will inform you about the process. When this process is complete, the AIFF version of your soundtrack is ready for the project in which you want to use it.

Converting the Soundtrack to MP3

Having your soundtrack in the MP3 format can also be useful. For example, you can choose an MP3 to use as a soundtrack when you play a slideshow in iPhoto. To convert your soundtrack into MP3, use the following steps.

Convert the Soundtrack into MP3

1. Launch iTunes.

2. Make sure that the MP3 encoder is selected on the Importing tab of the iTunes Preferences window (see Chapter 2 for more information).

3. Choose Advanced, Convert to MP3.

4. In the resulting Choose Object dialog, move to the QuickTime or AIFF version of your soundtrack, select it, and click Choose. The soundtrack will be imported into iTunes (see Figure 10.8).

5. Select your soundtrack and choose File, Get Info. The Song Information window will appear.

6. Click the Tags tab.

7. Enter your name in the Artist field (see Figure 10.9). You can also rename the track by editing the name that appears at the top of the Info window. This step makes your soundtrack easy to find amidst the many other tracks that are likely to be in your iTunes Library.

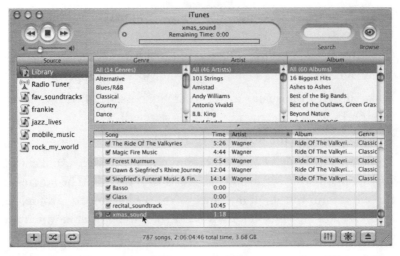

Figure 10.8 *The soundtrack I have created is now part of my iTunes Library.*

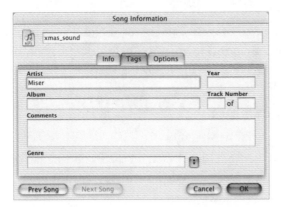

Figure 10.9 *By setting the artist name to your name, you can easily find your soundtrack by searching your iTunes Library for your name.*

8. Open the following folders: Home, Documents, iTunes, iTunes Music, Unknown Artist, and finally the Unknown Album folder. You will see the MP3 version of your soundtrack (see Figure 10.10).

9. Drag the MP3 file to a location from which you will use it (such as a folder for the project for which you have created it).

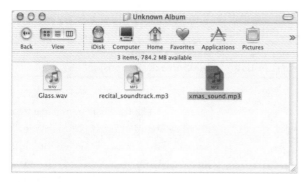

Figure 10.10 *While the album might be unknown, the soundtrack certainly isn't.*

TIP

If you want to leave the soundtrack file in your iTunes Library, make sure that you make a copy of it when you move it (hold the Option key down while you drag the file to a new location). If you don't want to keep the soundtrack in your iTunes Library, move back into iTunes and delete it.

Adding the Soundtrack to a Digital Lifestyle Project

Since you created your soundtrack for a project, you might as well use it. Table 10.1 provides a summary of how you can use the soundtrack in various digital lifestyle applications.

Table 10.1 How to Use Your Soundtrack in Various Digital Lifestyle Applications

Application	Soundtrack Format to Use	How to Add the Soundtrack to a project
QuickTime	.mov .aif	Open either version of the soundtrack. Choose Edit, Select All and then choose Edit, Copy. Move to the QuickTime movie to which you want to add the soundtrack and choose Edit Add. The soundtrack will be added to the QuickTime movie as a new soundtrack.

Table 10.1 How to Use Your Soundtrack in Various Digital Lifestyle Applications (continued)

Application	Soundtrack Format to Use	How to Add the Soundtrack to a project
iPhoto in Slideshow Mode	.mp3	Select the photos that you want to display in a slideshow. Click the Share button and then click the Slide Show button. In the Slide Show Settings dialog, choose Other on the Music pop-up menu. Move to the MP3 version of your soundtrack, select it, and click Open. Click OK. When the slideshow plays, so will your soundtrack.
iMovie	.aif .mp3	Import the soundtrack into the movie using the File, Import File command.
iDVD When Creating a Slideshow	.mp3	Drag the MP3 file to the Audio well in the Slideshow window.
iDVD to Add Sound to a Menu	.mp3	Drag the MP3 file onto the Audio well on the Customize tab.

TIP

You can also add the MP3 version of your soundtrack to iPhoto's Music pop-up menu. See Chapter 3 for the detailed steps to do this.

Creating Soundtracks Like a Pro

You can build very complex and complete soundtracks using the digital lifestyle applications, particularly iMovie. However, matching a soundtrack to a project's content and length can require a substantial amount of time and effort on your part. That is where Sonic Desktop's SmartSound Sonicfire Pro comes in.

This amazing application helps you create very high quality soundtracks for any QuickTime project. Because it is not part of the digital lifestyle applications and costs additional money, I didn't include a chapter on it in Part I. However, this third-party application is (one of the few actually) that warrants some coverage in this book even though it doesn't come from Apple.

SmartSound Sonicfire Pro actually automates the process of creating a soundtrack for a QuickTime movie project. The application's many cool features include the following:

◆ The Maestro feature helps you select and orchestrate music for a soundtrack.

◆ The music collection CDs that are available for the application include many types of royalty-free music (meaning that you can use the projects in which the music is included in any way you'd like).

◆ The application automatically adjusts music tracks to fit the segments of the QuickTime movie that you select. Instead of just chopping the music off or even fading it out, Sonicfire Pro actually changes the music to fit the length of the segment as if the music was designed for that segment (which is actually has been).

◆ The application's editing tools enable you to fine-tune various aspects of the music track, such as the volume levels of specific tracks as they play. For example, you can lower the volume level of a music track when narration is happening, no matter where in the track that occurs.

◆ Sonicfire enables you to save the soundtrack with the movie or you can export it separately, for example, to import it into iMovie or QuickTime Player Pro.

It is stunning how fast you can create professional sounding soundtracks. Not many applications impress me the way this one has. It is truly amazing.

Unfortunately, I don't have room in this book to give this application the coverage it deserves. However, to demonstrate how easy it is to use, the following steps show you the basics of creating a soundtrack in SmartSound Sonicfire Pro.

Create a Professional Sounding Soundtrack in Sonicfire Pro

1. Create the project for which you want to create a soundtrack and save that project as a QuickTime movie or as a DV file.

2. Launch Sonicfire Pro.

3. Choose File, Choose Video.

4. In the resulting dialog, move to the project for which you want to create a soundtrack, select it, and click Open. The movie will open in the applications movie window.

5. Choose Timeline, Maestro. The Maestro tool will appear (see Figure 10.11).

Figure 10.11 *The Maestro tool guides you through the creation of a soundtrack.*

6. Choose the style of music you want by checking one of the radio buttons and then clicking Next. You will see the options available for that music style along with a description of the music and where you might want to use it.

7. Choose the option you want by checking its radio button and clicking Next. You will see the sources you have for that music style and option.

8. Choose the source by clicking its radio button and then clicking Next.

9. Choose the length for the soundtrack and then click Next. If the music isn't already installed on your hard drive, you will be prompted to insert one of the SmartSound music collection CDs. The music will be imported, and you will see a dialog that presents several variations of music from which you can choose (see Figure 10.12).

10. Select the variation you want to preview and click the Play button. The music will play along with the movie in the application's movie window so you can see how well the music matches the project.

11. Continue previewing options until you find the one that is best.

12. Click Finish. The application will create the soundtrack for you and match it to the movie's length. You can then either save the music with the movie or export the soundtrack as a QuickTime movie.

This brief example just scratches the surface of what Sonicfire can do. For example, you can easily create segments of a soundtrack and include different music in each segment. As with an entire movie, the application automatically fits the music to the segment.

Note: You can also import your own music to use in Sonicfire, although the results you get aren't quite as spectacular as they when you use music from the SmartSound collection.

The only downside to the application is that it costs about $349 for the application and a couple of music CDs. Additional CDs are about $69 or $129 depending on the quality that you select. However, if you want to create amazing soundtracks that sound as if they came from a professional studio, the results you get will be more than worth the investment you have to make to get the application.

For more information about this great tool, visit www.smartsound.com/sonicfire/index.html. In addition to lots of detailed information about the application, you can also order a copy.

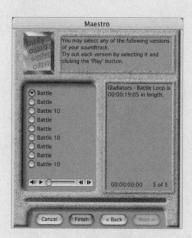

Figure 10.12 *This Maestro has composed several musical options for you to choose from.*

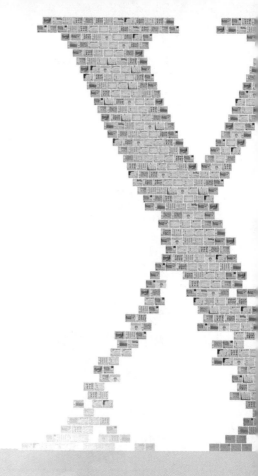

Chapter 11

Adding Video and Sound from Movies or Television Shows to Your Digital Lifestyle Projects

Since it is already Chapter 11, it's time for true confessions. I admit it—I am a television and movie nut (of course, I'm only crazy about certain movies and television shows, but the few that I do like, I *really* like). Of course, being a technology geek, I am required by law to enjoy all the science fiction classics, such as *Star Trek*, *Star Wars*, *Babylon 5*, The *Terminator* series, and so on. But I like lots of other great movies and television shows as well, such as *Braveheart*, *Gladiator*, *Henry the Fifth*, and so on.

For me, one of the most fun parts of the digital lifestyle is capturing great lines, sounds, images, or even entire scenes from my favorite movies and television shows to use in my digital lifestyle projects or to accent my desktop. If you enjoy any movies or television shows, I'll show you how to do this. (If you don't like any movies or television shows, you might want to skip to Chapter 12 now…)

NOTE

Before you start capturing content from VHS or DVD sources, you need to make sure that you remain aware of copyright issues. All content on commercially produced VHS or DVD is copyrighted in one form or another. Almost all content that you record from television sources is also copyrighted. This means that you need to be very careful about extracting this content and using it in your own projects, which is the whole point of this chapter. As I mentioned before, you are probably okay if you use this content *only* for your own amusement (this is usually referred to as "for your own use"). As soon as you start distributing such material, such as posting movies that include copyrighted material on the Web, you move onto dangerous ground from the legal perspective. Just respect material that other people have created as you would want your own work to be respected and you should be fine. A good rule of thumb is that if you are going to distribute a project so that more than one or two people can access it, don't include any material in it that is copyrighted by someone else—unless you have written permission to do so.

What You Need for This Project

To capture and use audio and video content from movies or television shows, you can use the following items:

◆ VCR

◆ DVD player

◆ DV camera

◆ DVD ripping software

◆ Snapz Pro X on a Mac that has an NVidia graphics card

◆ QuickTime Pro

◆ iMovie

Mining Sources of Content

There are lots of great sources of content out there. The four sources that you'll learn about in this chapter are the following:

◆ **Television**. While most of television, whether broadcast, satellite, or cable, is a wasteland, there are a few gems that contain material you might want to include in your digital lifestyle projects. With a VCR and a DV camera, you can capture television content easily.

◆ **Movies or television shows on VHS**. Most anything that is on a VHS tape can be easily brought into the digital lifestyle. And since there are so many types of tapes out there, the VHS world can be your oyster.

◆ **Movies or television shows on DVD**. The DVD format has taken the world by storm, and with good reason. With its amazing quality and great special features, DVD is the media of choice for audio and video enthusiasts.

◆ **QuickTime content**. As you have seen in other parts of this book, lots of great content is available in the QuickTime format. You can find this content primarily on the Web, but QuickTime is also widely used on CD-ROMs and other sources. Including QuickTime material in your projects is a trivial exercise.

Why a FireWire DV Camera Might Be the Only Digitizing System You'll Ever Need

In the olden, predigital lifestyle days, capturing content from VCRs, camcorders, and other sources so that you could work with it on a computer was a real pain. Because the content was *analog*, it couldn't be used directly on a computer. It had to be *digitized* first. And to digitize content, you needed a *digitizer*. These devices, usually in the form of a PCI card, were expensive and quite difficult to work with, and the software you used to work with these devices was no walk in the park either. After lots of money and tons of time and effort, the results were usually marginal—at best. Unless you were a professional and had access to the best hardware and software, capturing content at a decent quality level was almost impossible.

And then came DV. Because DV cameras capture content in a digital form, there is no need to digitize that content. With FireWire, this content can be moved onto a computer very easily. Thus, the digital lifestyle came into its own.

A side benefit of DV cameras is that in addition to capturing content through their lenses, they can often record content from an external source. This is way cool because you can connect a DV camera to a VCR or DVD player and record content onto a DV tape. After you do so, you can move that content onto your Mac and work with it just like content you shoot with the DV camera. For most people, a DV camera will prevent you from ever having to fuss with a digitizer, and trust me, that is a good thing.

Capturing Content from VHS

There are two sources of content on VHS tape that you can capture and use in your projects. One source includes television shows or movies that you record yourself. The other source is commercially produced VHS content. The process that you use to capture material from either of these sources is very similar. The only difference is how the content gets onto a VHS tape in the first place.

The following are the four general tasks you will do to capture content from a VHS source:

1. Obtain the VHS content that you want to use.
2. Connect the output of the VCR to the input of your DV camera.

3. Use the DV camera to record the segments containing the content that you want to use.

4. Import that content into iMovie.

NOTE

Some VHS content is copy-protected and your DV camera won't be able to record it properly. When you attempt to record a copy-protected VHS tape, wavy lines and other artifacts will usually destroy the image, and the images will usually appear in black-and-white. The images from a copy-protected VHS tape will generally be unusable. In such cases, you will probably have to resort to a digitizing system in order to be able to capture that content on your Mac (digitizing systems are beyond the scope of this book). However, you can usually capture good quality audio from VHS tapes, even if they are copy-protected.

Obtaining VHS Content

If you are going to use a commercially recorded VHS tape to capture content, you don't need to do anything to obtain the content—assuming that you have the tape that contains the material you want to use. If you are going to record the content yourself, record it as you would record anything else.

TIP

Using a VCR to record content is straightforward; however, one setting that you should check is the recording speed. Make sure that you choose the SP or standard option for recording. This option uses more videotape, but the quality of the recording will be better and thus the quality of the content you capture will also be better. (Most VCRs have at least two recording speed settings. The standard setting records less on a given tape length, while the extended play setting records more on a given tape length. However, the standard setting will provide a better quality playback so you should use that when you are capturing material for your digital lifestyle projects.)

Connecting a DV Camera to a VCR

To capture content from the VCR onto your DV camera, connect the output of your VCR (that normally goes into a television or A/V receiver) to the input of your DV camera. Usually, you can use the same cable that you use to record from the DV camera to the VCR. On many DV cameras, you even connect this cable to the same port, regardless of whether you are recording on the camera or outputting what you have recorded to a VCR. This port is usually called the Audio/Video (A/V) port, Input/output port, or something similar. The cable you need should have been provided with the camera. When you have the camera connected, your configuration should look something like that in Figure 11.1.

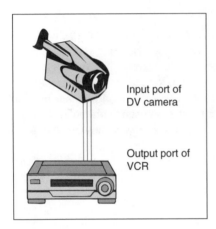

Input port of
DV camera

Output port of
VCR

Figure 11.1 *If you connect the output of your VCR to the input of your DV camera, you can record content from a VHS tape on a DV tape.*

Check the VCR's Connection to Your DV Camera

1. Power up the VCR and the DV camera.

2. Play the VHS tape. You should see its output in the Monitor screen on the DV camera. If you do, your capture system is ready to go. If not, check the connection to make sure that you are connected to the output port of the VCR. If the connection looks okay, make sure that your DV camera is capable of recording from an external source and that you have it set in the correct mode to do so (check the user manual).

Recording VHS Content on a DV Camera

Recording VHS content on a DV camera is trivial.

Record Content from a VCR on a DV Camera

1. Locate the content on the VHS tape that you want to capture.

2. Position the tape so that you are just before that content (allow some "wasted" space at the beginning of the capture).

3. Start recording on the DV camera.

4. Play the VHS tape until it finishes the segment you want to capture.

5. Stop the DV camera.

6. Repeat the previous steps until you have captured all of the content you want. You will have this content on a DV tape just as if you had recorded it using the camera's lens.

TIP

Many DV cameras have a passthrough feature. With this feature, the camera can output through the FireWire port whatever is coming into the camera through the A/V port. This means that you don't have to record the output from the VCR; you can simply pass it through the DV camera so that it goes directly into iMovie without having to record it to a DV tape. Of course, this requires that you have the camera connected to your Mac and a VCR at the same time.

Importing VHS Content into iMovie

After you have recorded content from VHS, you can import it into iMovie just like content you have captured using the camera's lens.

NOTE

For the detailed steps to import content from a DV camera into iMovie, see Chapter 4.

Import Captured Content into iMovie

1. Open iMovie and open or create the project in which you will use the content you have captured.

2. Import the content from the DV camera. When you are done, the clips will be just like those you captured with the camera itself (see Figure 11.2). You can edit them, place them in movies, and so on.

If the VHS content is from a 16 x 9 or widescreen version, the clip you capture will have black bars at the top and bottom of the screen, just as it does when you play that content on a 4 x 3 television. There isn't anything you can do about that with iMovie.

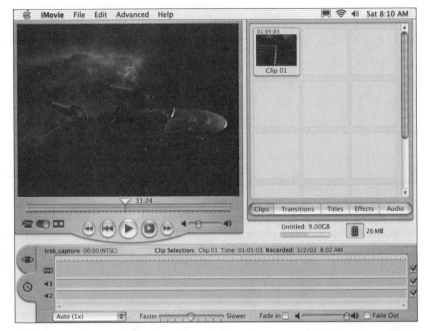

Figure 11.2 *I captured this clip from the VHS version of the movie "Star Trek: First Contact."*

NOTE

Some DV cameras enable you to capture content in the 16 x 9 format. If you are going to be mixing footage you shoot with content from a 16 x 9 or widescreen VHS, you should also capture content in the 16 x 9 format with your DV camera.

NOTE

You can also capture audio clips from the VHS content you imported into iMovie, such as to create an alert sound or sound effect. You'll learn how to do this in the next chapter.

Capturing Still Images From VHS Content

You can also capture still images from VHS content. For example, you might want to use such images as desktop pictures or you might want to print them. You can create an image from a clip you have captured by using the following steps.

Capture Still Images from VHS Content in iMovie

1. Select the clip that contains the image you want to capture.

2. Move the Playhead so that the image you want appears in the Monitor.

3. Choose File, Save Frame As (or press ⌘ + F).

4. In the Save Frame As Image dialog, choose the format for the image on the Format pop-up menu; for most purposes, you should choose JPEG.

5. Choose a location in which to save the file, name it, and click Save.

6. Open the image in a viewing application or import into the application in which you want to use it (see Figure 11.3). For example, you can view the image in the Preview application or you can import it into iPhoto.

Figure 11.3 *Here is an image of the Enterprise that I captured from the movie clip I imported into iMovie.*

Capturing Content from DVD

Because the DVD format offers so many benefits, all the best content comes on DVD these days. There are several ways to get DVD content onto your Mac. The easiest way is to record content from a DVD to a DV camera just like you do with VHS content. Unfortunately, because most DVDs are copy-protected, this method often does not work. The harder way is to rip a DVD. While this is much more work than recording, it almost always works.

Recording Content from DVD

For those DVDs that aren't copy-protected, you can use the same process to capture content as you do for VHS content. Simply connect the DV camera to a DVD player instead of a VCR. Otherwise, the steps are exactly the same.

If you try this with a DVD that is copy-protected, which most DVDs that contain recent movies are, the results will be terrible. The images will be distorted by wavy lines and will usually be in black-and-white. The video portion will be unusable. In such a case, you will need to use the ripping technique that is described in the next section.

TIP

If all you are interested in is the audio portion of a DVD's content, you might be able to record that successfully even from a copy-protected DVD. Even though the video track will be junk, the audio track often can be recorded just fine.

Ripping Content from DVD

There are applications that enable you to extract, more commonly called ripping, content from a DVD and create QuickTime versions of that content. After you have the DVD's content in QuickTime, you can use it in your digital lifestyle projects.

This process works on just about any DVD.

To rip content from a DVD, you need a DVD ripping application. There are several available on the Internet, and most of them are freeware.

However, there are complex legal issues surrounding the software that enables you to rip DVD content, especially if you live in the United States. In fact, in the United States, distributing such software is currently illegal.

Because of this, I can't tell you about the details of this process. However, I can describe it generally since talking about it isn't illegal.

Basically, you use a DVD extracting application to extract the video track and the audio track from the DVD. The tools that you use to do this are usually rough and sometimes don't work at all. And you need tons of disk space to be able to extract an entire DVD's worth of content—when it does work, the process takes a long time. If the process works, you end up with a file containing the video and another containing the audio.

You then use converters to decode these files into usable formats. For example, you convert the video file into QuickTime and the audio into AIFF or MP3. You can then open the video file in QuickTime Player, open the audio file and copy it, and then add the copied audio into the video file. Save the file, and you have a DVD movie in the QuickTime format. You can use this just like other QuickTime movies, such as copying parts of it, exporting sounds from it, and so on.

If you want to explore how this process works in more detail, search the Web for information on DVD ripping and Macintosh. You will find information resources and if you live in an area where the software isn't illegal, you can download a DVD extracting application. You'll also need to download decoding applications that you can use to translate files that you extract into usable formats.

Capturing Still Images from DVD

Because DVD content is encoded, you can't use the Mac's built-in screen capture feature to capture images from a DVD—if you try, all you will get is a black screen.

Even though ripping content from a DVD is problematic, you can capture images from a DVD fairly easily—if you have a Mac equipped with an NVidia graphics card that is. To determine if you have an NVidia graphics card, use the Apple System Profiler application or check the documentation that came with your Mac.

If you do have an NVidia graphics card, you can use Ambrosia Software's excellent screen capture utility Snapz Pro X to capture images when you play a DVD in OS X's DVD Player application. (In fact, all the screenshots in this book were captured with Snapz Pro). To download a copy of Snapz Pro, visit www.AmbrosiaSW.com, click the Utilities tab, and look for the Snapz Pro X section. Download and install the application on your Mac. (You can use the application on a trial basis for 30 days; after that you need to register it, which costs about $30 without QuickTime movie support.)

After you have installed and configured Snapz Pro, using it to capture a DVD image is simple.

Capture a Still Image from a DVD By Using Snapz Pro X

1. Insert the DVD containing the image that you want to capture and play it in the DVD Player application using the full-screen mode.

2. When you get to an image that you want to capture, pause the DVD using DVD Player's controls.

3. Hide DVD Player's Controller and Info window if they are visible.

4. Launch Snapz Pro X and activate it (by default, you press ⌘ + Shift + 3 to do so, but you can set any hot keys that you want). The Snapz Pro X window will appear.

5. Click the Screen button.

6. In the resulting dialog, name the image you are capturing.

7. Press Return. The image will be captured and placed in your Pictures folder—unless you tell Snapz Pro X to store it elsewhere (see Figure 11.4). You can use this image in your digital lifestyle projects or anywhere else for that matter.

Figure 11.4 *Here I captured an image from the excellent For All Mankind DVD*

Using Captured Content in Your Digital Lifestyle Projects

After you have captured content from DVD or VHS sources, there are lots of ways to use that content. These include the following:

◆ Import content into iMovie and extract audio clips from it for sound effects or system alert sounds.

◆ Add video or sound from content you have converted into QuickTime into your own QuickTime movies.

◆ Import content into iMovie and use it in your iMovie projects.

◆ Use images from your favorite movies as menu elements on a DVD that you create in iDVD.

◆ Add audio and video elements from your favorite movies and television shows to your desktop (you'll learn how in the next chapter).

Making a Resolution (Change That Is)

When capturing content from movies (whether on VHS or DVD), the format in which that movie was created becomes important. The standard format for analog television is 4 x 3 while movies are shot in 16 x 9 or widescreen format. If you mix the formats in an iMovie project for example, the results might not be too pleasing as the application scales the content to match its current format.

You can use QuickTime Pro to resize content to better match the format of the project in which you are using it. To learn how to do that, see Chapter 1.

Chapter 12

Customizing Your Mac OS X Desktop with Digital Media

If you are like most Mac users, you like to make your Mac reflect your own personality and preferences by customizing your desktop. The great news for Mac OS X users is that the digital lifestyle applications enable you to create and add all sorts of unique elements to your desktop. In this chapter, you'll learn how to customize your Mac by doing the following:

- Creating and using your own alert sounds
- Creating and applying your own desktop pictures
- Creating your own screen saver

What You Need for This Project

To create and use your own desktop elements, you need the following:

- QuickTime Pro
- iTunes
- iPhoto
- iMovie

Creating and Using Your Own Alert Sounds

When your Mac needs to get your attention, it plays an alert sound, and Mac OS X includes a number of different sounds that you can choose as your alert sound. But with the digital lifestyle applications, you can capture and use just about any sound as your alert sound.

Capturing Alert Sounds

The sources of alert sounds for your Mac are nearly endless. Following is a brief list of some possible sources of alert sounds for you to consider using:

◆ Movies or television shows (you can learn how to capture content from these items in Chapter 11)

◆ QuickTime movies that you create or download

◆ Your iMovie projects

◆ Sounds that you download from the Internet

◆ Sounds that you record in iMovie

◆ Music clips that you capture in iTunes

Whatever source you choose, you need to capture the specific sound you want to use in a file of one type or another. How you do this depends on the specific source file that you select. If you have read through many chapters of this book, you should have a good idea how to do this in the digital lifestyle applications. However, as a refresher, in the following sections, you'll see a summary of the steps you use for various types of sources.

Creating an Alert Sound in iMovie

You can create an iMovie project just to create an alert sound. The benefit of this method is that you can use iMovie's audio tools to create a complex alert sound. For example, you can fade sounds in, fade them out, and even layer sounds. (See Chapter 4 to learn how to create and work with sounds in iMovie.)

After you have created the alert sound "movie," you can export it as a QuickTime movie. Then you can use QuickTime Player to remove the video track and to convert the sound into the appropriate format. (See Chapter 9 to learn how to export QuickTime files in various formats.)

Capturing an Alert Sound from a QuickTime Movie

Capturing an alert sound from a QuickTime movie is simple. Just open the movie, crop the section of the movie that you want to use, and export that movie in the format you want to use the sound that you have selected as an alert sound. (To use QuickTime Player's tools to edit a QuickTime movie, see Chapter 1.)

TIP

A great source of QuickTime movies from which you might want to extract sounds for alert sounds are the QuickTime movie trailers that are available on www.apple.com/quicktime/.

Capturing an Alert Sound from the Internet

There are millions of sound files on the Internet that you can download to use as alert sounds. Many of these will already be AIFF files, in which case they are ready for you to use as alert sounds. If they aren't in AIFF (for example, many sounds are available in the WAV format), you can use QuickTime Player to convert those sounds into AIFF. (See Chapter 9 to learn how to convert sounds into AIFF.)

Preparing Alert Sounds

In order to use a sound as an alert sound, you need to first convert it into the AIFF format. To do this, you can use QuickTime Pro.

Convert a Sound into AIFF

1. Open the file in QuickTime Player Pro. If the file isn't of the .mov type, you might need to open it by choosing File, Import. Then select the file and click Open. The file will appear in a QuickTime Player window.

2. If you want to use only a part of the file as an alert sound, crop the file as needed until only the portion containing the alert sound remains. If the file also contains a video track, you can delete the track if you want to, but it isn't necessary to do because QuickTime Player will only export the audio portion when you choose to export to AIFF. When you are done, the movie should contain the alert sound you want to use (see Figure 12.1).

Figure 12.1 *This is a sound effect I captured from the movie "Star Trek: First Contact."*

3. Choose File, Export.

4. In the "Save exported file as" dialog, choose Sound to AIFF on the Export pop-up menu (see Figure 12.2).

5. Name the file, choose a location in which to save it, and click Save. The alert sound will be converted to the AIFF format and saved in the location that you selected.

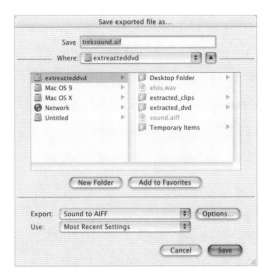

Figure 12.2 *When you use QuickTime Pro's Export feature, you can convert most digital audio files into the AIFF format.*

In a bit of Mac OS X quirkiness, you must use the .aiff file name extension for alert sounds even though most applications, including QuickTime Pro, append .aif to AIFF file names. You must change the name of the AIFF version of the alert sound that you created so that it has the required extension.

Change the .aif File Extension to .aiff

1. Move to the location in which you saved the alert sound (see Figure 12.3).
2. Select the .aif file and press ⌘+I to open its Info window.
3. Choose Name & Extension on the pop-up menu.
4. In the File system name box, change the file name extension from .aif to .aiff (see Figure 12.4).
5. Close the Info window. You will see a warning prompt explaining that changing the file name extension may cause the document to open in a different application.
6. Click Use .aiff. The file name extension will be changed to .aiff, and the sound will be ready for you to install.

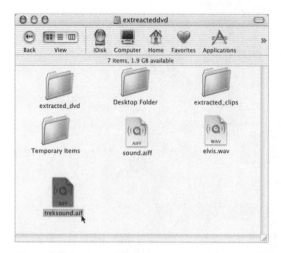

Figure 12.3 *QuickTime Player appends the .aif file name extension to AIFF files that you export.*

Figure 12.4 *What a difference an "f" makes.*

Installing Alert Sounds

There are two ways in which you can install alert sounds that you create. You can install them so that only specific users will be able to choose them, or you can install them so that anyone who uses your Mac will be able to choose them.

Installing Alert Sounds for Individual Users

Installing your alert sounds for individual users takes only a few mouse clicks.

Install an Alert Sound for a Specific User

1. Log in under the user account for which you want to make your new alert sounds available.
2. Open the User's Home folder (yours if you are currently logged in).
3. Open the Library folder.
4. Open the Sounds folder.
5. Drag the alert sounds into the Sounds folder. This makes them available for the currently logged-in user to choose as the alert sound.

Installing Alert Sounds for All Users

You can also add alert sounds to the system so that they will be available to all the user accounts on your machine. However, to do this, you must log in under the root account. Logging in under the root account is beyond the scope of this book. However, information on creating and using a root account under Mac OS X is widely available (for an example, see my book *Special Edition Using Mac OS X*).

Install an Alert Sound for All Users

1. Log in under your Mac's root account.
2. Open the Mac OS X startup volume.
3. Open the System folder on the Mac OS X startup volume.
4. Open the Library folder in the System folder (not the Library folder that is at the root of the Mac OS X startup volume).
5. Open the Sounds folder.
6. Drag the alert sounds into the Sounds folder.
7. Log out of the root account. The alert sounds that you installed will be available to anyone who uses your Mac.

Choosing an Alert Sound

To make your new alert sound active, do the following steps.

Choose an Alert Sound

1. Open the System Preferences utility.
2. Click the Sound icon to open the Sound pane.

3. Click the Alerts tab if it isn't already selected.

4. Scroll down the window until you see your new alert sound (see Figure 12.5).

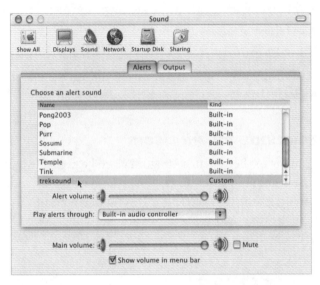

Figure 12.5 *Since I've added the treksound.aiff file to my Sounds folder, it is available as an alert sound.*

NOTE

Alert sounds that you have added to the system are indicated by "Custom" in the Kind column of the Sound pane. If you add the alert sound to the system by being logged in under the root account, the sounds you add would be of the Built-in kind.

---

5. Select your alert sound, and it will play.

6. Use the Alert volume slider to change its relative volume level.

7. Quit the System Preferences utility. When your Mac needs to notify you, it will play your custom alert sound.

Creating and Using Your Own Desktop Pictures

Most of us spend a lot time staring at our Macs. Why not see something you want to see rather than what someone else has made available to you? You can apply your own images to your desktop to make your Mac your own.

Capturing Desktop Pictures

You can use just about any image as a desktop picture, include JPEGs, TIFFs, and PICTs, and so on. Here are some ideas for some images that you might want to use as a desktop picture:

◆ Images in your iPhoto Library

◆ Frames from an iMovie that you have created

◆ Frames from a QuickTime movie that you or someone else has created

◆ Images that you download from the Web

◆ Images from your favorite DVD movie

◆ Images you created by using a scanner

Throughout the other chapters of this book, you have learned many ways to use the digital lifestyle applications to create your own images from many sources. Following are some reminders in case you have a short memory like I do:

◆ In iPhoto, select the images you want to export, click the Share button, and then click the Export button. Use the resulting dialog to set a resolution for the images you are exporting and choose a save location. (See Chapter 3 for the details.)

◆ In iMovie, view the frame that you want to export as an image and choose File, Save Frame As. In the resulting dialog, choose a format (JPEG is usually the best choice), name the file, choose a location, and save the frame.

◆ If you have an NVidia-equipped Mac and a copy of Snapz Pro X, play a DVD in full-screen mode and take a screenshot.

Preparing Desktop Pictures

After you have captured the image you want to use, there isn't much preparation that you need to do to it before you can use it as a desktop image. About the only factor of significance is the resolution of the image in comparison to the desktop resolution that you are using.

If you use a small image, such as 640 x 480, on a large desktop, such as 1280 x 1024, Mac OS X has to rescale the image quite a lot to make it fill the screen. Dramatic changes in size like this can reduce the quality of the image significantly. For best results, the image you use as a desktop picture should be equal to or slightly larger than the desktop resolution in which you most commonly work.

TIP

When you export images from your iPhoto Library, you can choose the size at which the images are exported. When exporting images for your desktop, choose your desktop's resolution as the size at which the images are exported.

Similarly, the orientation and proportions of the image that you use should be similar to your desktop. Since the desktop is in the landscape format, landscape images work best. You can use a portrait-oriented image, but Mac OS X will scale the image to fill the screen, which can result in the image being distorted or having only a portion of the image visible onscreen.

If the image you want to use is significantly different than the desktop resolution you use, consider using an image editing application to resize the image to better match your desktop resolution. If you want to use a portrait-oriented image, you can create a background for it and composite your image and the background together so that the total image has the landscape orientation and is sized appropriately.

TIP

Even if an image isn't sized similarly to the resolution of your desktop, you can quickly apply it to your desktop. If Mac OS X handles the resizing decently and the image looks okay to you, you can skip the editing step. If not, the time you took to preview the image on your desktop won't be significant.

Applying Pictures to the Desktop

You use the Desktop pane of the System Preferences utility to set your desktop picture.

Apply Images to Your Desktop

1. Open the System Preferences utility.
2. Click the Desktop icon to open the Desktop pane (see Figure 12.6). The image currently being displayed on your desktop is shown in the Image well.

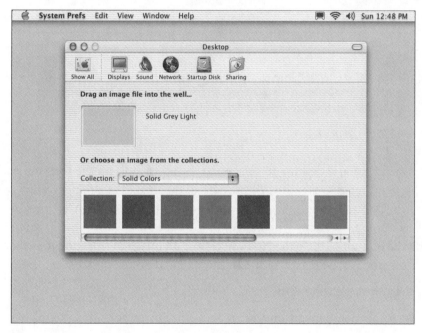

Figure 12.6 *The desktop picture I have to use while writing a book can be described in one word, boring.*

3. Drag the image that you want to apply to the desktop from a Finder window onto the Image well. The image will be applied to your desktop. To see it in its full glory, quit or hide the System Preferences utility (see Figure 12.7).

Figure 12.7 *Ah, that's better.*

You can also choose desktop images using the other tools on the Desktop pane of the System Preferences utility. To preview all the images in a folder (called collections in Desktop lingo), select the collection that you want to view on the Collection pop-up menu. The images in the collection will appear in thumbnails along the bottom of the pane. You can choose an image by selecting it—when you do, the image will be placed in the Image well and on the desktop.

The default image collections are the following:

◆ Apple Background Images
◆ Nature
◆ Abstract
◆ Solid Colors

The other options on the pop-up menu are Pictures Folder and Choose Folder. If you select Pictures Folder, you will see the images are at the root of your Pictures folder (if images are contained in subfolders, they won't be shown). If you select Choose Folder, you can select any folder that you can access. When you choose a folder, the images that can be used as desktop pictures will be shown.

TIP

When you use the Choose Folder option to select a folder, that folder is added to the Collections pop-up menu until you choose a different folder (the Collections pop-up menu remembers only one of your folders at a time).

Unfortunately, the current version of Mac OS X does not allow you to apply a folder of images, whereby your Mac chooses a different image each time you start up or log in. Previous versions of the Mac OS included this feature, so hopefully future versions will include it again. If you want to be able to rotate desktop images automatically, you will need to install an application to provide this feature.

NOTE

If you have multiple monitors attached to your Mac, each monitor can have its own desktop image. When you click the Desktop icon, a Desktop pane will appear for each monitor. You can drag different images into each Image well to apply those images to the various monitors you are using.

Creating and Using Your Own Screen Saver

Mac OS X's built-in screen saver enables you to create a custom screen saver by using your own images.

Capturing images for a screen saver is just like capturing images for the desktop. You can use the common image formats; for best results, your images should be sized and proportioned so that they look good with the desktop resolution that you use.

TIP

To create a screen saver consisting of images in your iPhoto Library, start by creating an album in iPhoto and placing your screen saver photos in that album. Then export the album into the screen saver folder that you created previously. When exporting the album from iPhoto, remember to choose a resolution that is close to the resolution that you use for your desktop.

To create your screenshot's content, create a new folder in the Finder and place the images that you want the screen saver to display in it.

To configure your custom screen saver, do the following steps.

Configure a Custom Screen Saver

1. Open the System Preferences utility.
2. Click the Screen Saver icon to open the screen saver pane.
3. Click the Screen Savers tab if it isn't selected already.
4. Select the Slide Show screen saver. The images in your Pictures folder will be selected automatically (see Figure 12.8).

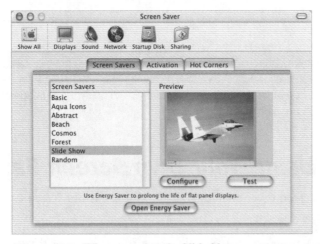

Figure 12.8 *When you select the Slide Show screen saver module, the Preview window in the Screen Saver pane shows the contents of your Pictures folder.*

5. Click Configure.
6. In the sheet that appears, move to the screen saver folder that you created previously, select it, and click Open. The contents of your screen saver folder will appear in the Preview window (see Figure 12.9).
7. Click Test to preview your screen saver. Move the mouse to stop the test.
8. Click the Activation tab (see Figure 12.10).
9. Use the slider to set the amount of idle time that passes before the screen saver is activated.

Figure 12.9 *I've switched the contents of the screen saver to be the images in my screen saver folder.*

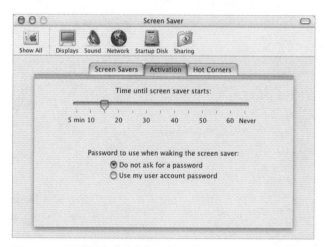

Figure 12.10 *Use the Activation tab to control when the screen saver is activated.*

10. Use the radio buttons to determine if a password is required to exit the screen saver.

11. Click the Hot Corners tab.

12. Use the tab's controls to set corners to which you can move the pointer to activate the screen saver (click a corner's checkbox once) or to prevent it from being activated (click a corner's checkbox twice).

13. When you are done configuring your screen saver, quit the System Preferences utility. Prepare to be impressed when your custom screen saver becomes active!

NOTE

When you use multiple monitors, different images are displayed on the screen saver in each monitor

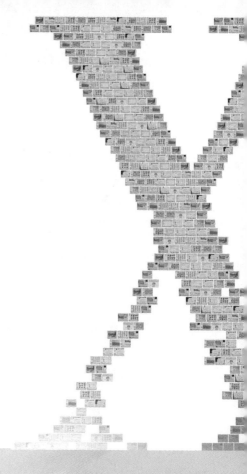

Chapter 13

Adding Digital Tricks to iMovie's Bag

As you learned back in Chapter 4, "iMovie: The Swiss Army Knife of Digital Video Software," and have seen in other places in this book, iMovie is a great application that enables you to do awesome things with your digital lifestyle movies. "Out of the box" iMovie includes lots of neat tools that you can use to create amazing movies. But wait, there's more.

You can add to iMovie's tool set to do even more with your movies. In this chapter, you'll learn how to do the following tasks:

◆ Add more transition, title, and special effects with Apple's iMovie Plug-in Pack

◆ Create titles over backgrounds other than the basic black that is available in iMovie by default

◆ Add sound effects that others have created

◆ Use iMovie to create sound effects

◆ Use other applications to create sound effects

◆ Add the sound effects that you create to iMovie's Audio palette so that you can easily include them in your movies

What You Need for This Project

To add to iMovie's bag of tricks, you need to have the following:

◆ iMovie (duh)

◆ Apple's Plug-in Pack

◆ An image editing or painting program (to create new backgrounds)

◆ QuickTime Pro to capture sound effects and to translate sound into AIFF

Adding Transitions, Titles, and Effects

As you've learned to use iMovie, you have seen how impressive its effects can be. iMovie includes a number of transitions, titles, and special effects that you can use in your movies. That's the good news. The even better news is that you can expand the effects available to you.

Adding the iMovie Plug-in Pack

Apple provides additional effects that you can download and install in iMovie to provide additional effects to you.

Download the iMovie Plug-in Pack

1. Move to www.apple.com/imovie.
2. Scroll down the page until you see the iMovie Plug-in Pack link (see Figure 13.1).
3. Click the iMovie Plug-in Pack link.
4. Follow the on-screen instructions to download the Plug-in Pack.
5. Double-click the iMoviePlugin.smi file that you downloaded.
6. Click Yes when you see the license agreement screen. The Plug-in Pack volume will be mounted on your Mac.

Figure 13.1 *Apple's iMovie Web site offers a wealth of iMovie information and tools.*

The steps you follow to install the tools in the Plug-in Pack depend on the version of iMovie that you are using. The current version of iMovie at the time of this writing is 2.1.1. To add the effects contained in the Plug-in Pack to this version of iMovie, do the following steps.

Install the iMovie Plug-in Pack

1. Quit iMovie if it is running.

2. Open the Library folder that is in your Home folder.

3. If you don't already have an iMovie folder in your Library folder, create a new folder and call it iMovie. If you already have an iMovie folder, skip this step.

4. Open the iMovie folder in your Library folder.

5. If there isn't a Plug-ins folder in the iMovie folder, create a new folder and call it Plug-ins. If there is already a folder called Plug-ins, skip this step.

6. Drag the iMovie Plugin Pack folder from the iMovie Plugin Pack volume and drop it inside the Plug-ins folder (see Figure 13.2).

7. Open iMovie again.

NOTE

Adding the Plug-in to other versions of iMovie is similar to the previous steps. Check the ReadMe file that comes with the Plug-in Pack for the details.

Figure 13.2 *These plug-in effects are ready to roll.*

To see the new tools on the palettes, open the Transitions, Titles, and Effects palettes. You will see a number of new tools on these palettes. You can use these tools just like those that are installed on the palettes by default (see Figure 13.3). (See Chapter 4 to learn how to use iMovie's effects tools.)

NOTE

The effects that you add to the Plug-ins folder in your Home directory are available only to you. In order to make those effects available to other user accounts, you will have to repeat the installation steps while logged in under those other user accounts.

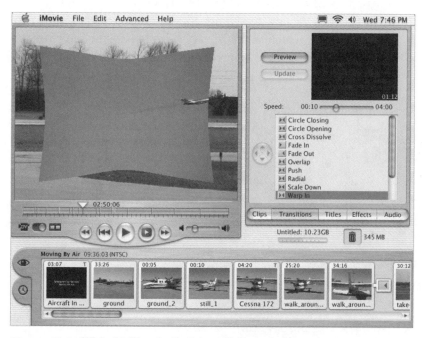

Figure 13.3 *With the Plug-in Pack installed, you have access to even more cool transitions (such as this Warp In transition), titles, and special effects.*

Manipulating iMovie Effects

iMovie's default effects are also provided by plug-ins, but the default plug-ins are part of the iMovie application bundle. You can use Mac OS X's information window to see the plug-ins that are installed and active for iMovie currently, and you can also disable those plug-ins should you want to do so.

One reason that you might want to disable some of iMovie's effects is that the more effects that iMovie loads when it opens, the more memory the application needs to work. As long as you have plenty of RAM installed, this won't be a problem. But if you have a machine that barely meets Mac OS X requirements, you might want to reduce iMovie's memory signature by disabling effects that you never use.

Disable iMovie Default Effects

1. Open your Applications folder, select the iMovie icon, and choose File, Show Info (or press ⌘+I). The iMovie Info window will appear.

2. On the pop-up menu, choose Plugins. You will see the list of plugins that are installed by default (see Figure 13.4). Some of the plugins are for individual effects (such as the Music Video.bundle that provides the Music Video title effect) while others contain multiple effects (such as the Basic Transitions.bundle that provides iMovie's basic transition effects).

Figure 13.4 *If you have used any of iMovie's effects, some of these names should look familiar to you.*

3. Uncheck the checkbox next to any effects that you want to disable.

4. Close the Info window. The next time that you open iMovie, the effects you disabled will no longer be available.

To enable effects that you have disabled, do the following steps:

Re-enable Effects That You Have Disabled

1. Point to the iMovie application icon, hold the Control key down, and click to open the contextual menu.

2. Choose Show Package Contents. You will see a window called iMovie that contains one folder called Contents.

3. Open the Contents folder (see Figure 13.5).

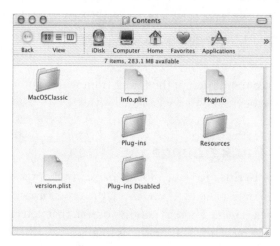

Figure 13.5 *The Contents folder contains various files that iMovie needs to able to function.*

4. Open the Plug-ins Disabled folder. You will see any plug-ins that you disabled by unchecking their checkboxes in the iMovie Info window.

5. Drag the plug-ins that you want to enable from the Plug-ins Disabled folder into the Plug-ins folder. The next time that you open iMovie, the effects will be enabled again (they also reappear in the iMovie Info window).

You can also disable effects that you added by the iMovie Plug-in Pack.

Disable Plug-in Pack Effects

1. Open a folder that is not located in your Library folder (use your Home folder for example) and create a folder called "iMovie Plug-ins Disabled."

2. Open the iMovie folder that is located in the Library folder that is within your Home folder. You will see plug-in pack folders for each plug-in pack installed in your Home folder.

3. Drag effects that you want to disable from the Plug-ins folder to the Plug-ins Disabled folder that you created in Step 1. The effects that you move will not appear on the respective Tool palette the next time that you launch iMovie.

NOTE

If the folder to which you drag an effect is not outside of the Library folder, it might still be loaded when iMovie starts up.

To enable the effects again, place them back in the folder from which you moved them. They will be available the next time that you launch iMovie.

Using Other Than Black Backgrounds for Titles

When you learned how to apply titles to your movies back in Chapter 4, you learned that you can apply them over a clip or, if you check the Over Black checkbox, the title appears over a black screen. There is another option that you can use if neither of these is exactly what you want. This option is to import another background and then apply a title over that background. For example, you might want to use a still image, or you might want to create a different color screen to use as the background for a title.

To create a different color background for a title, use the following steps.

Create a Title Over a Colored Background or an Image

1. Use an image editing application to create a 640 x 480 image filled with the color you want as a background.

TIP

You can use any image that you create as a background. For example, you can create a gradient image as a background, or you can use a photo.

---

2. Save the image as a JPEG file.
3. Move into your iMovie project.

4. Choose File, Import File.

5. In the resulting dialog, move to the image that you saved in Step 2, select it, and click Import. The image will be placed on the Shelf and will be selected (so it will appear in the Monitor).

6. Drag the background image from the Shelf to the Clip Viewer and place it where you want the title to appear.

7. Select the background image clip that you just placed in the movie.

8. Open the Title tools and use them to create a title for the background clip (see Figure 13.6). (See Chapter 4 to learn how to create titles.) Make sure that the Over Black checkbox is not checked or the title will be placed over a black background instead.

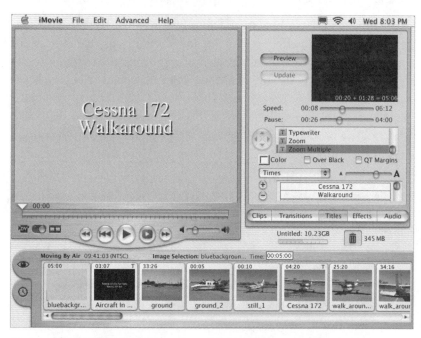

Figure 13.6 *This title appears over a light blue background (since this is a black-and-white book, you will just have to trust me on that).*

9. Drag the title onto the background image clip. The title will be rendered and will appear in the movie over the background image clip. If the duration of the clip is shorter than the length of the title you have created, the duration will be increased so that the title plays in full.

> **TIP**
>
> You can create interesting title clips by capturing an image from your movie to use as the background for the title. Display the frame that you want to use as a background and choose Edit, Create Still Clip. The frame will become a still image clip on the Shelf. You can use this image as a title's background by following the previous steps.

Adding Sound Effects to the Audio Palette

Adding sound effects is a great way to enhance your movies. In Chapter 4, you learned how to use the default sound effects that are included on iMovie's Audio palette, and you also learned how to import sounds to use as sound effects.

In this section, you'll learn how to add your own sound effects to iMovie's Audio palette. Adding a sound effect to the Audio palette means that it is available for you to add to any of your movies (instead of importing it each time you want to use it). You can also remove any of iMovie's default sound effects that you don't ever use.

> **NOTE**
>
> If you are going to use a sound effect only a time or two, it is better to import that sound effect into your movie project rather than adding it to iMovie's Audio palette. The more effects that are installed on iMovie's Tool palettes, the more resources iMovie requires to run.

Adding Sound Effects That Others Have Created

You can find millions (literally) of sound effects on the Internet. Because you can use QuickTime Pro to convert just about any audio file into AIFF, you can use just about any sound file as an iMovie sound effect. The possibilities are almost endless and include WAV, MP3, QuickTime, and many other file formats. Table 13.1 will give you a short list of places to look for sound files to use—if you do any exploring on your own, you will find lots more.

Table 13.1 Example Sources of Sounds You Can Download

URL	Description
new.wavlist.com	Wavelist.com contains thousands of sound files in the WAV format. You can preview these sounds and download any that you want to use.
www.apple.com/imovie/freestuff/audio.html	Apple's iMovie site contains a number of sound files that you can preview and download to your Mac. These include music files and sound effect packs.
www.wavplanet.com	Wavplanet.com also provides many, many sounds in the WAV format.

After you have downloaded sounds to your Mac, you'll need to convert any that aren't in the AIFF format into that format. To learn how to use QuickTime to convert sounds into AIFF, see Chapter 9, "Converting Digital Media into Formats You Need."

Using iMovie to Create Its Own Sound Effects

Using sound effects that other people create is fine, but it can be even more fun to create your own sound effects to install on the iMovie Audio palette. You can use iMovie to create its own sound effects.

First, create the sound effect.

Create a Sound Effect in iMovie

1. Create a new iMovie project.
2. Use the techniques that you learned in Chapter 4 to create the sound effect at the beginning of the project. For example, you can record a sound, add MP3 music, and so on. You can even create a sound effect that is layered (for example, it can include both recorded sound and music).
3. Use iMovie's sound tools to mix the sound. For example, you can fade the sound in, fade it out, change relative volume levels if you include multiple tracks, and so on.

Next, export the sound as a QuickTime movie.

Export the Sound Effect

1. Choose File, Export Movie.
2. In the Export Movie dialog, choose To QuickTime on the Export pop-up menu.
3. Choose CD-ROM Movie, Medium on the Formats pop-up menu.

NOTE

You can choose any format that you would like. Higher quality formats will provide better sound, but the file will also be larger.

4. Click Export.
5. Name the movie, choose a location in which you save it, and click Save. The movie will be exported to the location you selected.

Now use QuickTime Player to remove the video track and convert the sound into AIFF.

Remove the Video Track from the Sound Effect and Save as AIFF

1. Open the movie that you created in QuickTime Player.
2. Choose Edit, Delete Tracks.
3. Select the Video Track.
4. Click Delete. The video track will be removed, and your movie will contain only the sound effect.
5. Preview the sound effect by playing the movie.
6. Choose File, Export.
7. On the Export pop-up menu, choose Sound to AIFF.
8. Name the sound file, choose a location in which to save it, and click Save. The sound effect that you created is ready to be added to the iMovie Audio palette.

Using Other Applications to Create iMovie Sound Effects

You can also use the other digital lifestyle applications to create sound effects. For example, you can use iTunes to convert music from an audio CD into AIFF and then use that AIFF as a sound effect. You can use QuickTime Player Pro to crop the AIFF, and you can use iMovie to fade it. Or you can create sound effects from any file you can open in QuickTime Player (see Chapter 8, "Extracting Video and Audio Elements of Any QuickTime Movie for Your Digital Lifestyle Projects," for the details).

Adding Your Sound Effects to iMovie's Audio Palette

There are two ways to add sound effects to iMovie's Audio palette. One enables only you to access those sound effects, while the other makes them available to every one who uses your Mac.

Adding Sound Effects Only You Can Use

With this technique, only the users who perform the following steps will be able to use the new sound effects.

> **NOTE**
>
> This requires that you use iMovie 2.1.1 or later.

Add Sound Effects Only You Can Use

1. Quit iMovie if it is open.
2. Open the iMovie folder within your Library folder.
3. Create a folder called Sound Effects.
4. Place your AIFF sound effect files in the Sound Effects folder. The next time you open iMovie, the sound effect will appear on the list of available sound effects on the Audio palette (see Figure 13.7).

> **NOTE**
>
> You have to repeat these steps while logged in under another user account to make the sound effect available to that user.

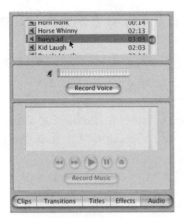

Figure 13.7 *I have added the sound effect called "hueys.aif" to my Audio palette.*

Adding Sound Effects Anyone Can Use

You can also add sound effects so that they appear on the Audio palette for everyone who uses your Mac.

Add Sound Effects So Everyone Can Use Them

1. In the Applications window, select the iMovie icon and open its contextual menu (by holding the Control key down while you click on the icon).

2. On the contextual menu, choose Show Package Contents.

3. Open the Contents folder that is contained in the iMovie folder.

4. Open the Resources folder. You'll see various resources that are available to iMovie (see Figure 13.8).

5. Open the Sound Effects folder. The contents of this folder should look familiar to you since they are the same as the sound effects you see on the Audio palette.

6. Place the sound effects that you want to add to the Audio palette in this folder (see Figure 13.9).

7. Close the folders you opened.

8. Open iMovie and then open the Audio palette. You will see the sound effects that you added (see Figure 13.10).

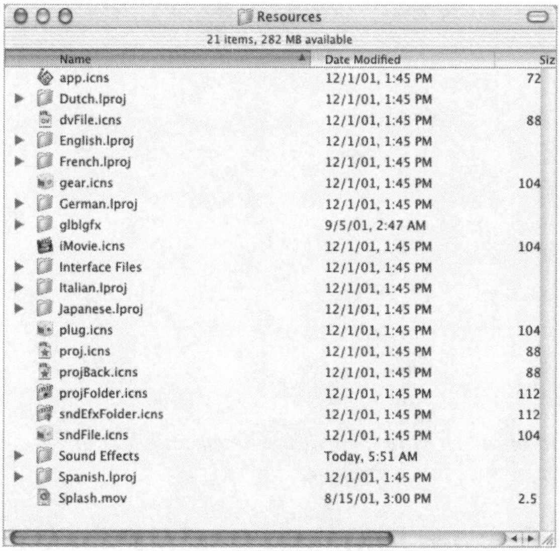

Figure 13.8 *As its name implies, the Resources folder contains iMovie resources.*

Figure 13.9 *I've placed the file called "symbol_crash.aif" in the Sound Effects folder so that it will appear on the iMovie Audio palette.*

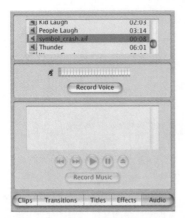

Figure 13.10 *Since I added this sound effect to the iMovie Resources folder, it is available to anyone who uses my Mac.*

Removing Sound Effects from iMovie's Audio Palette

You can also remove sound effects from the iMovie Audio palette. How you do this depends on how the sound effect was installed.

Removing Sound Effects Installed in Your Library Folder

To remove sound effects that are installed in your Library folder, do the following steps.

Remove Sound Effects from Your User Account

1. Open your Library folder, then the iMovie folder, and finally open the Sound Effects folder.

2. Drag the sound effects that you want to remove from this folder to a location outside of your Library folder. The next time you launch iMovie, these sound effects will no longer appear on the Audio palette.

Removing Sound Effects Installed in the iMovie Resources Folder

You can also remove the sound effects installed in the iMovie package (even those that are installed there by default).

Remove Sound Effects for All User Accounts

1. In the Applications window, select the iMovie icon and open its contextual menu (by holding the Control key down while you click on the icon).

2. On the contextual menu, choose Show Package Contents.

3. Open the Contents folder that is contained in the iMovie folder.

4. Open the Resources folder.

5. Open the Sound Effects folder.

6. Drag the sound effects that you want to remove from this folder and place them in another location (you can delete them if you will never want to use them again).

7. Close the folders you opened. The sound effects that you removed from the Sound Effects folder will no longer appear on the Audio palette.

Chapter 14

Creating Your Own Soundtrack CDs

Some great audio CDs have been produced from the soundtracks of equally great movies. In fact, some movie soundtracks are masterworks of music in their own right. Just as the digital lifestyle enables you to create your own movie masterpieces, you can also put your own movie soundtracks on an audio CD.

NOTE

Want some examples of great music that also happens to be an important part of a great movie? Here are some of my favorites: *Star Wars*, *Gladiator*, *Braveheart*, *Glory*, and *The Lord of the Rings: The Fellowship of the Ring*.

Creating your own soundtrack audio CD requires the following general steps:

1. Use iMovie to create the soundtrack.
2. Export the soundtrack as a QuickTime movie.
3. Use QuickTime Player to remove the video track from the movie and save it as an AIFF file.
4. Import the soundtrack into iTunes and burn the audio CD.

What You Need for This Project

To create your own soundtrack audio CD, you need the following:

◆ iMovie
◆ QuickTime Pro
◆ iTunes
◆ A CD-RW or CD-R drive

TIP

One of the best ways to use this project is to create an audio CD from a movie that you have made of a concert you attended or a recital of some kind. This is a great way to capture music that you have experienced in person so that you can listen to it on a CD.

Preparing the Soundtrack

Of course, the first step in putting a soundtrack on CD is creating the soundtrack that you want to put on a CD. The best tool for this is iMovie since you can have multiple soundtracks, including music, sound effects, narration, and so on. You can use iMovie's sound tools to create a soundtrack as part of a movie that you are creating, or you can create a soundtrack as an end in itself.

Using iMovie's tools for these purposes is covered elsewhere in this book. To learn how to use iMovie's audio tools during the creation of a movie, see Chapter 4, "iMovie: the Swiss Army Knife of Digital Video Software." To learn how to create a soundtrack for an audio CD or for other purposes, check out Chapter 10, "Creating Soundtracks for Digital Lifestyle Projects."

Exporting the Soundtrack

After you have created the soundtrack that you are going to put on an audio CD, you need to export it from iMovie as a QuickTime movie.

Export a Soundtrack from iMovie

1. Open your iMovie project if it isn't open already.
2. Do a final preview of your soundtrack by playing the movie and fixing any problems you find.
3. Choose File, Export Movie (or press ⌘+E).
4. In the Export Movie dialog, choose To QuickTime.
5. On the Formats pop-up menu, choose Expert.

6. In the Image Settings area, enter 10 for the width and the height of the movie's image. Since you aren't going to be using the video track at all, there is no reason to export a lot of data so you should make the video track very small.

7. In the Audio Settings area, click the Settings button to open the Sound Settings dialog (see Figure 14.1). You will use this dialog to maximize the quality of the soundtrack that you export.

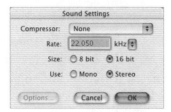

Figure 14.1 *You use the Sound Settings dialog to configure sound properties of the movie soundtrack that you are exporting.*

8. Choose None from the Compressor pop-up menu.

9. Click the pop-up button at the right end of the Rate field and choose 48 kHz. This sets the sampling rate to as high as possible.

10. Make sure that the 16 bit and Stereo radio buttons are selected.

11. Click OK to close the Sound Settings dialog.

12. Click OK to close the Expert QuickTime Settings dialog.

13. Click Export.

14. In the resulting Export QuickTime Movie dialog, name your movie, choose a location in which to save it, and click Save. iMovie will export your movie; the application displays a progress dialog to let you see how the export is proceeding. When the process is complete, you will have a QuickTime movie containing a very small video track and your soundtrack.

Finishing the Soundtrack in QuickTime

After you have created the QuickTime version of your soundtrack, you need to get rid of the video track and put it in a format that you can import into iTunes.

Finish the Soundtrack in QuickTime Player Pro

1. Open the movie containing the soundtrack in QuickTime Player (see Figure 14.2).

Figure 14.2 *This movie has a high-quality soundtrack, but a very tiny video track.*

2. Choose Edit, Delete Tracks.

3. In the Delete Tracks dialog, select Video Track and click OK. The video track is removed from the movie (see Figure 14.3).

Figure 14.3 *This is the same movie without a video track.*

4. Choose Export.

5. In the "Save export file as" dialog, choose Movie to AIFF on the Export pop-up menu.

6. Click the Options button. The same Sound Settings dialog that you saw in iMovie will appear.

7. Make sure that the quality is maximum (48kHz as the rate and the 16 bit and stereo radio buttons selected).

8. Click OK to close the Sound Settings dialog.

9. Name the file, choose a location in which to save it and click Save. QuickTime Player will export the file as an AIFF file. The progress dialog will inform you about the process. When it is complete, the file is ready for the next step.

Burning Your Own Soundtrack CD

After you have exported the soundtrack as an AIFF file, it is ready to go into iTunes so that you can burn a CD.

Add the Soundtrack to Your iMovie Library

1. Open iTunes.

2. Use the Importing tab of the iTunes Preferences dialog to choose the encoder and quality level that you want to use to import the soundtrack file. (See Chapter 2, "iTunes: Burning Down the House," and Chapter 9, "Converting Digital Media into the Formats You Need for Your Digital Lifestyle Projects," for the details of configuring the iTunes encoder.)

3. Choose Advanced, Convert to Format, where Format is the encoder that you have selected, such as MP3.

4. In the Choose Object dialog, move to the soundtrack AIFF file that you created earlier, select it, and click Choose. The soundtrack file will be imported into the iTunes Library. If the soundtrack is a large file, this process can take a while.

TIP

If you want to make the soundtrack easy to find, make yourself the artist. To do so, select the soundtrack and choose File, Get Info. Click the Tags tab and put your name in the Artist field. Click OK. Now you can find this soundtrack by searching the Library for your name.

After the soundtrack is in your iTunes Library, you can burn it onto a CD.

TIP

Before you burn your CD, make sure that you have set iTunes' Burning preference to either Audio CD if you want to be able to play the CD in standard Audio CD players or, MP3 CD if you want iTunes to put an MP3 version on the CD. See Chapter 2 for the details about this.

Burn the Soundtrack CD

1. Create a playlist for your soundtrack.

2. Drag the soundtrack onto the playlist you have created. You can place additional music in this playlist until you have enough music to fill a CD, or your soundtrack can be the only music in the playlist.

3. Select the playlist containing your soundtrack (see Figure 14.4).

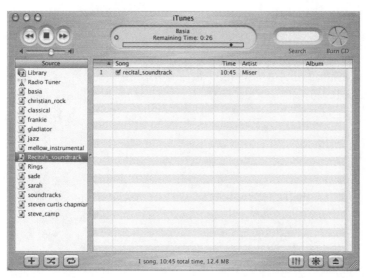

Figure 14.4 *This movie soundtrack is ready to go on CD.*

4. Click the Burn CD button. The CD tray will open, and you will be prompted to insert a blank CD.

5. Insert a blank CD and close the tray. The CD will be mounted on you Mac and after a few moments, you will see the Burn CD button change color.

6. Click the Burn CD button to create the CD. Depending on how much music your CD contains, this process can take a few moments. When the process has finished, iTunes will play a tone and then mount your new CD and start playing it.

If you chose to create an Audio CD, you can listen to your movie soundtrack CD in any CD player! If you chose to create an MP3 CD, you can play it in any device capable of playing MP3 CDs.

Chapter 15

Building Digital Lifestyle Slideshows

Photos are a great way to capture the important (and not-so-important) times in our lives. They are also a great way to express our creative selves. Using digital lifestyle tools, it is easy to capture all kinds of images and use them in many ways. One of the best ways to use your images is by creating a slideshow.

When it comes to the digital lifestyle applications, there are many amazing things you can do to transform a set of static images into an entertaining slideshow that not only makes those images more enjoyable to view, but also enables you to express yourself through the way you choose to present those images to the world.

What You Need for This Project

Creating great slideshows can involve the following tools:

◆ QuickTime
◆ iPhoto
◆ iTunes
◆ iMovie
◆ iDVD

Finding Your Way to Slideshow Paradise

Just like skinning cats, there are many ways to create slideshows. And all methods have their own pros and cons, pluses and minuses, good and bad, yin and yang, well, you get the idea. The three methods you'll learn about in this chapter are summarized in Table 15.1. This information will help you choose a method that you want to use when it comes time to put your images on the big (or not so big) screen. Of course, you don't really need to choose a single method because you can always choose a method that best serves your intentions for any particular slideshow you create.

Table 15.1 Slideshow-Building Techniques for the Digital Lifestyle

Technique	How it Works	Advantages	Disadvantages
The iMovie Method	Build the entire show in iMovie	Simplest method— do everything with one tool Can include transitions, titles, and special effects Easy to vary the time that images appear onscreen Can distribute the slideshow in many ways (QuickTime, DVD, videotape)	Only one, but it is a biggie; iMovie changes the resolution of your images— usually for the worse, making it tough to achieve good image quality
The iDVD Method	Build the slideshow in iDVD, create a soundtrack in iMovie	Easy Easily match slideshow duration to soundtrack (varies image display time automatically)	Just like iMovie, iDVD changes the resolution of the images in the slideshow, meaning that the quality of the images can be degraded significantly Distribution limited to DVD only More work to add title slides Very difficult to add transitions or special effects
The Combo Method	Build the slideshow in iPhoto (or QuickTime Player), create the soundtrack in iMovie, combine the two tracks in QuickTime Player	Only one really, but it is a biggie—using this method, you can maintain full image quality	Most work and complexity More work to add title slides Difficult to add transitions or special effects More work to distribute the slideshow on videotape

One of the most important factors that should drive the decision about which method you use for a given slideshow is the quality of the images you want to achieve. If having the highest quality is the most important thing to you, then you should usually choose the combo method. If you can live with slightly lower image quality and it is more important to be able to include transitions and special effects in your slideshow, the iMovie method is the way to go. If you are in a hurry and only need to put a slideshow on DVD, the iDVD technique can be a winner.

When it comes to image quality, the means that you choose to display your slideshow is a very important factor. For some examples of what I mean by this, consider the following scenarios:

◆ You are primarily going to display the slideshow on an analog television via videotape. The resolution of standard televisions and VHS tapes is fairly low. Creating a high-resolution slideshow for analog television won't do you much good because the images will be pared down when you show the slideshow on the television anyway. In this case, you should use the iMovie technique because it is the easiest, and it enables you to directly output your slideshow to videotape.

◆ You will primarily watch the slideshow on your computer. In this case, you will probably want to maximize the image quality since your computer is able to display high-resolution images. The Combo method is a good choice for this situation.

◆ You want most of your projects to be on DVD so you can view them on a computer or on your home entertainment system easily. The iDVD method can be a good choice for this situation, although the other methods can result in a QuickTime version of the slideshow (and you can use iDVD to put any QuickTime movie on a DVD).

NOTE

With all this focus on image quality, I have made an assumption that the images you capture, whether via a digital camera, scanner, or other technique, are of a relatively high resolution. For example, if you use a digital camera that captures images with a resolution of two-megapixels or more (more pixels is better), your images are "high resolution," and you are likely to want to maintain as much of that quality as you can. If you use a low-resolution device to capture images, such as a one-megapixel camera, the image quality will only be so-so to start with so the method you choose doesn't have much impact on image quality. In other words, when it comes to deciding about image quality, consider the image quality from which you are starting.

Building a Slideshow the iMovie Way

Creating a slideshow in iMovie is really not much different than creating a movie in iMovie. In fact, saying it is not much different is to emphasize the difference too much. There is only one difference, and that is setting the duration of the images, which is to set the amount of time that each image appears on the screen.

The iMovie method offers many benefits, such as being able to easily add transitions, titles, and special effects to your slideshow. Plus, you can use iMovie's audio tools to build the soundtrack at the same time that you build the slideshow itself. Also, you can export the slideshow in many formats. Finally, building a slideshow in iMovie is the easiest and fastest method.

The potential drawback to this method is the image quality of the slideshow (you'll learn more about this shortly).

Prepping Images for iMovie

Before you move your images into iMovie, it is a good idea to resize them to the 640 x 480 proportion; the images don't have to be this size, but they should have the same proportion (which is 1.33333 x 1). That is because iMovie will resize your images to 640 x 480 when you import them. If the proportions of your images match this, iMovie won't do any scaling. And, trust me on this one—you don't really want iMovie to scale your images. Sometimes, it will make a mess of otherwise decent images.

TIP

If you are using images from your iPhoto Library, create an album for the slideshow and place all the images that you will use in this album. Then you can easily export the images for the slideshow in one operation.

Also, if you include any portrait-oriented images in your slideshow, iMovie will place them in a black frame when it imports those images. It will also place a black frame around any images that don't fill the screen in both directions when scaled to 640 x 480.

TIP

When you export images from iPhoto, you can choose to scale those images to a maximum size. When it scales the images, iPhoto will attempt to fill up the 640 x 480 space in both directions. If you choose to scale the images no larger than 640 x 480 and the images that you export are not proportioned the same as 640 x 480, two sides (either top and bottom or left and right) will be less than maximum size (less than either 640 or 480). When this is the case, iMovie will add a black bar to fill up the space where the images are less than the maximum size.

If the black frames bother you, use an image editing application to resize all your images to be exactly 640 x 480 and place any portrait-oriented images in a 640 x 480 frame of your choosing.

NOTE

You can use iPhoto to crop your images to have the 640 x 480 proportion, but unfortunately, there is no way to crop a group of images at the same time. Select the first image that you want to crop and move into iPhoto's Edit mode. Choose 4 x 3 (Book, DVD) or 4 x 3 Portrait (Book) on the Constrain pop-up menu. (If you use the 4 x 3 Portrait (Book) option, portrait images will still have the black bars when you move them into iMovie. To get rid of the bar, use the 4 x 3 (Book, DVD) option, but be aware you will have to get rid of a substantial part of the image when you crop it). Then drag in the image to select as much of it as you can. Move the selection box to cover the area of the image that you want to keep. Click the Crop button. The image will be resized to 4 x 3 (which is the same proportion as 640 x 480). Repeat this for each image in the slideshow.

TIP

It is usually a good idea to make a copy of images that you are going to crop in iPhoto and then crop the copies. This assumes that you might want to make other changes to the same image. If you don't, you don't have to make a copy because you can always retrieve the original in iPhoto. Of course, if you resize the photos in an image editing application outside of iPhoto, such as Photoshop, you work on copies automatically (because you export them from iPhoto first). Such an application can also enable you to do batch editing, which can be much faster and less work.

To make importing your images easier, create a folder for your slideshow project and place the images that you will be using in the iMovie slideshow in this folder.

Adding Images to the iMovie Slideshow

You learned how to move still images into your movies back in Chapter 4. Just in case you have forgotten, here's how you do it.

Add Images to an iMovie Project

1. Choose File, Import File (press ⌘+I).

2. In the Import File dialog, move to the slideshow folder in which you stored the images for your slideshow.

3. Select the images that you want to import.

TIP

To select multiple images that are contiguous, hold down the Shift key, click the first image in the group, and then click the last image in the group. To select multiple images that aren't contiguous, hold the ⌘ key down while you select each image.

---

4. Click Import. The images will be placed on the iMovie Shelf (see Figure 15.1).

The big drawback to using iMovie to create a slideshow, the only one really, is that iMovie resizes images to be 640 x 480. When this happens, images can lose detail. For some images, such as landscapes, this loss of detail might not bother you. For others, it might cause images to appear to be blurry when you compare them to the originals fresh from your digital camera. If the quality of the images in an iMovie slideshow isn't good enough for your purposes, you will need to use the Combo method to create the slideshow.

Building the Show in iMovie

Building a slideshow in iMovie is just like building any movie in iMovie. For example, to place the images in the slideshow, drag them from the Shelf to one of

Figure 15.1 *These images are ready to be placed in the iMovie slideshow*

the viewers. Add transitions between the images if you want them, create titles, and so on. (For the details on building a movie in iMovie, see Chapter 4).

The one slight difference is that you can set the duration during which each image appears on the screen. When you import a group of images into iMovie, this duration is set to iMovie's default value (such as 5 seconds per image). You can change the duration for an image in the slideshow by doing the following steps.

Change the Display Duration for an Image in a Slideshow

1. Select the image on the viewer.
2. In the Time box, enter the length of time that you want that image to appear onscreen (see Figure 15.2). When entering the duration, remember to use the timecode format, which is minutes:seconds:frames. For images, you will likely only be changing the seconds value.

A slideshow can be more interesting if you do vary the duration for images. For example, you might want images containing less detail to appear on the screen for a shorter duration than those that contain lots of detail.

Figure 15.2 *The selected image will appear on the screen for 3 seconds.*

TIP

Because you can't change the duration for a group of images at the same time, you have to do so for each image individually. This can be a pain so make sure that the default duration is set to an appropriate value before you import your images into iMovie. You do this on the Import tab of the iMovie Preferences dialog.

Adding Music and Other Sound to the Show

Again, using iMovie to build a soundtrack for a slideshow is just like building a soundtrack for any other movie that you create. (See Chapter 4 for the details.)

TIP

Just as you can add still images to a movie, you can add video clips to a slideshow.

Exporting the Show from iMovie

After you have finished your slideshow, you can export it in the following three ways (again, just like movies that you create in iMovie):

◆ Export to Videotape
◆ Export to QuickTime
◆ Export for iDVD

The details of exporting movies and slideshows for each of these formats are explained in Chapters 16 through 18.

Building a Slideshow Using the iDVD Method

Putting your slideshows on DVD is a great way to be able to show them easily. Since most people now have a DVD player, you can take the slideshow almost anywhere. And, of course, you can also show the slideshow on any computer that is equipped with a DVD drive.

The iDVD method suffers from two major drawbacks and a few less major ones.

One is that using iDVD to build a slideshow causes the images to be resized, just like building one in iMovie does. The resulting loss in image quality might be acceptable to you or it might not be. The best way to tell if this is an issue for you is to try it to see for yourself.

NOTE

Of course, displaying images on an analog television screen will usually make the images look worse than they do on a computer monitor. A computer monitor usually is set to have much higher resolution than analog televisions (which are equivalent to a 640 x 480). When your images are displayed on an analog television screen, they will look fuzzy compared to the same images at a higher resolution on your monitor even if you create a slideshow using a higher resolution.

The other major drawback is that the slideshow you create can only be displayed on DVD; however, with the iMovie or Combo methods, you can choose from a variety of export options.

The minor drawbacks are that you have to work harder to add title slides and adding transitions or special effects is nearly impossible.

Prepping Your Images for iDVD

You prepare your images for an iDVD slideshow in the same way that you prepare them for an iMovie slideshow. See the section called "Prepping Images for iMovie" earlier in this chapter for the details.

Creating a Soundtrack to the iDVD Slideshow

As you learned in Chapter 5, iDVD enables you to add a soundtrack to a slideshow by choosing an audio file that you want to use as a soundtrack. You can add a single music track as a soundtrack, or you can use the techniques described in Chapter 10 to create a more complex soundtrack for the slideshow.

Creating a Slideshow in iDVD

Creating a slideshow in iDVD is covered in detail in Chapter 5, but a summary of the steps follows.

Create a Slideshow in iDVD

1. Create a new iDVD project or open an existing one.
2. Add a slideshow button to the project.
3. Double-click the slideshow button to open the iDVD slideshow mode.
4. Drag the images for the slideshow onto the iDVD window in the order in which you want them to appear.
5. Add a soundtrack to the slideshow.
6. Choose the duration of the slideshow—the best duration is to simply have the slideshow match the duration of your soundtrack.
7. Design the slideshow's button.
8. Preview the slideshow using iDVD's preview feature.
9. When the project is complete, burn the DVD.

Building a Slideshow Using iPhoto, QuickTime, and iMovie (AKA the Combo Method)

If nothing but the highest possible image quality is good enough for your slideshows, you can create your slideshows by using several of the digital lifestyle applications together.

The benefit of this approach is just that—your images can retain their maximum image quality because the tools you use won't resize the images, as happens with the previous two methods. You can choose the resolution of the images in the slideshow, and you can maintain that resolution in the final result.

There are several disadvantages to this method. The biggest is that it is simply more work than the other two methods. You have to manipulate more files, work in more applications, and use more of the techniques that you have learned throughout this book. Another drawback is that if you want to distribute the slideshow on DVD or via videotape, your work to achieve the higher image quality is wasted because the display devices you use won't be able to handle the image quality you achieve anyway; in other words, this method is really only beneficial for showing the slideshow on a computer or other high-resolution devices. And, adding title slides or special effects is much more difficult than the iMovie method.

Even though it requires more work on your part, this method isn't hard, and the image quality you can achieve can easily make this additional work worthwhile.

Building the Slideshow in iPhoto

Under the Combo method, you create the video track for your slideshow as a QuickTime movie. There are two basic ways of building the video track for the slideshow:

◆ Use iPhoto to export images in a QuickTime movie
◆ Use QuickTime Player to import a series of images to create a QuickTime movie

Before you start using either of these techniques, you need to do a bit of planning.

In addition to deciding what images you will be including in the slideshow, you need to decide if you want all of the images to have the same duration, or if you want to vary the duration. If you want the images to appear on the screen for the same amount of time, you will create a single QuickTime movie containing all of the images in the slideshow. If you want to vary the duration for which images appear on the screen, you will have to build your movie in segments, with the duration of images in each segment being different. Then, you can combine those segments to create the video track for the slideshow.

TIP

You can use QuickTime Player to add special effects to a QuickTime segment; while you probably don't want an entire slideshow to be created using one of the QuickTime effects, if you create a segmented movie, it can be useful to add some QuickTime effects to individual segments to add variety to the slideshow. To learn how to add QuickTime effects to a QuickTime movie, see Chapter 1, "QuickTime Pro: Making it All Happen."

Next, decide how large you want the images in the slideshow to appear. If you have captured your images using a high-resolution digital camera, they might be very large indeed, such as 2160 x 1440 pixels. You can maintain this resolution, which preserves all of the information in those images, or you can use a smaller size to make the file size smaller (possibly for display on smaller monitors). The larger the size (resolution) that you choose for your images, the higher the quality of those images will be in the slideshow. I prefer to take full advantage of my 3 megapixel camera and use its maximum image size (which is 2160 x 1440 or 1440 x 2160), but you can choose any size for your slideshow.

NOTE

Remember that you display a slideshow of any album in iPhoto by using its slideshow feature. However, that creates only a temporary slideshow. With this technique, you can create a permanent one.

Exporting the Slideshow in iPhoto

To use iPhoto to create the video track for your slideshow, do the following steps.

Create a Slideshow's Video Track in iPhoto

1. In iPhoto, create an album for each segment of the slideshow. If all the images in the slideshow will have the same duration, you will need to create only one album. If you want to vary the duration of the images in the slideshow, you will need to create an album for each segment of the slideshow.

2. Drag the images from the iPhoto Library to the albums that you have created.

3. Select the first album you created and arrange the images in the order that you want them to appear in the segment (see Figure 15.3). The images will be exported starting with the top left image and moving to the right, in the same direction and order as when you read a page of text in English. In other words, the image in the top left corner will be the first one in the slideshow, the image to its right will be the second, and so on.

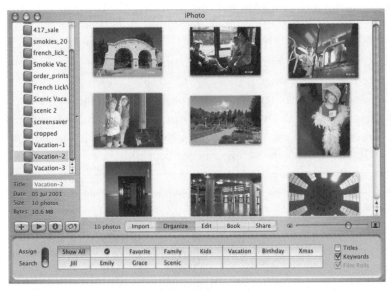

Figure 15.3 *I have created three albums for this slideshow (Vacation-1, Vacation-2, and Vacation-3) and have organized the images in the order in which I want them to appear in the slideshow.*

4. Repeat Step 3 for each album you have created for the slideshow.

5. Select the album that contains the images for the first segment of the slideshow and click the Share button to move into iPhoto's Share mode.

6. Click the Export button.

7. In the Export Images dialog, click the QuickTime tab (see Figure 15.4).

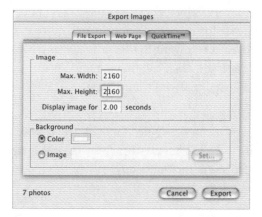

Figure 15.4 *Using the QuickTime tab of the Export Images dialog, you can configure the properties of the QuickTime movie you are creating.*

8. Enter the maximum size of the images (in either direction) that you are placing in your slideshow in the Max. Width and Max. Height boxes. If all the images are oriented in the same way (portrait or landscape), you can enter the maximum height and width values from those images. If you have both landscape and portrait images in the same slideshow, you should enter the same maximum size in both directions.

TIP

If you don't remember what the resolution of your images are, cancel out of the Export dialog and select images in your albums. When an image is selected, its size appears in the information area between the list of albums and the iPhoto controls area. Find the maximum dimension of all the images in your slideshow in either direction. If you have captured all the images with the same device, such as a digital still camera, the sizes should be the same for all images (although images that are oriented differently will have the two dimensions reversed).

9. Choose the duration of the images in the slideshow by entering a value in the "Display image for" box. The default value is 2 seconds.

10. Choose the background for any "blank" space around images by using either the color or image radio buttons. When an image doesn't fill the screen in either direction, the background you choose will be used to fill in the empty space. To choose a color as a background (I prefer black or white, but you might like another color), click the Color radio button and then click the color tab. The Color Picker will appear, and you can use it to select the background color. If you want to use an image as a background (such as a textured pattern), click the Image radio button and use the Set button to select the image that you want to use.

11. Click Export.

12. In the save sheet that appears, name the QuickTime movie, choose a location in which to save it, and click Save. A progress bar and image count shows you how the process is moving along. When the process is complete, the images in the selected album will be exported to a QuickTime movie.

13. Repeat Steps 5 through 12 for each album. When you are done, you will have a QuickTime movie slideshow of each album.

NOTE

If you don't want any "empty" space outside the images in your slideshow, you will have to use images that are the same size in both dimensions. This means either using images that are the same orientation or cropping images so that they fill the same amount of space.

After you have created QuickTime movies of each segment in the slideshow, you can use QuickTime Player to preview those movies and to combine those segments into a single QuickTime movie.

Preview and Combine QuickTime Segments in QuickTime Player Pro

1. Open the first segment of your slideshow in QuickTime Player. If you have used a large image resolution in your movie, prepare to be impressed—especially if you have created any slideshows in iMovie or

iDVD (those methods suffer by comparison). The image quality should be superb (see Figure 15.5).

Figure 15.5 *Because I was able to maintain the resolution of my images, the image quality of this slideshow is much better than the one I created in iMovie (although because of the low resolution of the images in the printed version of this book, it might not look that way to you).*

2. Play the movie to preview the slideshow segment.

3. Repeat Steps 1 and 2 for each segment of your slideshow.

4. Move into the movie for the second segment of your slideshow.

5. Choose Edit, Select All to choose the entire segment.

6. Choose Edit, Copy to copy that segment.

7. Move into the first segment and place the Playhead where you want to start the second segment (most likely at the end of the first segment).

8. Choose Edit, Add. The segment that you copied will be added to the first segment (see Figure 15.6).

9. Repeat Steps 4 through 8 for each segment of the slideshow, until you have added them all into one QuickTime Player window.

10. Choose File, Save As.

Figure 15.6 *Here, I have added the second segment to the first (the second segment is still selected and is indicated by the shaded area between the crop markers).*

11. In the Save dialog, name the slideshow, choose a location in which to save it, click the "Make movie self-contained" radio button, and click Save.

You now have a movie that contains all of the images that you want to be in your slideshow. If you used segments that have different image durations, each segment will be a video track in your movie (for example, if you had three segments with each having its own image duration, the complete movie will have three video tracks). As the movie plays, the amount of time that the images are displayed on the screen will change as each segment is played.

To finish the slideshow, you can add title slides and a soundtrack.

Creating the Slideshow in QuickTime Player

You can also create a slideshow directly in QuickTime Player. The results will be the same as when you export the images as a QuickTime movie from iPhoto, but the steps to get there are slightly different.

Create a Video Track for a Slideshow in QuickTime Player Pro

1. Collect the images that you will use in your slideshow in a folder. If the images are stored in iPhoto, export them as files. The resolution of the images will determine the resolution of the slideshow; you can use the highest resolution images that you have available to you.

2. Rename the image files so that the file names end with a sequential number; the sequence of the numbers determines the order in which the images will appear in the slideshow. End the name of the first image with a "1," the second with "2," and so on (see Figure 15.7).

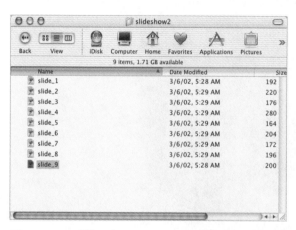

Figure 15.7 *These images are ready to be imported into QuickTime Player as a slideshow.*

3. If you want to vary the duration of images in the slideshow, organize the images into groups; each group will be used to create one of the segments for the slideshow. Place the images for each segment in a separate folder; the sequential numbers in the file names within that folder will determine the order in which the images appear in the segment.

TIP

If the groups of images from which you are creating the slideshow contain images in both orientations, include landscape-oriented images in separate groups from portrait-oriented images. When QuickTime Player imports the images, it will size the movie according to the first image you select. The rest of the images will be scaled to fit the orientation of that image. This can distort images that are of a different orientation.

4. Open QuickTime Player.

5. Choose File, Open Image Sequence.

6. In the Open dialog, move to and select the first image in the first segment of the slideshow.

7. Click Open. You'll see the Image Sequence Settings dialog.

8. On the Frame rate pop-up menu, choose the duration of the images in the segment, such as 3 seconds per frame.

9. Click OK. The sequence of images will be transformed into a QuickTime movie (see Figure 15.8).

Figure 15.8 *A group of images have been imported into QuickTime Player as an image sequence (in other words, a slideshow).*

10. Save the first slideshow segment.

11. Repeat Steps 5 through 10 for each segment of the slideshow.

12. Move into the movie for the second segment of your slideshow.

13. Choose Edit, Select All to choose the entire segment.

14. Choose Edit, Copy to copy that segment.

15. Move into the first segment and place the Playhead where you want to start the second segment (most likely at the end of the first segment).

16. Choose Edit, Add. The segment that you copied will be added to the first segment.

17. Repeat Steps 12 through 16 for each segment of the slideshow, until you have added them all into one QuickTime Player window.

18. Choose File, Save As.

19. In the Save dialog, name the slideshow, choose a location in which to save it, click the "Make movie self-contained" radio button, and click Save.

You now have a movie that contains all of the images that you want to be in your slideshow. If you used segments that have different image durations, each segment will be a video track in your movie (for example, if you had three segments with each having its own image duration, the complete movie will have three video tracks). As the movie plays, the amount of time that the images are displayed on the screen will change as each segment is played.

To finish the slideshow, you can add title slides and a soundtrack.

Adding Title Slides to the Slideshow

Adding title slides to a QuickTime slideshow can be a nice way to start the slideshow, end it, or introduce the various segments included in it. You can place your titles over images, over solid backgrounds, such as a black background, or over a pattern. To add title slides, you can use the following steps.

Add Title Slides to a Slideshow

1. Open your slideshow movie.

2. Select Movie, Get Movie Properties (or press ⌘+J). You'll see the Movie Properties dialog.

3. On the left pop-up menu, choose one of the movie's video tracks.

4. On the right pop-up menu, choose Size. The size of your slideshow's images will be shown next to the word "Normal" (see Figure 15.9). This size tells you the size at which you need to create your title slides.

Figure 15.9 *This slideshow has a resolution of 1440 x 1440, which is a lot better than the 640 x 480 it would have had in iMovie or iDVD.*

5. Use an image-editing program to open an image over which you are going to add text or to create a solid or patterned background.

6. If you create a background, size the background to the size of your slideshow that you determined in Step 4. If you are going to use an image, make sure that image is the size of the rest of your slideshow.

7. Use the image editing application's tools to create the title slide.

8. Save the image as a JPEG or TIFF files.

9. Repeat Steps 5 through 8 for each title slide that you will include in the slideshow.

10. Move back into QuickTime Player.

11. Choose File, Open Image Sequence.

12. In the Open dialog, move to and select the first title slide that you created.

13. Click Open. You'll see the Image Sequence Settings dialog.

14. On the Frame rate pop-up menu, choose the duration of the title slide, such as 3 seconds per frame.

15. Click OK. The title slide will be transformed into a QuickTime movie (see Figure 15.10).

16. Choose Edit, Select All (press ⌘+A).

17. Choose Edit, Copy (press ⌘+C).

18. Move into your slideshow movie.

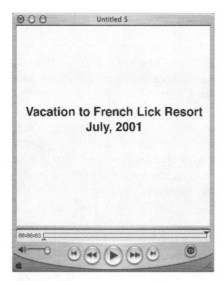

Figure 15.10 *Hopefully, your title slides will be a bit more creative than this one is!*

19. Place the Playhead at the point at which you want to add the title slide.

20. Choose Edit, Add (press Option+⌘+V). The title slide will be added to the slideshow at the Playhead's location.

21. Repeat Steps 11 through 20 for each title slide.

22. Save your slideshow movie.

Now, you have a slideshow that contains images and title slides. Next, add some sound to the slideshow.

Building a Soundtrack in iMovie

Your slideshows will be much more enjoyable if you add soundtracks to them. At the simplest, you can open a music file, select its contents, and add it to the slideshow. But, unless you are very lucky, the slideshow and the music file will be of different lengths. Plus, you might want to use more than one music track, and you might want to throw in some narration or sound effects. You can use iMovie to create as complex a soundtrack for your movie as you'd like.

TIP

You can scale a slideshow to fit a music file in QuickTime Player. First, open a music file, such as MP3, in QuickTime Player. Move into your slideshow movie and select and copy all of it. Move into the music file that is open in QuickTime, place the Playhead at the beginning of the music, and choose Edit, Add Scaled (press Shift+Option+⌘+V). The slideshow will be added to the music file and will be scaled so that it plays for the length of the music file. This means the slideshow and music will end at the same time, but the results might or might not be pleasing to you depending on how much scaling QuickTime Player has to do. For best results, the slideshow movie and the music file should be about the same length.

All the information you need to create a soundtrack in iMovie is contained in Chapter 10. Following are the general steps.

Create a Soundtrack for the Slideshow in iMovie

1. Export your slideshow as a DV Stream.

2. Open iMovie and create a new project.

3. Import the DV Stream that you created in Step 1.

4. Place the DV Stream file on the Timeline Viewer or Clip Viewer.

5. Use iMovie's audio tools to create the soundtrack. You can include music, sound effects, narration, and any other sound you'd like. You can time the sound to the slideshow because you can view it while you are creating the soundtrack, just like when you create any other sort of movie in iMovie.

6. When the soundtrack is finished, export the movie as a QuickTime file.

7. Open the soundtrack movie and delete the video track.

8. Select and copy the entire soundtrack file.

9. Move into the slideshow movie, position the Playhead at the beginning of the slideshow, and add the soundtrack to it. Because you used the slideshow to time the soundtrack, they are exactly the same length so you don't have any scaling issues to deal with.

10. Save the movie—make it self-contained.

Watching and Distributing the Slideshow

You can enjoy the fruits of your labor in QuickTime Player, just like any other QuickTime movie.

You can also distribute your slideshow movie in several ways.

- ◆ Copy the slideshow onto a CD (assuming it will fit, of course) to distribute it or to archive it.

- ◆ Copy the slideshow on a DVD (not created using iDVD).

- ◆ Post the QuickTime file on your iTools Web site.

- ◆ Create smaller versions of the slideshow by exporting it to a DV Stream file and then importing it to iMovie. From there, export it to videotape, for iDVD, or in as a QuickTime movie with different options (such as size or audio settings). Of course, when you import the movie into iMovie, the images are resized, and you will lose resolution, so you should only use this technique for special purposes.

- ◆ Place the slideshow on a DVD created in iDVD. As with the previous bullet, iDVD will resize the slideshow, so you will lose resolution in the images, but still, this can be a handy way to make the movie very portable.

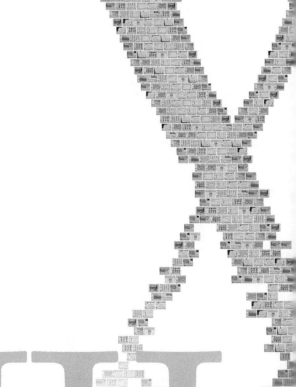

PART III

Displaying Your Digital Masterpieces

Chapter 16

Exporting Your Projects to Videotape

Putting your digital lifestyle projects on videotape is a good way to store and distribute them for the following reasons:

◆ **Almost every home has a VCR**. Because VCRs are ubiquitous, you can count on being able to distribute your projects on videotape to just about anyone. Unlike other distribution methods, such as DVD or over the Web, you don't have to be concerned with whether the person to whom you are sending the videotape will have the equipment needed to view it.

◆ **Videotape is inexpensive**. You can purchase blank videotapes for less than $1. That makes them a very inexpensive media to use to record your projects.

◆ **No technical savvy is required to play videotape**. Using a VCR is very basic, and there aren't any technical issues associated with playing one. You don't have to be concerned that the person receiving your videotape won't know what to do with it.

Videotape also has some drawbacks. One is that the resolution at which a standard television and VCR works is fairly low so you can't expect the same viewing quality that you can achieve on your Mac. Another is that videotape is linear; your viewer is locked into viewing the tape in a specific order (unlike other means, such as DVD, by which the viewer can choose the order in which to view your content).

There are two basic ways to put your projects on videotape: record your project to a DV camera via iMovie or output your project directly from your Mac to a VCR.

Using iMovie to Put Projects on Videotape

You can output *any* project that you can open in iMovie to videotape by exporting that project from iMovie to a DV camera. Then you can output the project from the DV to a standard VCR to put the project on standard videotape. Using iMovie to output projects to videotape is almost trivially easy.

Preparing an iMovie Project for Videotape

In iMovie, open the project that you want to put on videotape. If you have created the project in iMovie, you don't need to do anything but open the iMovie project file. If you didn't create the project in iMovie (perhaps it is a sideshow that you created using iPhoto and QuickTime), then you need to import that project into iMovie (see Chapter 4, "iMovie: The Swiss Army Knife of Digital Video Software" for information about importing content into iMovie).

After the project is in iMovie, use the application to get the project into the shape you want to record it in.

Recording an iMovie Project on a DV Camera

You can export any iMovie project to videotape by using the following steps.

Record an iMovie Project on a DV Camera

1. Put a tape on which you want to record in your DV camera.
2. Connect your DV camera to your Mac's FireWire port, turn the camera on, and put it in the "VCR" mode (often called VTR).
3. In iMovie, choose File, Export Movie (or press ⌘+E).
4. In the Export Movie dialog, choose To Camera on the Export pop-up menu (see Figure 16.1).
5. If your camera takes longer than 5 seconds to get ready to record (it probably doesn't), increase the value in the "Wait…" box.

Figure 16.1 *Exporting an iMovie project to videotape really is as simple as this dialog makes it appear.*

6. Input the amount of black screen before your project starts playing in the "Add __ seconds of black before movie" box. The default value is one second, but you might want to have more "empty" space before your movie starts. This can make it slightly easier to record on a VCR later.

7. Input the amount of black space after your movie by entering a value in the "Add __ seconds of black to end of movie" box. This black space makes a nice buffer between elements recorded on the same tape.

8. Click Export. iMovie will start your camera recording, pause the amount of time you entered in Step 5, play a black screen for the amount of time you entered in Step 6, and then begin recording your iMovie project on the DV camera. When the project has been recorded, iMovie will add the amount of black space that you entered in Step 7 and then stop the DV camera. Your project will be recorded on the DV's tape just as if you had recorded it through the DV camera's lens.

Recording from a DV Camera to VHS

After your project is on a DV tape, you can easily transfer it to a VHS tape.

Transfer a Project from a DV Camera to VHS

1. Connect the standard video and audio ports of your DV camera to input ports on the VCR; many VCRs have ports on the front to make this connection easier. Most DV cameras ship with the cable you need to make this connection.

NOTE

Some DV cameras require that you use a VTR, VCR, or dubbing mode to record the camera's output onto a VCR. If your camera requires this, place the camera in the appropriate mode when you connect it to the VCR. If you don't know which mode to use, see the user manual for your camera.

---

2. Set the VCR's input mode to be the ports to which you connected the DV camera in Step 1.

3. Move the DV camera to the black space before your iMovie project starts.

4. Put the VHS tape that you are going to record your iMovie project on in the VCR and get it in the position at which you want to begin recording.

5. Start recording on the VCR.

6. Play the tape in the DV camera.

7. When the project has finished, stop the DV camera and the VCR. Your project will be on the VHS tape, and you can view it on any VCR.

Outputting Projects to Videotape Outside of iMovie

For most projects, you should use the iMovie method to put that project on video-tape. Using iMovie is very simple, and there are few technical hurdles for you to overcome. However, in some cases, you might want to record the output of your Mac directly to videotape. For example, you might want to record action that is happening on the screen, such as a series of steps you are performing. Or you might want to record a QuickTime movie directly to videotape without going through iMovie first. Or you might want to record the output of a non-digital lifestyle application, such as a PowerPoint presentation.

Recording your Mac's output directly to videotape is either fairly easy if your Mac has the required video output hardware, or it will be a bit more complex if you will have to add hardware to your Mac to be able to do so. After you have the appropriate hardware, recording a project on videotape isn't hard.

Connecting Your Mac to a VCR

To be able to record your Mac's output directly to video (without using iMovie) requires that you can connect your Mac's video and audio outputs directly to a VCR or other recording device (such as an analog camcorder or your DV camera). There are two basic situations that might exist for you:

◆ You have a PowerBook with S-video output or an iBook with an A/V port.

◆ You have a desktop Mac to which you can add a graphics card that has an S-video or standard RCA output jack.

NOTE

There are some converters that will enable you to connect a standard video recording device to a Mac's video output port. However, because these devices are fairly unique and they are likely to be more hassle than they are worth, they are beyond the scope of this chapter.

Connecting a PowerBook or iBook to a VCR

Many PowerBook models have an S-video output port. You can connect this port to the input of a standard VCR just like you connect the output of your DV camera. Connect the PowerBook's audio output port to the audio input ports on the VCR, and you can also record the sound output from the Mac.

NOTE

You need a couple of adapters to be able to connect a PowerBook directly to a VCR. One adapter will be required to convert the S-video cable to a standard RCA jack if that is the input port provided on the VCR you are using. This adapter is included with the PowerBook. The other adapter you will need in all cases converts the stereo mini-jack audio output port to two standard RCA connectors to which you can connect the VCR's audio input ports.

After you have connected the PowerBook to a VCR, you can record its output directly on the VCR. If you want to record the same image that is displayed on the PowerBook's screen, you can use video mirroring to make the displays the same. Or you can treat the output to the VCR as a second monitor.

TIP

You can use the same setup to connect the output of the PowerBook to use a television as a second monitor. Just set up the system so that the television takes its input from the VCR. The signal from the PowerBook will play through the VCR and will appear on the television. You can also connect the PowerBook directly to a television if you only want to display the image rather than record it.

You can use similar techniques to connect the output of an iBook to a VCR. For example, newer iBooks have an A/V port that you can connect to a VCR or television. To learn how to do this, check out the documentation that came with the iBook (there is too much variation in iBook models for me to be able to include details here).

Connecting a Power Mac to a VCR

If you have a Mac capable of accepting a PCI graphics card, you can add a graphics card to enable you to output to a VCR or television. Most PCI graphics cards include an S-video or RCA video output port through which your Mac can output a signal.

> **NOTE**
>
> A great benefit of adding a second graphics card is that you can use two monitors at the same time.

While covering the variety of graphics cards is beyond the scope of this book, some simple research on your favorite Web retail site (such as www.smalldog.com) will turn up several from which you can choose.

Installing a PCI graphics card is a simple task that usually takes just a few minutes (most of the time required is to connect and disconnect your existing cables). After the card is installed, you connect its video output to the video input on the VCR. Then connect the Mac's audio output to the audio input on the VCR.

> **NOTE**
>
> Just like a PowerBook, you might need an S-video to RCA adapter to be able to connect to the video output of the graphics card to the video input on the VCR. You will also need a stereo mini-jack adapter to connect your Mac's audio output to the audio input on the VCR.

Recording Your Mac's Output to VHS

After your Mac is connected to a VCR, configure it to record.

You can choose to have the output to VCR be the same as what is displayed on your primary monitor, which is called video mirroring, or you can have the two outputs be independent. (For help configuring multiple monitors, see my book *Special Edition Using Mac OS X*).

After you have configured your Mac's output, you simply need to make the action that you want to record happen on the appropriate display (your Mac's main display if you use video mirroring, or on the second graphics card if you aren't using video mirroring). Some examples are the following:

◆ Play a QuickTime movie. (To make the movie fill the screen, use the Present movie comment.)

◆ Perform a task on your desktop and record your actions on videotape.

◆ Show the output of another application, such as a PowerPoint presentation.

To record the content on videotape, do the following steps.

Record a Power Mac's Output on VHS Tape

1. Check your system to make sure that your Mac's output is being played through the VCR. If it isn't, check your connections and try again.

2. Put the tape on which you want to record in the VCR and move to the location at which you want to start recording.

3. Start recording.

4. Make the Mac action you are recording happen. For example, play a QuickTime movie.

5. When the action is done, stop recording.

Chapter 17

Putting Your Projects on CD

Most modern Macs include a drive that enables you to burn your own CDs. CDs are a great way to distribute your digital lifestyle projects for several reasons:

◆ **CD-R discs are cheap**. If you pay attention, you can pick up blank CD-R media for less than $0.25 per disc!

◆ **CD players are common**. Almost everyone who has a computer will be able to experience the content that you put on a CD. Since Mac OS X and the digital lifestyle applications all support standard formats, you don't have to be concerned about what kind of computer is used to view your content either.

◆ **CDs are easy to create**. Because you can burn CDs directly from the Mac OS X desktop, you don't need to mess around with any dedicated CD burning applications. You can create a CD by simply dragging files onto a blank CD and then burning it. Or you can use iTunes to burn a CD directly.

Putting your projects on a CD does have a couple of downsides that you need to keep in mind.

◆ **CDs are limited to 700MB or so**. Depending on the specific CD-R media you use, you can only store around 700MB of data on a single CD. While that might sound like a lot, it isn't much when compared to how much data a single QuickTime movie of large size and high quality requires. Such a movie can easily require more than a GB of space, and sometimes, a lot more. You need to keep the size of your project files in mind when planning a CD.

◆ **While the technical requirements for a CD are minimal, they do exist.** For example, you need to make sure that the person to whom you distribute your CDs has the software necessary to view your content. For Mac users, this won't be an issue because all the software they need is part of Mac OS X (QuickTime, iTunes, and so on). However, not all Windows users have QuickTime installed so make sure that the recipients can handle the CD's contents before you send it to them.

◆ **CDs require that the user take action to view the content**. When you place files on a CD by using the Finder's burn feature, the user has to know how to view those files. For example, he has to know how to double-click a QuickTime movie to play it, and he has to understand how to use QuickTime Player's controls. While this is basic for most Mac users, some users might not know how to use the CD you provide to them.

NOTE

Even if your Mac doesn't include an internal drive that enables you to burn CDs, you can add an external USB or FireWire CD burner to your system. Check out www.smalldog.com to see the types of drives that are available and how much they cost. Mac OS X supports most external CD burners, but you should check out Apple's Web site to make sure that the burner you are considering is compatible with Mac OS X.

Preparing Digital Lifestyle Projects for a CD

There are lots of projects that you might choose to put on a CD; the ones you'll learn about in this section are the following:

◆ QuickTime movies

◆ iPhoto images

◆ iMovie projects

Using iTunes to Burn a CD

iTunes is the only digital lifestyle application that enables you to burn a CD directly. The most obvious use is to create your own CDs containing your favorite music. But as you learned in Chapter 14, "Creating Your Own Soundtrack CDs," you can also place content from iMovie, such as a soundtrack, in iTunes and then burn that content onto a CD.

Preparing QuickTime Content for a CD

A CD is a great way to distribute QuickTime movies. Because QuickTime is a standard on both Macs and Windows PCs, just about anyone who has a computer can view QuickTime movies that you put on a CD. No matter where the QuickTime movie comes from, such as an iMovie project or a slideshow, you should prepare that movie by doing the tasks described in this section.

Making a Movie Self-Contained

As you learned in Chapter 4, a QuickTime movie's file can include all of the actual content used in the movie, or it can include pointers to the files that make up the movie. The ability to include references to other files within a movie instead of including the actual content enables QuickTime movies to be created at smaller file sizes; QuickTime can include pointers to other files within the movie instead of replicating the content itself. However, if a movie that contains references is moved to a different location, such as onto a CD, the references will break, and the movie will not be able to be played (especially if not all the source files are included on the CD).

> **NOTE**
>
> In QuickTime, these references are called dependencies because one movie depends on the contents of another to play properly.

There are two ways to prevent this problem. One is to make the movie self-contained, which means that all the content in the movie is actually included in the movie's file. The other is to use the Movie Properties tool to determine which files are needed for the movie.

To make a movie self-contained, open the movie in QuickTime Player and choose File, Save As. Check the "Make movie self-contained" radio button and then save it as you normally would. When the movie is saved, all its content will be included in a single file, and you won't have to worry about dependencies.

You can also use the Movie Properties window to determine if a movie file has file dependencies.

TIP

If the "Make move self-contained" radio button is disabled, the movie doesn't contain any file dependencies.

Determine the File Dependencies for a QuickTime Movie

1. Open the movie in QuickTime Player.

2. Choose Movie, Get Movie Properties (or press ⌘+J).

3. In the Properties dialog, choose Movie on the left pop-up menu and choose Files on the right pop-up menu. In the resulting information window, you will see the files on which the movie depends (see Figure 17.1). If more than one file is listed, the movie has file dependencies.

Figure 17.1 *This movie depends on the two files listed in the information window (in this case, the soundtrack is a referenced file).*

4. To prevent problems from these dependencies, save the movie as a self-contained movie or make sure you put all of the files listed in the Properties window on the CD.

Making a QuickTime Movie Play Automatically

You can configure a QuickTime movie so that it plays automatically when the file is opened. This can be very useful if the person to whom you send the movie doesn't know how to use QuickTime Player, and it is a convenience for everyone else.

Make a Movie Play Automatically When Opened

1. Open the QuickTime movie that you are going to put on a CD.

2. Choose Movie, Get Movie Properties (or press ⌘+J).

3. In the Properties dialog, choose Movie on the left pop-up menu and choose Auto Play on the right pop-up menu.

4. Check the "Auto Play Enabled" checkbox.

TIP

Sometimes, the movie will start playing from the most recent position of the Playhead so move the Playhead to the beginning of the movie before you save it.

---

5. Close the movie and save your changes.

When the movie file is opened, it will play automatically.

TIP

When placing QuickTime movies on a CD, make sure that they always have the .mov file name extension. The tools you use to create them should add this extension by default, but you can remove it on the Mac, and the file will still open properly. Not so on the PC; if the file name extension is missing, the user will have to choose the appropriate viewing application.

Preparing iPhoto Images for CD

CDs are also a great way to distribute your photos. Using iPhoto, there are two ways to output your images for CD: you can export individual files and place those files on a CD, or you can create a photo Web site and put the Web site on a CD.

Unless you know that the recipient has a need for separate image files, using the Web page option is usually the most convenient way to put the images on a CD. If the recipient will want separate image files, such as to print the photos you provide, use the export file method so that you can include high-resolution versions of your images on the CD. (Of course, assuming you have enough space on the CD, there isn't any reason you can't include both versions on the same CD.)

Exporting Photos for CD

Back in Chapter 3, "iPhoto: Not Your Father's Photo Album," you learned about the many ways you can export photos from iPhoto. One of these ways is to export photos as separate files; once out of iPhoto, you can put the images on CD.

Export Images from iPhoto as Individual Files

1. Launch iPhoto.
2. Create an album to organize the photos that you want to export.
3. Add the photos to the album that you created in Step 2.
4. Select the album.
5. Click the Share button.
6. Click the Export button.
7. In the Export Images dialog, click the File Export tab (see Figure 17.2).

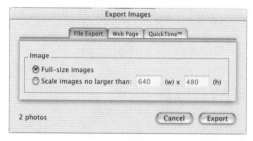

Figure 17.2 *iPhoto's File Export tab enables you to export your photos as separate image files.*

8. If you want to maintain the maximum resolution of your images, leave the "Full-size images" radio button selected. If not, click the "Scale images no larger than" radio button and enter values in the (w) and (h) boxes. To maintain the proportions of your images, be sure that the numbers you enter are in the same proportion as the original images.
9. Click Export.
10. In the save sheet that drops down, create a new folder, select it, and click OK or choose a folder in which to store the photos and click OK.
11. If you get a Directory exists warning dialog, click Add to folder. You will see a progress bar. When the process is complete, the image files will be placed in the folder that you selected.

> **NOTE**
>
> There seems to be a slight bug in the current version of iPhoto that results in the dialog mentioned in Step 11. If you don't see this dialog, don't worry about it. If you do, clear it by clicking the Add to folder button.

After the photos have been exported from iPhoto, you can place the image files on a CD.

Exporting an iPhoto Web Site for CD

An even better way to put images onto a CD is to create a Web site and then place the Web site on the CD.

Prepare an iPhoto Image Web Site

1. Create an album containing the images that you want to include on the Web site.

2. Click the Share button.

3. Click the Export button.

4. Click the Web Page tab (see Figure 17.3).

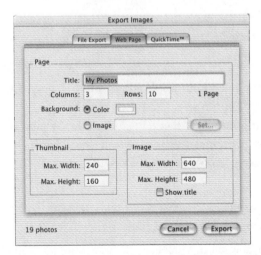

Figure 17.3 *iPhoto's excellent Web Page feature enables you to create a Web site from your images in a matter of moments.*

5. Enter the name of the Web site in the Title box.

6. Enter the number of rows and columns of thumbnails of your images that the pages of the site should have. When you do so, the number of pages in the site will change as needed.

7. Use the Background controls to set the Web site's background. Use the Color radio button and color chip to choose a color for the background, or use the Image radio button and Set button to select an image as the background. (All the pages in your Web site will have the same background.)

8. In the Thumbnail area, enter the maximum size of the thumbnails that will appear on the site (usually the default value is fine, but you can choose just about any size you would like).

9. In the Image area, enter the maximum size of the images themselves (that will be displayed when the viewer clicks an image's thumbnail). To maintain the highest resolution possible, use the maximum width and height of the images in the group. Otherwise, choose a smaller value, such as 800 x 600 (which is a good size for most displays).

10. If your images have titles, and you want them displayed on the Web pages, check the "Show title" checkbox.

11. Click Export. In the Save sheet, the Sites folder in your Home folder will be selected automatically. You can store your site here or choose another location.

12. Click the New Folder button and create a new folder for your Web site.

13. After the folder has been created and while it is still selected, click OK. You will see a progress bar as iPhoto builds your Web site. When the process is complete, you will return to the iPhoto window.

After your site is created, check it out.

View an iPhoto Web Site

1. Move to the folder in which you stored your Web site (see Figure 17.4).

2. Open the index.html file. It will appear in your default Web browser (see Figure 17.5).

3. Use standard Web browser tools to move around the site. To view full-size images, click an image's thumbnail.

Figure 17.4 *The file index.html is the home page of the Web site that iPhoto builds for you.*

Figure 17.5 *Have pictures? Create a Web site!*

You can add the photo Web site that you created by placing the folder in which you stored it on a CD.

TIP

When you create a CD, place an alias of the site's index file at the root level of the CD so the viewer can access it without having to open the Web site's folder.

Exporting an iMovie Project for CD

You can export your iMovie projects for CD by exporting them in the QuickTime format.

Export an iMovie Project for CD

1. Open the iMovie project that you want to put on a CD.
2. Choose File, Export Movie (or press ⌘+E).
3. In the Export Movie dialog, choose To QuickTime on the Export pop-up menu.
4. Choose CD-ROM, Medium on the Formats pop-up menu (see Figure 17.6).

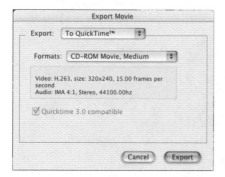

Figure 17.6 *This format's video and audio settings are suitable for most movies that you are going to place on a CD.*

5. Click Export.
6. In the Export QuickTime Movie dialog, choose a location in which to save the movie, name it (leave the .mov file name extension), and click Save. You will see a progress bar that provides you with an estimate of how long the process will take.
7. Use the techniques provided in the section earlier in the chapter called "Preparing QuickTime Content for a CD" to finish preparing the QuickTime movie you exported from iMovie for CD.

While choosing the CD-ROM Medium format is a good choice for many movies, there is no reason that you have to use this format for movies that you want to place on a CD. You can use any format or export settings to export a movie as a QuickTime movie. The predefined CD-ROM Medium format is simply a combination of settings that should work well for most movies to play decently from a CD.

You can configure a custom combination of settings used to export a QuickTime movie by doing the following steps.

Use Expert Settings to Export an iMovie Project for CD

1. Open the iMovie project that you want to put on a CD.
2. Choose File, Export Movie (or press ⌘+E).
3. In the Export Movie dialog, choose To QuickTime on the Export pop-up menu.
4. Choose Expert on the Formats pop-up menu. You will see the Expert QuickTime Settings dialog (see Figure 17.7). This dialog has three areas, which are Image Settings, Audio Settings, and Prepare for Internet.

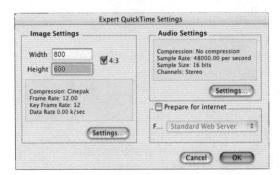

Figure 17.7 *Using the Expert QuickTime Settings dialog, you can custom configure the settings used to export a movie from iMovie in the QuickTime format.*

5. Use the controls in the Image Settings area to configure the image track of your movie. To set the image size, enter values in the Width and Height boxes. Check the "4:3" checkbox to keep the image in the 4:3 proportion. Click the Settings button to open the Compression Settings dialog (see Figure 17.8). Use the Compressor pop-up menus to choose the compressor used and the color depth that should be maintained (Best Depth is usually the appropriate choice). Use the Quality slider to set the image quality that is maintained when the images are compressed. Use the Motion controls to configure frame rate, key frames, and a data limit if applicable. Click OK to close the Compression Settings dialog.

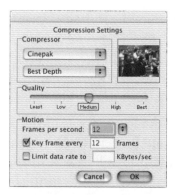

Figure 17.8 *Most of the time, you probably won't need to make changes to the compression settings you use, but you can if you want to.*

6. Click the Settings button in the Audio Settings area to open the Sound Settings dialog (see Figure 17.9). Use this dialog to configure the movie's soundtrack. Use the Compressor pop-up menu to apply compression to the soundtrack. Use the Rate box to enter a sampling rate (higher is a better quality and larger file size). Use the Size to choose the bit size (16 is better than 8, but the file will be larger). Use the Mono or Stereo radio buttons to choose a mono or stereo soundtrack. If the compressor you choose has options, the Options button will be available. Click the button and then configure the options for the compressor you have selected. Click OK to close the Sound Settings dialog.

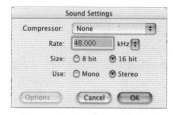

Figure 17.9 *Setting audio settings isn't as complex as setting video settings is.*

7. Click OK to close the Expert QuickTime Settings dialog.

8. Click Export.

9. In the Export QuickTime Movie dialog, choose a location in which to save the movie, name it (leave the .mov file name extension), and click

Save. You will see a progress bar that provides you with an estimate of how long the process will take.

10. Use the techniques provided in the section called "Preparing QuickTime Content for CD" earlier in this chapter to finish preparing the QuickTime movie you exported from iMovie for CD.

The compressors and other options that are available to you in the Expert QuickTime Settings dialog are fairly complex and are beyond the scope of this book. Most of the time, one of the predefined formats will be what you end up using anyway. However, you should experiment with some of the expert settings if you really want to fine-tune your movies.

A good way to start experimenting is by selecting each of the predefined formats. When you do, the settings used by the format will appear below the Formats pop-up menu. Use this information to learn how the default settings are configured. Then you can explore what effect these settings have by making changes to them in the Expert settings dialog. Frankly, configuring compressors, frame rates, and other settings isn't a lot of fun, but with some time and effort, you might be able to improve on the predefined formats.

Whether you export your movie using a predefined format or expert settings, keep the following two points in mind:

◆ **File size**. When you are exporting a movie for a CD, file size can quickly become an issue. You need to make sure that your movie will actually fit on a single CD.

◆ **File size versus quality**. Improving the quality of a movie that you export *always* increases the file size. When you choose less compression or increase the quality level of the compressor that you select, the image quality of the QuickTime movie will be better, but the file size will also be larger. This is also true when you choose a higher frame, more key frames, and better audio settings. Because iMovie doesn't tell you how big the file will be for a specific configuration, the only way to determine how big a file will be is to export it and see what happens. This can take a lot of time and effort, which is one reason that I suggested that you start with the default format settings.

Video CD and You

The Video CD (VCD) format enables video content to be recorded on and played from a CD, somewhat similar to presenting video content on a DVD. Video CDs can then be played on computers with software that can play VCDs as well as certain DVD players that can also handle the VCD format. Because the digital lifestyle applications don't support VCD natively, you have to obtain and use other applications to be able to create or view VCDs. Since this is a digital lifestyle book, I don't have room to cover VCD in detail here. If you are interested in this topic, use Sherlock to search the Web for Mac and VCD. You'll find many sites, and you can use those sites to learn about VCD and to obtain the software you need to play or create VCDs.

Using the Finder to Put Projects on CD

One of the cool features of Mac OS X is that you can burn CDs directly from the desktop by drag-and-drop (try that one on a Windows PC!). Burning CDs from the desktop is as simple as using a floppy disk was way back in the day when floppy disks were part of the Mac experience.

NOTE

CDs are a great way to archive projects on which you are no longer working along with projects files that you don't want to store on your hard drive, but that you want to save. You'll learn about organizing and archiving your digital lifestyle files in Chapter 20, "Organizing and Archiving Your Digital Media."

Burning a CD from the Finder requires the following general tasks:

1. Prepare the CD's contents by placing the files on the CD.
2. Burn the CD.
3. Test the CD.

NOTE

There are also CD burning applications, such as Roxio's Toast, that provide more features than the Finder's CD burning feature does (such as creating VCDs). To explore Toast, check out www.roxio.com. However, try using the Finder's CD burning capabilities before buying a dedicated application; you'll likely find that the Finder is the only CD burning application that you'll ever need.

Building the CD

After you have developed the content of your CD and prepared it as required, you will be ready to create your CD.

Build a CD

1. Insert a blank CD-R or CD-RW disc into your CD recordable drive.

2. At the prompt, name the CD you are creating by typing the name in the Name box.

3. Choose Standard (HFS+/ISO 9660) on the Format pop-up menu (see Figure 17.10).

Figure 17.10 *You can see that just under 700MB can be stored on this CD.*

4. Click Prepare. The CD will be mounted on your desktop.

5. Open a Finder window showing the contents of the CD.

6. Create folders to organize the contents of the CD. For example, you can place aliases to files contained in folders at the root level of the CD so that the viewer won't have to hunt for them.

7. Add a ReadMe file to explain what the contents of the CD are and to provide any special instructions (see Figure 17.11).

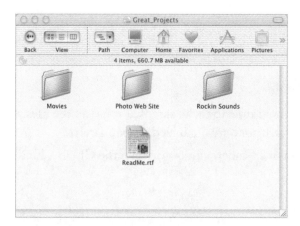

Figure 17.11 *This CD is starting to take shape.*

8. Drag files from other Finder windows to the folders that you created in Step 6. You can also place files at the root level of the CD if you prefer to leave them "loose."

9. Continue placing files and reorganizing the CD until you have it just the way you want it. Until you burn a CD, you can change its contents in any way, such as by removing files, creating new folders, moving files and folders around, and so on.

Building a ReadMe File

You should include a ReadMe file on your CD to explain its contents, to provide your contact information, or to provide any special instructions to the viewer (such as dragging QuickTime movie files to their hard drive for maximum performance). To create a ReadMe file, you can use any word processor, such as Microsoft Word or Mac OS X's TextEdit. When you save the version of the ReadMe file for the CD, make sure you save it in a format that is viewable by standard applications on any computer on which the CD will be viewed. The lowest common denominator is a plain text file because every computer contains at least one application that can open plain text files. Another viable option is the Rich Text Format (RTF) that enables you to include formatting. Mac OS X's TextEdit application has native support for RTF files so RTF is a good choice if you are sending the CD to other Mac users.

Burning the CD

After you have built the CD, it is time to make your work permanent.

Burn a CD from the Finder

1. Check the CD one more time to make sure that it has all the files you want to include and that they are organized appropriately.

2. Select the CD's icon in a Finder window or open the CD in a Finder window.

3. Choose File, Burn Disc.

4. In the resulting dialog, click Burn. You'll see a progress bar that tells you how the process is proceeding. The process will work through several stages including preparing the data, writing to the disc, and verifying the disc. Fortunately, you can use your Mac for other tasks while it is burning a CD because the Finder will continue to burn even when it is in the background. Depending on your Mac's speed, what else you are doing on the machine, and how much data is going on the disc, the process can take from several minutes to a half hour or so.

TIP

Activities that require heavy access to your Mac's drives, such as graphics or video work, can cause slight pauses in the CD burning process. Sometimes, these pauses can lead to problems, and the disc might not complete the burning process or might not work properly even if it does complete it. If you have trouble writing to a disc, close all open applications and try again. If the Finder has all the resources available to your Mac, it has the best chance of creating the CD properly.

Testing the CD

After the burn process is complete, eject the CD. Then reinsert it and open its files and folders to make sure that it works as you planned. For example, open QuickTime movies and play them. Try to move about a Web site on the disc. Open image files. Check the disc's organization.

If something is wrong, you will need to try again (fortunately, CD media is cheap!). For example, if a movie plays poorly, it might be that the image size is too large or the frame rate is too high to play back from a CD (try dragging it to your hard drive and play it from there). In such a case, you might want to adjust the settings you used for the movie until you achieve better performance. Or just add instructions to your ReadMe file to explain that the files should be moved to the hard drive for better performance.

After you are sure that the CD is what you were shooting for, it is ready to be sent to others or to be added to your own collection.

NOTE

If you want to get fancy, you can obtain blank CD labels on which you print to create your own custom labels. Or you can just write on the label side of the CD with a felt-tip pen

Chapter 18

Putting Your Projects on DVD

The DVD is on its way to replacing the CD (and most other removable media) as the standard way to provide large amounts of digital data (okay, that is a bit of an exaggeration, the CD will be around for a long time to come). DVDs really offer only one benefit when compared to other removable media, but it is a huge one (pun intended). DVDs provide a tremendous amount of storage space on a single disc—most DVD media provide 4.7GB of storage space. No other removable media even comes close to the DVD's combination of price and storage space.

The DVD's abundance of space and the fact that it is an all-digital media make the DVD the preferred choice for the distribution of commercial movies. And, with the introduction of DVD-R drives on the Mac (where Apple has again led the way), creating DVDs on personal computers has become a practical reality.

NOTE

One benefit that a CD does have over a DVD is the cost of each disc. Blank DVD media currently cost about 10 times what blank CD media do (around $5/disc compared to $.50/disc or less). However, the cost/MB difference is not all that much. And the prices of DVD media continue to tumble; it won't be long until the cost difference between the two media types is negligible.

Building DVDs in Mac OS X

There are two fundamental tools that you can use to get your projects onto a DVD:

- iDVD
- The Finder

Each of these tools has a set of advantages and disadvantages.

> **NOTE**
>
> While DVD-R drives are not yet as common as CD-R drives, the Apple SuperDrive (which can burn DVDs and CDs) is an available option on all Power Macs and iMacs. There are also external DVD-R drives that can be added to any Mac with a FireWire port (see Chapter 7, "Digital Lifestyle Hardware: Digital Rules, Analog Drools").

Using iDVD to Create DVDs

Using iDVD enables you to create very sophisticated DVDs that include features such as motion menus. Users don't have to figure out how to access your projects on DVD; they just insert the disc and use their DVD player's controls to get to the gems you have created for them. That's because the DVDs that you create can be played in most standard DVD players, which means that they can be viewed on computers as well as in most of the players that people use to watch DVD movies. Using iDVD to create a DVD is easy because it manages the media that goes onto the DVD for you.

Using iDVD does have a couple of drawbacks. The biggest is that it converts everything that you place on the DVD into the 640 x 480 format, which can lower the resolution of your images (in slideshows and QuickTime movies). If you view the DVD on a standard analog television, you probably won't notice, but the reduced resolution can be very noticeable on a computer. The other drawback to using iDVD is that you are pretty much limited to QuickTime movies or slideshows. (Of course, since you now know how many types of media you can convert into QuickTime, this isn't all that severe a limitation.)

Using the Finder to Create Your DVDs

Using the Finder to burn a DVD enables you to place any file on a DVD so there are no limits to what you can include on it. The Finder's other benefit is that you aren't limited to a specific resolution for your projects; using the techniques you learned earlier in this book, you can create high-resolution versions of your projects. Because you can store up to 4.7GB on a single DVD, it is likely that even the highest-resolution project that you create will fit on a single DVD.

The "cons" of using the Finder are significant. The biggest is that the DVDs you create can be used only on a computer. Another is that your projects won't have a cool interface like they do when you use iDVD to create a DVD; your disc will look and act just like any other volume opened in a Finder window. This means more work for the viewer, and the viewer has to understand how to use the files that you provide (such as how to view a QuickTime movie).

Choosing the Right Tool for the Job

Choosing which tool to use isn't all that tough. If you want the DVD to be viewable in most DVD players, the choice is simple—use iDVD. If you intend for the DVD to be used on computers only, the choice becomes just a bit more difficult. You have to balance iDVD's ability to create a "packaged" DVD with a slick interface versus the Finder's ability to maintain high-resolution versions of your projects.

NOTE

Of course, you don't really need to choose between the two tools. You can take the same projects and use both tools to create two different versions of the DVD. One can feature a slick interface and can be used on most DVD players while the other can be your "special edition" and feature high-resolution versions of your projects.

Whichever method you choose, the previous chapters in this book provide you with the knowledge you need to create your projects.

Creating a DVD with iDVD

Using iDVD to build a DVD enables you to do amazing things. Creating a DVD, popping it into your home theater system, and using the awesome motion menus and other features to view your projects is nothing less than a thrill. (Other people will enjoy them too so don't be stingy with your creations!)

Because iDVD is one of the core digital lifestyle applications, Chapter 5, "iDVD: The Power of a Movie Production House in Your Mac," explains all you need to know to use it to put your projects on DVD.

Creating a DVD with the Finder

Using the Finder to create a DVD is nearly identical to using the Finder to put your projects on a CD. The primary difference is that you have a lot more room in which you store your projects, so you can balance the quality/file size trade-off more in favor of quality.

The following are the four general steps to putting your projects on DVD:

1. Prepare your projects for DVD.
2. Build the DVD.
3. Burn the DVD.
4. Test the DVD.

Preparing Your Digital Lifestyle Projects for a DVD

Just as with a CD, you can store any file on a DVD, but for the purposes of this book, the following types are the most important:

- ◆ **iMovie projects**. By exporting an iMovie project as a QuickTime movie, you can put it on a DVD. When you export your project with the intent of putting it on a DVD, you can use larger image sizes, higher frame rates, and so on.

NOTE

Remember that hardware speeds can limit the playback of your QuickTime movies. If you create very large movies with high frame rates, the computer on which they are displayed might not be able to handle the high data rates required to present the movie in a smooth fashion. Make sure you check out your final product using equipment that is similar to what your audience will be using. Just because a DVD has room for huge, high-quality movies, your audience won't necessarily have the hardware that can play that movie in the quality that you provide it.

- ◆ **QuickTime movies**. You can place any QuickTime movie on a DVD just like you can place it on a CD.
- ◆ **Images**. You can place individual image files on a DVD.
- ◆ **Sounds**. Just like images, you can place sound files on a DVD.

◆ **Image Web sites**. You can use iPhoto to create a Web site for images and put that site on a DVD.

◆ **Slideshows**. Use the techniques you learned in Chapter 15, "Building Digital Lifestyle Slideshows," to create high-resolution slideshows as QuickTime movies.

Preparing these types of projects for a DVD is analogous to preparing them for a CD. For example, you need to make sure that your QuickTime movies are either self-contained or that you include any files on which they depend. For space reasons, I won't repeat the details here—you can find the details of preparing your projects for CD/DVD in Chapter 17, "Putting Your Projects on CD."

The one difference is that because you have more room on a DVD, you can often choose to create higher quality files. In other words, the quality versus file size trade-off can be shifted more towards quality since file size isn't usually a significant limitation for DVD.

Archiving Digital Media on DVD

Because DVDs can hold such a large amount of data, they are very useful as a way to archive the digital lifestyle projects on which you are no longer working, as well as the various digital media files that you develop as you create your projects. This use of DVDs will be described in detail in Chapter 20, "Organizing and Archiving Your Digital Media."

Building the DVD

After you have prepared your projects for a DVD, building a DVD is also quite similar to building a CD.

Build a DVD in the Finder

1. Insert a blank DVD-R disc into your DVD recordable drive.

2. At the prompt, name the DVD you are creating by typing the name in the Name box (see Figure 18.1).

3. Click Prepare. The DVD will be mounted on your desktop.

4. Open a Finder window showing the contents of the DVD.

5. Create folders to organize the contents of the DVD.

Figure 18.1 *You can store about 4.2GB of data on a DVD when you use the Finder to burn it.*

6. Add a ReadMe file to explain what the contents of the DVD are and to provide any special instructions (see Figure 18.2).

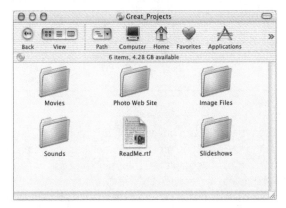

Figure 18.2 *Organize your DVDs so that the people to whom you provide them will understand what they have received.*

7. Drag files from other Finder windows to the folders that you created in Step 5. You can also place files at the root level of the DVD if you prefer to leave them "loose."

8. Continue placing files and reorganizing the DVD until you have it just the way you want it. Until you burn a DVD, you can change its contents in any way, such as by removing files, creating new folders, moving files and folders around, and so on.

Burning the DVD

After you have organized your DVD and added your projects to it, burning the DVD won't be a challenge for you.

Burn a DVD from the Finder

1. Check the DVD one more time to make sure it has all the files you want to include and that they are organized appropriately.

2. Select the DVD's icon in a Finder window or open the DVD in a Finder window.

3. Choose File, Burn Disc.

4. In the resulting dialog, click Burn. You'll see a progress bar that tells you how the process is proceeding. The process will work through several stages including preparing the data, writing to the disc, and verifying the disc. Fortunately, you can use your Mac for other tasks while it is burning a DVD because the Finder will continue to burn even when it is in the background. Depending on your Mac's speed, what else you are doing on the machine, and how much data is going on the disc, the process can take from several minutes to an hour or more.

TIP

Activities that require heavy access to your Mac's drives, such as graphics or video work, can cause slight pauses in the DVD burning process. Sometimes, these pauses can lead to problems, and the disc might not complete the burning process or might not work properly even if it does complete it. Because DVD media is relatively expensive, you probably don't want to trash many discs. For the best chance at creating a "good" DVD, don't burn the DVD until you don't need your Mac for anything else. Then quit all running applications before you click the Burn button so that the Finder has all your Mac's resources available to it.

Testing the DVD

After the burn process is complete, eject the DVD. Then reinsert it and open its files and folders to make sure that it works as you planned. For example, open QuickTime movies and play them. Try to move about a Web site on the disc. Open image files. Check the disc's organization.

If something is wrong, you will need to try again (unfortunately, DVD media isn't yet cheap so you should check your DVD as much as possible before you burn it). For example, if a movie plays poorly, it might be that the image size is too large or the frame rate is too high to play back from a DVD-ROM drive (try dragging it to your hard drive and playing it from there). In such a case, you might want to adjust the settings you used for the movie until you achieve better performance. Or just add instructions to your ReadMe file to explain that the files should be moved to a hard drive for better performance.

NOTE

Of course, expecting a user to have the room to store a 3GB movie on her hard drive probably isn't a reasonable expectation on your part.

After you are sure that the DVD is "done," it is ready to be shared with others or to be added to your own collection.

NOTE

Just as for CDs, you can obtain DVD labels on which you create custom labels for the DVDs that you print. Or you can just write on the label side of the DVD with a felt-tip pen

Chapter 19

Creating and Hosting
a Digital Lifestyle
Web Site with iTools

Creating a Web site for your digital lifestyle projects is a great way to share them with the world—literally. Anyone who can access the Internet can access your Web site and view the fruits of your labor. Using Apple's iTools services, you can create a digital lifestyle Web site easily and inexpensively (for no cost if you limit yourself to 20MB of content or less).

> **NOTE**
>
> In this chapter, I have assumed that you have read Chapter 6, "iTools: Maybe the Only Internet Tool You Ever Need," your iTools account is set up, you understand how to use your iDisk, and you are familiar with HomePage. If you haven't read Chapter 6, do so before continuing with this chapter.

Preparing Projects for the Web

Just like the other distribution options about which you have learned in this part of the book, you can use an iTools Web site to distribute all sorts of projects. And like the other chapters in this part, this chapter focuses on the following four types of content:

- iMovie projects
- iPhoto images
- QuickTime movies
- Files for downloading from an FTP page

Also like other distribution methods, you need to spend some time preparing your projects for the Web before you upload them to your iDisk (as you learned in Chapter 6, you place the content for your Web site in the various folders of your iDisk).

Unlike other distribution methods, file size is critical when you place your projects on a Web site. Exactly how critical file size is depends on an assumption you make about the people who will be visiting your site. If you believe that most of the people who will come to your site will use a slow Internet connection, such as a 56K modem, then it is imperative that you make files smaller even if that means that the quality of your projects suffers. People using a slow connection aren't likely to wait long periods of time that it takes to view large files. If you believe that most people visiting your site will be using a fast connection, such as a cable modem, then file size is still important, but not as vital as it is for those people who use slower connections.

The other reason that file size is important is because you are limited in the amount of storage space on your iDisk. The smaller the files sizes you use, the more projects you will be able to store on your site.

If you haven't upgraded your iDisk storage space, I strongly suggest that you do so before you start building your Web site. While it is generous of Apple to provide 20MB of storage space at no cost to Mac users, that isn't sufficient to build much of a site if you intend to include QuickTime movies on it. Even a small, short QuickTime movie can be 3MB or more. It doesn't take many to fill up 20MB of iDisk space. See Chapter 6 for the details of upgrading your iDisk.

Streaming Versus Downloading

When creating content for your Web site, especially for QuickTime movies, the concept of streaming as compared to downloading is important. When a file is streamed, it can be viewed as it is downloaded to a computer. The benefit of this is that the viewer doesn't have to wait until the file has downloaded completely before being able to view it. When a file is meant to be downloaded, it must be downloaded to a computer before it can be viewed. For those people who enjoy a high-bandwidth connection to the Internet, such as a cable modem, viewing streamed content is almost instantaneous and, in the best case, is similar to viewing a television channel (click the link and immediately view the content). However, for people who use a low-bandwidth connection to the Internet, such as a 56K modem, streaming is not all that much better than downloading it. This is because the connection has such a limited data transfer rate that most of the file has to be downloaded before the playback process can start (in order to be able to view the entire file without pausing). If you believe that most of the people who will be visiting your site use slow connections, you might consider providing files that can be downloaded along with the streamed version. With a slower connection, waiting for a file to download can sometimes be less frustrating than waiting for a file to "stream" enough so that it can be viewed.

One solution to the slow connection/low quality or fast connection/high quality tradeoff is to provide two versions of your project files on your Web site. One version can be a smaller, lower quality version for people who use a slow Internet connection. The other version can be a larger, higher quality version for those people who use a high-speed connection. This is a common practice on many Web sites, such as Apple's QuickTime Movie Trailer page. Most trailers are presented in various sizes for different connection speeds.

Preparing iMovie Projects for the Web

Preparing iMovie projects for the Web is similar to preparing them for other means of distribution. You use iMovie Export tools to export the movie in the QuickTime format, using settings that are appropriate for the delivery that you intend to use.

Prepare an iMovie Project for the Web

1. Open the iMovie project that you want to prepare for the Web.

2. Choose File, Export Movie (or press ⌘+E).

3. In the Export Movie dialog, choose To QuickTime on the Export pop-up menu.

4. Select the appropriate format on the Formats pop-up menu, such as Streaming Web Movie, Small (see Figure 19.1). (See the following discussion for information on the formats you might choose to use).

5. Click Export.

Figure 19.1 *The Streaming Web Movie, Small format is a good choice for iMovie projects that you will place on your Web site.*

6. In the resulting dialog, choose a location in which to save your movie, name it, and click Save. The movie will be saved using the settings that you select.

NOTE

When you use highly compressed formats, such as those Apple has designed for the Web, the export process can take a long time. Don't be surprised if exporting even a relatively short movie takes 20 to 30 minutes.

The only real nuances to preparing an iMovie project for the Web are the format settings that you choose to export it with. The default format settings that Apple has designed to be used for "online" movies are the following:

◆ **Web Movie, Small**. This format provides decent quality with a size of 240 x 180 pixels and a frame rate of 12 fps. The audio settings are also reasonable. However, this format is not designed for streaming so you should choose it only if you will be providing the movie for downloading rather than for streaming.

◆ **Email Movie, Small**. This choice favors small file size over movie quality. At a size of 160 x 120 pixels, a frame rate of 10 fps, and a compressed mono soundtrack, your movie won't be very high quality, but, the file size will be small.

◆ **Streaming Web Movie, Small**. This format is a good choice for most of your iMovie projects. It offers a fair compromise between movie quality and file size and results in a movie that is ready to be streamed. It features a size of 240 x 180 playing at 12 fps and with a reasonably high-quality soundtrack.

Again, you aren't limited to these default format settings. You can choose among the other default values or use the Expert settings to customize an exported movie. Just remember that people have to move the content of your exported movie over their Internet connection, and you need to always be conscious of that fact so that you keep your movie files to a reasonable size.

The Expert QuickTime Settings also work as they do for other distribution methods (see Chapter 17, "Putting Your Projects on CD," for more information about using the Expert QuickTime Settings). However, when using these settings for a Web movie, you should configure the movie so that it can be streamed.

When you open the Expert QuickTime Settings dialog, you will see the "Prepare for internet" section (see Figure 19.2). You use these tools to create a streaming version of your movie. To do so, check the "Prepare for internet" checkbox and select the type of streaming server for which you want to prepare the movie. For an iTools Web site, you should choose the QuickTime Streaming Server option.

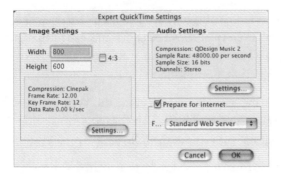

Figure 19.2 *A movie exported with these settings would be appropriate only for someone with a high-speed connection to the Internet (although the movie will stream, note how large the image size is).*

Preparing iPhoto Images for the Web

There are two ways to provide your iPhoto images on your iTools Web site: as individual files or as photo albums.

Preparing Individual iPhoto Images for the Web

To prepare images for the Web, you need only to decide the resolution at which you want to provide the images. The trade-off remains the same; higher resolution images require larger file sizes and more time for people to view. However, image file sizes generally won't be huge even if you export them at a relatively large size.

To prepare your iPhoto images for the Web site, simply export them from iPhoto at the resolution you desire (export them to a single folder so you can move that folder to your iDisk). (For a detailed explanation of exporting images from iPhoto as separate files, see Chapter 17.)

Preparing iPhoto Photo Albums for the Web

You can also upload photo albums from iPhoto to HomePage to make them available on your Web site. You can choose a specific page from which to make your album available and then publish the album to that page. For now, just create the albums that you want to put on your Web site. When you build the sites, you can move back into iPhoto and upload the album to your Web site.

Preparing QuickTime Movies for the Web

As with your iMovie projects, you need to prepare your QuickTime movies to stream from your Web site so that people can watch your movies as they download. You can also adjust a QuickTime movie's video and audio settings similarly to how you use the Expert QuickTime Settings in iMovie.

Prepare a QuickTime Movie for the Web

1. Open the QuickTime movie that you want to prepare for the Web in QuickTime Player.
2. Choose File, Export (or press ⌘+E).
3. In the "Save export file as" dialog, choose Movie to QuickTime Movie on the Export pop-up menu.
4. Click the Options button. You will see the Movie Settings dialog (see Figure 19.3). You can use this dialog to configure your movie for the Web, including setting its Video, Audio, and Internet Streaming properties.

Figure 19.3 *Using QuickTime Player's Movie Settings dialog is similar to using the Expert QuickTime Settings dialog in iMovie.*

5. Click the Settings button in the Video area. Use the resulting Compression Settings dialog to configure the video compressor, quality, frame rate, and other video parameters for the movie.

TIP

Just like your iMovie movies, more quality means larger file sizes. You need to weigh the quality of the movie as you export against the file size you end up with.

6. If you want to apply QuickTime effects to the movie, click the Filter button and use the Choose Video Filter dialog to apply and configure a video filter.

7. If you want to resize the movie, click the Size button, click the "Use custom size" radio button, and enter the size of your movie. Click OK, and the movie that you export will be the size you entered.

8. Click the Settings button in the Audio area and use the Sound Settings dialog to configure the audio compressor and audio quality of your movie.

9. Check the "Prepare for Internet Streaming" checkbox and choose the type of streaming that you want to use on the pop-up menu. The Hinted Streaming option is the best choice when posting a movie to an iTools Web site. When you choose that option, the Settings button next to the pop-up menu will become active. You can use this button to customize the streaming configuration of your movie; however, unless you really understand streaming, just use the default Hinted Streaming configuration.

10. When you are done, check your settings to make sure that your movie is configured the way you want it to be (see Figure 19.4).

11. Name the movie, choose a save location, and click Save. The movie will be prepared as you configured it and will be saved in the location you selected. The Exporting Movie progress window will show you when the process is complete.

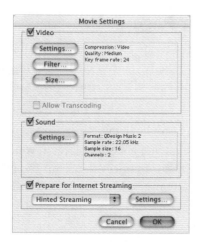

Figure 19.4 *This movie has audio compression applied to it and will be prepared for streaming from the iTools Web site I am creating.*

Preparing Files for Downloading from an FTP Page

A File Transfer Protocol (FTP) page enables you to provide files so that people can download them to their computer (instead of viewing them from the Web pages). There are many uses for this, and you can provide any file for downloading by creating FTP pages on your iTools Web site.

To prepare files for downloading, you can simply post the files as you have them, but you should compress those files so that the file size is as small as possible. You can also compress multiple files into a single compressed file so people can download all of them with a single click.

The dominant compression scheme on the Mac is the .sit file format, which is created by Aladdin Systems' StuffIt utilities. You can learn more about these utilities by visiting www.aladdinsys.com. You can also download trial versions of DropStuff or StuffIt Deluxe and use them for 30 days without charge.

The details of compressing files are beyond the scope of this book, but after you have a compression application, it isn't hard to do. (For detailed information, see my book *Special Edition Using Mac OS X.*)

Preparing Images for Each Project Page

When you create a Web site, you can choose to create a Site Menu page that acts like that site's Home page. On this Site Menu page, you can include an image to represent each project's page. You store these images in the Pictures folder on your iDisk.

To make the creation of your Site Menu page faster later, take the time to select or create an image to represent each project that you are going to place on your Web page. For example, capture a frame from an iMovie project to use on the Movie page for that movie, select an image from an album to use to preview that album's page, and so on.

Place all of your preview images in a folder.

Uploading Files to Your iDisk

After you have prepared the content of your site, you upload the files you will place on your Web pages to the various folders on your iDisk.

Upload Files for the Web Site to Your iDisk

1. Open your iDisk (see Chapter 6 if you don't know how to do this).

NOTE

Remember that you will only be able to place files on your iDisk, and thus on your Web site, up to your iDisk's size limit (which is only 20MB if you haven't upgraded it).

2. Place your movies in the Movies folder.
3. Place any folders containing images that you exported from iPhoto in the Pictures folder.
4. Place the folder containing your preview images in the Pictures folder, too.
5. Place the files that you want to provide on an FTP page in your Public folder (see Figure 19.5).

Figure 19.5 *You can see some of the contents that will be available for my Web site in my iDisk.*

NOTE

For those of you who use a low-speed connection to the Internet, such as a 56k modem, it's good news/bad news time. The good news is that you have a chance to really develop your patience. The bad news is that you have a chance to really develop your patience. When you build an iTools Web site, you move relatively large amounts of data around. Moving this much data over a slow connection can be maddening. Not only do large files seem to take forever to upload to your iDisk, sometimes even opening windows or moving to the next HomePage screen can take what seems to be an eternity. Unfortunately, there isn't much you can do about it (if a high-speed connection option is available to you, now might be the time to upgrade). You can lower your frustration somewhat by working with iTools during "off-peak hours," which are typically early morning hours for the west coast of the United States (U.S. Pacific Time). When fewer people are using iTools services, these services will work a little faster for you. But, the main problem is the size of the "pipe" through which you are moving data. Unless you can increase this, it will help to have the patience of Gandhi to build a large site. (For those of you who enjoy a high-speed connection to the Internet, such as with a cable modem, you'll really appreciate the speed at which you can build a Web site.)

Building Your iTools Web Site

After you have your site's content prepared, you can use the HomePage service to build your Web site. First, start by logging into HomePage. Then, you create the Web sites that you will be providing. After that, you create the pages that make up each Web site.

Logging into HomePage

To get started, log into your account and move to the HomePage page.

Open the HomePage Web Page

1. Launch your Web browser and move to itools.mac.com.

> **TIP**
>
> Internet Explorer includes a link to the iTools page on the default Favorites bar.

2. Click the HomePage button or the HomePage tab. If you aren't logged into your account already, you will see the iTools Login page. If you are logged in already, you will move directly to the HomePage page (and you can skip step 3).
3. Log in to your iTools account.

You will see your HomePage page, and you are ready to begin building your Web site (see Figure 19.6). In the upper part of the page, you see the Sites window and the Pages window. The Sites window lists the sites that are part of your iTools Web site. The Pages window shows the pages that are part of the site selected in the Sites window. For example, in Figure 19.6, the site called "miser_photos" is selected and it contains the three pages shown in the Pages window.

Designing Your iTools Web Site

Your iTools Web site can consist of multiple Web sites with each site having multiple Web pages (see Figure 19.7). Each Web site within your iTools Web site will have its own URL that people can use to move to that site. Once you have created

Figure 19.6 *The HomePage page enables you to build your iTools Web site (you can see that I already have several Web sites as part of my HomePage Web site).*

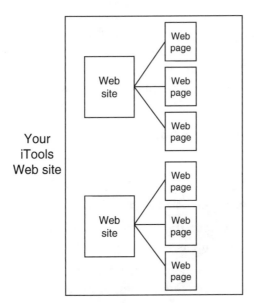

Figure 19.7 *An iTools Web site can include multiple subsites with each subsite having multiple pages.*

a site, people can use the links that you will create with HomePage to move around.

Your Web site will be much better if you design it before you start clicking HomePage buttons to build it. A site design does not have to be complex. A simple sketch that identifies each site and its component pages will take only a few minutes to create and will save you time while creating your site—not to mention enabling you to create a site that makes more sense to people who visit it.

Within each site, plan the types and numbers of pages you are going to create. You can start each site with a Site Menu page that provides a top-level view of the site and acts as that site's Home page. Then determine which other page types will be included. In this chapter, you will see examples of Movie, Photo Album, and FTP pages, but there are others you can add as well.

One other factor to decide is whether you want to protect any of your sites with a password. If you protect a site, a viewer will have to have its password in order to be able to view the site. This enables you to control who has access to your Web site. If you want just anyone to be able to browse your site, leave it unprotected.

TIP

Your iTools Web site can include both protected and unprotected sites.

When your site is designed, you are ready to use HomePage's tools to build it.

Creating Sites on Your iTools Web Site

Start by creating each site that will be part of your iTools Web site.

Create the Sites that Compose Your iTools Web Site

1. Under the Sites list area of the HomePage page, click the + button. You will see the HomePage Create a Site page (see Figure 19.8).

2. Enter the name of the site you are creating. You can't use any spaces in the site name, but you can use underscores, hyphens, and so on. The site name is case-sensitive so enter it just as you want it to be in the URL. Try to make the name appropriate for the contents of your site.

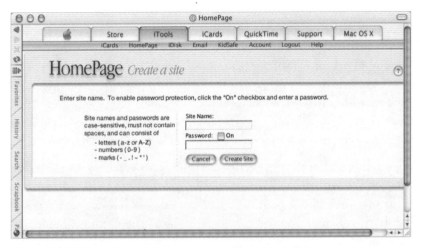

Figure 19.8 *Use this page to create sites on your iTools Web site.*

3. If you want to password protect the site, check the On checkbox and enter the password for the site in the Password box.

4. Check the information you have entered, and if it looks good, click the Create Site button. The site will be created, you will return to the HomePage page, and you will see the site in the Sites window.

5. Repeat Steps 1 through 4 for each site that will be part of your Web site. When you are done, you will have a list of sites, although each site will not have any content (see Figure 19.9).

NOTE

If you look carefully at Figure 19.9, you can see that one of my Web sites, called dig_life_files, is marked with the padlock icon. That indicates that the site is password protected. (In case you are curious, this is the site on which I stored the chapter files for this book when they were ready for editing.)

Creating Pages on Your Sites

After you have created some sites, you can create pages on those sites. In the following sections, you will see examples of several types of pages. After you have worked through these examples, creating pages of other types will be just as straightforward.

Figure 19.9 *Here, you can see the sites I have created. The selected site (digital_life_rocks) contains no pages yet.*

Creating Movie Pages

Create movie pages to display your QuickTime movies; you need to create one page for each movie on your site.

Create a Movie Page

1. On the Site list, select the site on which you want to create a movie page.

2. Click the + button under the Pages window. You will see the HomePage Select a theme page.

2. Click the iMovies tab. The designs that are available for iMovie pages will appear (see Figure 19.10).

3. Click the page design that you want to use. That design will appear in an Edit your page window.

4. Click the Edit button at the top of the window. The fields on the page will become editable, and you will see the QuickTime icon and Choose button in the movie display area.

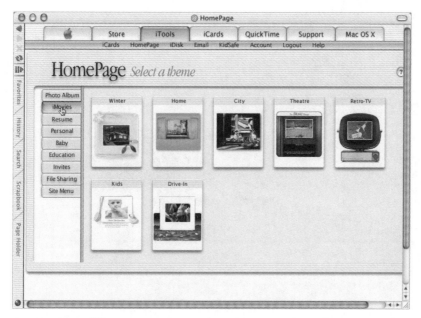

Figure 19.10 *When you create a movie page, you can choose from among these designs.*

5. Edit the text that appears on the page by selecting it and typing the text you want to appear. Most iMovie pages have a page title, movie title, and movie description that you can enter. You might have to scroll up and down the window to see all of the text fields.

6. If you want the page to have a counter that tells you how many times that page has been viewed, scroll down until you see the zero icon and check the Show checkbox next to the icon.

7. In the movie display area, click the Choose button. You'll see the movies contained in the Movies folder on your iDisk. The first movie in the list will play in the Preview window.

8. Select the movie that you want to place on the page and click the Preview button to preview it. The page will be refreshed, and you will be able to preview the selected movie (see Figure 19.11).

9. Select the movie that you want to provide on the page and click Choose. You will return to the Edit your page screen; now the movie area will say, "Click here to play movie." If you click in this area, the movie will begin to play.

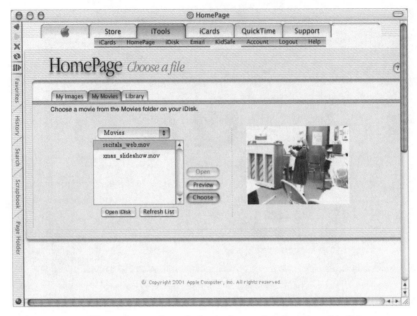

Figure 19.11 *Here, the movie recitals_web.mov is selected and is being previewed.*

10. Continue editing the text on the page or select another movie until the page is done.

11. Click the Publish button. The page will be created as part of the site you selected in Step 1. You will move to the Congratulations page that shows you the URL to the page you have created, enables you to announce the page via an iCard, or lets you return to the HomePage screen by clicking Return to HomePage. When you move back to the HomePage screen, you will see the page you created on the Pages list.

Creating Picture Pages

Creating a page to display individual image files, such as those that you have exported from iPhoto or that you have from other sources, can be done with the following steps.

Create a Picture Page

1. On your HomePage page, select the site to which you want to add a Picture page.

2. Click the + button under the Pages list. You will move to the Select a theme page.

3. Click the Photo Album tab.

4. Click the album theme that you want to use for the page. You will move to the Choose a folder page.

5. Select a folder that you placed in the Pictures folder on your iDisk.

TIP

You can preview the images in a folder by selecting it, clicking open, choosing the images that you want to preview, and clicking Preview.

---

6. Select the folder containing the images you want to publish and click Choose. You will move to the "Edit your page" page.

7. Click the Edit button. The text fields on the page will become editable.

8. Edit the text on the page. Most picture pages contain a page title, an album title, and a description. You can also edit each image's title, which is the file name by default.

9. Uncheck the Show checkbox for any images that you don't want to appear on the page.

10. Check the Show checkbox next to the counter symbol if you want the number of visitors to the page to be tracked.

11. Click the Preview button. You will see your page as it will appear on the Web (see Figure 19.12).

12. If something isn't right, click the Edit button to return to the Edit mode.

13. Continuing making changes and previewing the result until the page is right.

TIP

You can even change the theme applied to a page. Click the Themes button to move to the Change your theme page. Select a new theme and when you return to the Web page, it will have a whole new look.

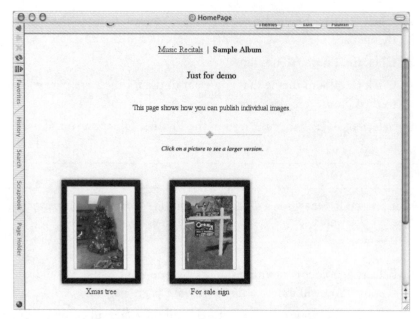

Figure 19.12 *This Photo Album page certainly won't make anyone proud—but you get the idea I'm sure.*

14. Click Publish. You will move to the confirmation page that tells you the page is now on the Web; its URL is also provided. You can visit the page by clicking the URL, send an announcement by clicking the iCards button, or return to the HomePage by clicking the Return to HomePage button.

Creating Photo Album Pages

A better way to publish photos from your iPhoto Library is to publish them directly from iPhoto.

Publish a Photo Web Page from iPhoto

1. Open iPhoto.
2. Select the album that you created for the Web.
3. Click the Share button.

4. Click the HomePage button. iPhoto will connect to HomePage, and you
will see the Publish HomePage screen (see Figure 19.13). The photos in
the album that you selected will appear on the page. The available themes
appear just above the tool bar at the bottom of the window. All the text
on the page, such as the page title, description, and image titles, will be
editable.

Figure 19.13 *Publishing images from iPhoto to the Web is a fast and inte-
grated operation.*

5. Edit all the text on the page. To edit a piece of text, select it and replace it
with the text you want to appear on the page.

6. Click one of the theme buttons to apply the theme to the page. The page
will immediately appear in the theme you select.

7. Choose the Web site to which you want to publish the page on the
Publish to pop-up menu (see Figure 19.14).

8. When the page is done, click Publish. iPhoto will connect to HomePage
and will upload the photos in the selected album along with the Web
page itself. A progress bar will appear to show you how the process is
going. When the process is complete, you will see a confirmation dialog.
To visit the page you have published, click the Visit Page Now button. To
return to iPhoto, click the OK button.

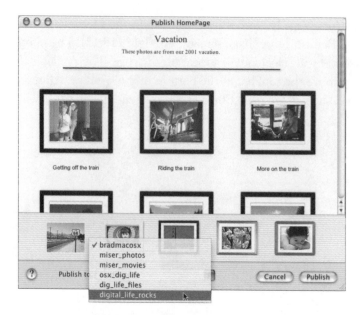

Figure 19.14 *The Web sites that make up your iTools Web site will be listed on the Publish to pop-up menu.*

Creating an FTP Page

An FTP page is a great way to share files with people. The files you place on an FTP page can be downloaded by anyone who visits the page. The files that appear on the FTP page are those contained in the Public folder on your iDisk.

Create an FTP Page

1. On the HomePage page, select the site to which you want to add an FTP page.
2. Click the + button.
3. On the Select a theme page, click the File Sharing tab.
4. Choose a theme for your FTP page.
5. On the "Edit your page" page, click the Edit button.
6. Edit the text on the page, which includes the page title and description.
7. Click Preview to preview the page.
8. Click Publish to publish the page. When the page is published, you will see the confirmation screen. You can visit the page, announce it, or return to HomePage (see Figure 19.15).

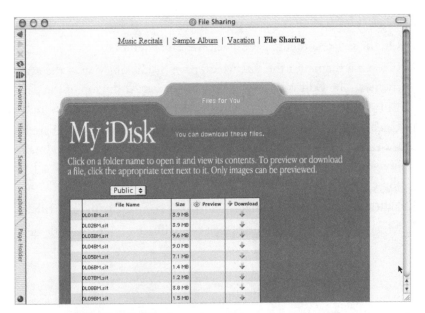

Figure 19.15 *While file Sharing pages aren't much to look at, they are a great way to share your files with others.*

Creating a Site Menu Page

A Site Menu page provides visitors with a "menu" of the contents of that site. If you have more than one page on a site, it should include a Site Menu page. On the Site Menu page, each page on your Web site will be represented by a page preview.

> **NOTE**
>
> In a bit of counter-intuitiveness, you should actually create the Site Menu page last because you can't complete it until the other pages on the site are available.

Create a Site Menu Page

1. On the HomePage page, select the site for which you want to create a Site Menu page.

> **NOTE**
>
> Notice that when you select a site, its URL appears at the top of the window.

2. Click the + button to add a page to the selected site.

3. On the Select a theme page, click the Site Menu tab.

4. Choose a theme for the Site Menu page by clicking one of the available themes. The Edit your page page will appear. At the top of the page, you will see all of the pages contained in the Web site you selected in Step 1.

5. Click Edit. The page's text will become editable, and you will see boxes for each page on the Web site. You can place preview or thumbnail images in each box to represent that page on the site menu. By default, these boxes are linked to the other pages on the site.

6. Edit the site menu's text fields, including the page name and title.

7. Move to the box for the first page; you will see each page's title below its box (see Figure 19.16).

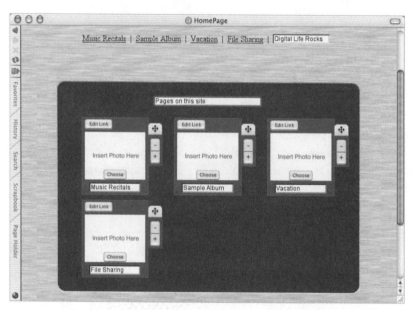

Figure 19.16 *Use a Site Menu page to make your Web site easier to navigate.*

8. Click the Choose button. You will move to the Choose a file page, and you will see the contents of your Pictures folder on the My Images tab. In addition to this tab, you will see the My Movies tab and the Library tab. The Movies tab will contain the contents of your Movies folder. The

Library tab contains some images provided by Apple that you can use to represent your Web pages.

9. To select an image to represent the page, select the file that you want to use to represent the Web page. If you created a preview image folder and uploaded that folder to your Pictures folder on your iDisk, this is a simple task because all of your preview images will be in this folder. To open a folder, select it and click Open. You can preview images by selecting them and clicking Preview.

TIP

As you move into folders, the pop-up menu above the list of folders will become active. You can open this pop-up menu to choose other folders within the currently selected folder.

---

10. Select the image that you want to use and click Choose. You will return to the "Edit your page" page, and the image will appear in the Web page's box (see Figure 19.17).

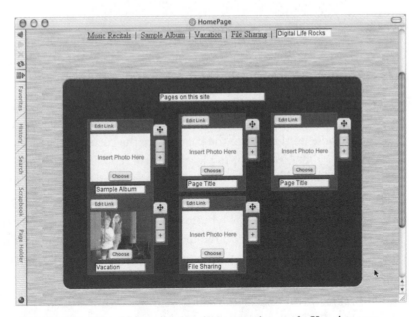

Figure 19.17 *Here I have added an image preview to the Vacation page.*

11. Continue developing your site menu page using the information that follows these steps.

12. When your Site Menu page is complete, click Publish to publish it. You will see a confirmation screen similar to those you have seen before.

The Site Menu tools are a bit more complex than those you use to create other pages, but that is because the pages themselves are a bit more complex. Following are some of the tasks you might want to do for a Site Menu page and the steps you need to do to accomplish those specific tasks.

The controls you have for each page preview are shown in Figure 19.18.

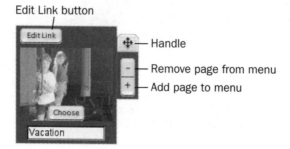

Figure 19.18 *You can use the controls you see here to configure each page as it appears on your site menu page.*

The tools you see for each page on the menu are the following:

◆ **Handle**. Drag a page's handle to move it around on the site menu. The site menu is organized by a grid. To move a page to another location, drag its handle until it is over the page where the current page resides in the location that you want to place it. It will replace the existing page; the current page will move into the place where the page you were moving was.

◆ **Add page to menu**. Click the + button to add a page to the site menu. A new, blank page will appear on the menu. You can then use the Edit Link button to link that page to a page on your site or to a Web page located elsewhere.

◆ **Remove page from menu**. Click the – button to remove a page from the menu. When you do this, the page itself is not affected. It just no longer appears on the site menu.

◆ **Edit Link button**. You use this button to link a page preview to a Web page. When you create a site menu page, each page on your Web site is represented on the site menu. However, you can add more pages to the site menu. When you click a page's Edit Link button, you will see the Edit your links page. This page has three tabs: My Pages, Other Pages, and Email. To link the preview to one of your pages, click the My Pages tab, select the page to which you want to link the preview, and click Apply. To link the preview to a page elsewhere on the Internet, click the Other Pages tab, enter the URL for the site to which you are linking it, and click Apply. To link the preview to an email address, click the Email tab, enter the email address, and click Apply.

To choose one of your movies as the page preview, do the following steps.

Choose a Movie as a Page Preview

1. Click the Choose button for the page.

2. On the Choose a file page, click the My Movies tab.

3. Select the movie that you want to use as a preview of the page and click Choose. You will return to the Edit your page page, and the QuickTime logo will appear in the page preview.

To use an image from Apple's Library to represent a page, do the following steps.

Choose an Apple Library Image to Represent a Page

1. Click the Choose button for the page.

2. On the Choose a file page, click the Library tab. You will see a list of folders containing images that you can use.

3. Select a folder and click Open. The images in the folder you selected will be shown.

4. Select an image and click Preview to preview it.

5. Continue previewing images until you find the one you want to use.

6. Select the image and click Choose. The image that you chose will be applied to the Web page on the Edit your page page.

Lastly, after you have created a Site Menu page, make it your Web site's Home page (which iTools calls a start page).

Make a Menu Page the Site's Home Page

1. Select the site containing the Site Menu page.

2. Drag the Site Menu page up on the list of pages on the selected site until it is the topmost page. The HomePage will be refreshed, and the Site Menu page will be in bold to indicate it is now the start page for the site.

Testing Your iTools Web Site

After you have completed your Web site, you need to test it to make sure it is something that you want others to see.

Test Your iTools Web Site

1. Select the site that you want to test—make sure that the Site Menu page is selected.

2. Click its URL that appears at the top of the HomePage page. You will see your Web site; you should see the Site Menu page that you created (see Figure 19.19). If you have used a movie as a page preview, it will begin to play in the page preview box.

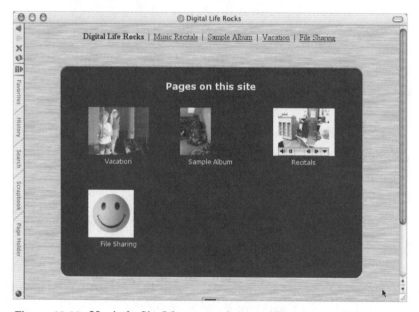

Figure 19.19 *Here's the Site Menu page that provides access to all the pages on my Web site.*

3. Click the page preview images to move to those pages to preview each one.

TIP

A link for each page on your site appears at the top of each page. Click a link to jump to that page.

If you find any problems, fix them by using the techniques you have already learned and those described in the next section.

Now, all you have to do is to provide the URL for your site to those whom you want to visit it. To make sure that you provide the URL to your Site Menu page, select it and use the URL that you see at the top of the HomePage page.

TIP

If you want to send iCards announcing your site and providing the URL, click the Announce Site button. Use the resulting screens to create and send an iCard that provides your new URL.

Maintaining Your iTools Web Site

After you have published your Web site, you can change it as you need to by doing the following tasks:

◆ To add more sites or more pages to an existing site, use the techniques you learned earlier in this chapter.

◆ To delete a site, select it and click the - button.

◆ To change a site, select it and click Edit. On the resulting Edit your site page, you can rename the site, make it password protected, and make the site the start site for your iTools Web site (similar to making a page a start page on a specific Web site). When you are done making changes, click Apply Changes to update the site.

◆ To delete a page from a site, select it and click -. After you confirm the deletion, the page will be removed from your site.

◆ To edit an existing page, select it and click Edit. You will move to the familiar Edit your page page.

◆ You move pages between Web sites by selecting a page and dragging it to another site.

Other Ways to Create and Post a Digital Lifestyle Web Site

With Mac OS X, you aren't limited to using HomePage to build and host a Web site. Here are some of your other options:

◆ **Use a Web site tool to create your own Web site**. You can use any Web page/site creation tool to build a Web site. Put the Web site in the Sites folder on your iDisk, and the site that you create will be available like sites that you create with the HomePage tool. This means that you can use more sophisticated tools, such as Adobe's GoLive, to build a Web site that is more distinctly yours. To learn how to post a Web site that you created outside of HomePage, check out the help available to you on the iTools site.

◆ **Use Mac OS X's built-in Web server to host a Web site**. Mac OS X includes the Apache Web server software that enables you to host Web sites right from your Mac. While the details of this process are beyond the scope of this book, a couple of sentences will give you the general idea. You build your site by using any tools that you would like. Then you place your site in the Sites folder located in your Home folder. Lastly, you use the Sharing pane of the System Preferences utility to turn Web sharing on. At that point, your Web site becomes available to anyone who can access your Mac, such as from a local network or even from the Internet (assuming your Mac is connected to the Internet in a way that makes this possible). For more detailed information, see my book *Special Edition Using Mac OS X*.

◆ **Use other hosting services**. There are thousands of other companies that will host a Web site that you create. Some of these companies also provide software that you can use to build your site, similar to Apple's HomePage service, while others require that you use your own tools to build a site. Some of these services are free, but the free sites usually offer limited storage space or require that you allow advertising on your site. Some services will also register a domain name for you so that the URL to your site can be something that you choose. To learn about some of these companies, use Sherlock to search the Internet for Web hosting services

Chapter 20

Organizing and Archiving Your Digital Media

After the fun and excitement of creating lots of digital lifestyle projects, you'll discover some not-so-pleasant facts about living the digital lifestyle. One is that many projects generate a lot of files. Another is that some of the files are big, and some are *really* big. Yet a third discovery will be that no matter how much hard drive space you have, you don't have enough disk space to keep all of the files that you generate.

All these discoveries should lead you to the conclusion that even the digital lifestyle requires some housecleaning now and again. After you finish projects, you should take some time to figure out what to do with the files that those projects have generated.

Housecleaning in the digital lifestyle consists of three general tasks:

◆ Cleaning up after projects to determine what to do with the files you have generated

◆ Organizing and cataloging the files you will keep

◆ Archiving the files that you don't want to store on your working drives

NOTE

Because creating projects is a lot more fun than organizing and archiving your files, you might be tempted to skip over the tasks in this chapter. However, the first time that you realize you need to find a specific file out of the hundreds you have generated, you might regret such a choice. Your digital lifestyle will be more enjoyable and more productive in the long run if you learn to practice good data management techniques.

Cleaning Up After Your Projects

After you have finished a project and distributed it in all the ways you want, you should let that project sit where it is for a while. Invariably, you will find that you want to distribute it another way or that you want to make some change to it.

After some time has passed during which you have not "touched" the project's files, you need to go back and evaluate the files that your project has generated.

The files that are generated by a project include the "final product," such as a QuickTime movie, a Web site, and so on. But there are likely dozens of other files that you created along the way, such as an iMovie soundtrack that you combined with a QuickTime slideshow. Then there are source files that you used to create a project, such as narration that you recorded for an iMovie project.

As you explore the files you have created, classify each in one of the following categories:

- **Trash**. You'll never, ever need these files again.
- **Accessible**. You want to keep these files available by leaving them on one of your hard drives.
- **Archive**. You want to keep these files, but you don't want to consume precious hard disk space with them so you need to archive them in one way or another.

Files in the first category are the easiest to deal with—just drag them to the Trash and be done with them. Files in the other two categories require that you take more complicated action with them.

TIP

Consider creating a "holding" folder for the files that you consider to be trash. Place the "trash" files in the holding folder for some period of time. Should you need them within that period of time, you can easily retrieve them, and then you might want to reconsider your classification of those files. Should you not need them during this period and they are truly trash, you can move them to the Trash and get rid of them.

Organizing and Cataloging Your Media Files

As you work with lots of files, you need to keep them organized in some logical way so that you can easily find the files you need. The need to organize and catalog files applies to both files that you want to keep accessible and those that you want to archive.

Using the Finder to Organize and Catalog Your Media Files

The Finder is your first stop on the organization trail. Mac OS X gets you started down this path by providing your Home folder that contains subfolders that, amazingly enough, are organized into convenient digital lifestyle categories such as Movies, Pictures, and so on.

Using these Finder folders provides you with a good starting point. Within those folders, you can create subfolders and organize them according to your preferences. For example, in the Movies folder, you might choose to create subfolders for your movie projects by date, by subject, and so on.

While the Finder isn't really a cataloging tool, with some logical and consistent naming on your part, you can make your files easy to find.

> **TIP**
>
> Remember that you can use Mac OS X's Sherlock application to search for files and folders by a number of different parameters. See my book *Special Edition Using Mac OS X* for information about using Sherlock.

Organizing and Cataloging Files with the Digital Lifestyle Applications

Each of the of the digital lifestyle applications provides different aspects for the organization and cataloging of your files.

QuickTime Player

When it comes to organizing your QuickTime movies, QuickTime Player offers no help. QuickTime movie files exist only independently of the application. You will have to use the Finder or another tool to keep control over your QuickTime movie files.

iTunes

iTunes helps you organize and catalog your music files automatically. For example, when you add music to your iTunes Library, you can add that music to playlists to make it simple to find. Even if you don't add music to a playlist, you can always use iTunes' search tools to find that music in the Library. With the Info window tools, you can apply various information to music files to make them even easier to find.

iPhoto

iPhoto also excels at keeping your files organized. Similar to iTunes, all the photos that you work with in iPhoto are added to the Photo Library, and you can use iPhoto's tools to organize and catalog them (such as adding them to albums or associating keywords with them).

iMovie

iMovie does a great job of helping you organize files for a *specific* project. As long as you maintain a project's folder as iMovie created it, you can easily access the files you used in that project. Unfortunately, iMovie project folders tend to be huge since they usually include DV files. This means it is unlikely that you will want to store your iMovie project files on your working hard drives.

Generally, when you finish with an iMovie project, you should evaluate any of the media files that are part of that project to see if you want to keep any individual media files accessible. If so, you need to locate those files in the project's Media folder and then copy those files to an accessible location.

After you have made accessible copies of the media files, you should archive your projects, if possible. If that isn't possible, for some reason, be sure to keep any original source files before trashing the project.

iDVD

iDVD project files are huge, and you aren't likely to want to keep them around after you have created a DVD. Just like iMovie, iDVD does a great job of organizing files within a project, but is no help organizing multiple projects.

Generally, after you have created a DVD (as many copies as you need), you should make sure that you maintain the source files that you used in that project, such as QuickTime movies, saved in some fashion, such as by archiving them. Unless you have a very high capacity archiving system, you will probably have to trash iDVD projects that you have finished.

Since the DVD project that you create is permanent, it serves as its own archive. As long as you maintain all of the source files for your iDVD projects, you can recreate a specific DVD without too much work should you ever need to do so.

iTools

When you use iTools to create a Web site, you are forced to organize the files that you use for that site, such as by placing the movie files in the Movies folder on your iDisk. Until you replace the files, the files on your iDisk are maintained for you. Since you don't really create files using iTools, you won't generally need to do much organization of your iTools projects; this is done automatically when you create the project online.

Using a Media Cataloging Application to Organize and Catalog Your Media

There are several media cataloging applications available that you can use to organize and catalog your media files. You can include any type of digital media file in these applications and then search for and preview them wherever they are stored on your Mac. (These applications are somewhat similar to iTunes and iPhoto except that they can handle all types of files.)

Media cataloging applications offer several benefits, including the following:

◆ **Organize all your files in one place**. Since you can organize different types of files with the same tool, you don't need to move all over your Mac to find files. You can open your media catalog and quickly search for the files you need.

◆ **Preview files easily**. Media catalog applications enable you to preview files from within the application. For example, you can see thumbnails of your images, listen to sound files, and so on.

◆ **Exist independently of storage location**. You can include files that are stored in many different locations (different hard drives, on CD, and so on) in the same catalog.

Media cataloging applications also have a few drawbacks, such as the following:

◆ **Another application to learn and maintain**. Media cataloging application are *applications*, meaning that you have to learn how to use them, keep them updated, and so on.

◆ **Don't integrate with the digital lifestyle applications**. Because they are separate applications, cataloging applications don't integrate with the digital lifestyle applications. For example, if you use iPhoto, you probably aren't going to want to also maintain your image files in the media cataloging application. This detracts somewhat from the benefits of using a cataloging application.

◆ **Cost**. Of course, these applications aren't free.

TIP

If you want to explore a media cataloging application, you can download and use one such application, iView MediaPro, at no cost for 30 days. To get information about iView MediaPro and to download a copy, go to www.iview-multimedia.com.

Organizing and Cataloging Your Source Tapes

When you organize and catalog your project files, don't forget about source tapes, such as your DV tapes. You should organize and catalog source tapes so that you can return to any source material that you need.

This doesn't have to be a hard process.

Create a Tape Log to Organize Your Source Tapes

1. As you use a tape, name it. A simple way to do this is to use the current year and a sequential number, such as 2002-1, 2002-2, and so on.

2. When a tape is full, review the tape and record its contents in a log. You typically will review a tape when you create an iMovie project from it anyway so this step doesn't add much work.

TIP

I recommend that you never record over a source tape. Tapes are relatively cheap and easy to store when compared to the fact that you usually can't recreate the material that they contain. Source tapes should be their own archive.

Your source tape log can be fairly simple, such as an Excel spreadsheet or a simple database. In most cases, you should include the tape name, the date on which the material was recorded, the start and stop timecode for each segment, and a brief description of that segment's content. Even a simple tape log like this makes finding source material relatively easy. (If you have ever stared at a pile of tapes and had no idea what they contained, you will see why a tape log is a very good idea.)

TIP

Generally, you shouldn't remove a tape on which you are recording from your DV camera until the tape is full. If you don't remove it, the tape's timecode will be consistent from start to finish. If you do remove a tape, so as to record on another one, the tape's timecode will probably be reset to 0:00:00 when you start recoding on it again. This makes your catalog a bit messy because you can have multiple segments that start at the same timecode (that being 0:00:00).

Archiving Your Digital Media

Unless you have the money to add more hard drive space to your system after every big project, it is unlikely that you will have the room to keep all of your digital lifestyle files on a working hard drive. There will simply be too many of them, and some of them will be too big. Unless you want to delete those files and so lose them forever, you will need to archive them in some fashion. To archive files means to move them from your working hard drive space to some other storage media.

NOTE

If you took my earlier advice and never recorded over your source tapes (such as DV tapes), you will have that material archived automatically. Just keep your tapes organized with the log that I described, and you will always be able to retrieve the source material should you need it again.

Using CD-R, CD-RW, or DVD-R to Archive Your Media

If your system includes a recordable drive, such as a CD-RW or DVD-R, you can use that drive to archive files onto CD-R or DVD-R discs.

NOTE

For archiving purposes, I don't really recommend that you use CD-RW discs because they are more expensive than CD-R discs. Archives should be permanent so there is no need to be able to erase an archive disc.

The primary difference between these two options is the amount of data that you can store on a single disc. A CD-R will enable you to store around 700MB or so while a DVD-R will enable you to store around 4.2GB. CD-R is a practical option for individual files, but probably won't enable you to store complete projects, such as an iMovie project, on a single disc. DVD-R, on the other hand, will be able to store many of your iMovie projects intact.

Archive Files on CD or DVD

1. Identify the files or projects that are ready to be archived.

2. Insert blank CD-R or DVD-R media in your drive.

3. At the prompt, name the disc and choose the appropriate format on the Format pop-up menu. You should select and use a consistent naming convention for your discs, such as Archive_1, Archive_2, and so on. The appropriate format choice depends on the media you are using. For CD-R, you will choose Standard (HFS+/ISO 9660) (see Figure 20.1). For DVD, you will choose HFS+ DVD 4.2 GB.

3. Click Prepare. The disc will be mounted on your Mac, and you can work with it by opening the Computer folder in a Finder window.

4. Drag the files or folders that you want to archive onto the disc. For example, if you are archiving an iMovie project (and have enough space for it on the disc), drag the project folder onto the disc.

Figure 20.1 *When you create an archive disc, use a consistent naming scheme.*

5. Organize the disc by placing files into appropriate folders if you want to. One way to organize your archive discs is to mirror the organization of the files on your hard drive (which you have organized already, right?).

6. When the disc has the files you want to archive and is organized appropriately, burn it.

7. Eject the disc and label it with the name that you gave it.

8. Insert the disc again and open it.

9. Open some of the files on the disc to make sure that they were recorded properly.

10. When you are *sure* that you have captured the files on a disc, delete them from your hard drive.

11. Eject the disc and store it so that you can find it when you need to.

TIP

Ideally, you will store your archived discs and your original source tapes in the same location for easy access.

The trick to having an effective archive system is to know which files are archived on which discs. The simplest solution to this need is to create an archive log that is similar to the log you keep for your source tapes. In the log, list the archive disc name, the files or folders that it contains, and a brief description of each file or folder's contents (trust me, in six months when you need to retrieve the file again, you won't remember the name, but a brief description will help you find a file quickly).

TIP

If you use Excel to keep your logs, create one worksheet for your source tapes and another for your archived files and folders and store them in the same workbook. This will make all your log information available in one file.

Using a Back-Up System to Archive Your Media

If you have a back-up system (and you really should, you know), you can also use that system to archive your files. For example, if you use a tape back-up drive and the excellent Retrospect back-up software, you can archive your files automatically. The software manages all the work for you; you simply tell it what files you want to archive and where you want to store those files. Describing how to set up and use a back-up system requires more space than I have here—for more information, see my book *Special Edition Using Mac OS X*.

TIP

In back-up software, the only difference between an archive and a backup is that when files are archived, they are removed from the hard drives on which they are stored. When files are backed up, a copy is moved to the back-up media

Index

If it revolves around a Mac, Small Dog has it.
You might say we're a virtual Mac universe.

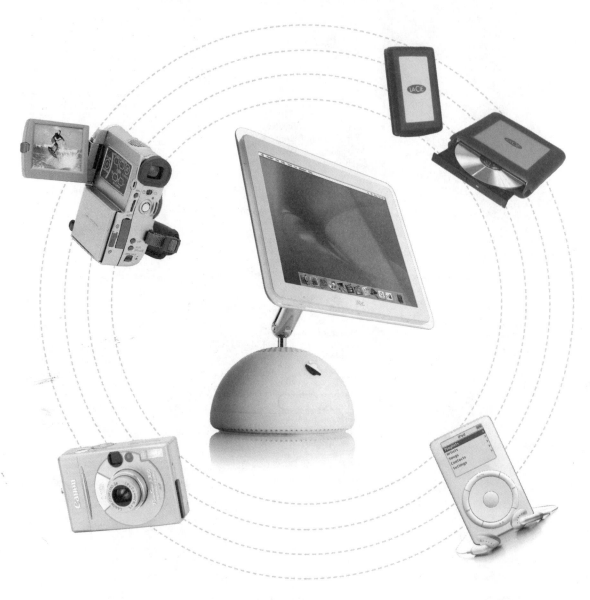

SmallDog.com has everything that you might want or need. From digital camcorders and cameras to iPods, hard drives and more! All this high technology for low prices makes it easy for you to create a little Mac universe of your own.